Geography of Michigan and the Great Lakes Basin

Geography of Michigan and the Great Lakes Basin

RICHARD A. SANTER
Professor of Geography
Ferris State University

 KENDALL/HUNT PUBLISHING COMPANY
4050 Westmark Drive   Dubuque, Iowa 52002

*Cover: Muskegon River south of Paris, Michigan.
Log Relics from the 19th century and canoe
design from the early Amerind period.*

This edition has been printed directly from camera-ready copy.

Copyright © 1993 by Kendall/Hunt Publishing Company

ISBN 0-8403-9089-0

Printed in the United States of America
10 9 8 7 6 5 4 3 2 1

TABLE OF CONTENTS

LIST OF FIGURES

LIST OF TABLES

We are by nature observers,
and so learners.
> Ralph Waldo Emerson

PREFACE

This book is the result of a modern-day exploration and research of the Great Lakes Basin (the Basin). The goal of the book is to describe comprehensively the Basin/watershed features to readers including those with a **casual browsing interest** and the **serious student** whether of the classroom or home plus provide a **basic reference document** for school, community and business libraries. The author endeavors to nurture a "spirit of place" focused on the Great Lakes Region. Also encouraged is responsible citizen decision-making and behaviors now affecting the watershed and its future.

Helpful convenient features of the book's fourteen chapters to aid its use include:

- Short end of chapter summaries;
- Key words and concepts italicized;
- Provocative chapter heading quotes;
- 3 photo essays;
- Reflections and Self-Learning questions to stimulate reasoning and analysis beyond recalling of data;
- Tearout pages and maps for **workbook** use;
- 54 tables -- Rivers, Counties, Peninsulas, Islands, Communities (Port and Hinterland), Lakes, Population, Crime, Colleges and Libraries, *etc.*;
- 116 photos to illustrate points and author's Basin exploration;
- 96 maps to show distributions and relationships;
- 525 item list of Sources;
- Index.

The book interweaves the Basin's social-demographic-economic features plus its physical-environmental elements to form a holistic geographic description of the primary parts of the watershed's ecosystem. Throughout the chapters, questions are raised and contrasting points of view are given to stimulate thinking -- especially to apply to the present and the future. The wise answers to those questions may foster the use of the Basin's resources to allow life to be sustained in it forever. Helpful aids in studying with the book might be a dictionary and general road atlas.

The book is an extension of the author's previous work, especially *Michigan: Heart of the Great Lakes* (Kendall/Hunt 1977) which in a few places has been quoted. However, the value of this new work comes from the author's five traverses of rediscovery in 1985 and 1986 which led around each of the Great Lakes, to each of the major connected and connecting water bodies plus in many places to the edge of the Basin (Fig 1). Bracketing those travels were several other short interior traverses made in the 1970's and 1990's. Wherever possible, a map delineated with the

Great Lakes Basin divide has been used to illustrate features. The diversity of graphics and writings other than the author's photographs and findings have been adapted from many sources to help expand the knowledge of the richness of the Basin's printed resource materials and to lay a foundation for their further use. The last chapter presents a proposal for an international freshwater grant college as a complement to the Basin's existing higher education institutions as a means of fostering the wise use of the land and freshwater within the Basin's 185 major watersheds.

Explorers and authors expect, in time, others to follow and make improvements. Toward that end, this book provides an initial contemporary effort in which others will further the process of thinking and caring for the "Great Lakes" as an entire Basin ecosystem of the planet earth.

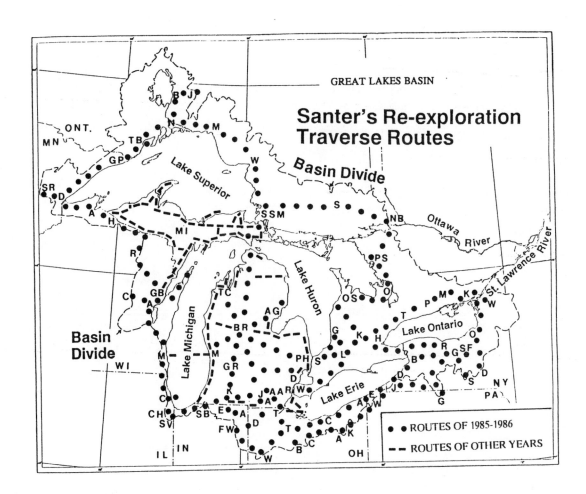

Key to Places

IL	**Illinois**	J	Jellicoe	D	Dryden	W	Wapakoneta
SV	Sauk Valley	M	Marathon	S	Spencer	D	Defiance
CH	Chicago Heights	W	Wawa	G	Geneva		
C	Chicago	SSM	Sault Ste Marie	SF	Seneca Falls	**IN**	**Indiana**
		S	Sudbury	R	Rochester	FW	Fort Wayne
WI	**Wisconsin**	NB	North Bay	B	Buffalo	A	Angola
M	Milwaukee	PS	Parry Sound	D	Dunkirk	E	Elkhart
A	Appleton	O	Orillia	J	Jamestown	SB	South Bend
C	Custer	OS	Owen Sound				
GB	Green Bay	G	Goderich	**PA**	**Pennsylvania**	**MI**	**Michigan**
R	Rhinelander	S	Sarnia	G	Gold	TC	Traverse City
H	Hurley	W	Windsor	W	Waterford	AG	Au Gres
A	Ashland	L	London	E	Erie	BR	Big Rapids
		K	Kitchener			M	Muskegon
MN	**Minnesota**	H	Hamilton	**OH**	**Ohio**	GR	Grand Rapids
D	Duluth	T	Toronto	A	Ashtabula	K	Kalamazoo
SR	Swan River	P	Peterborough	C	Cleveland	J	Jackson
GP	Grand Portage	M	Madoc	T	Toledo	A	Adrian
		K	Kingston	K	Kent	AA	Ann Arbor
ONT	**Ontario**			A	Akron	R	Redford
TB	Thunder Bay	**NY**	**New York**	C	Crestline	D	Detroit
N	Nipigon	W	Watertown	B	Bucyrus		
B	Beardmore	O	Oswego	T	Tiffin		

Figure 1. Author's Field Traverse Routes 1970's - 1990's

Thank you...

Acknowledgments

First, recognition is extended to all whose work assisted in the creation of this text. All reasonable effort has been made to identify and credit maps, photographs, table data and quotes. Fairness and accuracy has been strived for. If an error or omission has occurred, it was unintentional and the author would appreciate further information to make corrections when possible.

This work is the result of: the dedicated efforts of dozens of former teachers; more than a quarter-century of teaching and research experience with the advantage of receiving the encouragement and help from scores of professors, administrators, secretaries and librarians; plus the comments of former students.

During the research and Basin traverse stages, people from many walks of life, including those employed, some without paid occupations and others discouragingly unemployed from over eighty-five communities, gave their individual time -- most often unscheduled -- to share concerns, insights and specialized knowledge. These people "made the system work" so as to provide, in a timely manner, both historical and contemporary materials. Their aid individually, although unnamed, is sincerely appreciated and here acknowledged.

This work was accomplished with neither public nor private foundation grant funds or support. However, the approval of a one-year sabbatical leave at partial pay by Ferris State University (FSU), during 1985-86, was the critical factor in undertaking this research.

Dale Hobart, Sidney Sytsma, Sharon Octernaud, Susan Cherry and Coleen Hunsanger of the Ferris academic support staff provided timely professional computer assistance. Geraldine Hurt, Sara Krumins, Larry Martin, Anne Breitenwischer, Linda Creaser, Mary Gallagher, Keitha Breault, Lyle Mourer, Elaine Nienhouse and Raymond Dickinson of the Ferris - Timme Library, provided reference and prompt inter-library loan assistance. Jerry Sholl and the Ferris media production staff processed many photo requests. This work benefits from the extraordinary assistance received at the City and Port of Thunder Bay, Great Lakes Forest Research Centre, many community planning or chamber of commerce offices and the Map Library of University of Western Ontario. The several Sea Grant College staffs also provided timely useful materials. Terry Nerbonne and James Samuels shared their professional knowledge. I am especially indebted to three elders who reviewed and shared their wisdom on the proposal for the innovative Freshwater Grant College before their deaths -- John R. Smith, former President of FSU; Robert Huxol, former Vice-President Academic Affairs FSU; Leland Jacobs, Professor Columbia University plus Jean Kelly, retired Social Studies teacher. Gratefully, Rosalyn Jorgensen performed seeming miracles in processing the final layout and copy-ready draft with calm professional steadfastness. Finally, my wife Ruth who accompanied me on each of the Basin traverses, is especially acknowledged for her untiring work and continuous support.

Richard A. Santer
Big Rapids, Michigan

Chapter One

A REDISCOVERY OF THE LAND OF FRESHWATER

Wapakoneta, Ohio is situated close to the edge of the Great Lakes Basin. There one finds an abundantly watered plain of bountiful food land. That place, near the headwaters of the Auglaize River, a tributary of the Maumee which flows into Lake Erie at Toledo, was the home of Neil Armstrong. In being the first from planet earth to explore by foot the waterless surface of the moon, Armstrong was supported by the cooperative and competitive efforts of hundreds of specialists around the world which culminated with his historic words: "That's one small step for man, one giant leap for mankind". Now, scientists, engineers and technicians with dreams, add to the store of knowledge which outer space exploration reveals about the earth and its universe. Some risk their lives and die as did so many early explorers. Still others are challenged by the question of the use of space exploration -- for knowledge or war?

Perhaps Gary, Indiana native, astronaut Frank Borman's observation provides the astute perspective on the continual need for the people of *geo*-earth to educate themselves in the ecological relationships of the world.

> When you are privileged to view the earth from afar, when you can hold out your thumb and cover the earth's whole image with your thumbnail, you realize that we are really, all of us around the world, crew members on the space station earth...If nothing else, it should impress all humans with the absolute fact that our environment is bound, that our resources are limited, and that our life support system is a closed cycle.[1]

Now we can only ponder how Christa McAuliffe would have described the Great Lakes in relationship to the waterless universe had she survived the risk of being the first teacher to ride into outer space .

Water on the Earth

Over seventy percent of the earth's surface is covered by oceans, seas and lakes. Yet, the perspective of the poet, "Water water everywhere, nor any drop to drink," still holds true.[2] The concern for freshwater has led to conferences on the feasibility of moving shelf ice from the Antarctic to California and Saudi Arabia. For years there have been reports and photos from Africa dramatizing drought. Further, those who have sought a more comfortable life by migrating

---

[1]Frank Borman, Commander Apollo 8 Lunar Circumnavigation Mission, December 1968.
[2]Samuel D. Coleridge, *The Rime of the Ancient Mariner,* Part II Line 39-40, 1978 in Burton Stevenson, *Home Book of Verse* (9th edition, New York: Holt, Rinehart and Winston, 1953), p. 2751; Marlin Falkenmark, Carl Widstand, "Population and Water Resources: A Delicate Balance," *Population Bulletin*, Vol. 47 No. 3 (November, 1992), 36 pp.

into the Upper Amazon River Basin, have been disappointed with little hope for food abundance because of the laterization of the soil into a hardpan.[3]

United States and Canada Water Concerns

The situation of an emerging shortage of freshwater and land to meet the food, sanitation and employment needs of the earth's 5.6 billion people, with 85-100 million added each year or 10,000 births over deaths each hour, is not just another foreign relations task for the U.S.A. and Canadian political, religious and charitable organizations. There are ample warning signs in North America that the location, quality and shortage of freshwater is a serious situation. The examples listed now call for a new consensus for the managing of freshwater and the land it drains.

1. In spite of a bold line on maps to indicate its natural location, the Colorado River is a thin trickle when it flows into Mexico;

2. Some developers of housing complexes in the sun/drought belt include clauses in their sale contracts stipulating that the water supply is not assured for over a century;

3. In parts of Arizona the water table has been lowered 119 m (400 ft) since the mid-1930's;

4. The Ogalla aquifer on the high plains has become a less reliable source of water. Corn is giving way to crops requiring less water such as wheat and milo. Given the past depletion rate and no hope for recharge, the Internal Revenue Service grants food raisers there a depletion allowance. Figured on past usage, estimates indicate that the Ogalla may provide another 10 to 50 years of relatively abundant water (Fig 1-1).[4]

James Michener, in 1976, wrote in the concluding pages of *Centennial* of the large cattle herd's relocation back to the humid east as a result of depletion of freshwater. On balance, a change in the "national diet" from red meat to poultry which requires less freshwater may mitigate some of the anticipated freshwater hardship.

Freshwater for the Future

In comparison to the freshwater plights affecting most regions of the world, the Great Lakes Basin has the earth's largest area of concentrated freshwater.[5] Thus, it persists as a region of vast potential for sustained living, but only if the citizens in and outside the Basin choose to learn of its relationships, and then manage it with permanent, long-term democratic wisdom (Fig 1-2).

[3]Tom L. McKnight, *Physical Geography: A Landscape Appreciation.* (2nd ed., Englewood Cliffs, New Jersey: Prentice Hall, Inc., 1984), pp. 275-276.
[4]Ontario Government, *Futures in Water: Proceedings Ontario Water Resources Conference,* (Toronto: Ontario Government, June 12-14, 1984), pp. 2, 7 and 9.
[5]Edward B. Epenshade, Jr., editor, *Goode's World Atlas,* (16th ed., Chicago: Rand McNally, 1983), p. 242.

Figure 1-1. The Arkansas River no longer flows at Dodge City, Kansas. Source: *Conserving the Ogalla*, D. Kromm and S. White, Kansas State University. Copyright 1985.

Concerns of People of the Great Lakes

The people of the Basin, as other regions, have a considerable number of concerns. In addition to taxes and politics, many thoughts of citizens relate to: (1) resource depletion; (2) economic, employment, and entrepreneurial opportunities; (3) lake levels; (4) air, water, and soil pollution; (5) crime; (6) toxic waste disposal; and (7) education.

Examples of Concerns

At Orient Bay, on the shore of Lake Nipigon, a fishing guide talks in a hushed tone about the quietness of the forest. Not from solitude, but that the birds are gone. He is worried about sprayings to control insects -- "better natural methods," he said.

In Thunder Bay, middle-aged loggers discuss outside the Polish Royal Canadian Legion Hall a worry that their sons will not find jobs in the woods because of cutting practices and spruce bud worm losses.

3

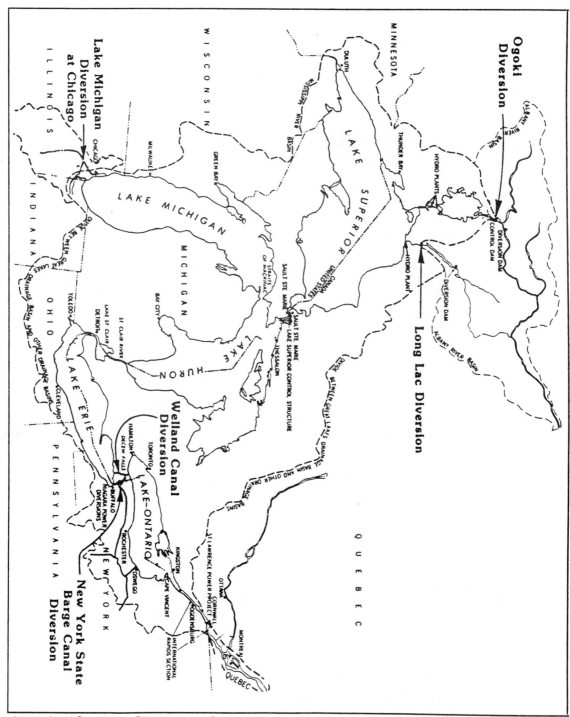

International Great Lakes Diversions and Consumptive Uses Study Board

Figure 1-2. The Great Lakes Basin and diversion sites: Ogoki and Long Lac (into), Chicago (out of), Welland and New York State Barge Canal (within). Source: International Joint Commission.

4

At the harbormaster's office of the Port of Milwaukee, a manager says firmly, "We need to understand once and for all that while the Great Lakes hold tremendous amounts of water which can support many activities, it is a system. What happens in one place relates to, and impacts, the entire Great Lakes System."

At the University of Western Ontario in London, a scholar shakes his head and says, "I don't care what the reports indicate -- from my observation of operations, I prefer to have my family's cottage north of the nuclear plant."

At Buffalo, a Chamber of Commerce vice-president speaks candidly, "No, the need isn't so much for growth, but having a comfortable living for our people. You know, we have enough resources -- if people don't get greedy with them."

At Sarnia, an economic development official responds to a hypothetical question with a simple reply -- "The days of limitless resources for exploitation are gone."[6]

Cognizant vs. Operation Perception

In an era of seeming abundance, an economic system can successfully work with an *operational perception*, that is, what one thinks the environment is. Now, realities of the *information/service* age, or global village age, require for survival, a *cognizant perception*, that is, decisions based on what the ecosystem actually is or, as nearly as possible, to a holistic understanding of it.

Initiating a New Era of Knowledge and Cooperation

For over a century and a half, the people of the Basin have lived peacefully and with essentially unfortified borders. Yet, the relics of war at the bottom of Lakes Erie and Ontario, old forts and historic markers, provide contemporary evidence of times when the United Empire Loyalists, the American Revolutionaries, as well as American Indians (Amerinds) sacrificed their lives to contest the political control of the Great Lakes.[7]

During 1984, the bicentennial year of the arrival of the United Empire Loyalist settlers into Ontario, the Province Premier, William Davis, welcomed a group of delegates from both the U.S.A. and Canada to a "Future in Water" conference, perhaps the first international conference on water *quantity*. The meetings helped to break misperceptions and further heal U.S.A.-Canadian patriotic wounds. They also focused on the Basin's water as: (1) a valuable long-term resource, (2) a limited supply, plus (3) relationships of water diversion. In introduction Premier Davis observed:

> No doubt some of those early settlers would be surprised if they could see us now, Canadians and Americans sitting together discussing how best to manage the Great Lakes and our other water resources.

[6]Author interviews with understanding of anonymity, Summer 1985.
[7]Forts of the Great Lakes Basin 1776-1815; Dearborn (Chicago), Defiance (Defiance, Ohio), Erie (Ft. Erie, Ontario), Fredrick/Henry (Kingston, Ontario), George (Niagara-on-the-Lake), Lernoult-Shelby (Detroit), Mackinac, Michillmackinac, Malden (Amherstburg, Ontario), Niagara (Youngstown, New York), Ontario (Oswego, New York), York (Toronto) Kamistiqula (Thunder Bay, Ontario), Grand Portage (Minnesota), St. Joseph (Niles, Michigan), and naval ports -- Sackets Harbor (New York), Wayne Blockhouse (Erie, Pennsylvania).

In giving further perspective on the need to overcome provincialism and expand geographic awareness, he said:

> I'm sure many Ontario residents view these vast bodies of water as being solely Canadian. And I wouldn't be surprised if many of our American neighbors also saw the Great Lakes as being solely American.[8]

Evidence that provincialism is waning and joint initiatives are expanding can be found in three notable comprehensive publications:

1. *Decisions for the Great Lakes*, by Great Lakes Tomorrow, a bi-national organization with headquarters in Hiram, Ohio and Toronto,

2. *Our Great Lakes Connection*, a 1985 elementary grades curriculum guide jointly funded by private (the Joyce Foundation) and public (Wisconsin Coastal Management Program) sources.

3. *The Great Lakes: An Environmental Atlas and Resource Book.* Environment Canada and USA Environmental Protection Agency, Chicago-Toronto. (Jointly with Brock University and Northwestern University), 1987 (revised 1994).

Persistence of the Legacy of Incomplete Focus

In the past and present-day, works on the Great Lakes, whether academic, encyclopedic or general publication, had the weakness of being focused on a fragment of the Basin area, included considerable non-Basin territory or centered on a narrow range of topics. Further, graphics used to illustrate the Great Lakes region have frequently been incomplete or misleading.

Examples of Incomplete Representation

Maps and logos of Great Lakes organizations sometimes omit the Basin boundary or connected waters of Lakes Nipigon and Nipissing. So what?, one might pointedly ask. First, Lake Nipissing, with its French River outlet, was the historic route of Europeans into the Great Lakes. Second, Lake Nipigon is four times larger than Lake St. Clair and has water diverted into it from the Arctic watershed. Further, care in use of area statistics has to be exercised because some Basin publications while illustrating the Basin border cite for its "total area" only the surface area of the five large lakes.[9] The books associated with the region are usually limited to a single state or the lakes in relationship to shipping, shipwrecks, fishing, boating, history or the shoreline beauty and shore communities. Unfortunately also is that government and education materials typically omit Canadian data. While the publications have merit; collectively they tend to perpetuate the non-holistic perception of the Basin and Basin wide relationships.

---

[8]*Op. Cit.*, Futures in Water, pp. 2, 7 and 9.

[9]The Marine Advisory Service, *Great Lakes Basin*, Ext. Bull. E1865 Mich. U-SG-85-500, (E. Lansing; Michigan Sea Grant College Program and Cooperative Extension Service, 1985). Folder; Great Lakes Governors Task Force, *Water Diversions and Great Lake Institutions*, January 1985.

Advancing a Holistic Perception of the Basin

This section is organized to help develop a holistic perception of the Basin by describing its location and areas, activities found near the edge of the watershed, comparisons of the Great Lakes with other major lakes of the world, the connecting water bodies, plus listing the Basin's principal peninsulas and islands.

Location, Extent and Divide Activities

The Great Lakes Basin is located in the east-central area of the North American continent. The Strait of Mackinac (45.50 N-84.40 W) is situated near the mid-point of the oblong-shaped Basin (Fig 1-2). The watershed is relatively small, reaching 1360 km (850 mi) east-west and 1160 km (725 mi) north-south. Near the northern edge of the Basin are Whiteclay Lake and the Arctic water diverting Ogoki Reservoir situated at about 50.30 N-88.30 W -- a similar latitude as Kiev, Ukraine. A short distance southwest of Wapakoneta lies New Bremen, Ohio on the St. Mary's River which forms the Basin's southern border at 40.30 N-84.15 W -- a similar latitude as Beijing (Peking), China. Swan River, Minnesota is a hamlet situated about 80 km (50 mi) west of Duluth and overlooks a wilderness swamp that provides habitat for moose, deer, bear, eagles, raccoon and ducks. The actual western divide has been artificially fixed by the roadbed of M-65 (47.10 N-93.15 W) above the naturally shifting headwaters formed by beaver dams (Fig 1-3). Cartographers vary in placing the eastern edge of the Basin. This geographer prefers to use as the boundary, Alexandria Bay, New York (44.20 N-75.55 W), at the foot of Lake Ontario where the water becomes shallower in the vicinity of the Thousand Islands (Fig 1-4).

Other Watershed Divide Communities

An interesting variety of settlements ranging in size from sub-hamlets to metropolitan cities are sited along the divide. On the southwest is an economically depressed and racially isolated industrial suburb, East Chicago Heights.[10] Chicago Heights is also situated in an overpopulated area coping with the timely delivery of survival health services and food. In dairy farmland astride US-10 on the west central divide is Custer, Wisconsin. From the Custer hilltop one has an inspiring view of the Great Lakes watershed and the Mississippi River Basin. The nearby eastward flowing Tomorrow River provides a stress-relieving name for those caught-up in the unrelenting deadlines of contemporary society. Jellicoe, Ontario, the last northern community on a paved road (KH-11), is sited a few kilometers west of the actual Great Lake/Arctic Divide. Here the moose roam on a glacially sculptured landscape of swamps, bogs and marshes sliced by clear, cold streams such as the Sturgeon River. Crestline, Ohio, formerly thought to be the highest elevation in that state, is on the edge of thriving farms and the urban/industrial sprawl of Mansfield. A modern highway overpass elevates automobiles above the complex of railroad tracks which still sparkle in the sun in this historic rail center. In "up-South" New York, in an area of wooded, round top low mountains and planted flat bottom lands, is North Spencer in the county of Tioga, which means in Iroquoian "gateway." Also on the southeast edge of the Basin is found a gravel pit operation and -- Michigan Hollow Road -- a road perhaps taken by pioneers out of the forest-stripped confining hills into the heart of the Great Lakes. Gold, Pennsylvania, is a farm hamlet at the head of the renown Genesee River (Photo Essay A). Surprising to most travelers, North Bay, Ontario, a diversified metropolitan community is sited near the portage at the east end of Lake Nipissing. Here Etienne Brulè and Samuel de Champlain became the first European officials to

---

[10]Irving Cutler, Chicago (2nd edition, Dubuque, Iowa, Kendall/Hunt Publishing Company), p. 53.

Figure 1-3. Basin divide at Swan River, Minnesota.

enter the Great Lakes Basin in the second decade of the 17th Century. Here also is one of the former glacial lake outlets to the St. Lawrence (Fig 1-5). At the head of the French River and foot of Lake Nippising is a Dokis settlement and reservation. The ancestors of these people welcomed the French explorers into the Basin."[11]

[11]Michael Barnes, *Gateway City*, (North Bay, Ontario: North Bay and District Chamber of Commerce, 1982), pp. 4-7.

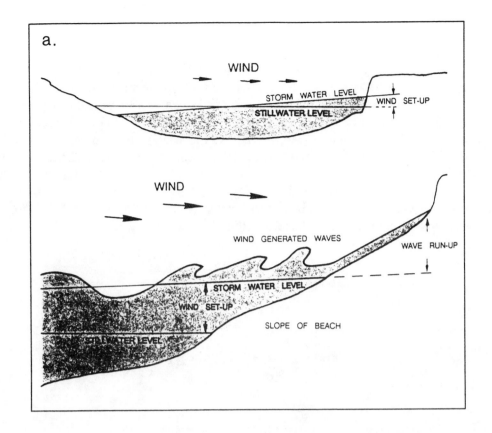

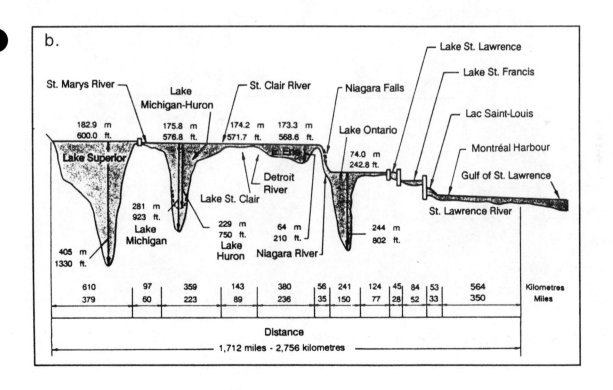

Figure 1-4. Great Lakes Depth Profile. (See Appendix for bottom topography.) Source: IJC.

Basin Area in Water and Land

The area of the Great Lakes Basin is 765,000 km^2 (295,000 mi^2), but somewhat smaller than Mozambique's 786,000 km^2 (302,329 mi^2). Varying with annual precipitation, the Great Lakes and three major connected lakes have an area of 253,170 km^2 (97,363 mi^2), a surface large enough to submerge the United Kingdom, 244,982 km^2 (94,224 mi^2). In volume, the Great Lakes alone hold six quadrillion gallons of freshwater, over 20 percent of the world's surface freshwater. The land area of the Basin is not precisely known but is estimated to be about 509,600 km^2 (196,000 mi^2), an area less than half the size of Quebec, 1,546,636 km^2 (594,860 mi^2). It is important to note, especially when relating Ontario statistics to the Basin, that only about one-quarter of the total area of the Province is located within the Great Lakes watershed.[12]

Figure 1-5. Basin divide at North Bay, Ontario. Portage area from Trout Lake to upper creeks of Lake Nipissing.

[12]The Marine Advisory Service, *Great Lakes Basin, op. cit.*: Epenshade, *Goode's World Atlas* (16th ed.), *op. cit.*, pp. 237-242; "Great Lakes," *Academic American Encyclopedia*, (Vol. 9, Princeton, New Jersey, Arete Publishing Co., Inc., 1980), pp. 319-320.

TABLE 1-1

Large Natural Freshwater Lakes of the Earth

| | | Surface Area | |
Lake Name	Location	sq mi	sq km
The Great Lakes			
Lake Superior	North America	31,820	82,414
Lake Huron	North America	23,010	59,596
Lake Michigan	North America	22,400	58,016
Lake Erie	North America	9,940	26,745
Lake Ontario	North America	7,540	19,529
Connected Lakes			
Lake Nipigon	North America	1,872	4,848
Lake St. Clair	North America	460	1,191
Lake Nipissing	North America	321	831
Canadian Great Lakes			
Great Slave Lake	North America	11,031	28,570
Lake Winnipeg	North America	9,417	24,390
Rift Valley Lakes			
Lake Victoria	Africa	26,828	69,484
Lake Tanganyika	Africa	10,965	23,399
Lake Nyasa	Africa	10,900	28,231
Lake Rudolf	Africa	2,473	6,405
Others			
Lake Baykal	Russia	12,159	31,491
Lake Balknash	Kazakh	6,678	17,296
Lake Titicaca	South America	3,500	9,065
Lake Eyre	Australia	3,700	9,583
Lake Torrens	Australia	2,200	5,698
Lake Biwa (est.)	Japan	1,600	4,144

Source: *Goode's World Atlas* (16th ed.), p. 242.

Russia's Asian Lake Baykal is smaller in surface area than Lake Superior but has a greater volume because of its mile depth. Similarly, Lake Ontario, the smallest of the Great Lakes, has the second largest volume because of its depth (Fig 1-4). Lake Titicaca is the largest of South America's few modest-sized water bodies. Australia possesses two periodic large lakes, Eyre and Torrens. In world comparison one of the economic advantages of the Basin is that the lakes are naturally connected and easily improved for navigation. In describing accurately the connecting waters, a bit of mental gymnastics is necessary. At several places the English word *river* is used topographically to identify what may be better termed a *strait* -- a narrow waterway connecting two large bodies of water. A map review of the Basin shows that physiographically many of the well-known rivers actually fit the common definition of a strait:

1. The Detroit River connecting Lakes St. Clair with Lake Erie,

2. The French River connecting Lake Nipissing with Georgian Bay,

3. The Niagara River connecting Lake Erie with Lake Ontario,

4. The Nipigon River connecting Lake Nipigon with Lake Superior,

5. The St. Clair River connecting Lake Huron with Lake St. Clair,

6. The St. Mary's River connecting Lake Superior with Lake Huron.

Navigation does not seem to be a factor in the namings, as the St. Clair and Detroit are navigable while the St. Mary's and Niagara are not. An interesting place name evolution is the Detroit River -- an English/American term which was derived from *de troit*, the French word for *the strait*. Thus, today we have bilingually the waterway as both a "strait" and "river."

Engineered Projects and Canals

To enhance economic development, with improved access, and protect residents from water transmitted diseases, several locks and canals have been constructed. In spite of the fact that these engineering projects affect natural run-off and lake levels, individually and collectively they appear incapable of controlling satisfactorily water levels of the entire ecosystem. Summarized here are the eight major projects.

The Chicago Sanitation and Ship Canal (1889) and Calumet Sag Canal (1922) are important because they set two precedents -- an understanding that pollution kills and it should be controlled for health reasons, plus under certain conditions, diversion of freshwater out of the Basin is reasonable. Combined, these two projects provide a controlled amount of water to: (1) help treat and flush the sewage wastes of metropolitan Chicago, and (2) allow direct barge interaction with the Gulf of Mexico. To assure a reliable supply of water for the systems, the flow of the Chicago and Calumet rivers has been reversed by locks at Lake Michigan. By artificially linking the Chicago and Calumet rivers to the Mississippi Basin, some may observe that parts of Chicago are no longer technically a part of the Great Lakes watershed. Nevertheless, because of its shoreline site, it remains an integral part of the Basin's ecosystem.[13]

The Soo Locks and dams at Sault Ste. Marie on the St. Mary's River provide a limited means to regulate the level of Lake Superior and a by-pass around the 6.2 m (20 ft) falls to facilitate inter-lake shipping.

The Welland Ship Canal, first opened in 1829, allows ships to by-pass Niagara Falls.

The New York State Barge Canal (NYSBC) is the 20th Century modernization and expansion of the historic 1825 Erie Canal system which linked the Hudson River near Troy with the Niagara River at Tonawanda.

The Trent-Severn Waterway, completed in 1920, links the Bay of Quint on Lake Ontario with Georgian Bay. Historically, this lake, river and canal-lock system was used for commercial

---

[13]Cutler, *Chicago, op. cit.*, pp. 31, 32 and 114-118.

and military purposes. Today it serves pleasure craft enthusiasts.[14]

The Rideau Canal connects Lake Ontario at Kingston with Ottawa on the river of the same name. This system also has been adapted to extensive recreational use.[15]

The St. Lawrence Seaway Project combines the Soo Locks and Welland Canal with other canals and locks to facilitate ocean shipping between the Atlantic and the mid-continent cities of Thunder Bay and Duluth-Superior on Lake Superior.

The Long Lac and Ogoki Reservoir works are designed to divert water into Lake Superior from the Albany River Hudson Bay watershed of the Arctic Basin some of which is used for hydro electricity production.

Of the connecting projects, two divert water into the Great Lakes Basin (Ogoki and Long Lac), three divert water within the Basin (Trent-Severn, Welland, NYSBC) and two divert water out of the Basin (Chicago-Calumet and Rideau). Several municipal water systems also divert small quantities of water outside the Basin and requests to divert more in years to come can be expected.[16]

Islands and Peninsulas

In creating a holistic perception of the Basin, islands and peninsulas are important features which are frequently left off or mislocated on modern maps (Tables 1-2, 1-3).[17] Yet, as a group, they contribute much to the Basin's economy and are especially significant as recreation areas. In some instances control of islands has shifted in modern times from national to state jurisdiction.

Each of the features identified in this section may provide a basis for leisure-time activities, journalism stories, video presentations and books which can advance the understanding of the ecosystem through the dissemination of information.

Political Geographic Divisions of the Basin

The Amerinds who occupied the Basin at the time of contact with the Europeans were organized with considerable independent operation into a few levels of political association. Two culture groups formed the top level -- the Iroquois with a power-base in New York and the Algonquian centered at Lake Superior. About two dozen major tribes, which will be described in Chapter Two, functioned with nation status for legal purposes. Semi-autonomous bands and clans formed minor political units. Similarly, in the present-day, the Basin is divided into a half-dozen levels of political geographic units:

1. Two national governments -- the United States of America and Canada;

[14]Parks Canada, *Historic Trent Severn Waterway*, (Minister of the Environment, 1985) a folder.

[15]Parks Canada, *Rideau Canal*, (Minister of the Environment, 1985) a folder.

[16]Great Lakes Governors Task Force on, *Water Diversion and Great Lakes Institutions*, (Final Report, January, 1985), p. 19; Bob Campbell, "The Great Shrinking Lakes", *The Detroit Free Press* (September 25, 1990) p. 10A; Mike Magnar, "Plan for Lake Pipeline", *Grand Rapids Press* (February 28, 1992) p. 3A.

[17]United States Bureau of the Census, *County and City Data Book 1983* (10th ed., Washington, DC., U.S. Department of Commerce, 1983), p. 968 -- this map illustrates a non-existent island between the Keweenaw Peninsula and Isle Royale; Michigan Department of Commerce, "Yes Michigan!" and "Say Yes to Michigan" -- both omit islands or mislocate Isle Royale; Robert W. Karrow, Jr., "Lake Superior's Mythic Isles," *Michigan History* (January-February 1985) pp. 24-31 and Satellite Image, p. 48; Richard A. Santer, "Where is Isle Royale?" *Michigan History* (May-June 1985), pp. 2-3.

TABLE 1-2

Selected Islands of the Great Lakes Basin

Island or Group	Lake/Strait	Comment
Apostle Islands	Superior	National Lakeshore Park, remnants of pre glacial hills
Bass Islands	Erie	Perry's victory and International Peace Memorial
Beaver	Michigan	Historic kingdom of James Strang -- ferry service.
Belle Isle	Detroit	Continent's most used and largest urban island park.
Bois Blanc	Huron	13,000 ac. with 25 deer per mi^2, 40 inland lakes.
Drummond	Huron	Recreation, mining.
Fox Islands	Michigan	Deer herd management.
Goat	Niagara	Niagara Falls recreation complex.
Green Bay Islands	Michigan	Border established by decision of U.S. Supreme Court 1920's.
Grosse Isle	Detroit	High class residential, industrial waste site.
Harsens	St. Clair	Seasonal homes, water fowl hunting.
Isle Royale	Superior	Largest island in lake, National Park, no motors, frequently mislocated.
Kellys	Erie	Notable glacial grooves in bedrock.
Mackinac	Huron	Historic fur trade center and fort, State Park, ferry, no motor vehicles.
Manitou Islands	Michigan	Part of Sleeping Bear Dune National Lakeshore Park.
Manitoulin	Huron	Largest in Basin, bridge and ferry service, seasonal recreation homes.
Michipicoten	Superior	Forested.
St. Ignace	Superior	Aesthetic beauty.
St. Joseph	St. Mary's	Amerind settlement.
Sleeping Giant	Superior	Spirit of Anishinabe.
Sugar	St. Mary's	Amerind settlement.
Thirty Thousand Islands	Georgian Bay	Boat tour.
Thousand Islands	Ontario/ St Lawrence	Boat tours, foot of Great Lakes Basin.
Walpole	St. Clair	Amerind settlement, outdoor recreation.
Wolfe	Ontario	Ferry service, residential.

Sources: Author; Official State and Province Highway/Transportation Maps; *Road Atlas: United States, Canada, Mexico,* Rand McNally, 1980; *Michigan Travel Pages,* Troy, Michigan, Ameritech Publishing Enterprises, Spring/Summer 1986, pp. 22-24.

TABLE 1-3

Selected Peninsulas of the Great Lakes Basin

Peninsula	Associated Lake and Bay
Bayfield	L. Superior - Chequamegon Bay
Bruce	L. Huron - Georgian Bay
Door	L. Michigan - Green Bay
Essex	L. Erie - L. St. Clair
Garden	L. Michigan - Big Bay De Noc
Keweenaw	L. Superior - Keweenaw Bay
Lakes Lowland	L. Huron - Georgian Bay - Lake Erie
Leelanau	L. Michigan - Grand Traverse Bay
Lost	L. Erie - Maumee Bay - Ottawa River
Lower	L. Michigan - L. Huron - L. Erie
Marblehead	L. Erie - Sandusky Bay
Niagara	L. Erie - L. Ontario
Old Mission	L. Michigan - Grand Traverse Bay
Point/Pillar	L. Ontario - Chaumont Bay - Black River Bay
Presque Isle	L. Erie - Presque Isle Bay
Prince Edward	L. Ontario - Bay of Quinte
Red Rock	L. Superior - Black Bay - Nipigon Bay
Sibley	L. Superior - Thunder Bay - Black Bay
Stonington	Green Bay - L. Bay De Noc - Big Bay De Noc
Thumb	L. Huron - Saginaw Bay
Upper	L. Superior - L. Michigan - L. Huron

2. Eight states and one province -- Illinois, Indiana, Michigan, Minnesota, New York, Ohio, Pennsylvania, Wisconsin and Ontario;

3. Two hundred thirty one counties (Fig 1-6);

4. Various regional organizations, and

5. Thousands of townships and municipalities, plus their school districts.

To identify the areas of the states and province within this text the term "district" will be used.

Cities and Capitals, Contemporary and Future

Of the nine state/province capitals, only two, Lansing and Toronto, are located in the Basin. Several cities have grown into complex metropolitan areas. One now can observe indications of overpopulation in Chicago, Detroit, Cleveland, Buffalo and Toronto. Alternatives to agglomerating more people in the largest urbanized areas might be: Thunder Bay, North Bay, London, Grand Rapids or Appleton. While not noted as a leadership center in the past, Toledo

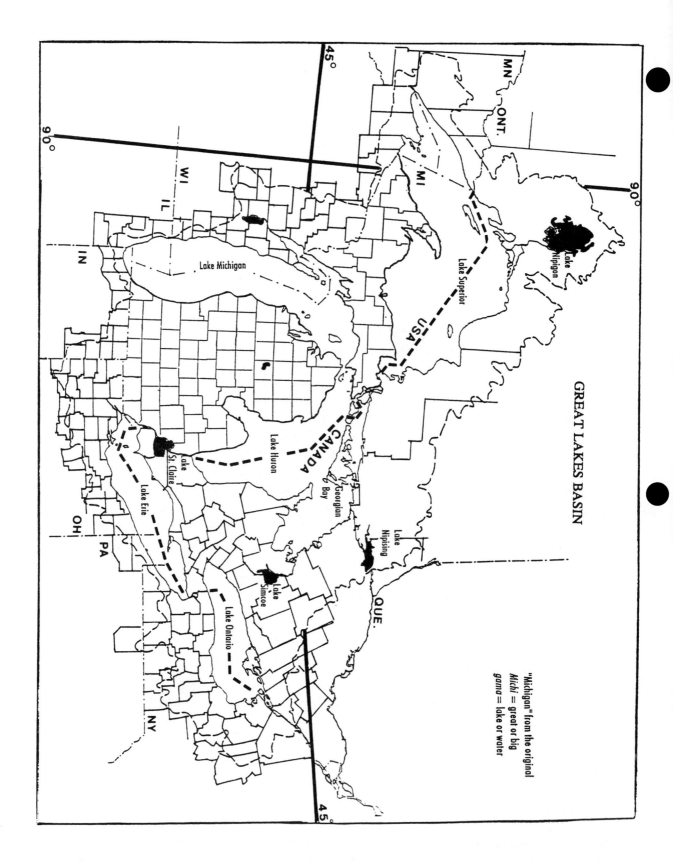

Figure 1-6. Basin, National, State/Province and County borders. Counties based on: Geography Division, Bureau of Census, Dept. of Comm. US Maps, GE-50 No. 47 and Ontario Ministry of Agriculture and Food. (Base Map IJC.)

16

gives evidence that it is emerging as the "capital" of the Basin in addition to its central port facilities.[18]

Nurturing Thoughts about the Future

Perhaps today with the computer and electronic transfer of data, growth communities do not have to be appended to metro cities -- especially the old military strategic sites of Toronto, Detroit and Chicago. Consider and think about a site like Reed City, Michigan:

1. It has road access to traditional metro-centers, US-10 (Detroit-3 1/2 hours), US-131 (Grand Rapids-1 hour);

2. It has rail service;

3. It is on low potential food land;

4. It, like London, Ontario is on a small river and 80 km (50 mi) from a Great Lake, to pipe in water;

5. Its attractive environment has a relatively low snowfall.

The point here is to stimulate thinking related to where the citizens of the Basin, acting democratically, will locate their economic activities to assure a comfortable living for themselves and posterity.

Identity, Geocentricism and Spirit Nurturing

It is suggested here that if resources of the Great Lakes Basin are to be maintained to sustain life with liberty, equality, justice and beauty for people, then identity with the Basin has to be nurtured.[19] To have an identity with a place, the territory of the place must be generally known. Such is not the case today because of the lack of educational materials which focus comprehensively on the Basin as a distinct area. In the past, most non-local place identity has been associated with one's state/province or their regional groupings (East, North, Midwest, Old Northwest, Southern Province Area, Great Lakes State or North-Central). The weakness of trying to fit the Basin to such regions is that its natural area does not fit the geometric boundaries of state/provinces. For example, Cincinnati, Ohio, could be classified as being in a Great Lakes State, Midwest and North-Central, but in reality, its spirit flows with the Ohio River outside the Basin. Further, as settlement patterns change, so must regional identities. Michigan today cannot be considered a "Western" or "Northwestern" state as it was when it was a Territory.

A regional place affiliation can be identified with university and professional sport teams. Kent State University, on the Summit and Portage edge of the Basin, identifies itself with the Great Lakes region through its football schedule (Figs 1-7, 1-8). Evidence that regional identity is

[18]Capital-like functions include: university with international business program, metropark system, regional shopping centers, rail-highway inter-modal network, daily-Sunday regional newspaper, significant urban renewal activities, major port and a "we'll do it" spirit.
[19]Serge Chermayeff and Alexander Tzonis, *Shape of Community: Realization of Human Potential*, (Middlesex, England, Penguin Books, 1971), pp. 4-5. Mortimer J. Adler, *Six Great Ideas*, (New York: Collier Books, 1984).

Figure 1-7. Kent State University (Kent, Ohio) football schedule indicates Basin and regional linkages.

Figure 1-8. Near Basin divide at Kent, Ohio, Kent State University, Summit and Portage Streets.

18

changing can be detected in the groupings for professional sport leagues and sport tournaments. In the past most professional baseball teams in the Basin were in the "east" division while the more recently established football and basketball league teams were "central". By the mid-1990s only Detroit, Buffalo and Toronto teams remained designated "east" while all others are grouped as "central" (Table 1-4). Nowadays in tournament basketball, the "Midwest" site can be in Texas or Colorado while Cincinnati or Louisville, Kentucky are "Mideast" sites which indicates a holistic perception of the nation and continent emerging.[20]

TABLE 1-4

Great Lakes Cities and Pro-Sport Divisions

City	Baseball			Football			Basketball				Hockey			
	W	E	C	W	C	E	P	W	C	A	P	C	NE	A
Milwaukee		*	X						X					
Green Bay					X									
Chicago AL	*		X											
Chicago NL		*	X		X				X			X		
Detroit		X			X				X			X		
Cleveland		*	X		X				X					
Buffalo						X							X	
Toronto		X										X		

KEY: W = West, E = East, C = Central, P = Pacific, A = Atlantic, NE = Northeast, * = Pre-1994 baseball division.

Perhaps by simply using the term Great Lakes Region, Great Lakes Watershed or Great Lakes Basin, residents, whether Canadian or U.S.A., can equally identify and share in nurturing the spirit of this unique place of east-central North America.

Spirit of Place

Extending to the remotest beginning of time of Homo sapien life, individuals have probably possessed in varying degrees of awareness, the importance of place. The Great Lakes and their land still hold a potential for enduring life. Yet, what may be needed to attain life in its fullest and sustain it, is to relink in part with the residual consciousness of the Basin's original inhabitants who have survived on its land for ten millennia.[21]

By rekindling and embracing a "spirit of place" -- a reverent sacredness of a territory's land, water and people -- one can then perhaps successfully reflect upon the primary meaning for life in the Basin, how it relates to other places and communities of people on the earth -- the Third Planet from the sun of our solar system, Milky Way Galaxy of the Universe, Cosmos. To ignore the power of a spirit of place is to risk hideous illnesses and revolting death from toxic pollution, overpopulation and villainous strife.

[20]Martha Thierry, "Where is the Midwest?", *Detroit Free Press* (February 12, 1989), p. 8J, 6 maps.
[21]See: Valerie Andrews, "Rekindling a Sense of Place," *Common Boundary*, (November/December 1990), 24-28.

A picture is worth a thousand words.
                Chinese Proverb

Photo Essay A

Scenes near the Great Lakes Divide:

1. Tip of Door Peninsula, Wisconsin
2. Custer, Wisconsin
3. Divide Southeast of Hurley,
   Wisconsin - Ironwood, Michigan
4. Swan River, Minnesota
5. Orient Bay, Ontario
6. Divide near Jellico, Ontario
7. Alexandria Bay Bridge, New York
8. North Spencer, New York
9. Gold, Pennsylvania (Headwater
   area Genesee River)
10. Crestline, Ohio (Railroad Center)
11. Chicago Heights, Illinois
12. Wapakoneta, Ohio (Armstrong Space
    Museum)
13. Divide South of Erie, Pennsylvania

21

22

23

24

Reflections and Self-Learning: Chapter 1 and Photo Essay A

1. How can geography help to rebalance Carson's concern of an "age of specialists"?

2. Why is the study of the land uses of the Basin as important as the study of the water of the Great Lakes?

3. Translate *Geo.*

4. Describe the similarity and difference of the terms: Basin/Watershed and Height of Land/Divide.

5. Why is the drying up of the Arkansas River an important relationship to the Basin?

6. Contrast the value of a cognizant versus an operational perception.

7. How can intra-basin communication and co-operation benefit the long-term survival of the people of freshwater?

8. List one community in each state/Province that is located at the edge of the Basin (Height of Land).

9. List the major islands and peninsulas with their associated water bodies.

10. Rank the Great Lakes in depth and area.

11. What are the major canal projects of the Basin? When and at what cost will they have to be maintained, replaced or removed?

12. What are the total units for the major political divisions of the Basin?

13. What are the advantages/disadvantages of Toledo as a regional capital? Does the Basin need a capital?

14. How would a change in diet (meat to poultry) effect the demand for water?

15. Contrast strait with river.

16. What would be the advantages of focusing settlement in cities other than the largest in the Basin?

17. What are the historic regional names and best contemporary regional name for the Basin?

18. How can a "spirit of place" be advanced economically/ecologically to assure survival in the Basin?

19. What is your concern for the Basin?

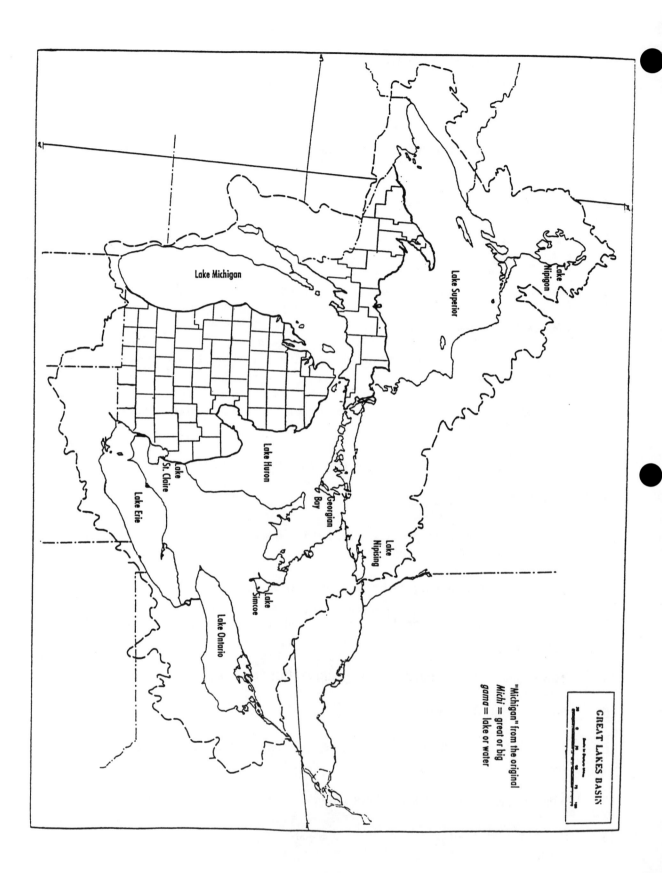

Lake Michigan

Lake Superior

Lake Nipigon

Lake Huron

Lake St. Claire

Lake Erie

Georgian Bay

Lake Nipising

Lake Simcoe

Lake Ontario

GREAT LAKES BASIN

Scale in Statute Miles

"Michigan" from the original
Michi = great or big
gama = lake or water

26

*"The utmost good faith shall always be observed
towards the Indians; their lands and property shall
never be taken from them without their consent ... they
shall never be invaded or disturbed, unless in just
and lawful wars...."*

Article III, Northwest Ordinance, 1787

*"Restoration will not only go a long way to solving the
immediate problem, but will also rectify a past wrong."*

P. J. Lucey 1973
Governor of Wisconsin

Chapter Two

EARLIEST INHABITANTS AND HISTORIC TRIBES

Notre Dame University is situated between two inland lakes near the south bend of the St. Joseph River. Most know of the University as a respected Catholic institution, its football team, or its Golden Dome. Yet, to those who travel to the edge of the Great Lakes Basin, awesome inspiration can be gained from the campus' twelve lesser known huge murals depicting the career of Christopher Columbus which line the narthex of the golden domed administration building.

Others may claim European contact with the Western Hemisphere prior to Columbus. However, his voyages mark the period of basically continuous intercontinental knowledge and contact between peoples of the two hemispheres. Predating Columbus, the ancestors of the Amerinds adapted to immense changing physical and cultural conditions to inhabit the Basin for over ten millennia. Thus, "new" to the Great Lakes watershed were the 17th Century explorers through the 19th Century pathfinders. Their maps and visions set the stage for the cultural patterns found today.

The Pre-Historic Amerind Periods

Archaeologists have identified three pre-historic periods of cultural activity: the Paleo-Indian Hunter Period, the Archaic Period, and the Woodland Period. Although here these periods have precise dates, variations occur between authorities and changes occur with interpretations of relics.

To totally identify or map the areas occupied by the prehistoric and Amerind people who came into contact with the explorers is subject to error. The Basin's earliest inhabitants were wanderers, not unlike contemporary residents (Fig 2-1). Territoriality existed as a shifting core area and jointly shared zones with undemarcated frontiers which were sometimes contested. Tecumseh, the eloquent Shawnee chief perhaps best stated the aborigines' concept of territoriality:

--- land, as it was at first and should be yet; for it was never divided, but belongs
to all for the use of each. That no part has the right to sell, even to each other...[1]

[1]T. C. McLuhan, *Touch the Earth, A Self-Portrait of Indian Existence*, New York: Promitory Press, 1971), p. 85.

Figure 2-1. "Wanderer", Indiana automobile license plate holds true for both people of the past and present.

The Paleo-Indian Hunter: 11,000 BP-4500 BP

The earliest inhabitants of the Basin were the Paleo-Indian hunters. These people probably did not continuously occupy the region. Instead they most likely wandered in and out in relationship to opportunities for hunting, fishing and gathering of food which were closely linked to the post-glacial environment. It can be surmised that these people were off-spring of those that migrated out of Asia. As always, survival depended upon the combined cooperative efforts of both males and females. Between 9000 BP and 4500 BP the lake levels rose to drown shoreline forests and expand swamps. Archaeologists hypothesize that in this period the population declined as the recorded number of Paleo-hunter sites found are few and material retrieved meager.

People of the Archaic Period: 4500 BP-2500 BP

Approximately 4000 BP the environment again favored hunting, fishing and gathering activities. At that time emerged biological associations similar to the present environment. Responding to the changes, people increasingly migrated into the Basin, primarily from the south. Their artifacts frequently consisted of magnificent copper tools of native copper from the vicinity of Lake Superior (Fig 2-2). Other items included gray flint "turkey tail" points from Indiana, carved stone objects and shell gorgets from the Gulf Coast of Florida. From their relics it may be surmised that the people, at times, had both a nomadic and somewhat settled life style.

The Woodland Indian Period: 2500 BP-Contact

This period is set apart from earlier cultures in that pottery was produced and by the Woodland peoples' distinctive mounds and garden beds. The landscape and cultural artifacts of the *Early Woodland* stage is dominated by burial mounds which contained thick pottery with cord impressions. Based on fingerprint size, it is surmised that women were the crafters of pottery. The *Middle Woodland* stage, (in Illinois and Ohio the Hopewell or "Mound Builder" period), commenced about 100 BC. In this stage are found more skillfully decorated pottery, worked copper and mica ornaments, plus typical arrowheads, hammers, knives, drills, hoes, spades, pipes and effigies. In the *Late Woodland* stage after about 1200 BP (700 AD) participation began in the Neolithic agricultural revolution. Seasonal ways of life became closely associated with planting, cultivating and harvesting. While the overall population was sparse, large assemblies of families would periodically come together at rewarding fishing sites. At the onset of winter, families and clans would disperse to survive on the success of hunting and trapping plus their stored processed foodstuffs. Trepanning of skulls, one custom rarely found north of Mexico, is sometimes uncovered at sites in the Basin.

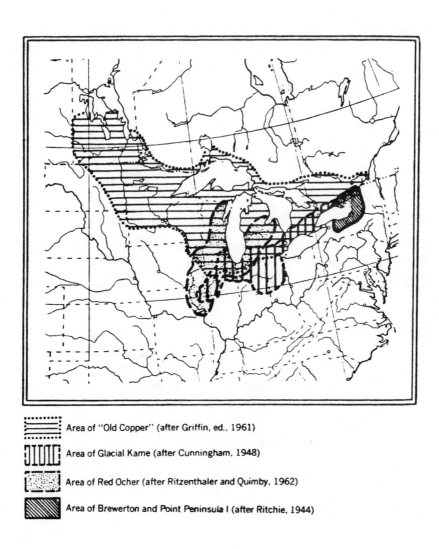

Area of "Old Copper" (after Griffin, ed., 1961)

Area of Glacial Kame (after Cunningham, 1948)

Area of Red Ocher (after Ritzenthaler and Quimby, 1962)

Area of Brewerton and Point Peninsula I (after Ritchie, 1944)

Figure 2-2. Approximate range of copper complexes. Source: J. E. Fitting, *The Archaeology of Michigan*, Cranbrook Institute of Science, p. 88. Citing: I. L. Fogel, *The Wisconsin Archaeologist*, Vol. 44, No. 3, p. 144. (Courtesy of The Wisconsin Archeological Society).

Continuing the Pre-Historic Knowledge Quest

The quest to expand the knowledge about the earliest people continues, but two basic related problems face archaeologists. One is attitude. There still exists a disregard for sites and relics of the aborigines. The unwitting disturbance of prehistoric sites not only angers the contemporary Amerind descendants, but also reduces scientific analysis based on the cooperative efforts between finders, landowners, concerned Amerinds and archaeologists. A second problem is the unabating destruction of aboriginal sites in the process of construction. Today, residents of the Basin, as caretakers of the region's cultural heritage, are responsible for preventing the loss of the fragile record of the first inhabitants.

The Amerind Tribes and Locations

In contrast to the knowledge about Paleo-Indians, Amerind history is voluminous, constantly being added to and studied. A summary of the locations and distinctive activities of the immediate ancestors of the Basin's aboriginal people is a way to illustrate similarities and contrasts with the present-day inhabitants. The Algonquian group occupied an area northwest from the headwaters of the Ohio River Valley and Niagara Strait to James Bay and the Upper Mississippi Basin. The Canadian Department of Indian Affairs and Northern Development lists fourteen major linguistic groups of the Algonquian language (Table 2-1). The United States Smithsonian Institution's *Handbook of North American Indians* generalizes the Algonquian language family into thirteen groups within the Basin plus several outside the watershed.

TABLE 2-1

Great Lakes Basin Tribal Groups and Language Families

Algonquian-Canada	Algonquian-USA	Iroquoian-USA	Siouan
1. Abenakis	1. Chippewa/Ojibway	1. Cayuga	1. Winnebago
2. Algonkin	2. Cree	2. Erie	
3. Blackfoot	3. Fox	3. Huron/Wyandot	
4. Cree	4. Illinois	4. Oneida	
5. Delaware	5. Kickapoo	5. Onondaga	
6. Malecite	6. Mascouten	6. Pentun	
7. Micmac	7. Menominee	7. Seneca	
8. Montagnais	8. Miami	8. The Neutrals	
9. Naskapi	9. Nipissing	9. Tuscarora	
10. Ojibway	10. Ottawa	10. Wenro	
11. Ottawa	11. Potawatomi		
12. Potawatomi	12. Sauk		
13. Acadia	13. Shawnee		
14. Saulteaux			

SOURCE: *Handbook of North American Indians*, ed. Bruce C. Taylor, Vol. 15-Northeast (Washington, DC.: Smithsonian Institution, 1978). *Canada Indian Bands with Linguistic Affiliations*, a map (Ottawa: Department of Indian Affairs and Northern Development, 1968).

Iroquoian speaking people occupied the Basin from southeastern Michigan and southern Georgian Bay east to the Finger Lakes Region of New York. There are at least sixteen Iroquoian groups which can be separated linguistically and politically; again, not all of these people lived in the Great Lakes watershed (Fig 2-3).

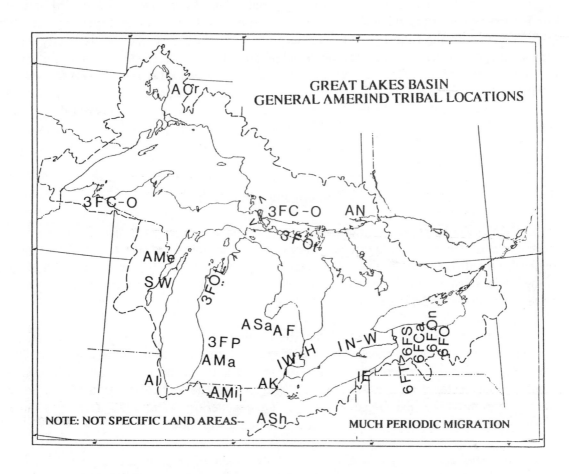

Figure 2-3. General Amerind Tribal Locations (Base Map: IJC).

Key

Algonquian:
Three Fire - Anishnabeg
  3FC-O Chippewa/Ojibway
  3FOt Ottawa
  3FP Potawatomi
ACr Cree
AF Fox
AI Illinois
AK Kickapoo
AMa Mascouten
AMe Menominee
AMi Miami/Plankashaw/Wea
AN Nipissing
ASa Sauk
ASh Shawnee

Iroquoian:
Six Fire Nations
  6FCa Cayuga
  6FO Oneida
  6FOn Onondaga
  6FS Seneca
  6FT Tuscarora
IE Erie
IN-W Neutral/Wenro
IW-H Wyandot/Huron

Siouan:
SW Winnebago

31

The Siouans

Throughout late pre-history and early history, Siouan people were the significant people on the western side of Lake Michigan and Lake Superior. Winnebago oral tradition places their origins at *Mogasuc*, red banks of the Door Peninsula. The Winnebago also occupied parts of the Fox River Valley and the vicinity of the large inland lake of their name at Appleton. Jean Nicollet made contact with the tribe in 1634. These people were first described as sedentary and more dependent upon horticulture than were their neighbors. The French tried to open up fur trade with the Winnebagos through Ottawa envoys. Peace and trade overtures failing, several Algonquian tribes united in war against the Winnebago. Yet, their strength was probably broken by an epidemic which swept their clustered villages soon after Nicollet arrived. Present-day individuals with Winnebago ancestry are found in Minnesota's Twin Cities, Albert Lea plus Milwaukee and Chicago.

The Algonquian People

This section provides a brief description of environmental conditions, social and historical antecedents of the major Algonquian groups which occupied the Basin. It is important to emphasize the diversity of tribes so as to better grasp the complex relations between all the people of the Basin. Further it is hoped, these summaries will facilitate progress in maintaining the peace between all people of the Basin and in furthering economic progress.

Canadian Michigan Quest.--After the signing of the 1783 Treaty of Paris, British fur merchants were reluctant to transfer control of the western Basin to the Americans. A 1791 map prepared by Montreal merchants outlined six international boundaries, one of which they felt should be substituted for the treaty boundary (Fig 2-4). The key point which the fur merchants wanted to control was the Grand Portage of Lake Superior. The 1795 Treaty of Greenville affirmed the 1783 boundary but Tecumseh, considered it worthless:

> But hear me: a single twig breaks, but the bundle of twigs is strong. Someday I will embrace our brother tribes and draw them into a bundle and together we will win our country back from the whites.[2]

Even the "bundle" broke in the War of 1812-15; yet, since then, peace has replaced warfare. Today, Grand Portage is reconstructed as a National Park trading post complex. A kilometer east, a modern low-rise lodge and conference center with decor of the local tribes provides employment opportunities for Amerinds and also is a dramatic landscape indication of the entrance of that area into the service economy era.[3]

The Shawnee -- the Last to Fight for Control of the Basin

During the years of transition between French and American control of the Great Lakes, the Shawnee were located on the Wapakoneta, Ohio periphery of the Basin. They vigorously resisted American expansion during and after the Revolutionary War. Chief Tecumseh was the last

---

[2]*Ibid.*, p. 116.

[3]Elizabeth Ebbott, *Indians in Minnesota*, 4th ed. Judith Rosenblatt, ed., (Minneapolis: for the League of Women Voters of Minnesota, University of Minnesota Press, 1985), pp. 97-98.

great Amerind organizer to fight for control of the Great Lakes area. His brother, The Prophet, also had great regional influence. Until their defeat at the Battle of the Thames near Windsor in 1813, the United States' hold on the west and south and parts of the watershed remained in question. In respect for his intelligence and loyalty, two communities, one in Lenawee County, Michigan, the other in Essex County, Ontario, retain the name Tecumseh.

BOUNDARY PROPOSALS OF MONTREAL MERCHANTS

Figure 2-4. Fur merchant boundary proposals 1791. Source: A. E. Perkin, *The Historical Geography of Detroit*, Michigan Historical Commission.

The Nipissing: Welcomers to the Great Lakes

The Nipissing ("little water of the big water") occupied the area in the vicinity of the lake which bears their name. When Champlain arrived in 1615 the Nipissing were living along the shore in seven or eight groups of about 100 each (Fig 2-5). He described them as a somewhat slender people who "refused to whip children" and as kindly and hospitable. Even though situated on the shield near the northern limit of corn cultivation; moose, fish, small game, duck and swan provided a secure food supply. Complementarily, the Nipissing maintained trading ties with the Cree and the Iroquois-Huron, especially bartering beaver pelts and fish.

Today conflicting feelings emerge when one travels for three hours across beautiful Lake Nipissing. The lake shimmers, but small oil slicks flash reflective warning signs of the age of pollution. As the modern ship Chief Commanda II approaches the boat landing of the Dokis reservation, a decrepit "French fry" stand with oil drum trash cans and a tourist store come into view. The latter, reflecting the world economy, is chockfull of imported souvenirs plus some very exquisite fur items.

Figure 2-5. Sunset Point, North Bay, Ontario. Wave "arrow" points to entrance to French River across Lake Nipissing.

The Cree: People of the Arctic Periphery

The Cree (Christinaux and Kilisinon) straddled the Arctic margin of the Basin. In later historic time, they primarily lived along the coastal areas of Hudson and James bays. Traditionally, they came upstream and portaged into the Great Lakes watershed to trade and hunt moose. In 1656 Cree were found to be living south of the Ogoki River (near the current water diversion) and in 1732 along the east shore of Lake Nipigon. During the Wars of the mid-17th Century, the Nipissings took refuge with the Cree near James Bay. Finding the environment too fragile to feed the rapidly increased population (of war refugees) and not wanting to overstay a friendly welcome, the Nipissings moved back into the Basin and temporarily settled on the east side of Lake Nipigon. Several years later they returned to their traditional homeland (Fig 2-6). In a sober vein, one could ponder the question, "If war came today to the Basin, where would you seek refuge to survive?"

Figure 2-6.

The Chippewa/Ojibway: The Largest Tribe -- Fishing

The Chippewa/Ojibway are a closely related people, though separated by the national border and by some researchers into two groups. These people, conservatively estimated to number over 35,000 in 1635, occupied the largest area in the Basin. As recently as the 1970's, this was the largest tribe north of Mexico. At contact, their many autonomous bands were widely scattered. Today over 110 reservation sites remain in operation with fishing a mainstay in the economy. As in the past, most of the tribal descendants live in Ontario (Fig 2-7). The establishment of gambling facilities on their reservations and treaty fishing rights litigations most frequently headline them and other tribes in the news (Fig 2-8). Historically, because of their location, resources and willingness, the Chippewa/Ojibway were extensively involved and affected by the boom and bust fur trade economy. During that period for mutual satisfaction, extensive intermarriage occurred resulting in many modern-day Chippewa/Ojibway women having French or English surnames. The rapids at Sault Ste. Marie was the focal point "gathering place" to gain the rewarding sustenance catch of whitefish and lake trout. About 1700, several of the tribal bands moved into southern Ontario. These movements coincided with the refocusing of fur trade activities from the Upper Straits-Mackinac to the Lower Straits-Detroit, founded by Cadillac with Count Ponchartrain's backing in 1701.

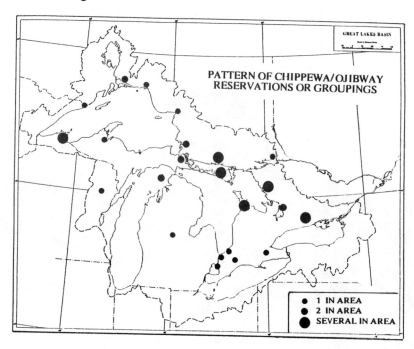

Figure 2-7. Sources: State Highway Maps and Canadian Department of Indian Affairs, 1968.

The Potawatomi: Cross Border Linkage

The Potawatomi and Ottawa are close associates of the Chippewa/Ojibway known collectively as the Anishnabeg -- the original people. The Anishnabeg probably migrated westward from the east coast.

Under Iroquoian pressure the Potawatomi left western Lower Michigan for a refuge with others on the Door Peninsula and nearby islands. They returned after the fur wars. At the time of Indiana and Illinois statehood (1816-1818), the tribe numbered about 10,000 living in about 135 villages (Illinois 14, Indiana 21, southwest Michigan 11, Wisconsin 80) ranging in size between 50 to 1500 individuals. Their homes, domed-shaped wigwams covered with mats of birch bark or cattails, sheltered, depending on size, single or extended families.

In political activity they challenged the Ottawa and carried on trade which included contact with the Spanish. For transportation they used both dugout and bark (birch, white elm, basswood) canoes (8 m by 1.7 m), but usually not for long distances. Later they easily adapted to horse transportation. In war they allied themselves with Pontiac in the siege of Detroit in 1763. In the War of 1812 they sided with the British and Loyalists and many Potawatomi continued to travel to

Treaty Waters Fishing Agreement

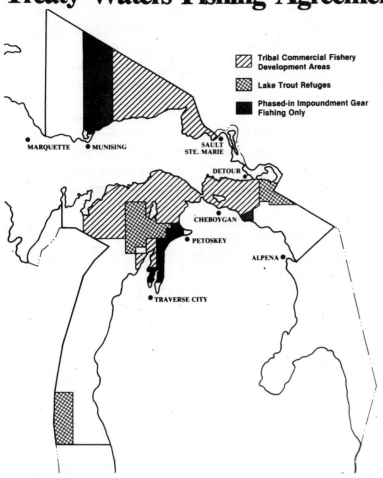

Figure 2-8. Source: Michigan Department of Natural Resources *Natural Resources Register*, Vol. 5. No. 5. May 1985, p. 7.

British posts at Amhersburg, Sarnia, Drummond and Manitoulin Islands for gifts and rations throughout the 1840's. In the mid-19th Century the Potawatomi were forced into harsh choices between (1) reservation living to the west, (2) adaptation to a new culture on the ancestral homelands, or (3) amalgamation with other tribes. Today their reservations are found in Oklahoma (Citizens Band), Kansas (Prairie Band), Michigan (Hannahville, U.P.) and Wisconsin (Forest County). The off-spring of those that resisted going to the reservations are found in clusters, especially at Wisconsin Rapids plus in the Michigan counties of Cass and Calhoun.

In Canada, somewhat mimicking the earlier loyalist migration, about 2000 Potawatomis relocated at Sarnia and Walpole Island. More recently they have been found at ten other locations closely identified with Chippewa/Ojibways at Kettle Point, Orillia, Cape Croker, Saugeen and Manitoulin Island. During the late 19th Century when an Amerind from any tribe arrived in Canada, they held no treaty rights, no crown grant "homeland", nor received annual land sales payments. In time, cross border Amerinds have been gradually accepted and some have gained reserve tribal membership.

The Ottawa (Sable): The Peacemakers

At the risk of over generalization, the Ottawa, were notable as peacemakers, liaisons and traders. Warfare was not their romance in life even though their chief Pontiac has become renowned for leading the 157-day siege of Detroit in 1763. The modern history of the Great Lakes and actual European contact with the "big waters" at Georgian Bay began with the Ottawa, for it was they that Brulè and Champlain first met at the mouth of the French River below Lake Nipissing. Although the Ottawa moved often, they lived within the Basin except for 1650-60 when they sought refuge at Pepin on the Mississippi River. Fishing by nets was a mainstay of their survival as they always lived on lake shores or at river mouths. From gardens the women raised many foods and were noted for making corn meal baked on hot sand or ashes. Marriages were described as stable with polygamy dependent on the husband's economic condition. Women were isolated in separate huts during menstruation and childbirth. At death, family members either buried, cremated or placed the remains on scaffolds.

The Ottawas occupied for the last 300 years a zone of environmental transition of the mixed coniferous-deciduous forest between sub-Arctic north and the humid continental long summer climate zone to their south near LaArbre Croche, Michigan. In conjecture, from an environmental determinist point of view, by occupying a transition zone, i.e. "middle-ground," is it easier or necessary to develop the go-between-peace keeper role because of the opportunity to evaluate and adopt ways of doing things from both bordering environments. Perhaps with skilled social scientists studying in detail the nuances of the Ottawa culture, additional insights may be gained on how to advance peacemaking in today's global villages.

The Menominee: Cohesive and Wildrice People

The Menominee people were noted as the "wildrice gatherers". More significant geographically is that, in contrast to most other tribes in the Basin, the Menominees have maintained a territorial cohesiveness. Further, their auto license plate directly implies a special status as a "nation" (Fig 2-9).

The Menominee in central Wisconsin and the Chippewa in central Michigan contrast in land cohesiveness. Each reservation originated in similar environments. The reservation at Mt. Pleasant has diminished from a six survey township-sized area to 450 ac (180 ha) of which half now lies outside the original reserve. In contrast, the Menominee ten township area has remained intact. In 1961 the federal status of the reservation was terminated which stripped the people of treaty rights and special recognition as an Indian.[4] In the following months economic, health and education crises abounded. Under the privately operating Menominee Enterprises Inc. (MEI), sale of land to non-Amerinds threatened to "checkerboard" the reservation. In 1965, 600 positive cases of tuberculosis were identified from 2000 tested in a population of about 4000. Infant mortality rose to three times the state average. In a hallmark Amerind legislation movement, DRUMS (Determination of Rights and Unity for Menominee Shareholders) led a challenge to restore the tribe and reservation. Restoration was approved on April 23, 1975. Evidence of vitality and educated leadership can be seen and heard at the tribal offices. Economic development is linked to a sawmill located at Neopit. Additionally, leather goods, plastic items, production of aluminum arrow shafts plus tubing activities complement a diversifying economy.

---

[4]Patrica K. Ourada, *The Menominee Indians: A History*, (Norman: University of Oklahoma Press, 1979), p. 202.

Refreshing to the traveler is the ancestral forest which has shaded the land for thousands of years and hugs W-42. In the forest are huge virgin stately pines plus deciduous species. In slowly traversing the route through the reservation, one can ponder the implications of dense development and what is the balance between human needs and nature?

Figure 2-9.   Menominee nation license plate.

The Illinois: The Walkers

The Illinois lived in the vicinity of the Chicago portage which linked the Great Lakes and Mississippi watersheds. The French gave the name Lac Illinois to Lake Michigan and found the tribe primarily along the river which retains their name. The Michiganea, a sub-tribe of the Illinois, were found outside the Great Lakes Basin, living in northeast Arkansas.

The Illinois culture was transitional between the Algonquian and the prairie Siouan. They were not known to be skilled in canoe making or in its use -- preferring to walk to battle sites. In many ways the Illinois were typical of the Basin's core tribes: (1) they had war and peace chiefs, (2) their subsistence activities revolved around hunting, fishing and gathering, and (3) women established productive gardens of beans, squash, melons and varieties of corn which were harvested in late July and August. Buffalo hunting, with kills numbering in the hundreds, challenged the survival skills of the men. Extended families and polygamy were frequently observed, mating males with females of the first wife. Both Marquette and Deliette observed that boys who showed a preference for female utensils were dressed as girls and became transvestites. Significantly, in later life, they became Manitous and were advisers at council gatherings.

The Miami: Loyalty in War and Peace

The Miami also had a transitional culture based on the wooded northern environment and the tall grass prairies. Factional groups, subsequently recognized as independent tribes, divided the tribe into the southern Piankashaw and the Wea which sometimes were found in Michigan. The Miamis fought as loyal allies of the British in the Revolutionary War and continued warfare for a decade after the Treaty of Paris. Under war chief Little Turtle, they had several victories over American forces including: de la Balme (1780), Hamar (1790) and St. Clair (1791) in which over 625 Americans were killed. In 1794, astride the picturesque steep banks of the Maumee River Little Turtle lost his life in the battle of Fallen Timbers. This American victory at present-day Toledo was led by General Anthony Wayne who determinedly guided his troops, down river from his tenaciously and strategically built Fort Defiance. Fallen Timbers resulted in the beginnings of peace through the Treaty of Greenville (Ohio 1795) and directly led to the transfer to American control in 1796 of British occupied Fort Lernoult (Detroit) and Fort Mackinac. Further, the Miami accepted American rule and did not ally with Tecumseh during the War of 1812-15 and even remained non-combative after their villages were overrun by Americans (Figs 2-10, 2-11).

The Mascouten: Migrate to Survive

Prior to 1655, the somewhat obscure Mascouten occupied the area between Michigan's Grand and Kalamazoo rivers. Later, although their culture was semi-sedentary, the tribe in response to Iroquois attacks, shifted their camps to northern Indiana and Illinois, then north to Milwaukee and finally west to Iowa. By 1800, due to population declines, they amalgamated with the Kickapoo. Similar to the Illinois, they did not extensively use canoes.

The Fox: A Clouded History

By 1683 the Fox came into contact with the French in the Wolf and Fox river valleys of Wisconsin. Their former core area was evidently at the eastern end of Lake Erie. Their independence as a separated tribe is clouded by the United States government policy which links them directly with their close cultural associates, the Sauk (Sac), with whom they and the Kickapoo share a single dialect.

The Sauk (Sac): Memorialized in Bay and Trail

The Sauk were skilled canoe users and lived at several locations. Most often, in historic time, they were located on the southwest periphery of the Basin. They were closely allied with the Fox and Kickapoo with whom they shared a similar way of life. The Sauk frequently had hostilities with the Fox in Illinois. Yet, all three tribes' cultures indicate a one-time linkage with the Shawnee. Women held some forms of political leadership which extended to speaking for the tribe in its 1804 treaty meetings that led to the ceding of their lands in Illinois. Today, Sauk are found predominantly in Iowa, Kansas and Oklahoma. Saginaw Bay derives its name from the tribe. The Sauk were a minor influence in the Basin; yet, the trail leading from their large Rock Island village near the head of Lake Michigan to Detroit is an enduring landscape feature and paralleled by several modern highways (Fig 2-12).

The Kickapoo: Southwest to Texas and Mexico - Use the Law

In historic time, the Kickapoo wandered often and cannot be linked to a specific core area. In the late 1600's, they were located in southern Wisconsin and moved out of the watershed through central Illinois, Mississippi, Oklahoma, Kansas, Missouri, Texas and into Mexico. In time, they became the most closely associated with the Mexican-Spanish of all the Algonquian tribes. One hypothesis for the tribe's divisions and extensive shifts is that the Kickapoo population increased too rapidly, partly through consolidation with the Mascoutens-Wabash-Vermilion bands, to establish an uncontested territory.

Law has become a key factor in tribal survival strategy. Today several hundred Amerinds hold law degrees. In recent years the Native American Rights Fund (NARF) based in Colorado, staffed with Amerind lawyers and a multi-million dollar budget, has been involved with contemporary issues of historic Great Lakes Basin tribes. In addition to providing trained legal aid

Figure 2-10. Fort
Defiance, Ohio.
Confluence of Augaize
and Maumee Rivers.
Starting point for land
surveys.

Figure 2-11. Fallen
Timbers Monument,
Toledo. "Onward in
Peace".

to the Menominee concerning its reservation and to the Chippewa of Michigan concerning fishing rights, the NARF was active in establishing a homeland for the Kickapoo in Texas.[5]

Figure 2-12. Sauk Village and Trail, Illinois.

The Northern Iroquois Tribes

The Finger Lakes region of New York is the core area of the northern Iroquois tribes (Table 2-1, Fig 2-3). In sharp contrast to other Iroquois, were the power wielding and warfare embracing members of the Five Nations or Five Fires --Seneca, Cayuga, Onondaga, Oneida, and Mohawk. The latter lived east, outside the Great Lakes watershed. Less warfare-prone Neutrals dominated the elephant-shaped southern Ontario Peninsula. After 1722 the Tuscarora, a southern USA Iroquois tribe, joined the core tribes forming a Six Nation Confederacy. The Five/Six Nations, in time, either expelled, absorbed or destroyed their culturally related peripheral tribes (Huron-Wyandot, Wenros, Petuns and Eries). Senate Concurrent Resolution 76 of the One Hundredth Congress notes the continuing government to government relationship between the Indian Tribes and the Federal Government and the linkage of the Constitution to concepts in the Iroquois Confederacy.

[5]R. J. Margolis, "The White Man's Laws" (as section of) Steven Cornell, "The New Indian Politics," *The Wilson Quarterly*, X.2 (New Year's 1986), p. 125.

Common Iroquois Culture

The Iroquois are classified by anthropologists as part of the Eastern Woodland complex. The Iroquois longhouses were clustered in village groups of 30 to 150 with a distinctive arched roof averaging 4.3 m wide by 25-66 m (25 ft by 80-200 ft) in length with 3-5 hearths serving two family groups of their extended families. Their women are known to have been the Basin's best horticulturists, as well as for slash and burn agriculture which they guided. Females gathered berries, nuts and roots which were eaten fresh or dried for winter use in baked goods. Tobacco, *Patun* in French, was commonly raised and remains a specialty crop of the Basin. Corn was milled by mortar and pistil, fashioned from a log (l8 in by 30 in) and a limb (6 ft). Salt evidently did not come into food preservation use until after European contact. The practice of arranged marriages and the absence of a rite of passage ceremony into adulthood contrast with the tribes of the western part of the watershed.

One of the most devastating impacts to affect the Ameriands were epidemics of diseases after contact with Europeans. Smallpox outbreaks between 1635 and 1641 reduced the Huron from an estimated 20,000 to 10,000 people. Ravaging losses also affected the Seneca, Petun, Wenro and Neutrals. As late as 1662, 1000 of the Five Fire people died from smallpox.

The Iroquois Wars. -- The causes of the wars, starting about 1630 and lasting until 1667 which the Five Fire confederacy waged against the Algonquian and the frontier Iroquois tribes are impossible to determine. However, they clearly appear to be related to the depletion of beaver and the control of fur trade. By 1649-51 with the Huron-Petun-Neutrals subjugated, the Five Fire tribes controlled the southern Ontario swamps, streams and lakes, and entrance into the Upper Great Lakes fur trade routes. In 1657 with the Erie defeated, control of fur out of the Ohio valley was gained. In reflection, the warfare and greed to gain control of the Basin's natural resources and trade network led to the demise of the prolific beaver and to economic poverty. Perhaps in the history of the powerful Iroquois, there is a contemporary lesson in the folly of turning on your cultural partners to gain temporary economic reward. What is there to be gained in the long run by one state of the Great Lakes Basin raiding another state for industrial plants?

The Seneca: Keepers of the Western Door

The Seneca territory was on the western edge of the Five Fire confederacy lying between Canadaigua Lake and the Genesee River. Their relative location provided their name "keepers of the western door." The Seneca maintained three to four consolidated villages which were relocated about once a decade in response to declining soil fertility and forest resources. During the fur wars they expanded their territory into Ohio and southern Ontario. In relationship to population and number of warriors, they controlled a very large area.

Today the thriving center of Geneva is found on the shore of Lake Seneca. The nearby town of Phelps and Preemption Road can provide some insight into the transition history from the Seneca to contemporary era. The Treaty of Paris assigned Seneca lands to the United States. Both Massachusetts and New York made claims which in 1786 led to a compromise with New York gaining jurisdiction over all the Iroquois treaty lands; while Massachusetts was granted new military land tract preemption rights (Fig 2-13). In 1788 Massachusetts sold the rights to a land company formed by Oliver Phelps and Nathaniel Gorham. These and other transactions opened the rich farmland of central New York to settlement and today lead many genealogists to visit the area in search of records of ancestors whose families migrated further west. Yet, Seneca Chief

Red Jacket, over 165 years ago, raised a fundamental question with the New York pioneers which is still raised in present-day politics:

You tell us your claim to our land and that you have purchased it from your state. How has your State, which has never owned our land, sold it to you?[6]

Figure 2-13. Preemption Road, Geneva, New York. The marker reads: "Preemption Line boundary drawn between Massachusetts & New York December 16, 1786 cause of long controversy in western New York."

Innovation of Handsome Lake and Mormon Religion

In 1799 Handsome Lake, a Seneca chief, received the first of several visions. In them messengers from the Creator revealed how the Iroquois should live. For fifteen years Handsome Lake preached what today is known as the Code of Handsome Lake -- the good message. The Code includes admonishments against alcohol, witchcraft, adultery and abortion plus encouragement for the kind care of children and elderly. Also in the Seneca lands at Palmyra, the Golden Tablets of Morani were revealed to Joseph Smith in 1827 which were translated into the Book of Mormon, a foundation of The Church of Jesus Christ of Latter Day Saints of Utah.

The Cayuga: Skilled Hunters

The Cayuga with three major villages controlled the land between the Seneca and Onondagas north to Lake Ontario and south from Lake Cayuga. As a distinction, Cayuga men did more hunting than the other league members, especially of deer and pigeons. At the onset of the

[6]*Ibid.*, p. 125.

Revolutionary War, the Cayugas, similar to the others in the five nations, may have tried to remain neutral; however, soon they allied themselves with the British. As a result, the American forces carried out devastating retaliatory raids against their warriors, villages and crops. The military actions totally reduced the war power of the Iroquois.

The Onondaga: Firekeepers and Conveners

The two historic main villages of the Onondaga occupied a relatively safe situation in the center of the five nations near present-day Syracuse. In their role as firekeepers of the league, they were responsible for primary governmental activities such as convening council meetings and maintaining wampum (archival) records. On the Onondaga reservation a stone marker identifies the grave of Handsome Lake. Today, perhaps benefiting from their historic interior geographical situation, the Onondaga continue to hold 6500 acres of ancestral land. Some Iroquois live on the land, many in single-family homes without central plumbing or electricity.

The Oneida: From Eastern to Western Basin Edge

The historic area of the Oneida was the vicinity of Oneida Creek and Oneida Lake on the eastern edge of the Basin. When discovered by Europeans, they lived in a single village of 66 dwellings. During the 17th and 18th Centuries, their culture was modified by contact with the Swedes, Dutch, French and English: fur/skin clothing gave way to textiles, clay pots were replaced by copper and iron ones. In the woods, stone materials were discarded for iron traps, guns and metal hatchets. In the Post-Revolution period, the family organization shifted to a male-dominated nuclear family, replacing the matrilineal extended family. In the 1820's, under the leadership of the Rev. Eleazar Williams, an Oneida group relocated near Green Bay (Michigan Territory), Wisconsin without approval of the local Menominees. In the 1850's, the Oneida-Mohican secured on the western side of the Basin the two southwest townships of the original Menominee Reservation at Stockbridge. Not surprisingly, there is little interaction between the "Stockie" and Menominee, even though they share a common border. By the 1970's the Oneidas' tribal roll was 6684. A second group of Oneidas remained in New York. By 1976 only 32 acres of their former communally held land remained with the tribe. A third group migrated to Ontario and located on a 5000-acre reserve near London. Today this group numbers over 2000 with over half still living on reserve land. Most earn a living by working in urban communities. Hereditary council membership has given way to an elected chief and councilors. In 1988 the 2nd U.S. Circuit Court of Appeals rejected a claim of 13,000 Oneidas of New York, Wisconsin and Canada to 5 1/2 million acres of land in New York.

The Tuscarora: Southern Member of the Six Nations

The Tuscarora originally occupied land in North Carolina. They experienced random killings on their traditional hunting land and women and children were taken into slavery. In part, they may have participated in their debilitation by the immoderate use of rum. In 1713, after the loss of 950 men, women and children, a few hundred families moved into New York between the Oneida and Onondaga villages. After a ten-year refugee process, they became the League's sixth member. In the 1780's they relocated near the Niagara strait where they maintain a reservation and tribal council.

The Six Nations of the Grand River, Ontario

At the same time that the Crown Loyalists migrated into Ontario, the Six Nation Reserve on the Grand River was established for allied Amerinds who also chose to avoid American government. The reserve lay six miles on both sides of the Grand from its headwaters to mouth, about 270,000 ha (675,000 ac). Over the years many controversies have occurred concerning rights of land sale. By 1847 the reserve was consolidated into a 44,900-acre holding plus a 6000-acre parcel for the New Credit Band Mississauga. Some Iroquois began the acculturation process by clearing the land and farming, engaging in road building and education. Others adhered to the traditional longhouse practices. Today the people of both cultures are having again to adapt; this time to the stress of urban development, which also challenges the governments as to how to continue to guide acculturation with justice. In 1991 a Canadian Royal Commission was appointed to study the social, economic and cultural situation of the Aboriginal peoples. Its logo illustrates a circle of unity of all ages and sexes, the never ending journey and a centered bear paw symbolizing healing energy.

The Erie and Iroquois of the Ontario Frontier

The Huron/Wyandot: Excellent Corn Growers

The Huron/Wyandot tribe, which later included the Petuns, occupied settlements adjacent to the Canadian Shield at the southeast end of Georgian Bay in a zone of mixed forest and extensive swampland. A complex network of moist trails beneath the climax forest connected as many as 135 villages. Indicating fear of raids, most villages were fortified 4 to 5-acre sites near a permanent water supply, with firewood, and arable soil. Corn, not meat, was their food staple. The Jesuits estimated when yields dropped below 7-12 bushel from a 27 bushel per acre average they relocated their village. Table 2-2 illustrates the seasonal cycle of activities, division of labor and culture traits.

The original Huron tribe disintegrated in 1649 as a result of the spread of diseases and warfare. Some members regrouped as the Huron of Lorette near Quebec, others intermarried with Ottawa, or were assimilated by the Erie and Neutrals. After 1649 the Wyandot emerged as a regrouping of Huron and Petuns. The Wyandot temporarily occupied areas at Mackinac, 1652; north central Wisconsin, 1658-1665 and left Chequamegon in 1665; and Detroit-Wyandotte after 1701. Currently a small Wyandot reserve is located in northeast Oklahoma and other Wyandot are found scattered in east Kansas.

The Neutrals and Wenro: Tried to Live in Peace

The Neutrals lived in villages sited to facilitate hunting in the area north of Lake Erie and southwest of Lake Huron. They were comprised of people from several Iroquois-speaking groups. They were named by the French based on their observation that they tried not to take sides and endeavored to maintain peace during the fur wars. They were dispersed by the Five Nations and no record of them appears after 1656.

The Wenro, who associated with the Neutrals, lived east of Niagara Falls and were the first Iroquois tribe to be forced out of their homeland by the Five Nation-Seneca. In their attempt to survive, they sought refuge with the Huron/Wyandot. No cohesive group of these people appear to have survived. One notable skill which the French reported was the Wenros ability to remove an arrow and heal a wound.

TABLE 2-2
Seasonal Cultural Cycle of the Huron/Wyandot

Activity	J	F	M	A	M	J	J	A	S	O	N	D
Fishing*	M	M	M	M	M	M	M	M	M	M	M	M
Hunting*		M	M	M	M	M			M	M	M	M
Trading						M	M	M	M	M	M	
Warfare						M	M	M	M			
Firewood-Gather				F	F							
Field-Prep*				F	F							
Planting					F	F						
Weeding						F	F	F				
Harvest								F	F	F		
Gathering-Food						F	F	F	F			
Manufacturing	MF	MF	MF	MF								MF
Socializing	MF	MF	MF								MF	MF

Key: M = male, F = female - major provider of labor
　　　　* = complementary sex - minor labor role
Note: Children were involved in weeding and food gathering.
SOURCE: *Handbook of North American Indians*, Vol. 15, p. 379.

The Erie: Casual Quarrel, Revenge, Annihilation vs. Peace

Records relating to the Erie are meager. What is evident is that they lived in sedentary villages and maintained linkages with the Huron/Wyandotte. They seem to have been concentrated north of the Portage escarpment of western New York and northern Pennsylvania.

Francis Parkman in his monumental work *The Jesuits in North America* describes the destruction of the Erie. The Erie in 1653 had made a peace treaty with the Seneca and sent, the following year, 30 deputies to a Seneca village to reconfirm it. While at the village, in an unwitting casual quarrel, one of the Erie killed a Seneca. The Seneca, in quick retaliation, murdered the 30 Erie. Soon afterwards, in guilt by association reprisal, the Erie captured an Onondaga chief. As an alternative to the planned burning of him alive, the chief pleaded under common tribal law to be given to one of the sisters of the slain Erie deputies. Temporarily this was agreed to and most expected the sister to accept this gentler solution. However, she rejected him and insisted that he should be burned -- and he was. The chief's death enraged the Onondaga who with other league members, sent 1200 warriors to retaliate. The Erie retreated with women and children to a fortification with perhaps 2000 Erie warriors. The Erie met the attack and fought with poisoned arrows, the only tribe reported to use them. The Onondaga, using their canoes as shield and cross supports as ladders, surmounted the stronghold and overwhelmed the Erie with mass butchery.[7]   The Erie vanished as a tribal entity with some of their survivors joining the Susquehannock. Perhaps the moral of the story is -- casual quarrels and lack of compromise may lead to annihilation of both sexes.

[7]Frances Parkman, *The Jesuits in North America in the Seventeenth Century* (Boston: Little, Brown and Co., 1925), pp. 542-545.

A Summary of the Amerind in the Basin

Complexity and pluralism characterize the habitation of Amerind people in the Basin. Perhaps DNA studies will reveal the origins of the first peoples in the Basin -- did they descend from a single group or many migrations? The pre-history evidence is from people of the Paleo-Indian hunter and Archaic culture groups. The Woodland people developed a distinct culture including pottery and mound building. The pre-history way of life blended with tribal life which began to be recorded on contact by the 17th Century Euro-Americans. The Amerinds of history can be described by their three distinctive linguistic stocks which varied east to west: Iroquoian, Algonquian and Siouan. These three cultures comprised about 25 independent social tribes, not all of which survived the aboriginal wars, European diseases and cultural changes.

Family life varied with both matriarchal and patriarchal authority and lineage. Marriages varied by tribe with both monogamous and polygamous associations approved. Housing included single family wigwams-teepees and extended family huge longhouses. Extensive trade and networks complemented the hunting, fishing, and gathering economy. Transportation included short and long distance walking and limited and skilled long distance water travel by canoe. Four chiefs emerged as notable leaders in the struggle to maintain a control in the Amerind homeland: Pontiac (Ottawa) 1763, Little Turtle (Miami) 1794), Tecumseh (Shawnee) 1814 and Black Hawk (Sauk) 1832.

The unique historical geography of the Amerind people coupled with their increasing college-educated leaders who possess the remnants of native spirit and wisdom, provide outstanding choices and opportunities for people of all heritages to share in the continued development of the Great Lakes Basin as a significant part of the global village and in the search for enduring peace.[8]

---

[8]In the development of this chapter the *Handbook of North American Indians*, ed. Bruce C. Taylor, Vol. 15-Northeast (Washington, DC.: Smithsonian Institution, 1978) has been extensively relied upon for factual data.

Reflections and Self-Learning: Chapter 2

1. Who were the first people to live in your area?

2. What peoples wandered through or temporally occupied your area?

3. Describe their culture:
   Housing, food activities, transportation, roles of sexes, political organization, economic and trade activities.

4. Identify the imprint of the Amerinds of your area on the landscape.
   Townsite(s), burial/sacred grounds, place names.

5. Interview/talk with a descendent of the first people -- what are their concerns for the future?

6. How can the development of more knowledge of the people and cultures of the original inhabitants help lead to a better community, world and survival of all?

7. What is the difference between BC and BP? Why?

8. What should you do if you discover Amerind relics on a lot where you are having a home constructed?

9. How can the Basin be considered an innovation site for modern-day religions?

10. What was left out of this chapter that you want to know of or more on about the Amerind people of the Great Lakes Region?

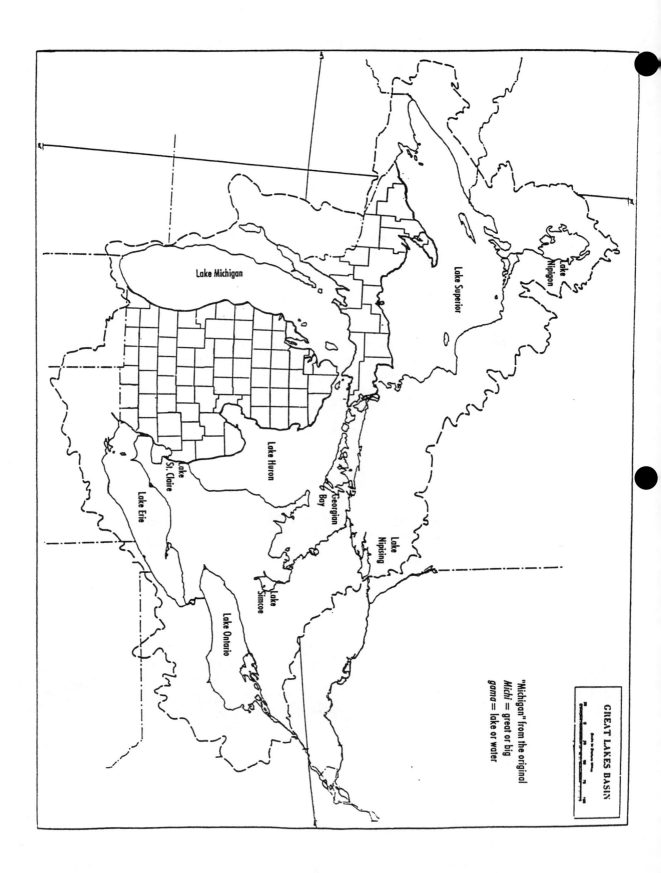

GREAT LAKES BASIN

"Michigan" from the original
Michi = great or big
gama = lake or water

Lake Michigan

Lake Superior

Lake Nipigon

Lake Huron

Lake St. Claire

Lake Erie

Georgian Bay

Lake Nipising

Lake Simcoe

Lake Ontario

"To explore is to: risk travel, traverse, wander, view,
talk to, record, search, inquire, photograph, map; gather data,
study, describe, feel, deal with misleading, enjoy.
R. Nare
Discovery 1956

Chapter Three

THE EUROPEAN EXPLORERS
1534-1855 AND PRESENT

Today, as in the past, those willing to take on the task of exploring the unknown, little known or forgotten places run enormous risks. On or off the well-traveled route one misjudgment, one misspoken word or one misstep can lead to shunting, injury or instant death. Indeed exploration nowadays has high risks, yet they pale in comparison to the body-wearing travel of the pre-automobile age. Explorers willingly accept what appear to be reasonable risks in order to gain comprehensive data about a place plus arrive back home to write and tell others of their experiences and insights. Explorers' rewards come, in part, from following generations memorializing them and using their work in ordering and advancing the body of knowledge of earth and the universe.

French Explorers of the Great Lakes Watershed

The age of recorded exploration into parts of the Great Lakes watershed began in the mid-1500's. In the centuries since then, about a score of men have received acclaim for their explorations. Sometimes these men worked virtually alone; however, in fairness, many were supported by parties of countrymen and natives, which at times, included women. Generally, the explorers came from a relatively few backgrounds: government officials, religious missionaries, surveyors and entrepreneurs (Table 3-1).

Jacques Cartier (1491-1557)*

Between 1534 and 1542 Cartier, a navigator, made three voyages to North America. His discoveries were the basis for France's claim to Canada. Although he gained credit for the discovery of the St. Lawrence River, fishing ships were already off its mouth.[1] His well-documented voyages up the St. Lawrence to Montreal set the stage for others who began to penetrate into the Basin proper three-quarters of a century later. Initially it was the quest to find a water route to the known riches of Asia which acted as a magnet for exploration. During the next two centuries, the fine fur pelts which Cartier and associates reported, plus the land claimed, became most important in shaping the region's history.

*Birth-Death Dates

[1]Ralph H. Brown, *Historical Geography of the United States*, ed. J. R. Whitaker (New York: Harcourt, Brace and World, Inc. 1948), p. 10.

TABLE 3-1

Selected List of Great Lakes Basin Explorers

Name	Background	Key Exploration Dates
French		
Jacques Cartier, navigator		1534
Etienne Brulè, interpreter-agent		1610-1614
Samuel de Champlain, governor-cartographer		1615
Jean Nicolet, government agent		1634
Groseilliers and Radisson, entrepreneurs		1659-1660
Father Menard, missionary		1660-1661
Dollier and Golineè, missionaries		1668
Louis Joliet, hydrographer - Jacques Marquette, missionary		1672
Daniel Graysolon (Duluth), government agent		1678-1688
Sieurde LaSalle, visionary		1679-1682
British		
Alexander Henry, adventurer-trader		1760-1796
Alexander Mackenzie, fur trader		1789-1793
Henry W. Bayfield, navy cartographer		1825-1830
American		
Henry Schoolcraft, agent		1820
Lewis Cass, governor		1820
Douglas Houghton, geologist		1837-1845
Father Baraga, missionary		1850-1853

Etienne Brulè (1592-1632)

As an emissary-interpreter for Governor Samuel de Champlain, Brulè probably was the first Frenchman to enter the Great Lakes Basin. Between 1610-1614 he undoubtedly reached Lake Huron. After Champlain followed his route in 1615 which brought the governor into contact with the Nipissing and Ottawa, Brulè returned to the Basin to continue his advanceman role. According to Gabriel Sagard's *Histoire du Canada*, published in 1636, Brulè is alleged to have wintered near Sault Ste. Marie in 1618-19. Perhaps two years later he was accompanied by Grenoble up the St. Mary's River into Lake Superior. Their return with copper nuggets give credibility to the assumption that they were also the first Europeans to sense the potential mineral wealth of the Upper Lakes area.

In 1629 he betrayed Champlain by guiding a British flotilla up the St. Lawrence to Quebec which led to its capture. Champlain spent four years as a prisoner in England. Brulè faired worse. In 1632, a quarrel with members of the Huron tribe with whom he was living, resulted in his death. His remains perhaps were eaten by some of them.

Samuel de Champlain (1567-1635)

Known simply as the "Father of New France," Champlain was also extremely interested in gaining accurate and first-hand knowledge about the land and water resources for which he was responsible. A cartographer by training, and being the son of a sea captain, provided him with a skilled background and respect for observation and description. In 1603 he sailed into the St. Lawrence. He was the first to write about Niagara Falls. In 1608 he established and named Quebec where he died as governor. Although many others contributed to the task, he articulately saw his leadership role which resulted in the opening of the Great Lakes Basin. His duty he wrote was:

> ...to extend my travels over the country in order by means of its numerous rivers, lakes and streams, to obtain at last a complete knowledge of it, and also to become acquainted with the view of bringing them (Amerinds) nearer to God (Fig 3-1).[2]

His epic journey across the divide into the Great Lakes watershed established the major French trade route of the voyageurs. Using the knowledge Brulè had gained from the natives, his route took him up the Ottawa River to Mattawa, west to Trout Lake, then over the muddy portage to LaVase Creek to Lake Nipissing (North Bay). In the early 1600's, Champlain began to submit reports on the natural conditions of New France which were realistically frank in comparison to those of Cartier. He repeatedly warned against inferring that the climate was similar to that of the homeland simply from the resemblances of vegetation and latitude. His reports that the interior areas held a potential, with their abundance of fur-bearing animals, found interest with the government. This was especially so when it was noted that the Amerinds, when treated with a semblance of respect, would cooperate in trade of pelts. Champlain's missionaries' and other people's analyses resulted in setting into motion the flow of valuable furs from the Great Lakes region to the profitable markets in Europe.

Jean Nicolet (1598-1642)

Another of Champlain's talented agents was Jean Nicolet who came into government service at the age of twenty. At first, he lived for eleven years as an Amerind, learning the several Algonquian dialects, social systems, farming methods and forming a family; in the process he gained respect as a trader and peacemaker. In 1634 Champlain sent Nicolet west to establish a peace between the aggressive Siouan-Winnebago and the eastern tribes. In his journey he passed through the Strait of Mackinac and is credited with being the first European official to travel on Lake Michigan (Lac Illini). The vastness of the lake and his misjudging the freshness of the water or perhaps misinterpreting the vague Amerind stories maybe led him to conclude that he had found the passage west to Asia. Regardless of his error, when his party made landfall on the red bank shoreline someplace along Green Bay, he dressed himself in a fine robe, shot pistols, "thunder in the hand," to demonstrate his authority to be guided to meet an emperor. Time and continued exploration revealed somewhat humorously the truism that *discoverers make bold unintentional errors*. Unfortunately, eight years later while again returning home, he drowned when a storm overturned his boat in the St. Lawrence River. Apparently the only extended account of his mission was written shortly after his death for the *Jesuit Relations* on the basis of his conversations with Jesuit Vimont.

---

[2]Michael Barnes, *Gateway City: The North Bay Story*, (North Bay: North Bay and District Chamber of Commerce, 1982), p. 6.

Figure 3-1. Samuel de Champlain, Couchiching Beach Park, Orillia. Vernon March, sculptor.

Guidelines for Explorers

Father Jean de Brebuf, a Jesuit who journeyed in 1635 with four other missionaries to work among the Huron/Wyandotte, set down these guidelines for canoe travel with the native Amerind:

1. Be prompt to embark or disembark.
2. Tuck up your gowns -- prevent wetness.
3. Do not track sand or water into canoe.
4. Keep your legs and feet bare.
5. While portaging at rapids you may wear shoes (the aborigines go barefoot).
6. Be careful not to annoy anyone -- especially with your hat.[3]

M. C. des Groseilliers and P. E. Radisson

Groseilliers and Radisson were unrestrained independent entrepreneurs. These brothers-in-law, in 1659 and 1660, skirted and intensely explored the south and west areas of Lake Superior. However, because of their difficulties with French-Canadian authority, they associated themselves with the British. Their most notable exploits are tied to the economic development of the Hudson Bay watershed and the opening of fur trade operations of the Hudson's Bay Company (Fig 3-2).

Louis Joliet (1645-1700), Jacques Marquette (1637-1675)

Joliet, a hydrographer, and Marquette, a missionary, were unexpectedly teamed in the awesome task of exploring and mapping the "great western river" (the Mississippi) which four decades after Nicolet's journey, was still thought to empty into the Pacific Ocean. In 1672 Joliet was assigned to the project by Jean Talon, the Intendent of Canada. As Joliet was preparing to leave Quebec, Father Claude Dablon, Jesuit Superior General, ordered Marquette to accompany him. Marquette was eager to join Joliet because in 1669 at Chequamegon Bay, he had heard from visiting Illinois of the great river.

The small party of six in two canoes (2 Frenchmen, 2 Amerind and the 2 leaders) began their journey from St. Ignace on May 17, 1673. Their route took them along the west side of Lake Michigan to Green Bay, then up the Fox River to the flatland portage to the Wisconsin River. Then, floating downstream at its confluence, they made their epic discovery of the great river -- Mississippi. Continuing down the broad river to below the Arkansas, they met, in July, a party of Amerind armed with Spanish muskets. Prudently, they turned around, paddling back against the mighty river's current. Following the geographer's adage, "whenever reasonable return by a different route," they turned up the Illinois River, portaged into the Chicago River. On Lake Michigan they followed the unexplored west shore to Green Bay where an ill Marquette wintered, while Joliet continued on to Sault Ste. Marie. Misfortune struck in 1674. First, Marquette, holding to a promise, returned to the Illinois village at Chicago. There he again fell ill and began a hurried return trip to the Upper Straits. He chose to journey along the east side of Lake Michigan and died en route, near the mouth of the Pere Marquette River. Joliet, on his return to Quebec, lost his maps and notes of the expedition when his canoe overturned in the Lachine Rapids. Surviving, he remade several remarkable maps from memory.

[3]Lynn Entine, *Our Great Lakes Connection: A Curriculum Guide for Grades Kindergarten through Eight*, ed. Ellen Fisher (Madison: University of Wisconsin-Extension Environmental Resources Center, 1985), p. 97.

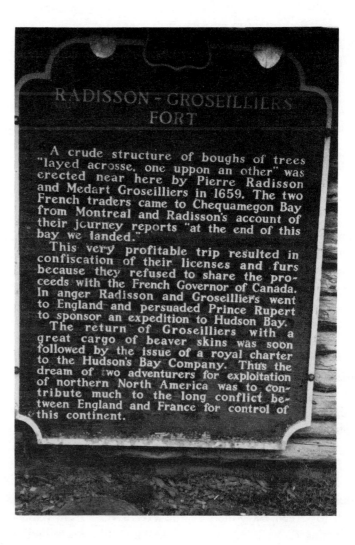

Figure 3-2. Groseilliers and Radisson historic marker, Chequamegon Bay near Ashland, Wisconsin.

Rene-Robert Cavelier, Sieur de La Salle (1643-1687)

La Salle was a visionary in foreseeing the economic importance of using large ships rather than canoes for transportation on the Great Lakes and the linking of the Lower Mississippi Valley to Canada. At age 26, he began an aborted attempt to find the water route to the Orient via the Ohio River. Thwarted in his Orient venture, ten years later he shifted his interest to large-scale shipping on the middle Great Lakes. At a site near Niagara Falls he assembled a diverse crew of 34 men to build a sturdy ship which could be used in a bold venture in shifting the fur-trade to shoreside mini-ports on the big lakes. His ship, the *Griffon*, weighed anchor in 1679, laden with trade goods, and set sail as the first ship to ply the adjoining middle lakes. The *Griffon* successfully cleared Lakes Erie and Huron and reached Mackinac Island. In the second week of September, La Salle met an advance party of his men on Rock Island, Green Bay. There they secured enough pelts to fill the ship's holds. He directed a skeleton crew of six to return the *Griffon* to Niagara. After sailing out of sight, the *Griffon* disappeared and the crew members were never heard from again. It is speculated that an early autumn storm sent the ship to the rocks two miles west of the modern-day Mississagi lighthouse on Manitoulin Island. This opinion is based on a 1890 finding of six skeletons and period relics on the island. Undismayed, La Salle, in 1681 and 1682, led a diversely skilled party of men by canoe around the Lower Peninsula and down the

Illinois River to the Mississippi and to its delta. In 1687 he met an unexpected death in modern-day Texas at the hands of disillusioned mutineers, who killed him in frustration of his not finding the Mississippi mouth from the Gulf of Mexico nor by land.

Daniel Graysolon, Sieur Duluth (1639-1710)

While La Salle was toiling at the mouth of the Mississippi, Sieur Duluth was exploring in the region near its headwaters, especially around Lake Superior. He was engaged in active exploration work for about ten years ending in 1688. In 1687 he served as an officer in Governor Denonville's 200-man *coureurs de bois* expedition against the Iroquois launched from Fort St. Joseph (Port Huron). However, his most noted work was in developing trade alternatives to the Hudson Bay Company. The furthest inland city connected to the Atlantic Ocean, Duluth, Minnesota bears his name.

Other Notable Explorers -- Missionaries

In addition to the explorations and records produced by government agents and entrepreneurs were the extended travel accounts of Jesuit missionaries. Father Rene Menard, in 1660-1661, journeyed into the distant Algonquian country as a part of the effort to expand posts in the Upper Great Lakes. Following the Nipissing (Brulè) route to the Sault; he continued west to the Keweenaw. Rather than navigate around the peninsula, he crossed at its base. At the end of the decade Dollier and Golineè made a grand circle from Quebec hugging the south shore of Lake Ontario, passing west of the Niagara strait to the north shore of Lake Erie and north along the east shore of Lake Huron to the Sault and returned via Brulè's route. Golineè's journal also describes for the first time in French, Lake St. Clair and the St. Clair and Detroit straits.

Father Fredrick Baraga, "the snowshoe priest" of the Upper Peninsula, made a lasting contribution, not only through his 30 years of observations, preaching and teaching, but also in compiling the authoritative grammar (1850) and dictionary (1853) of the Algonquian language, especially the Chippewa dialect. Unlike most other early explorers who were native French or French-Canadians, Bishop Baraga, who has been recommended for sainthood, was born in Dobernig, Austria; later a part of Yugoslavia.

British Explorers

In the transition period following the French explorers and missionaries, two British adventurers entered the Great Lakes region and made lasting contributions to the early historical-geographic record by publishing their travel observations. In 1809 the Englishman, Alexander Henry, released his *Travels and Adventures in Canada and the Indian Territories Between the Years 1760 and 1796.* In it he emphasized sixteen years devoted to ventures taking him into parts of the northern Great Lakes and central Canada. His lasting observations relate to topography, natural history and the tribal groups.

Alexander Mackenzie (1764-1820), a Scotsman and fur trader, is known for the river named in his honor. However, most notable were his explorations to the Arctic Ocean and becoming the first European to travel across North America above Mexico, reaching the Pacific Ocean in 1793 after having originally started from Montreal and traversing the upper part of the Basin. His exploits were published in 1801 in *Voyage from Montreal on the River St. Lawrence, through the Continent of North America: to the Frozen and Pacific Oceans in the Years 1785-1793.* Today, as one speeds along the Trans-Canada Highway west of the gold-rich mines at

Marathon, which passes through great roadcuts and vistas of awesome beauty, Mackenzie's words ring true:

> The country on the north and east parts of Lake Superior is very mountainous and barren. It is a continued mountainous embankment of rock, from three hundred to one thousand five hundred feet in height.[4]

In the Henry and Mackenzie era the typical cultural process of re-identifying places by changing their names continued. In their time Amerind and French names switched to English names.[5]

H. W. Bayfield, in 1828, explored and undertook the monumental task of producing a navigation chart of the 30,000 islands in the vicinity of Parry Sound on the east coast of Georgian Bay. He named that bay after King George IV (Fig 3-3).

Figure 3-3. Parry Sound -- Detail of H. W. Bayfield chart, 1828. (Lake Huron Series III). Source: Map Library, University of Western Ontario Facsimile No. 89.

[4]Henry R. Schoolcraft, *Travels through the Northwestern Regions of the United States*, copy of: *Narrative Journal of Travels*, 1820 (March of America Facsimile Series, No. 66, Ann Arbor: University Microfilms, Inc., 1966), p. 198.
[5]Canadian history has at least four prominent Mackenzies, two Alexanders (explorer and a Prime Minister), two Williams (a railroad builder and the journalist-reformer) plus Roderick, also a trader-explorer and cousin of Alexander, the explorer of the north.

In the early decades of the 1800's several forces were working which relate to the current shape and political-cultural-economic conditions of the present. These included:

1. The War of 1812-15 which reassured American control of the area south of the Great Lakes;

2. The rapid settlement by pioneers on the fertile lands of the defeated Iroquois confederacy;

3. The expansion of settlement by Loyalists in Ontario;

4. The conclusion of several treaties with the Amerind tribes and subsequent land divisions (Figs 3-4, 3-5);

5. The admission of Ohio (1803), Indiana (1816) and Illinois (1818) into statehood under provision of the Northwest Ordinance of 1787, plus the creation of Michigan Territory (1805) which was later expanded west to the Mississippi River, including Iowa, Wisconsin and the north-east half of Minnesota (Fig 3-6).

Two men, Henry Rowe Schoolcraft and Lewis Cass, followed by Bishop Baraga, were most active in recording the early American view of the Basin from a government leader point of view. The expansion into the former Iroquois territory was so rapid that Schoolcraft, in 1820, estimated that 90,000 people lived in Ontario (Geneva) County alone. He also noted with a keen eye that the progress of settlement was so swift that it:

> ---rendered it difficult to distinguish between those tumuli ancient fortifications, and other antiquities which owe their origin to an anterior race of inhabitants, and those marks of occupation left by the Iroquois or attributable to the French.[6]

In 1814 Lewis Cass was appointed territorial governor of Michigan. He concluded on arrival that, "such a forlorn district could not have been pointed out in America."[7] In time he became anxious to explore the remote area which was his responsibility and might provide economic stability.

Cass-Schoolcraft 1820 Expedition

With the permission of John Calhoun, U.S. Secretary of War, Cass organized a party of 42 men to explore the area south and west of Lake Superior to the headwaters and divide of the Mississippi River. In spite of the earlier Louisiana Purchase, the area was still considered to be in error, "the extreme northwestern regions of the union."[8] Starting from Grosse Pointe, after the wind calmed, at about noon May 26, 1820, Cass and his support group began their journey --

---

[6]Schoolcraft, *Travels, op. cit.*, p. 30.

[7]Henry R. Schoolcraft, *The Indian Tribes of the United States*, ed. Francis S. Drake, Vol. II (Philadelphia: J. B. Lippincott and Co., 1884), pp. 338-339.

[8]Schoolcraft, *Travels, op. cit.*, p. xii.

Figure 3-4. Treaty Land Cessions -- Michigan. Source: *County Evolution in Michigan*, Michigan Department of Education. Author added dates for Wisconsin and Minnesota.

signaling a new era.[9] The expedition paddled north to the Thumb and across the open-risky water of Saginaw Bay and followed the west shore of Lake Huron to Fort Mackinac. There the party and provisions were divided into three canoes and proceeded to the Sault. In addition to staples, pigeons, bear meat, fresh and dried sturgeon provided variety and protein to their diet. Floating along the south shore of Lake Superior they were awed by the beauty and pictographs of the Pictured Rocks -- now a National Lakeshore Park. At Ontonagon copper was found, as had been reported by earlier pathfinders. Forty-one days into the journey the party hoisted sails and let a

[9]The expedition included: Governor Cass; Captain D. Douglas, geographer-civil engineer; H. Schoolcraft, historiographer- geologist; A. Wolcott, medical doctor; Lieutenant A. McKay, U. S. Artillery-Troop Commander; J. Doty, Secretary; C. C. Trowbridge and A. R. Chace, assistant topographers; 10 Canadian voyageurs; 7 U.S. soldiers; 10 Ottawa-Shawnee; and 2 interpreters. At Fort St. Joseph (Port Huron) two sick soldiers were replaced by five others.

northeast wind blow them into the mouth of the St. Louis River at present-day Duluth-Superior. Here the great mineral wealth of the Basin became affirmed in Schoolcraft's mind:

> No part of the union presents a more attractive field for geological investigations or mineral discoveries. Copper, iron, lead promise to become important items in the future commerce...[10]

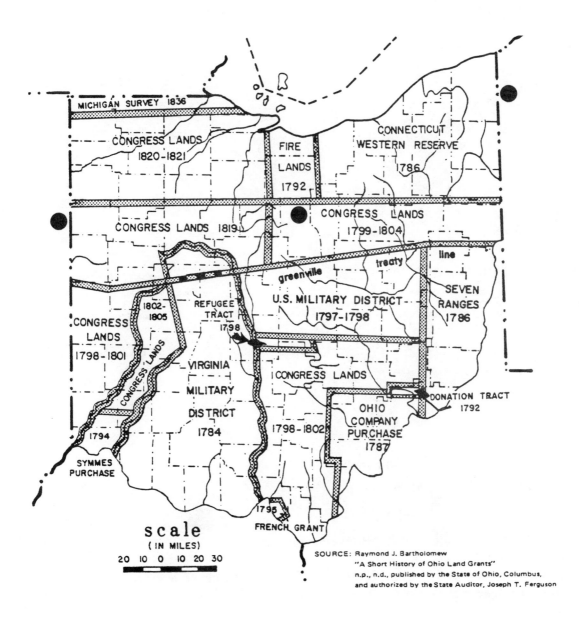

Figure 3-5. Land Divisions -- Ohio. The Greenville Treaty Line was south of the Great Lakes - Ohio basin portages. Dots added by author. Source: H. Raup, C. Smith, *Ohio Geography*, Kendall/Hunt Publishing Co., 1972. Used with permission.

[10]Schoolcraft, *Travels, op. cit.*, p. 199.

As the expedition approached the indistinct Sandy Lake-Savanna River portage, the men formed into two groups to assault the murky, swampy divide. After completing the five-day fatiguing trudge, Schoolcraft incorrectly surmised that the area would never be traversed by road (Fig 3-7). On July 15, the regrouped party entered the Mississippi Basin. After reaching the great river they followed it north and west to Cass Lake (located east of present-day US-2 and US-71) in the Leech Indian Reservation.

AREAL DEVELOPMENT

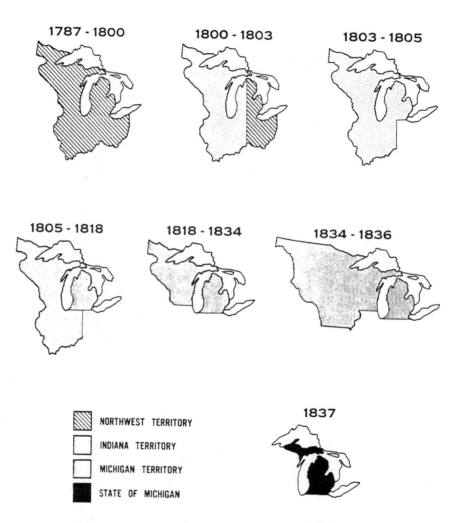

Figure 3-6. Areal Development -- Northwest Territory - Michigan. Source: E. J. Senninger, *Atlas of Michigan*, 3rd edition.

The Return to Detroit. -- Reaching what they thought was the headwaters of the Mississippi and naming it for the governor, the expedition traveled downstream to the Wisconsin River, portaged to the Fox which carried them to Green Bay. There the men again formed into two groups, one to return to Detroit via Mackinac, the other to proceed to the Chicago River. At Chicago another regrouping took place with Schoolcraft and Douglas leading a contingent along the east shore of Lake Michigan to Mackinac and then retracing their route to Detroit. Cass and a few others completed the circuit by horseback following the old Sauk Trail (US-12). They arrived in Detroit with its 250 buildings and 1400 residents on September 13, having journeyed 4200 miles. Schoolcraft rejoined him ten days later with his detachment. In 1822 Schoolcraft returned to the Upper Great Lakes, married a Chippewa who had attracted his discerning eye and served notably, with her support, until 1841 as United States Indian Agent for Michigan. Today numerous landscape features bear the names of Cass and Schoolcraft, including education institutions, highways, counties and communities.

Figure 3-7. Savanna Portage.
Floodwood, Minnesota.

Explorations to the Depths of the Lakes

In the continuing quest to gain or reaffirm knowledge about the Great Lakes, a risky exploration project was begun in 1985. The project was a joint Michigan State University-Connecticut University project which focused on Lake Superior in 1985, Lake Huron in 1986 and Lake Michigan in 1987. Of special scientific interest was, for the first time, reaching the extreme depth of Lake Superior with a human-operated submergible craft. Additionally, water quality, aquatic life, natural spawning sites for lake trout, bottom sediments and cultural artifacts were concerns of data collection and photography (Fig 3-8).

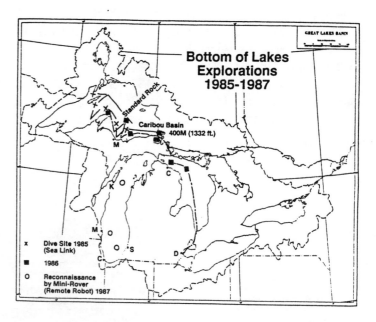

Figure 3-8. Michigan State University - Connecticut University, Bottom of Lakes Exploration Routes and Sites 1985-87. Base Map: IJC: Map - FSU Media Production.

The words that describe explorers of the past remain appropriate and set the standard for continued exploration: self-denial, self-discipline, self-motivation, self-gratification, toleration of critics, alertness, hyper-observational, risk taker, mediation skills, leadership abilities, perseverance and recorder. Today's explorations like the explorations of the French, British and pathfinder Americans invariably guided by Amerinds; the reports of discovery are not as important as what the people of the earth do with the newly revealed knowledge and how they expand upon it in the coming years.

Reflections and Self-Learning: Chapter 3

1. What are the risks of exploration?

2. Compare the means of exploration in the 1600-1800's to the present-day?

3. List 5 places that you would like to explore.

4. Compare the needs of explorers/travelers in the 1700's with the 1900's.

5. Which explorer/exploration of the Great Lakes Basin would you like to know more about?

6. Why are there more notable French than American explorers?

7. How can re-explorations of the present-day Basin lands and water help to solve problems of life in the "land of freshwater?"

8. Explore the backyard/block/area around where you live -- describe the beauty and concerns you observe.

9. What would you explore in or with a sea rover?

10. Who is given credit for exploring your district in the pre-pioneer period?

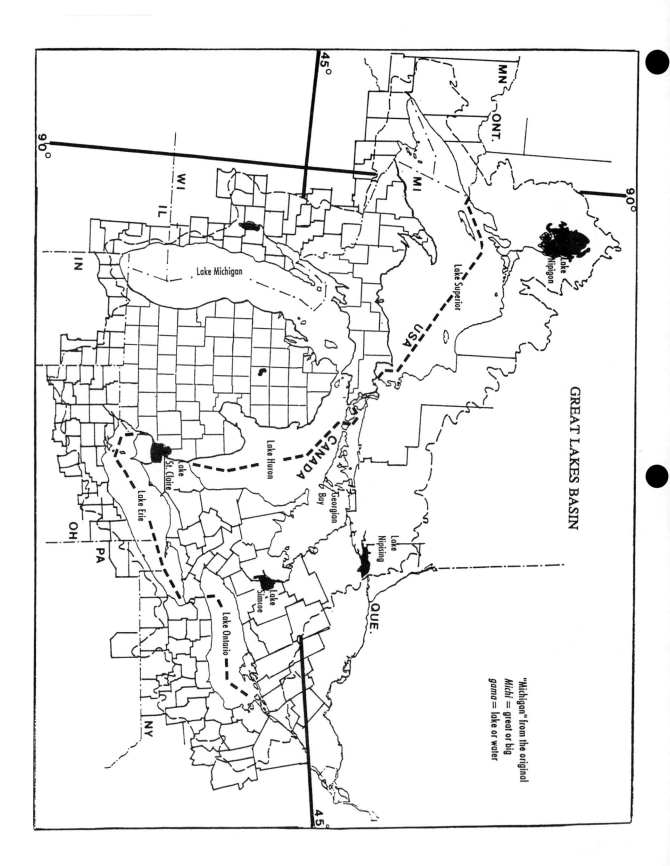

GREAT LAKES BASIN

"Michigan" from the original
Michi = great or big
gama = lake or water

Lake Nipigon

Lake Superior

Lake Michigan

Lake Huron

Georgian Bay

Lake Nipising

Lake St. Clair

Lake Erie

Lake Simcoe

Lake Ontario

MN

ONT.

MI

USA

CANADA

QUE.

WI

IL

IN

OH

PA

NY

45°

90°

66

"Enough for everyone's needs -- not everyone's greed."
Mother Teresa (attributed)

Chapter Four

CONTEMPORARY DEMOGRAPHY

The purpose of this chapter is to describe aspects of the contemporary human population, to stimulate thinking concerning their numbers and trends in relationship to the resources of the watershed and earth. Statistical data relating to cities, counties and watersheds will be used to aid, in part, the development of an awareness of and contrasts between the units of government.

Population and Political Units

Depending on one's point of view the demographic contrasts with the past are both astonishing and alarming, but also in some instances, quite similar. Today, rather than the Basin being divided into two dozen undemarcated tribal areas with a combined Amerind population of perhaps less than 100,000, the contemporary population of about 37 million is organized into 231 well-demarcated counties. In contrast to the frequently relocated villages of a few hundred people, today, there are approximately ninety-five metropolitan-sized communities of at least 50,000 extending from Thunder Bay in the north to Fort Wayne and Akron on the south, and Milwaukee in the west to Syracuse in the east (Tables 4-1, 4-2, 4-3, Fig 1-6).

Population Trends

Study, analysis and review of the county and community statistics should reinforce the notion that generalizations about the watershed's population have to be made with care and qualifications in order to prevent misperceptions. Further, in many instances, recent population trends and conditions are in fact different from popular assumptions, uninformed comments and media reports. As a primary basis for understanding the demographic situation, it is vital to emphasize that the total population of the Basin has had and continues to have substantial increases in number of people in spite of out of the Basin moves and relatively low percentage rates of inter-census growth for some political geographic units.

The Michigan Example.--Michigan is a prime example of the need for care in use of census statistics. During the late 1970's and early 1980's a national joke and bumper sticker message was: "The last one out of Michigan turn out the lights." Michigan was described along with other "frost belt/rust belt" states as a loser based on its "slower rate" of growth 4.3 percent population increase between 1970 and 1980 and its 40th rank among the 50 states in that category.[1]

---

[1]Lawrence M. Sommers *et al.*, *Michigan: A Geography* (*Geographies of the United States*, Gen. ed. Ingolf Vogeler; Boulder: Westview Press, 1984), p. 17.

TABLE 4-1

Great Lakes Basin and State/Province Population by County:*

County	1980 Population	% Change 1970-80	# Change + or - 1980-90	% Urban 1980	Race/Ethnicity/Gender % White 1980	Change 1980-90	Sex Ratio 1980
Illinois							
(Cook)	5,253,655	-4.4	-148,588	98	67	-4	92
(McHenry)	147,897	33.0	+35,344	59	99	-2	99
Lake	440,372	15.1	+76,046	89	90	-3	105
Basin Total	5,841,924		-37,198				
State Total	11,427,000		+3,602		81	-3	
Indiana							
Allen	294,335	5.0	+6,501	80	90	-2	95
De Kalb	33,605	9.0	+1,719	46	99	--	97
Elkhart	137,330	8.5	+18,868	64	95	-1	94
LaGrange	25,550	22.3	+3,927	--	99	--	97
(Lake)	522,965	4.3	-47,371	95	72	-2	95
(LaPorte)	108,632	3.1	-1,566	59	91	-1	99
Noble	35,443	12.9	+2,434	29	99	--	96
(Porter)	119,816	37.5	+9,116	65	98	--	98
St. Joseph	241,617	-1.3	+5,435	84	90	-2	94
Steuben	24,694	23.0	+2,752	22	99	--	102
Basin Total	1,543,988		+1,815				
State Total	5,490,000		+54,159		91	--	
Michigan							
Alcona	9,740	36.9	+405	--	99	--	97
Alger	9,225	7.7	-253	33	97	-3	100
Allegan	81,555	22.5	+8,954	20	96	--	99
Alpena	32,315	5.2	-1,710	38	99	--	95
Antrim	16,194	28.4	+1,991	--	99	-1	97
Arenac	14,706	31.9	+225	--	99	-1	98
Baraga	8,484	8.9	-530	30	90	-2	105
Barry	45,781	20.0	+4,276	14	98	+1	101
Bay	119,000	2.2	-7,277	65	97	-1	95
Benzie	11,205	30.4	+995	--	98	-1	96
Berrien	171,276	4.5	-9,898	55	84	+1	93
Branch	40,188	6.0	+1,319	24	99	-2	97
Calhoun	141,557	-.3	-5,575	68	89	-2	94
Cass	49,499	14.3	-22	18	90	+1	97
Charlevoix	19,907	20.3	+1,661	33	98	--	96

68

TABLE 4-1 (Cont'd.)

Great Lakes Basin and State/Province Population by County

County	1980 Population	% Change 1970-80	# Change + or - 1980-90	% Urban 1980	Race/Ethnicity/Gender		
					% White 1980	Change 1980-90	Sex Ratio 1980
Cheboygan	20,649	24.6	+749	25	99	-2	97
Chippewa	29,029	-10.4	+5,575	49	90	-8	104
Clare	23,822	42.7	+1,130	14	99	--	94
Clinton	55,893	15.3	+1,990	27	98	--	98
Crawford	9,465	46.0	+2,795	--	98	-2	99
Delta	38,947	8.4	-1,167	49	98	-1	96
Dickinson	25,341	6.7	+1,490	65	99	--	96
Eaton	88,337	28.2	+4,542	50	96	-2	96
Emmet	22,992	25.4	+2,048	27	97	-1	94
Genesee	450,449	1.1	-19,990	77	81	-3	94
Gladwin	19,957	48.1	+1,939	--	99	--	98
Gogebic	19,686	-4.8	-1,634	66	98	-1	95
Grand Traverse	54,899	40.1	+9,374	28	99	-1	94
Gratiot	40,448	3.1	-1,466	41	98	-1	94
Hillsdale	42,071	13.2	+1,360	18	99	--	97
Houghton	37,872	9.3	-2,426	40	99	-2	116
Huron	36,459	7.0	-1,508	8	99	--	97
Ingham	275,520	5.5	+6,392	85	89	-4	94
Ionia	51,815	13.0	+5,209	30	96	-3	109
Iosco	28,349	13.8	+1,860	27	96	--	102
Iron	13,635	-1.3	-460	--	99	--	93
Isabella	54,110	21.3	+514	44	97	-1	93
Jackson	151,495	5.7	+28,261	54	91	-1	102
Kalamazoo	212,378	5.4	+11,033	73	91	-3	94
Kalkaska	10,952	103.9	+2,845	--	99	--	101
Kent	444,506	8.1	+56,125	82	91	-2	93
Keweenaw	1,963	13.3	-262	--	99	--	108
Lake	7,711	36.2	+872	--	82	+3	96
Lapeer	70,038	33.8	+4,730	9	98	--	99
Leelenau	14,007	28.8	+2,520	--	98	-1	101
Lenawee	89,948	9.8	+1,528	38	97	-3	95
Livingston	100,289	70.1	+15,356	13	99	-1	103
Luce	6,659	-1.9	-796	--	96	-2	99
Mackinac	10,178	5.4	+496	26	91	-7	99
Macomb	694,600	10.9	+22,800	95	97	--	96
Manistee	23,019	12.9	-1,754	33	98	--	95
Marquette	74,101	14.6	-3,214	59	97	-1	105
Mason	26,365	16.6	-828	34	98	--	96
Mecosta	36,961	32.0	+347	39	97	-1	105

TABLE 4-1 (Cont'd.)

Great Lakes Basin and State/Province Population by County

County	1980 Population	% Change 1970-80	# Change + or - 1980-90	% Urban 1980	Race/Ethnicity/Gender		
					% White 1980	Change 1980-90	Sex Ratio 1980
Menominee	26,201	6.6	-1,281	39	99	-1	98
Midland	73,578	15.4	+2,073	50	98	-1	100
Missaukee	10,009	40.5	+2,138	--	99	--	100
Monroe	134,659	13.0	-1,059	39	98	-1	98
Montcalm	47,555	19.9	+5,504	17	98	-2	97
Montmorency	7,492	42.8	+1,444	--	99	-1	97
Muskegon	157,589	.1	+1,394	71	86	-2	94
Newaygo	34,917	24.7	+3,285	11	97	-1	97
Oakland	1,011,793	11.4	+71,799	90	93	-3	95
Oceana	22,002	22.3	+452	--	96	-2	96
Ogemaw	16,436	38.1	+2,245	--	99	--	95
Ontonogan	9,861	-6.5	-1,007	--	99	-1	102
Osceola	18,928	27.6	+1,216	--	99	-1	98
Oscoda	6,858	45.1	+984	--	99	--	96
Otsego	14,993	43.9	+2,961	20	99	--	96
Ottawa	157,174	22.6	+30,594	43	97	-1	97
Presque Isle	14,267	11.1	-524	28	99	--	100
Roscommon	16,374	65.5	+3,402	--	99	--	97
Saginaw	228,059	3.8	-16,113	67	80	-2	94
St. Clair	138,802	16.4	+6,805	52	97	-1	95
St. Joseph	56,083	18.3	+2,830	29	97	-1	96
Sanilac	40,789	15.9	-861	--	99	-1	97
Schoolcraft	8,575	4.2	-273	46	94	-1	91
Shiawassee	71,140	12.8	-1,370	34	99	-1	97
Tuscola	56,961	17.2	-1,463	12	98	-1	99
VanBuren	66,814	18.9	+3,246	14	90	--	96
Washtenaw	264,748	13.1	+18,189	78	86	-1	100
Wayne	2,337,891	-12.5	-226,204	98	63	-6	92
Wexford	25,102	27.3	+1,258	41	99	--	93
Basin Total	9,262,078		+33,219				
State Total	9,262,078		+33,219		85	-2	
Minnesota							
(Carlton)	29,936	6.6	-677	37	97	-2	100
Cook	4,092	19.5	-224	--	92	--	105
(Lake)	13,043	-2.3	-2,628	53	99	--	107

TABLE 4-1 (Cont'd.)

Great Lakes Basin and State/Province Population by County

County	1980 Population	% Change 1970-80	# Change + or - 1980-90	% Urban 1980	Race/Ethnicity/Gender % White 1980	Change 1980-90	Sex Ratio 1980
(St. Louis)	222,229	.7	-24,016	73	98	-1	96
Basin Total	269,300		-27,545				
State Total	4,076,000		+299,099		97	-3	
New York							
(Allegany)	<51,742	11.4	-1,272	21	98	--	97
(Cattanangus)	<85,697	4.9	-1,463	35	97	-1	93
Cayuga	79,894	3.2	+2,419	41	97	-2	97
(Chautauqua)	<146,925	-.3	-5,030	53	97	-1	92
(Chemung)	<97,656	-3.8	-2,461	73	95	-2	93
Erie	1,015,472	-8.8	-46,940	85	88	-2	91
Genesee	59,400	1.2	+660	36	97	--	95
(Herkimer)	<66,714	-1.0	-917	49	99	--	94
Jefferson	88,151	-.4	+22,792	36	99	-8	91
(Lewis)	25,035	5.5	+1,761	13	99	--	100
Livingston	57,006	5.5	+6,366	31	99	-3	93
(Madison)	65,150	3.5	+3,970	44	98	--	97
Monroe	702,236	-1.4	+11,732	88	87	-3	93
Niagara	227,354	-3.5	-6,598	72	93	--	93
(Oneida)	253,466	-7.2	-2,630	63	96	-3	93
Onondaga	463,920	-1.3	+5,053	82	92	-3	92
Ontario	88,905	12.8	+6,196	29	97	--	98
Orleans	38,496	3.2	+3,350	29	94	-2	97
Oswego	113,901	12.5	+7,870	29	98	+1	97
Schuyler	17,686	5.7	+976	-	98	--	96
Seneca	33,733	-3.8	-50	38	98	-1	97
(Steuben)	--	--	--	--	--	--	--
(Tioga)	<49,812	7.1	+2,525	28	98	--	97
Tompkins	87,085	13.0	+7,012	49	94	-4	99
Wayne	84,581	6.5	+4,542	21	96	-1	96
Wyoming	39,895	5.9	+2,612	26	97	-3	107
Yates	21,459	8.2	+1,351	24	99	--	90
Basin Total	3,562,829		+23,832				
State Total	17,558,000		+432,455		80	-6	
Ohio							
Allen	112,241	1.0	-2,486	67	89	-1	94

71

TABLE 4-1 (Cont'd.)

Great Lakes Basin and State/Province Population by County

County	1980 Population	% Change 1970-80	# Change + or - 1980-90	% Urban 1980	% White 1980	Change 1980-90	Sex Ratio 1980
					Race/Ethnicity/Gender		
Ashtabula	104,218	6.1	-4,397	51	96	--	95
Auglaize	42,554	10.2	+2,031	50	99	--	96
Crawford	50,075	-.6	-2,205	62	99	--	94
Cuyahoga	1,498,400	-12.9	-86,260	99	76	-3	90
Defiance	39,987	8.2	-637	52	97	-3	97
Erie	79,655	4.9	-2,876	64	92	-1	96
Fulton	37,751	14.2	+747	42	97	-1	96
Geauga	74,474	18.3	+6,655	15	98	--	99
Hancock	64,581	5.5	+955	61	97	--	94
(Hardin)	32,719	6.2	-1,608	43	99	--	96
Henry	28,383	4.9	+725	30	97	-1	96
Huron	54,608	10.1	+1,632	44	98	+1	94
Lake	212,801	7.5	+2,698	90	98	-1	96
Lorain	274,909	7.0	-3,783	85	90	-1	95
Lucas	471,741	-2.4	-9,380	94	84	-2	92
Medina	113,150	36.8	+9,004	55	99	--	99
(Mercer)	38,334	7.8	+1,009	35	99	--	97
Ottawa	40,076	8.0	-47	24	98	--	96
(Paulding)	21,302	10.2	-814	13	97	--	98
Portage	135,856	7.5	+6,729	53	97	-1	98
Putnam	32,991	6.0	+828	12	96	+2	99
Sandusky	63,267	3.7	-1,304	48	96	-2	96
Seneca	61,901	2.0	-2,168	50	97	-1	95
(Summit)	524,472	-5.2	-9,482	91	88	-1	92
(Turnbull)	<241,863	4.0	-14,050	71	93	--	94
Van Wert	30,458	4.3	+6	47	99	-1	95
Williams	--	--	--	--	--	--	--
Wood	107,372	19.7	+5,897	57	97	--	93
Wyandotte	22,651	3.8	-397	42	99	--	93
Basin Total	4,370,924		-102,982				
State Total	10,798,000		+49,115		89	-1	
Pennsylvania							
Erie	279,780	6.1	-4,408	72	95	-1	93
(Potter)	<17,726	8.1	<-1,009	16	99	--	99
Basin Total	279,780		-4,208				
State Total	11,864,000		+17,643		90	-1	

72

TABLE 4-1 (Cont'd.)

Great Lakes Basin and State/Province Population by County

County	1980 Population	% Change 1970-80	# Change + or - 1980-90	% Urban 1980	Race/Ethnicity/Gender		
					% White 1980	Change 1980-90	Sex Ratio 1980
Wisconsin							
(Ashland)	16,783	.2	-476	54	93	-3	95
(Bayfield)	13,832	18.0	+176	-	93	-2	102
Brown	176,280	10.8	+18,314	81	97	-1	96
Calumet	30,867	11.8	+3,424	49	99	--	100
Door	25,029	24.5	+661	35	99	--	101
(Douglas)	44,421	-.5	-2,663	68	98	-1	96
Florence	4,172	26.5	+418	--	99	--	103
Fond du Lac	88,964	5.2	+1,119	56	99	--	94
Forest	9,044	18.0	-268	-	94	-5	106
(Green Lake)	< 18,370	8.8	+281	29	99	--	96
(Iron)	6,730	3.0	-577	-	99	--	97
(Kenosha)	123,137	4.4	+5,044	73	96	-3	96
Kewaunee	19,539	3.0	-661	33	99	--	102
(Langlade)	19,978	4.0	-473	43	99	--	96
Manitowoc	82,918	.8	-2,497	57	99	-1	97
Marinette	39,314	9.8	+1,234	38	97	+2	96
(Marquette)	< 11,672	32.0	+649	-	99	--	101
Menominee	3,373	29.0	+517	-	11	--	100
Milwaukee	964,988	-8.5	-5,713	100	82	-7	91
Oconto	28,947	13.3	+1,279	24	99	--	100
Outagamie	128,799	7.9	+11,711	71	98	-1	97
Ozaukee	66,981	23.0	+5,850	74	98	--	98
(Portage)	57,420	20.8	+3,985	49	99	-1	99
(Racine)	173,132	1.3	+1,902	77	90	-3	95
Shawano	39,928	10.0	-2,771	19	96	-1	99
Sheboygan	100,935	4.4	+2,942	64	99	-2	97
(Vilas)	16,535	51.0	+1,172	-	92	-1	97
(Walworth)	--	--	--	--	--	--	--
Washington	84,848	33.0	+10,480	46	99	--	99
Waukesha	280,326	21.2	+24,389	78	98	--	99
Waupaca	42,831	13.4	+3,273	32	99	--	97
(Waushara)	18,526	25.2	+859	1	99	--	99
Winnebago	131,709	1.4	+8,611	80	99	-1	95
Basin Total	2,836,275		+92,191				
State Total	4,706,000		+185,769		94	-2	

TABLE 4-1 (Cont'd.)

Great Lakes Basin and State/Province Population by County

County	1982 Population	# Change + or - 1982-91	Area (km²)
Ontario			
(Algoma)	--	--	--
Brandt	99,036	+6,303	91,662
Bruce	58,373	+2,710	394,065
Dufferin	31,536	+7,240	148,958
RM Durham	288,153	+120,917	242,184
Elgin	68,413	+4,323	187,985
Essex	311,441	+14,547	186,194
Frontenac	114,642	+14,825	381,972
Gray	73,427	+6,584	450,470
RM Haldimand and Norfolk	87,211	+11,496	282,725
RM Halton	254,085	+59,051	98,305
Hastings	105,242	+5,157	586,955
Holburton	11,117	+1,912	452,282
Huron	55,913	+2,629	340,273
Kent	104,231	+2,384	248,131
Lampton	120,651	+3,352	283,091
Lennox and Addington	32,440	+1,990	284,071
RM Lincoln and Niagara	367,738	+26,198	179,828
Metropolitan Toronto	2,140,347	+135,424	63,831
Middlesex	327,788	+42,413	228,812
RM Muskoka	36,746	+11,259	381,619
(Nipissing)	--	--	--
Northumberland	64,605	+9,364	209,325
Oxford (restructured)	84,302	+5,704	196,373
Parry Sound	--	--	--
RM Peel	506,421	+226,377	126,312
Perth	67,712	+1,538	219,015
Peterborough	102,078	+13,910	394,236
Prince Edward	21,966	+299	104,820
Simcoe	224,893	+49,469	480,000
RM (Sudbury)	157,856	+3,354	279,244
(Thunder Bay)	--	--	--
Victoria	48,724	+12,053	306,690
RM Waterloo	314,069	+63,693	134,270
Wellington	134,504	+19,605	265,928

TABLE 4-1 (Cont'd.)

Great Lakes Basin and State/Province Population by County

County	1982 Population	# Change + or - 1982-91	Area (km²)
RM Wentworth Hamilton	414,175	+37,490	112,136
RM York	266,128	+238,853	171,869
Basin Total	7,404,505	+1,162,423	
Province Total	8,625,000	+1,459,885	
Basin Grand Total = 36,513,150	35,371,603	+1,141,547	

KEY: * Ontario Area data substituted for unavailable %, and sex ratio data.

RM = Regional Municipality

( ) Portion of county situated outside of Great Lakes Basin.

< Population center or most of county population resides outside of Basin.

SOURCES: *Statistical Abstract of the United States 1985*, 105th ed. (Washington, DC.: Bureau of Census, 1985); *County and City Data Book 1983*, (Washington, DC.: U.S. Bureau of Census, 1983), Table B. *Ontario Municipal Directory 1985 and 1993*, (Toronto: Ministry of Municipal Affairs and Housing, 1985 and 1993). *Ontario Statistics 1984*, (Toronto: Ministry of Treasury and Economics, 1984).

Sources consulted: *1993 County and City Extra* edited by C. M. Slater and G. E. Hall, (Lanhan, MD, Bernan Press, Second Ed. 1993); *Canadian Almanac and Directory, 1993*, 146th Ed. (Toronto, Canadian Almanac and Directory Publishing Co. Limited, 1993).

Note: Population totals for 1991 Regional Municipalities and Metro Toronto differ between the *Canadian Almanac and Directory* (CA&D) pages 5-181/183 and the *Ontario Municipal Directory* (OMD) page 130 by a total of 260,000. The CA&D was relied on for RM and Toronto changes in population numbers and the OMD for county data.

TABLE 4-2

Ontario - Great Lakes Basin Population
by Watershed Area 1981

Watershed	Population 1981	Density sq. km.*	Urban Population
Belleville-Napanee Area, Lake Ontario	178,300	25	104,000
Trent System	217,500	17	112,000
Oshawa-Colborne Area, Lake Ontario	197,500	103	159,000
Toronto	2.642,700	866	2,574,500
Hamilton	704,700	306	636,400
Niagara Peninsula	611,100	238	550,800
Grand River	583,000	82	465,700
Erie Shoreline	490,100	67	337,200
Thames River	464,900	80	381,900
Sydenham River	83,300	25	43,200
South Huron	294,800	21	161,600
Georgian Bay, Lake Simcoe	384,400	16	217,900
North Huron	371,800	7	291,100
Lake Superior	180,400	2	145,100
Basin Sub-Total	7,404,500		
Province Summary			
Urban	7,047,030	(32.3%)	
Rural	1,578,075	(26.7%)	
Total	8,625,105	(35.4%)	

SOURCE: *Ontario Statistics 1984*, (Toronto: Ontario Ministry of Treasury and Economics), Table 1.6. *sq. km. x 0.4 = sq. miles

TABLE 4-3

Great Lakes Basin Metropolitan Communities
with Associated Cities over 50,000

Community	Population 1980	1970-80 % Change	# Change + or - 1980-90
Illinois			
Chicago CMSA	7,937,000	.2	+128,633
Chicago PMSA	6,060,000	.1	+9,974
Chicago (3)	3,005,072	-10.8	-221,346
Indiana			
Elkhart-Goshen MSA			+17,198*
Elkhart	41,305	-4.3	+2,322
Goshen	19,665	10.0	--
Fort Wayne MSA	354,000	.6	+7,811
Fort Wayne (99)	172,000	3.4	+1,072
Gary-Hammond MSA/PMSA			-35,000
Gary	151,953	-13.4	-35,307
Hammond	93,714	-13.2	-9,478
South Bend-Mishawaka MSA			+8,052*
South Bend	109,727	-12.6	-4,216
Mishawaka	40,201	11.5	+2,407
Michigan			
Battle Creek MSA			-2,018
Battle Creek	53,724	-8.2	-184
Benton Harbor MSA			-2,622*
Benton Harbor	14,707	-10.8	--
Detroit CMSA	4,753,000	-.1	-87,764
Ann Arbor	107,966	7.9	+1,626
Dearborn	90,660	-13.0	-1,374
Dearborn Heights	67,706	-15.0	-6,868
Detroit (7)	1,203,339	-20.5	-175,365
Farmington Hills	58,056	N/A	+16,596
Livonia	104,814	4.6	-3,964
Pontiac	76,715	-10.0	-5,549
Roseville	54,311	-10.3	-2,899
Rochester Hills	--	--	+17,737*
Royal Oak	70,893	-17.8	-5,483
St. Clair Shores	76,210	-13.6	-8,103
Southfield	75,568	9.1	+160
Sterling Heights	108,999	77.6	+8,811

TABLE 4-3 (Cont'd.)

Great lakes Basin Metropolitan Communities
with Associated Cities over 50,000

Community	Population 1980	1970-80 % Change	# Change + or - 1980-90
Taylor	77,568	10.8	-6,757
Troy	67,101	70.2	+5,783
Warren	161,134	-10.1	-16,270
Westland	84,603	-2.5	+121
Flint MSA	430,000	.1	+459
Flint	159,611	-17.4	-18,850
Grand Rapids MSA	602,000	1.1	+86,399
Grand Rapids	181,343	-8.0	+7,783
Wyoming	59,616	5.4	+4,275
Jackson MSA			+756*
Jackson	39,739	-12.6	-2,293
Kalamazoo MSA			+22,411*
Kalamazoo	79,722	-6.8	+555
Lansing MSA	420,000	1.0	+12,674
Lansing	130,414	-.8	-3,093
East Lansing	51,392	8.1	-715
Muskegon MSA			+4,983*
Muskegon	40,823	-8.5	-540
Saginaw MSA	422,000	.5	-22,680
Bay City	41,593	-15.9	-2,657
Midland	37,250	5.9	+803
Saginaw	77,580	-15.6	-8,068
Minnesota			
Duluth MSA	267,000		-27,029
Duluth	92,811	-7.7	-7,318
New York			
Buffalo CMSA	1,243,000	-.8	-53,712
Buffalo (50)	357,870	-22.7	-29,747
Cheektowaga	92,145		--
Niagara Falls	71,384	-16.6	-9,544
North Tonawanda	35,760	-.7	-771
Tonawanda	18,693	-14.6	--
West Seneca	51,210	5.8	--
Rochester MSA	971,000	.1	+31,410
Brighton	35,776	2.0	--

TABLE 4-3 (Cont'd.)

**Great lakes Basin Metropolitan Communities
with Associated Cities over 50,000**

Community	Population 1980	1970-80 % Change	# Change + or - 1980-90
Irondequoit	57,648	-11.2	--
Rochester	241,741	-18.1	-10,105
Syracuse MSA	643,000	.1	+16,864
Syracuse	170,105	-13.8	-6,245
Ohio			
Akron PMSA			+6,000*
Akron	237,177	-13.9	-14,158
Cleveland CMSA	2,834,000	-.6	-74,177
Cleveland (23)	573,822	-23.6	-68,206
Cleveland Heights	56,438	-7.1	-2,386
Euclid	59,999	-16.1	-5,124
Lakewood	61,963	-11.7	-2,245
Parma	92,548	-7.7	-4,672
Lima PMSA	--	--	+1,340*
Loraine-Elyria PMSA	275,000	.7	-3,874
Elyria	57,538	7.7	-792
Loraine	75,416	-3.5	-4,171
Toledo MSA	617,000	.2	-2,872
Toledo	354,635	-7.4	-21,692
Pennsylvania			
Erie MSA	280,000	.6	-4,428
Erie (179)	119,123	-7.8	-10,407
Wisconsin			
Appleton MSA	291,000	.5	+24,121
Appleton	59,032	4.7	+6,663
Green Bay MSA			+14,594*
Green Bay	87,899	.1	+8,567
Kenosha MSA			+6,000*
Kenosha	77,665	-1.4	+2,687
Milwaukee CMSA	1,570,000		+37,183
Milwaukee (17)	636,212	-11.3	-8,124
Waukesha	50,319	26.8	+6,639
Wauwatosa	51,308	-12.6	-1,942
West Allis	63,982	-10.6	-761

TABLE 4-3 (Cont'd.)

**Great lakes Basin Metropolitan Communities
with Associated Cities over 50,000**

Community	Population 1980	1970-80 % Change	# Change + or - 1980-90
Oshkosh	49,620	--	+5,386
Racine PMSA	173,000	.1	+2,000
Racine	85,725	-9.9	-1,472
Sheboygan			
Sheboygan	48,085	-.8	+2,877*

	Change 1976/81	1981 Population	# Change 1981-1991
Ontario			
Hamilton Metro	+	542,095	-90,430
Hamilton	-	306,434	+2,065
Brentford	+	74,315	+7,682
Burlington	+	114,853	+14,722
Kitchner Metro	+	287,801	--
Kitchner	+	139,754	+28,528
Cambridge	+	77,183	+15,589
Guelph	+	71,207	+21,565
London Metro	+	283,668	--
London	+	254,280	+48,885
Oshawa Metro	+	154,207	--
Oshawa	+	117,519	+12,132
St. Catherine-Niagara Falls Metro	+	304,333	+89,603
St. Catherine	+	124,018	+5,282
Niagara Falls	+	70,960	+4,439
Sudbury Metro	-	149,923	+11,287
Sudbury	-	91,829	+6,055
Thunder Bay Metro	+	121,379	--
Thunder Bay	+	112,486	+1,460
Toronto Metro	+	2,998,947	--
Toronto	-	599,217	-36,178
Brampton	+	149,030	+85,415
Markham	+	77,037	+76,774
Mississauga	+	315,056	+148,332
Oakville	+	75,773	+38,897
Windsor Metro	-	246,110	--
Windsor	-	192,083	-648

TABLE 4-3 (Cont'd.)

Great lakes Basin Metropolitan Communities
with Associated Cities over 50,000

Community	Change 1976/81	1981 Population	# Change 1981-1991
Metropolitan-sized cities (50,000+)			
Barrie	+	48,287	+14,441
East York	-	101,085	+1,611
Etobicote	+	302,973	+7,020
Kingston	-	52,616	+3,981
North Bay	-	51,268	+4,137
North York	-	556,297	+6,267
Peterborough	+	60,620	+7,322
Sarnia	-	50,852	+23,524
Sault Ste. Marie	+	82,697	-1,221
Scarborough	+	484,676	+39,924
Waterloo	+	58,718	+12,463
York	-	135,401	+5,124

Key: CMSA = Consolidated Metropolitan Statistical Area
PMSA = Primary Metropolitan Statistical Area
MSA = Metropolitan Statistical Area
Metro = Metropolitan Region
NL = Not listed
* = Change based on 1983 census estimate
(2) = Rank of Central City in Nation 1990

SOURCES: *United States Statistical Abstract 1985*, (Washington, DC. U.S. Bureau of Census, 1983), Table 22, pp. 19-21 and Appendix II, pp. 876-879; and 1992 Table 38, pp. 35-37. *County and City Data Book 1983* (Washington, DC. U.S. Bureau of Census, 1983), Table D, Appendix A, pp. 930-943 and maps pp. 959-995. *Canada Year Book 1980-81*, p. 132 and *Canada Year Book 1985* (Toronto: Statistics Canada), pp. 53-54.

SOURCES CONSULTED: *1993 County and City Extra*, edited by C. M. Slater and G. E. Hall (Lanhan, MD, 2nd Ed., 1993); *Canadian Almanac & Directory*, 146th Ed., (Toronto, 1993); pp. 5-41/76.

It can be documented that large numbers of people migrated out of the state and that the percent increase and rank figures are accurate. What is overlooked is the significant fact that between 1970 and 1980, Michigan added more individuals -- that is people to house, feed, educate, employ and govern -- than five of ten highest rate of increase states in the USA and more people than during the state's "pioneer boom" of 1830-1850 when Michigan added 366,015 people in leading the nation in percent of population increase. Additionally, by the mid-1980's a reverse migration from the Sun-Drought Belt became visible and continues.

Perhaps of more concern is the fact that Michigan in the 1970's reached an inhabitant-to-land density that is greater than China's was at the turn of the 20th Century, perhaps it would now be folly to encourage the state or region to attain higher growth rates (Fig 4-1). Further, to slow population growth even more may be reasonable, for Michigan has a population greater than two-thirds of the approximately 170 nations of the world. Similarly, Ontario's Great Lakes watershed area population alone of 8,566,928 (1991) is greater than half of the earth's countries. Thus, what

Figure 4-1

Lake/People Density Comparisons
Michigan 1980 and China 1900

a. $$\text{Density (People Per Square Mile)} = \frac{\quad\quad\quad\quad}{\text{Area / Population}}$$

b. China 1900

$$101 \text{ Density} = \frac{\quad\quad\quad\quad}{3{,}691{,}500 \ / \ 375{,}000{,}000 \text{ est. Population}}$$
sq. miles

c. Michigan Land and Great Lakes Water Area 1980

$$95 \text{ Density} = \frac{\quad\quad\quad\quad}{96{,}791 \ / \ 9{,}258{,}344 \text{ Population}}$$
sq. miles

d. Michigan Land Area Only 1980

$$159 \text{ Density} = \frac{\quad\quad\quad\quad}{58{,}216 \ / \ 9{,}258{,}344 \text{ Population}}$$
sq. miles

perhaps is needed in the region is not more people, but (1) population stability, (2) increased occupational skill development, (3) greater employment opportunities related to world markets, and (4) increased purchasing power in the service sector.

Residential Characteristics and Trends

Since the Industrial Revolution, migration from low-density rural settings to high-density urban places has been typical in western cultures. The 1920 and 1930 census reports of both the U.S.A. and Ontario show that the shift to a majority of people living in cities had been completed; however, today the trend has shifted and the flow is divided. Most movement is out of urban central cities to urban suburbs and, not uncommonly, to small cities in rural settings or rural home sites in planned developments or waterfront condominiums.

U.S.A. and Ontario Contrasts

The most apparent contrast between U.S.A. cities and Ontario's is that in the latter, low, medium and high-rise housing complexes with nearby parks are commonly sited within easy walking distance of central business districts (CBD). The advantage of locating residential housing near downtown CBD's include: (1) transportation cost reduction (2) the reduction of political loyalty fragmentation between places of work and place of residence, (3) post-work hours' aliveness in inner cities, and (4) marketing bases for a greater diversity of activities in the CBD (Fig 4-2).

Figure 4-2. Windsor central business district and high-rise.

Urban.--In comparing Ontario populations with the U.S.A., the data confirms observations that Ontario is more urbanized than the U.S.A. part of the Basin. In Ontario, all of the 14 provincial watershed areas have urban populations over 50 percent (Tables 4-1, 4-2). In Michigan more than two-thirds of the counties have less than half their residents in urban places. In the other seven state Basin districts, 48 of 97 reporting counties have urban populations under 50 percent. Overwhelmingly, it can be seen on both the landscape and in statistics, that in Ontario, economic and political processes operate to concentrate residents in urban places. Significantly also, all of its Basin counties increased in population during the 1980's while the Illinois, Minnesota, Ohio and Pennsylvania parts of the Basin decreased. In comparison of the state/provincial segments of the Basin, only the Illinois portion witnessed a population decrease between 1970/1980.

Livable Safe Cities vs. Move from Cities.--The critical elements in maintaining low-crime, healthy, successful, urban places, with higher personal space densities, may be related to attention to social organization and to a commitment to providing for human needs such as: employment and transportation plus close access to schools, libraries, parks, culture, recreational areas, sensitive accessible leadership and a sensitive community planning process plus gun use discipline. Probably this can be attained by people working and talking to each other in a non-combative manner and with a determined *commitment* to make life better.

In contrast, much of the still occurring move out of American cities is related to unresolved racial conflicts plus crime, especially violent ones, related to illegal use of guns and drugs. Insensitive leadership or styles of management in the political, corporate and education sectors may also underlie the *retreat* to the suburbs and beyond or "stacking-up" problems in housing projects. Like any wartime retreat, the resource loss is not immediately calculated, and so it is with the retreat out of the cities.

Density and Overpopulation

The highest ground level micro-densities occur in temporary use campgrounds. In analysis, it is difficult, with permanently occupied cities to determine the role of crowding and density in human quality of life, decision-making on where to live. However, for the survival of society, overpopulation is a most critical concept, and thoughtful reflection is called for to evaluate if the out-migrations are the inability of an area to viably support its local population or other factors.

Rural Comparisons and Place Name Duplications

In shifting the focus to very low density places, the problem of name duplication arises. In Michigan, 327 civil townships out of 1245 have the same name as another in the state. At the county level within the Basin, there are five Lake counties (Minnesota, Illinois, Indiana, Ohio, Michigan) plus several other county name duplications including: Monroe, Erie, Livingston, Menominee, Iron, Genesee, Cook, Portage, Wayne, Crawford and Seneca. Not unexpectedly, Ontario has been unaffected by carrying as "cultural baggage" county names from New England and New York west; however, the province's counties of Kent, Niagara, Huron and Ontario are duplicated in either Michigan or New York.

Largest, Lowest, Fastest and Stable County Populations

Cook County, Illinois' has the highest density of people, in contrast, Cook County, Minnesota has the lowest population density in the Basin and the second lowest number of people. As a physical side note, Cook County, Minnesota encompasses that state's highest place of elevation while Cook County, Illinois is the lowest place of elevation in that state. Keweenaw County, Michigan is adjoined by a water boundary to Cook County, Minnesota and is the least populated county in the watershed, with 1701 residents. The fastest growing counties in percent and actual numbers of people in population indicates migration to both metropolitan and non-metropolitan areas with urbanization occurring in rural northern settings. Most of the highest growth rates are attributable to relatively low population bases.

The Future: Striving for Balance and Survival

Whether it was three centuries ago when the dislocated Nipissing had to separate from their Cree kinsmen in order to survive because of the rapid population increases overwhelming the local economy and food supplies, or today, citizens and leaders cannot escape demographic-economic-realities and evaluations.

Sex Ratios

The sex ratio (SR) for a place is the number of males per 100 females. When a sex ratio for total population exceeds 100, it generally indicates in-migration for employment by males and male-dominated activities such as mining. Through the World War II era, sex ratios of 103-110 were frequent in most parts of the Basin. Today, less than ten percent of the counties have a SR over 100. In contrast to the U.S.A., Ontario continues to have relatively high sex ratios indicating a strong attraction to the province of foreign nationals and non-Basin residents (Figs 4-3, 4-4).

Newest Arrivals and Ethnic/Race Distribution

Maps of United States county distribution of people by race, ethnic heritage and age reveal similar patterns. African Americans are located in greatest number in the lakeshore counties of southeast Wisconsin, northeast Illinois, northern Indiana, Ohio, Pennsylvania and New York plus south of the Bay - Muskegon line in Michigan. Wayne (MI), Cook (IL), and Lake (IN) rank highest in Black citizens. Hispanic residents form much the same pattern. However, because of departures from the migrant labor flow, their distributions extend somewhat northward and inland into the agricultural areas of Wisconsin and Michigan. Asian and Pacific Islanders whose total numbers are low, but whose percent of increase is high are most concentrated in seven urban counties in Wisconsin (1), Illinois (2), Ohio (1), New York (3) and six in lower Michigan. The largest number of Amerind people are in Milwaukee, Cook, Wayne and Erie (NY) counties.[2] Yet, Menominee county , Wisconsin has the highest percentage (Table 4-1).

The highest growth rates for the elderly tend to be in rural counties. Their numbers are also becoming a larger portion of the total population reflecting a post-Baby Boom aging trend. In contrast, is the more recent growth in births to unmarried child deliverers and teenage minors.

---

[2]William P. O'Hare, "America's Minorities - The Demographics of Diversity", (*Population Bulletin*, Washington, DC.: Population Reference Bureau, Dec. 1992) pp. 20-26.

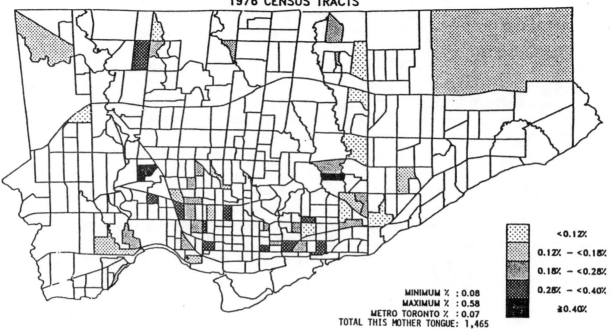

	<0.12%
	0.12% – <0.18%
	0.18% – <0.28%
	0.28% – <0.40%
	≥0.40%

MINIMUM % : 0.08
MAXIMUM % : 0.58
METRO TORONTO % : 0.07
TOTAL THIS MOTHER TONGUE: 1,465

NATIVE INDIAN MOTHER TONGUE, 1976

Figure 4-3. Residential areas of native Indian speakers -- Toronto 1976. Source: Census of Canada 1976.

Population Stability — Safety Valve?

Ontario County, New York provides an interesting comparison. In 1820 Schoolcraft noted the population for the county as 90,000. That was five years before the completion of the Erie Canal which flows through it and acted like a magnet to draw people into the western part of the Basin and for the development of Buffalo. Now, 18 decades later, the population of the county is 95,000 after increasing 6,196 during the '80's. Did continual migration out of the county act as a safety valve to more or less stabilize the population and help preserve a strong agricultural economy? Are there lessons to be learned from this county in attaining stable population and a viable economy? In reviewing and further studying Table 4-1, perhaps additional insights into demographic and economic relationships of the Basin can be determined.

If Charlevoix, who evaluated Detroit in 1721, and Schoolcraft, who judged its prospects in 1820, were to return to explore today, how would they alter their original descriptions?

> ---this is the finest portion of all Canada, and really, if we may judge it by appearances, nature seems to have refused it nothing. ... The islands seem placed in the river on purpose to enhance the beauty of the prospect; the rivers and lakes

abound with fish, the air is pure and the climate temperate and extremely wholesome.

Charlevoix 1721

It is gratifying, however, to behold, that Detroit...is rapidly becoming the seat of its [region's] commerce, the repository of its wealth, and the grand focus of its moral, political and physical energies.

Schoolcraft 1820[3]

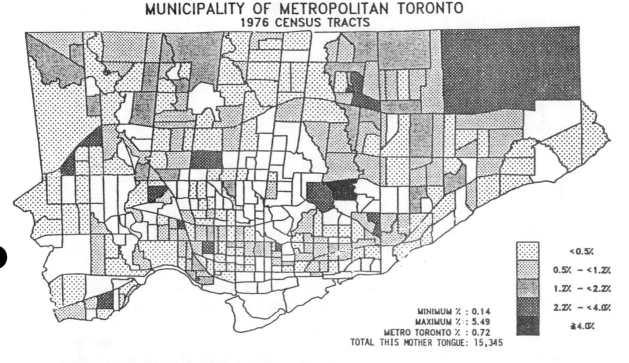

MUNICIPALITY OF METROPOLITAN TORONTO
1976 CENSUS TRACTS

MINIMUM % : 0.14
MAXIMUM % : 5.49
METRO TORONTO % : 0.72
TOTAL THIS MOTHER TONGUE: 15,345

< 0.5%
0.5% - <1.2%
1.2% - <2.2%
2.2% - <4.0%
≥4.0%

INDO-PAKISTANI MOTHER TONGUE, 1976

Figure 4-4. Residential areas of Indo-Pakistani speakers -- Toronto. Source: Census of Canada, 1976.

Forever Mindset and Choices Now

No generation can escape making decisions and choices and even doing nothing is a *de facto* decision and choice. Now, there are numerous demographic questions for this era's educated people to think through and in the democratic process make wise decisions and choices relating to the Basin and earth including:

1. How many people should or can live in the Basin?

[3]Schoolcraft, *Travels, op. cit.*, p. 53, 64-65.

2. What is an acceptable growth rate?

3. Where should people live?

4. Where should new cities be located?

5. How and what parts of established cities should be preserved or renewed?

6. How much in and out-migration can be economically and environmentally tolerated?

7. Should or in what ways can the economy be altered to assure a reasonable quality of life?

8. How can peace and tranquillity be attained and maintained in the communities of the Basin and at what monetary and human cost?

9. How do we stop the killing of each other, especially in the largest cities, and assure justice?

10. How can the conflicts of urban sprawl development, agricultural land loss, and racial and upward mobility relocations be resolved?

A final question: when will it become comfortable to say, "We can't do this, the people of 2994 AD have a right to this, we can not destroy it?" To be sensitive to needs a thousand years ahead is not so far into the future. It is only 8 percent of past time based on the 12,000 years of evidence since the Paleo-Indians left their earliest relics on the landscape. In the scale of a week, 8 percent is a little over one day -- NOW! Perhaps then the best mindset in people-land/water relationships is -- forever!-- a thousand years is too short a time period.

Maybe in reflecting on these questions the words of Father Pere Zenobe Membre, who accompanied La Salle through the Great Lakes Region and down the Mississippi, can provide a clue and springboard for discussion.

A nation may grow powerful through force of arms. It may grow rich through commerce, but if it does not grow equally strong in things of the spirit -- it can never be called civilized and it must remain forever a wilderness.[4]

Ultimately, we have to: Get beyond thinking globally and acting locally to thinking responsibly and acting justly for our posterity.

[4]"The Voices of La Salle: Expedition II: Reliving the Past to Explore the Future," a 12-in. Recording (Chicago: La Salle Expedition II, 1977) Side 1 Cut 3.

The photographer's "....way of changing nature was elastic
and always left things in their original form when he finished. "
The Bridges of Madison County

Photo Essay B

Urban Scenes:

1. Toronto - World Trade Centre
2. Toronto - Freeway home
3. Jackson - Graffiti
4. Chicago - Lock and Skyline
5. Detroit - Skyline from Windsor Waterfront Park
6. Port Huron - Waterfront Park
7. Cleveland - Men Working
8. Thunder Bay - Port (Source: Thunder Bay Harbor Commission)

90

91

Reflections and Self-Learning: Chapter 4 and Photo Essay B

1. What is the advantage of population change statistics by actual number versus percent?

2. Why have Ontario counties all increased in population in comparison to several declines in the USA portion?

3. What are the implications of Michigan's density of population being similar to China's at the turn of the century?

4. What are the factors needed to have a reasonable quality of life in a large city?

5. How would Charlevoix and Schoolcraft describe your community?

6. Discuss with others and answer the 10 questions related to "Forever Mindset and Choices Now".

7. Evaluate Pere Zenobe's statement.

8. Graph population growth for your community. What is its age-sex composition and trend? Why?

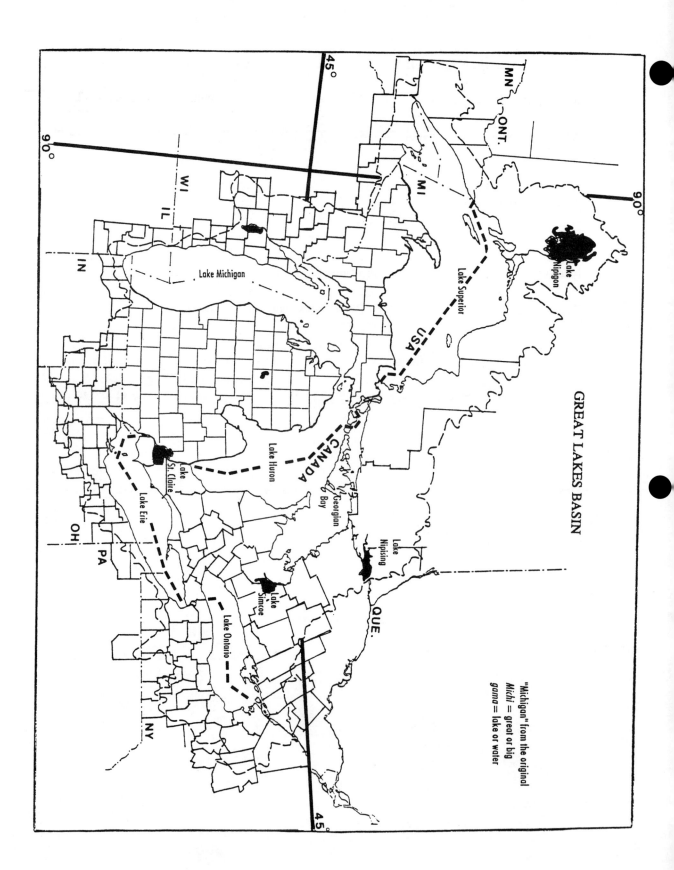

GREAT LAKES BASIN

"Michigan" from the original
Michi = great or big
gama = lake or water

94

Chapter Five

GEOLOGIC RESOURCES OF THE PRECAMBRIAN AND PALEOZOIC BEDROCK

Introduction

From Nipigon at the northern most indentation of Lake Superior to east of Marathon, "The Magnificent 100 Kilometers" unveils itself as one of the earth's most spectacularly beautiful places of continuous scenery. Here, the modern-day traveler, at hourly rates double the voyageur daily water distances, speeds along the Trans-Canadian Highway (KH-17) completed in the 1960's which is linked to the U.S. highway system forming the Lake Superior Circle Route through the continent's primary metallic mining district. As one rides through expanding communities and back to the open road of the Precambrian Shield the pavement is hugged by road-cut portals blasted through rugged hills and low mountains with sheer cliff escarpments. The discerning eye can detect the work of the glaciers in ice sculpturing the ancient folds and faults. The untamedness of the landscape is made apparent by rapid flowing rivers and occasional rock falls. Curves and steep downslopes demand a driver's undivided attention and a firm hold on the steering wheel even though the eyes are dangerously attracted to shimmering Lake Superior bays and stunning offshore islands or inland waterfalls. Undoubtedly, to maintain the beauty as development of the Basin resources continues, progress will have to be made in altering operational perceptions of "the solution to pollution is dilution," and mindsets that to hold a contemporary deed to real estate is ownership. Rather, it is advocated here, ownership is temporary with each generation as in: *We have not inherited the land from our parents -- We have borrowed it from our children.*

Geologic Processes

Scientifically, the geology and geomorphology of the Basin described in this chapter are related to four major events:

1.   The formation of the Precambrian, Laurentian, or Canadian Shield
       sometimes simply the Shield.

2.   The formation of the sedimentary Paleozoic rock layers of the Michigan
       Basin.

3.   The several advances and retreats of the Pleistocene glaciers.

4.   The recent natural and human erosion and excavations of the earth's surface.

How each of the natural processes worked are presented by earth scientists as fact. Nevertheless, geologic explanations carry with them an element of conjecture as scientific work is still underway which may alter accepted findings.

Precambrian Rocks and Minerals

The Precambrian igneous-granitic rock of the Michigan Basin is the basement rock formation of the earth's crust on which the Great Lakes Basin watershed rests. The resources from this structure and the Paleozoic layers are fundamental to manufacturing in the Industrial Age. Table 5-1 summarizes the mineral activities in the Basin.

Origin of the Resources

In the remote past of 600 million to 2 billion years ago mountain ranges pierced the skyline of the western Upper Peninsula, northern Wisconsin and Minnesota, the area north of Lake Superior and at other areas along the edge of the 5.2 million km^2 (2 million mi^2) U-shaped Precambrian Shield centered on Hudson Bay. The Shield, Appalachian and Ozark Highlands formed a rim of a vast saltwater sea which occupied a deep basin or syncline. The deepest part of the former ocean is in Lower Michigan. It reaches a depth of 5240 meters (17,466 ft) at a site near Ithaca, Michigan (Fig 5-1, 5-2).

Iron Mining Operations

Iron ore is the primary metallic resource mined in the Basin. Most activities focus on the western Lake Superior area and the eastern Ontario Shield area. Although iron mining maps continue to show areas basically unchanged since the ranges were first identified, it should be noted many mines and ranges functionally do not exist because of depletion, the deposits are too low-grade or too deep for economic retrieval. Since World War II, the depletion of high-grade direct ship hematite ore (65% iron) has resulted in the establishment of nearby concentration or beneficiation plants. The Marquette Range in Michigan and Minnesota's Mesabi are the major contemporary benefication mining sites. In contrast, iron mining in Wisconsin ceased in 1965 with the closing of the Cary Mine at Hurley. As a result of investments in beneficiation plants, a potential of 16.5 million tons of pelletized ore can be shipped annually.

The Iron Rich Minnesota Ranges.--The fabulous iron mines of Minnesota have always been economically linked to the Great Lakes; however, none of the four major ranges lie wholly within that state's district of the Basin. The Gunflint Range has a greater portion of its formation in Ontario while the Vermilion and Mesabi ranges, as a result of glaciation, are situated with parts in both the Great Lakes and Mississippi watersheds. The Cuyuna Range is entirely outside the Great Lakes Basin. It was the lure of gold in the Soudan area in 1865 which led George Stuntz to confirm the existence of iron in commercial quantities. The rushers, perhaps blinded by the glint of gold in their own minds, hurried along the old Vermilion Trail beyond the divide and passed over the continent's richest hills of iron -- the Mesabi Range. Henry Eames, the state's first geologist, is alleged to have said when he spoke of the fine deposits of iron on the divide near Babbitt: "To hell with iron. It's gold we're after." By 1893 ten mines were in operation. Now, a century later, six of the Mesabi's eight taconite beneficiation plants are located in the Great Lakes Basin: Hibbing, Mountain Iron, Virginia, Eveleth, Hoyt Lake and Silver Bay.

TABLE 5-1

Mineral Sites and Production

Mineral Site	Production Site
Lead	
Manitouwadge	E. Chicago
Sturgeon Lake	
Zinc	
Manitouwadge	
Sturgeon Lake	
Balmat, NY	
Copper	
White Pine, MI	White Pine, MI
Manitouwadge	Sudbury
Batchawana Bay	
Sudbury	
Platinum	
Sudbury	
Uranium	
Elliot Lake	Elliot Lake
	Port Hope
Salt	
Manistee	Goderich, Ont.
Montague	Sarnia, Ont.
Gratiot Co.	Ojibway, Ont.
Midland	Akron, OH
Marysville	Painesville, OH
(Detroit)	Retsof, NY
	Syracuse
	Watkins Glen
Potash	
Hersey, MI	Hersey, MI
Sulphur/Sulfur	
Sudbury	Toledo

TABLE 5-1 (Cont'd.)

Mineral Sites and Production

Mineral Site			Production Site	
Iron-Steel-Beneficiation (B)				
Hibbing (B)			*O E	Chicago
Chisholm			O b	E. Chicago
Buhl			O E b	S. Chicago
Mountain Iron (B)			E	Chicago Heights
Eveleth (B)			E	Morton Grove
Virginia (B)			b	Burns Harbor, IN
Aurora			b	Gary
Hoyt Lake (B)			E	Ft. Wayne
Babbitt			E	Jackson
Iron River			b	Dearborn
Wawa (B)			b	Ecorse
Moose Mt. (Sudbury)			E b	Trenton
Falconbridge (B)			E	Warren
Marmora (B)			E	Ferndale
Ishpeming (B)			BF	Toledo
Tilden (B)			b	Lorain
Palmer (B)			b E	Cleveland
Negaunee (B)	E b	Trenton	E	Syracuse
	E	Warren	E	New Hartford
	E	Ferndale	E	Marmora
	BF	Toledo	E	Whitby
	b	Lorain	E	Guelph
	b E	Cleveland	E	Kitchener
	E BF	Erie	E	Orillia
	E	Dunkirk	E	Owen Sound
	b	Buffalo	E BF	Sudbury
	b O	Lackawanna	O E	Sault Ste. Marie
		N. Tanawanda	O E	Hamilton
	E	Lockport	E	Welland
	E	Alburn	BF	Pt. Colborne

* O = open hearth
  E = electric
  b = basic oxygen
  BF = blast furnace

TABLE 5-1 (Cont'd.)

Mineral Sites and Production

Mineral Site		Production Site
Nickel		
Sudbury		Sudbury
Falconbridge		Port Colborne
Chromium		
		Hammond, IN
		Painesville, OH
		Niagara Falls, NY
Manganese		
		Ashtabula
		Welland
Cobalt		
Sudbury		Sudbury
Gold		
Ishpeming		Chicago
Hemlo		
Manitouwadge		
Sudbury		
Silver		
Manitouwadge		Chicago
Sudbury		Toronto
Balmar, NY (small)		
Beryllium		
		Elmore, OH
		(e. of Toledo)
Zirconium/Hafnium	Cleveland	Akron, NY
	Ashtabula, OH	Dresden, NY
	Falconer, NY	Pt. Hope, Ont.
	Niagara Falls, NY	

SOURCES: R. A. Santer, Field Traverses 1985-1986. R. McNeill, G. Telfer, R. Santer, Air Photography of the Michigan Shoreline 1980-1981, (Ferris State University, 1980-1981). *Oxford Regional Atlas of the United States and Canada*, 2nd ed., (Great Britain: Oxford University Press, 1975).

Selected Minerals By Geological Formation

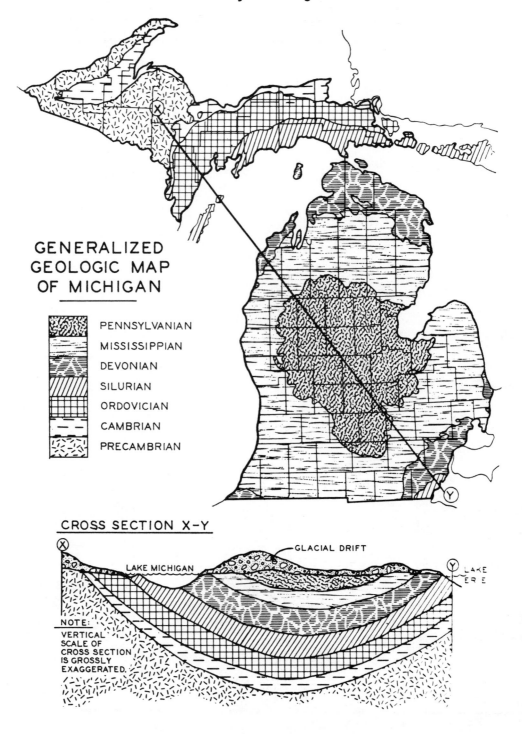

GENERALIZED GEOLOGIC MAP OF MICHIGAN

PENNSYLVANIAN
MISSISSIPPIAN
DEVONIAN
SILURIAN
ORDOVICIAN
CAMBRIAN
PRECAMBRIAN

CROSS SECTION X-Y

GLACIAL DRIFT
LAKE MICHIGAN
LAKE ERIE

NOTE:
VERTICAL SCALE OF CROSS SECTION IS GROSSLY EXAGGERATED.

Figure 5-1. Michigan Basin geological formation of bedrock. Source: J. D. Lewis, *Michigan Mineral Producers 1975*, Michigan Geological Survey Division.

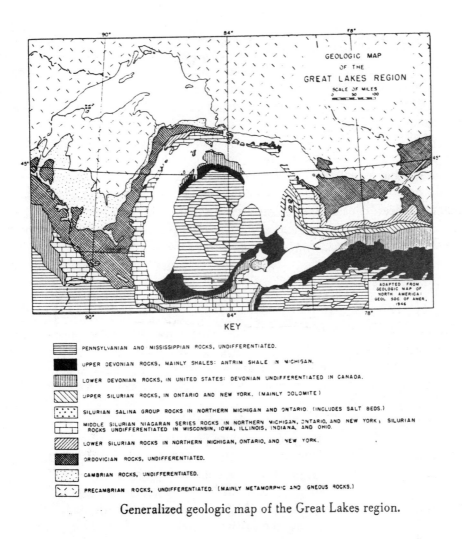

KEY

PENNSYLVANIAN AND MISSISSIPPIAN ROCKS, UNDIFFERENTIATED.

UPPER DEVONIAN ROCKS, MAINLY SHALES: ANTRIM SHALE IN MICHIGAN.

LOWER DEVONIAN ROCKS, IN UNITED STATES: DEVONIAN UNDIFFERENTIATED IN CANADA.

UPPER SILURIAN ROCKS, IN ONTARIO AND NEW YORK. (MAINLY DOLOMITE)

SILURIAN SALINA GROUP ROCKS IN NORTHERN MICHIGAN AND ONTARIO. (INCLUDES SALT BEDS.)

MIDDLE SILURIAN NIAGARAN SERIES ROCKS IN NORTHERN MICHIGAN, ONTARIO, AND NEW YORK; SILURIAN ROCKS UNDIFFERENTIATED IN WISCONSIN, IOWA, ILLINOIS, INDIANA, AND OHIO.

LOWER SILURIAN ROCKS IN NORTHERN MICHIGAN, ONTARIO, AND NEW YORK.

ORDOVICIAN ROCKS, UNDIFFERENTIATED.

CAMBRIAN ROCKS, UNDIFFERENTIATED.

PRECAMBRIAN ROCKS, UNDIFFERENTIATED. (MAINLY METAMORPHIC AND GNEOUS ROCKS.)

Generalized geologic map of the Great Lakes region.

Figure 5-2. Generalized Geologic Map of the Great Lakes Region. Source: R. Welsh. *Great Lakes Basin*, American Association for the Advancement of Science, Pub. 71, H. J. Pincus (ed.). Copyrighted by AAAS 1962. (See also Fig 5-1).

Since 1884 Minnesota iron mines have produced more than three billion tons of ore (90% from the Mesabi), over twice the combined total of Michigan and Wisconsin. In 1942, a record 64 million tons of high-grade ore were mined from the Mesabi. In the 1990's production from all mines still exceeded 50 million tons with 80 percent in taconite pellets.

Reserves of iron ore are great on the Vermilion Range, but they are deep, making them presently uneconomical to mine. The Mesabi high-grade direct ship ore is near depletion. However, taconite reserves, in 1978, were figured to be about 43 billion tons -- at a mid-1970's rate of uses, about a 240-year reserve. If new technology (plastics) and an altered economy (recycling) emerge, resulting in a tripling of the estimates, a 750-year supply is held -- a short period in comparison to the 12,000 years of inhabitance in the Basin.

The Iron Range Interpretive Center, in the divide town of Chisholm, visually illustrates a summary history of the people, engineering accomplishments and geology of the iron mining district.

Ontario Shield Iron Activities.--The province of Ontario ranks second in Canada in mineral production based largely on metallic resources of the Shield. Again, not all the deposits are located in the Great Lakes watershed. Iron ore ranks about fifth in Ontario's value of minerals produced, double the production of Michigan and with a greater diversity of mining. Ontario's mineral industry includes products from the following seventeen earth's resources in general descending order of value: nickel, uranium, copper, gold, zinc, cement, iron ore, silver, salt, lime, clay, natural gas, sulphur, oil, quartz, gypsum, and peat.

The Steep Rock Lake Mine opened during World War II near Atikokam in the Gunflint Range. It has been the province's most productive mine. It and the Griffith Mine near Red Lake lie outside the Basin, but their beneficiated pellets are marketed through the Port of Thunder Bay. The reserves are now small and may easily be depleted. Hamilton receives iron pellets from the Sherman Mine plant near Timagami. The steel mill at Sault Ste. Marie sometimes receives pellets formed as a by-product from the Sudbury copper-nickel tailings. The Michipicoten Range near Wawa holds a small reserve of occasionally mined iron ore.

The Historic and Innovative Marmora District

The mining operations at Marmora are located 50 km (30 mi) north of Trenton and Lake Ontario. Several isolated incidents combined to lead to the opening of the Marmora Iron Works in 1822: especially the 1815 eruption of the Tambora volcano, the "year without summer" in 1816, and the disruptions of the 1812-1815 war. As a result, the Upper Canada government was determined to have developed an iron works safe from possible U.S. invasion and to assure residents cast iron stoves. Within a few months after the completion of a primitive road from Stirling, the ironworks and company town came into production with an initial pouring of 90 tons of cast iron goods. Little demand doomed this venture and three others through 1875. Fayette State Park, in Michigan's Upper Peninsula, preserves a similar cast iron works.

The World War II innovation of the fluxgate magnetometer used to detect submarines provided an instrument which significantly improved geological mapping. In 1949, after a province-sponsored aeromagnetic survey, the distinctive outline of the presently operated Marmora Mine deposits appeared on the new geological maps as an anomaly. To utilize the ore, North America's first iron ore beneficiating plant was opened in 1955 with an annual capacity of 453,000 tons of pellets. Currently at Marmora, basalt is quarried and crushed to produce roofing granules (Fig 5-3).

Iron Ore Benefication and Environment Impact

As early as 1918, Edward Davis of the University of Minnesota became concerned about depletion of the Mesabi high-grade ore. His research led to the innovation of drilling techniques using kerosene and oxygen flame with a piercing jet of water to spill the ore in the drill hole. More recently, tungsten-carbide "buttons" on drill bits with 25-ton weights are used to flake the extremely hard low-grade ores. After blasting, the loose ore is taken to the beneficiation plant for crushing and grinding into fine dust, particles of about .044 mm. To separate the iron grains from inorganic tailings requires one of several methods, depending on the type of ore: taconite, jaspolite, limonite or magnetite.

In Minnesota, at Michigan's Empire Mine and at Marmora *magnetic separation* is used. Michigan's first pelletizing operation, pioneered at the Republic Mine, used a *liquid flotation* process which allows both magnetic and non-magnetic iron grains to be skimmed off the top of a ferrosilicon mixture. The Tilden Plant, opened in 1972 in Ishpeming, separates hematic particles *off the bottom* of a vat of caustic soda, cornstarch and water.

The finely ground iron dust is formed into marble-sized pellets of about 65 percent iron using bentonite clay as a bonding agent. The soft balls are hardened in kilns heated to 1338°C (2440°F). The dry, uniform pellets can then be easily loaded anytime of the year for transport which has raised demand for extensions of the lake shipping season.

The disposal of fine tailings has vexed mine managers and ecologists for years. From the mid-1950's until 1980 at Silver Bay, the site of the world's first taconite plant, 60,000 tons of wastes per day were deposited in Lake Superior. The discovery of asbestos-like cummingtonite fibers in the municipal water supply of Duluth and other Lake Superior communities prompted a demand for land deposition of tailings which was ordered by a federal court in 1976. Reserve Mining Company, after an initial investment of $370 million, now operates an on-land tailing site 11 km (7 mi) from the lake shore, connected by pipeline to a huge evaporation pond.

Land disposal problems of tailings occurring in Michigan include: (1) filling of wetland swamps, (2) run-off into streams, (3) blowing dust, and (4) stack emissions. These problems, coupled with greater environmental awareness, have led to corporate projects to reclaim land by revegetating inert tailings with grasses, shrubs and trees.

Figure 5-3. Marmora mine, Ontario.

Other Precambrian Resources

Uranium

Near Mahtowa, 40 km (25 mi) southeast of Duluth, uranium is found at a former gold and graphite mine buried in erosional unconformities. Similar formations are found in Michigan, but as of yet, the potential reserves have not been opened. At Bancroft and Wilberforce, near Peterborough, is a major activity. These mines provide uranium for both the United States and Canada nuclear electrical power production. At Elliot Lake, uranium mining, since the late 1950's, has led to the development of a modest sized city.

Copper on the Keweenaw Fault

The copper-rich spine of the Keweenaw Peninsula was thrust upward over 200 meters by a massive fault which can be traced for over 240 km (150 mi) in an area 1.6-13 km (1-8 mi) wide between Copper Harbor and northern Wisconsin. This copper and other valuable minerals were deposited in three ways as the materials cooled: (1) in dikes, fissures, and veins of otherwise solid basalt rock (Phoenix Central Mine, Central); (2) in amygdaloids or gas bubble voids in the basalt rock (Quincy and Pewabic Mines, Hancock); and (3) in the mixed conglomerate rock (Calumet and Hecla Mine, Calumet). In 1841 Michigan's first State Geologist, Douglas Houghton, mapped and reported on the economic potential of the copper country. By 1844 the first of the modern-day miners arrived at Copper Harbor and Eagle River from Cornwall, England, bringing with them mining skills and also the regionally distinctive lunch bucket pasty. The original copper mines tapped fissures and veins in the basalt in comparison to present-day mining of stratified deposits in shales, conglomerates and lava flows.

Copper Production.--Since the opening of commercial mining, 5.5 million tons of native copper and one million tons of lower-grade copper ores have been shipped to refining plants. Through the 1800's Michigan was the nation's leading copper-producing state and reached a peak in production in 1916. Only two active mines are still in production, Centennial, north of Calumet, and White Pine. Yet, the reserves of inferred copper have been judged to be the largest in the United States (Fig 5-4). Other minerals with commercial potentials in the Upper Peninsula are: zinc, lead, nickel, cobalt, platinum, gold and silver.

Copper and Nickel at Sudbury

The unusual Sudbury geological formation is synonymous world-wide with copper and nickel. Since its initial mine was opened in 1880, production has been continuous and has led to the opening of the 20 mines now found on the edge of the formation (Fig 5-5). Towering above Sudbury, a regional metropolitan city which has grown to over 145,000 people, is the world's tallest emissions stack which provides evidence of the city's role as a primary refining center. To overcome negative images, efforts have been made to more wisely manage stake emissions and to regenerate vegetation. Experiments with soil and water catchment terraces have led to some visual success.

Nickel refineries operate at Sudbury and Port Colborne on Lake Erie. Falconbridge has traditionally sent nickel-copper matte to Kristiansand, Norway. To help overcome local boom-bust economic gyrations, a tourist-service activity has been initiated at Sudbury focused on Science North (Fig 5-6). Science North, in addition to its hands-on, high quality northern environment orientation and science activities, is unique in its adaptive design. During construction it was found that the building, in part, was sited on a fault. Rather than relocate, the fault was cleared of natural debris and adapted into an intriguing aspect of the Centre.

Discovery of Copper in Wisconsin

Perhaps as early as 1636, Sagand mentioned copper at Keweenaw Point. Father Dablon, in 1669, wrote the following about copper while in the vicinity of the Apostle Islands and Chequamegon Point:

> Near that place are some islands, on the shores of which are often found Rocks of Copper, and even slabs of the same material. Last spring we bought from the Savages a Slab of pure Copper two feet square, and weighing more than a hundred livres (100 pounds, troy weight). It is not thought, however, that the mines are found in the Islands, but that all these Copper pebbles probably came from Minong (Isle Royale)...It is true that on the Mainland (Bayfield Peninsula), at the place where the Outaouaks raise Indian corn, half a league from the Water's edge, the women have sometimes found pieces of Copper....[1]

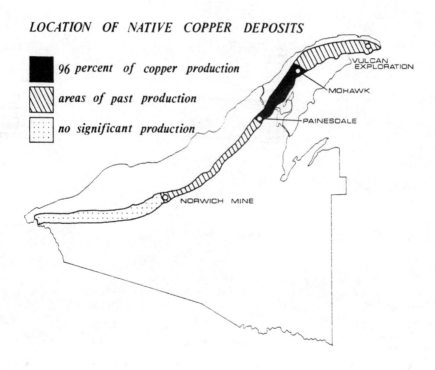

Figure 5-4. Keweenaw copper region of Michigan. Source: Western Upper Peninsula Planning and Development Region.

[1]Lawrence Martin, *The Physical Geography of Wisconsin*, (Madison: University of Wisconsin Press, 1916 and 1974), p. 446.

Figure 5-5. Sudbury mining area. Source: Ontario Ministry of Natural Resources.

Figure 5-6. Science North - Sudbury.

Minnesota Copper and Nickel

The Duluth Complex formation is a 5 km (3 mi) wide 80 km (48 mi) long zone of basalt northeast of Hoyt Lake on the edge of the watershed. It is estimated that the deposits make up about 25 percent of the total U.S. reserves of copper and 12 percent of the world reserves of nickel. Also found in the Complex are small, refinable, amounts of cobalt, gold, silver, platinum and titanium. These are low-grade ores of less than 1 percent ore content, similar to modern-day mined copper deposits. To mine these ores requires huge tailing holding sites (Fig 5-7).

Gold and Silver

Depending on price, gold when mined is found at three sites in Ontario and at the Ropes Gold Mine near Ishpeming, Michigan. The latter yielded $700,000 worth of gold between 1883 and 1897 at $28 per ounce. At fluctuating prices, of $300-600 per ounce, millions of dollars' worth remain in the small deposit which is well guarded, sporadically mined, refined and marketed.

107

Figure 5-7. Copper tailing site -- White Pine, Michigan on the Keweenaw Peninsula extending about 4 km (2.5 mi). Source: R. McNeill, G. Telfer, R. Santer, Air Photography of Michigan Shoreline, 1980, Ferris State University.

Historically gold was Ontario's most important mineral. Ontario's first gold discoveries occurred in Hastings County at Eldorado which was "rushed" in 1866. Other mines have been briefly operated in central Lennox and Addington counties. However, much activity is now centered around the Hemlo gold mine east of Marathon which began producing in the mid-1980's. This mine also indicates the growing economic influence of the West because the operation was developed with Vancouver capital (Fig 5-8).

The largest silver mining operation in the Lake Superior area took place at Silver Islet between 1868 and 1884. The small island in Ontario waters, 75 km (45 mi) northeast of Grand Portage, yielded $3,350,000 in historic dollars. On the mainland, silver also has been taken from Rove slate of middle-Precambrian age. The "Point of Rocks," a gabbro formation in the city of Duluth, has been periodically evaluated for silver mining.

The Paleozoic Seas: Deposits and Contemporary Resources

The Paleozoic Era lasted for about 380 million years. During that time several oceans alternately separated and contracted leaving their sediments which formed into layers of bedrock. Geologists identify the divisions of time of the Era by the names of the six major seas which occupied the Precambrian Syncline (Fig 5-1, Table 5-2). The Cambrian Sea was 735 km (460 mi) in diameter and about 5 km (3 mi) deep while the Pennsylvanian Sea was only 200 km (125 mi) wide and 180 meters deep. Intervening the ocean periods were desert and rainforest conditions.

Figure 5-8. Hemlo Gold Mine, near Marathon, Ontario.

Characteristic of the Paleozoic Era are the remains of aquatic life which were fossilized in the bedrock. The Basin possesses a wide diversity of types of fossils which are classified as follows:

1.   Fossilized plants;

2.   Crinoids (pronounced "cry-noids") including starfish, sea urchins and sand dollars;

3.   Solitary corals and colony corals;

4.   Cephalopods (pronounced "sef-a-lo-pods"), creatures with tentacles about the head. The octopus and chambered nautilus are modern examples of the ancient life of the Michigan Basin;

5.   Brachiopods, clams, and snails;.

6.   Trilobites, perhaps related to modern-day lobsters, crabs, crayfish and scorpions.[2]

---

[2]Robert W. Kelly, *Guide to Michigan Fossils*, Michigan Geological Survey Pamphlet 3 (Lansing: Michigan Department of Conservation, 1962), pp. 1-16.

The Paleozoic Era is best known for non-metallic minerals, especially sedimentary rocks plus fossil fuels, water and liquid chemicals.

In the sections describing the resources of the Paleozoic Seas which follow, an attempt has been made to relate the development of the bedrock resources to contemporary production locations and uses (Fig 5-2).

TABLE 5-2

Generalized Geologic Time Scale

Era	Period	Epoch	Time (million years ago)
Cenozoic	Quaternary	Recent	0.004
		Pleistocene	0.5-2.0
	Tertiary		58
Mesozoic			63
Paleozoic	Permian		220
	Pennsylvanian		280
	Mississippian		310
	Devonian		345
	Silurian		405
	Ordovician		425
	Cambrian		500
Precambrian	Proterozoic		600
	Archeozoic	(oldest rock date)	3,500
	Origin of earth		4,500-5,000

SOURCE: Adapted from J. A. Dorr, Jr. and D. F. Eschman, *Geology of Michigan* (Ann Arbor: The University of Michigan Press, 1971).

The Cambrian Sea and Pictured Rocks

Cambrian sandstone underlies the Basin south and east from Marquette, Michigan, Waupaca, Wisconsin, and Georgian Bay. At Sault Ste. Marie the formation is the physiographic basis of the international waterway political divide. In central Wisconsin it is physiographically related to the watershed divide. The fossil imbedded Cambrian sandstones have attained international prominence in the Pictured Rocks at Munising, Michigan, one of the Basin's four National Lake Shore Parks. The hard outer layer of the formation provides a less-easily erodible escarpment face over which sparkling streams tumble creating picturesque falls which delight photographers, local Chambers of Commerce area promoters and earth scientists.

The Ordovician Sea and Soft Limestone

The Ordovician sediments solidified into limestone and shales. The deposits form the east and west divides of the watershed. Alexandria Bay, Green Bay, Bay DeNoc and North Channel along Manitoulin Island are a result of the glaciers and lake water which easily eroded the relatively soft limestone.

Since 1837 at historic Madoc, Ontario, near the interface of the Precambrian and Ordovician formations, fourteen minerals have been identified at sixty-four separate sites including: rhyolite, limestone, granite, slate, marble, marl, garnet, fluorite, pyrite, iron, lead, copper, gold and talc.

Canada Talc Industries, Ltd. at Madoc operates the talc mines and initial processing. Currently the 1899 site is the oldest mining site in continuous operation in Ontario. The high quality talc is mined at several open pit and underground sites. The ground talc is used in the processing of paint, paper, plastics, rubber and cosmetics, plus talfil for striping athletic fields. During the removal of over-burden in 1982, earth scientists were able to cooperatively work with the owners to gain a direct view of the results of ancient weathering of the basement Precambrian rock and the deposition of Paleozoic sediments.

The Silurian Sea:
Limestone, Salt, Niagara Falls and Peninsulas

The warm Silurian Sea provided nutrients for rich growths of corals including barrier reef structures and narrow patch reef column formations. Several of the Basin's major peninsulas are directly related to the physiographic conditions of the Silurian period such as the Door, Garden, Bruce and Niagara.

Limestone is the basic rock of the Silurian sediments which are revealed most spectacularly in the steep cliffed *cuestas* of the *Niagara Escarpment* (Fig 5-2). The awesome vistas of the escarpment were exposed by the weathering away of the less-resistant Ordovician limestone. The Niagara Escarpment can be experienced inland as it parallels the south edge of Lake Ontario in New York, then spectacularly as it crosses into the Province as the underlying cap rock of the gigantic, powerful, roaring, attractive Niagara Falls. At Blue Mountain near Collingwood the highest elevations (322 m, 1000 ft) of the formation have been turned into thrilling ski slopes adjacent to 50 m (150 ft) cliffs, while at Owen Sound city engineers and crews must perform seeming miracles of snow and ice removal every wintertime to prevent automobiles from turning into unsteerable wheeled toboggans as they travel the streets. The escarpment terminates at the Door Peninsula. Here, the tourist economy of Wisconsin is strengthened by the millions of travelers who come to the peninsula to not only enjoy the natural beauty of the area, but also the artist colonies, fruit and wines, evening fish boils, and perhaps to reminisce on Nicolet's thoughts that he had reached China when he met the Winnebago.

The Silurian limestone formation continues below the surface through eastern Wisconsin and Illinois. However, it lies near the surface providing for easy quarrying in Indiana, western Ohio plus Monroe and Wayne counties in Michigan which are marked by characteristic landscape features (Fig 5-9 and 5-10).

Niagara Falls and Gorge -- the Future

Since the meltback of the glaciers, the Niagara River has cut a great notch in the Niagara Escarpment (Fig 5-11). By about 1000 BP (900 AD), the falls had cut back to the site of the

American Falls. There a complete separation occurred when the gorge reached Goat Island. Since then nearly all the waterflow has been in the Canadian Branch. The unequal flow has resulted in the Canadian Horseshoe Falls eroding back nearly 1000 m (3000 ft) while the American Falls has receded slightly. Given similar waterflows of the past, a reasonable estimate may be that in another 2500 years the escarpment in the strait will be totally cut. Such an event would cause another change in the shape of the lakes and bring the bottom of Lake Erie very close to the surface level of Lake Ontario.

Figure 5-9. Quarry and Sibley Road sign, Riverview, Michigan.

The Future of the Falls.--Since the Pleistocene Ice Age, millions of people, for innumerable reasons, have been attracted to the spectacular falls at Niagara. The falls' awesomeness brings out in individuals both inspirational reward and challenges to conquer in some manner its power. To others, it is the place to end life. Some people after visiting the Niagara Falls area with its clutch of motels, viewing towers, changing colored lights, train rides, busy parking lots, eateries, flashy souvenir shops and auto traffic remark about the place's over-development and commercialism. Such descriptions raise a question for pondering -- What is reasonable development around a natural wonder? With an increasing population and a steady adaptation to a service economy it can be anticipated in the near future, natural waterfalls throughout the Basin will be targeted for further development by both the sensitive community spirited individuals and those tending more toward unbridled, greedy hucksterism.

Figure 5-10. Sibley-Detroit Edison limestone quarry, Riverview, Michigan.

Silurian Sea Salt Products

The most important mineral resources from the Silurian period are its brines and rock salt which support a diversifying international chemical products industry. By locating near the shore of the former sea, where the brines and rock salt were deposited closest to the surface, Dow Chemical -- headquartered in Midland, BASF -- of Wyandotte, plus plants of other companies have been able to gain a competitive edge in extraction costs. The brines are most valuable for sodium salts such as iodine, fluorine, bromine, caustic soda and soda ash. Natural brines are a source of sodium chloride -- table salt. Since the mid-1800's, Michigan has ranked first in the production of natural salines. Rock salt mining occurs at Windsor and Goderich in Ontario, plus Cleveland. In the past, Detroit and Rochester, New York, were important sites (Fig 5-12).

During the 1950's consideration was given in case of war to sheltering the entire population of Detroit in the huge mine opened in 1912. The idea continues to be rejected because there are only two entrance/exit shafts which would restrict timely entrance in the case of an unexpected missile attack. Further, they could be easily sealed with a blast. In reaction to modern salt mining competition from Cleveland and Windsor operations, the Detroit mine was taken out of production in January, 1983. As a transitional enterprise until 1986, Crystal Mines, Inc. operated the mine as a tour activity. Potential alternate commercial uses include storage, mushroom culture, trash filling or toxic waste storage in its 14 C° (58 F°) with 56 percent humidity environment.

113

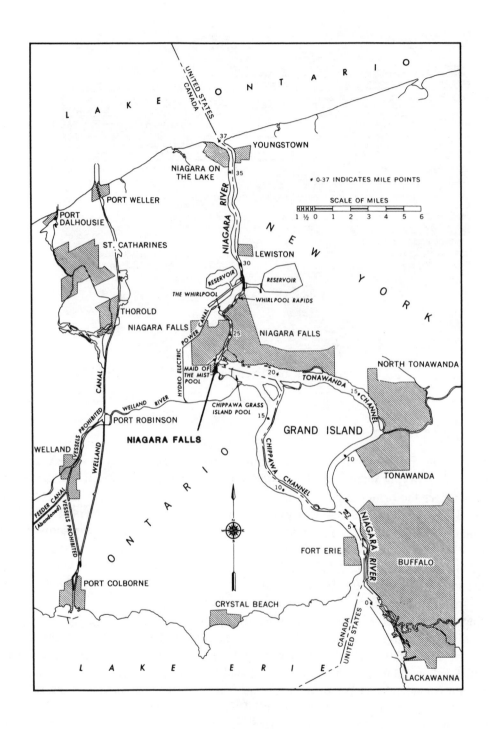

Figure 5-11. Map of Niagara Falls area. The original Falls were at Lewiston. Source: *Great Lakes Water Level Facts*, 1986, U.S. Army Corps of Engineers, Detroit District.

Figure 5-12. Goderich salt monument.

The Safety of Salt Mines for Waste Storage.--It is sometimes reported in articles relating to hazardous waste storage that salt formations are a stable place within the earth. Neither the geologic history nor mining history in Michigan support the assertion. An underground waste site on the north end of Grosse Isle collapsed in 1971 and is now filled with a watery liquid. During the original opening of the Detroit salt mine which began in 1906, work was slowed by dangerous hydrogen sulfide gas and much flowing water. The separation of the Upper and Lower Peninsulas has been attributed to water which entered the salt strata between Lakes Michigan and Huron which dissolved the rock salt up to 100 meters thick. As a result, limestone and shale above collapsed forming the initial strait. With such a record of instability, it is questionable whether salt beds as sites for long-term storage of radioactive wastes, can be considered as safe, especially with their proximity to the world's foremost bodies of fresh water.

The Devonian Sea: Coral, Limestone and Petroleum

The Devonian Sea deposit consists of thick layers of corals, limestone and shales. The Devonian limestone quarrying and cement manufacturing have become one of this region's most important activities. Quarries operated for the production of both portland and masonry cement are located at Alpena, Charlevoix and Dundee. In Ontario, plants are found at Clarkson, Belleville, Bath, Picton, St. Mary's and Woodstock. Much of Indiana's famous limestone is outside the Great Lakes watershed. Similarly only six of Ohio's 57 primary counties with quarries are located in the Basin: Sandusky, Erie, Wyandot, Ottawa, Lucas and Seneca. The world's largest limestone quarry now considerably reduced in activity and employment is located at Rogers City, Michigan, where

115

calcite is secured to provide a flux for steel-making. Oil, natural gas, railroad ballast, stone aggregate and stone for the chemical industry also come from the Devonian bedrock formation. The French La Farge Corporation is significantly involved in limestone, gypsum and cement activities.

Karst Topography.--Sinkholes, with uniformly round and steep sides, are formed from water eroded limestone. One Basin karst or sinkhole area is located north and west of Alpena, in Long Rapids Township (T32N R6E-Mich.) at Lachine and Fletcher plus in the narrow outlet channel of Long Lake. Most of the 30 prominent sinks are 15-30 m (50-100 ft) in diameter with vertical rock walls of 25-30 m (75-100 ft). Two *warnings*: (1) the sinkholes are a dangerous landscape feature, especially when investigated with unsure footing and inattention, and (2) most sinkholes are on private property requiring owner's permission to traverse the land.

The Mississippian Sea: Sandstone and Gypsum

The Mississippian Sea disappeared when dry arid winds of a desert climate evaporated its water (Fig 5-1). Sandstone and gypsum have become the most used deposits from this formation. In addition, colorful shale in pastel blue, greenish-yellow and black, plus salt, alabaster and limestone were formed from the Mississippian sediments. Gypsum beds appear as outcrops at Grand Rapids, National City and Alabaster in Michigan, which are easily mined for use in gypsum-plasterboard/drywall and fertilizer. During the Vietnam War, an underground mine in Grand Rapids was adapted for constant temperature storage use.

Mississippian age sandstone has been frequently used for fences, stepping stones, fireplaces and other decorative or functional purposes. The 20th Century's world's largest walled prison is made of brick. However, its mid-19th Century predecessor located in the city of Jackson, Michigan, was constructed from rock split from the Marshall sandstone formation (Fig 5-13).

Figure 5-13. Mississippian - Jackson sandstone used for State Prison wall -- currently National Guard Armory.

The Pennsylvanian Sea: Low-Grade Coal

The Pennsylvanian Sea was the last of the six major Paleozoic Seas which occupied the Michigan Basin until about 280 million years ago. Coal formations of Pennsylvanian age in the Appalachian Region overshadow the minor low-grade deposits which appear as extensive on geologic maps of Michigan. In total Michigan holds about 110 million tons in useful reserve which could be easily reached by strip mining some agricultural land. Ohio coal deposits have always been more productive than the Michigan field within the Basin; however, the Ohio fields outside the watershed are even more productive. Ontario produces no coal and imports 87 percent of its consumption from the Appalachian field.

Petroleum

Massive anticlinal domelike geologic formations have proven worldwide to be the best source of natural gas and crude oil. The concaved syncline of the Michigan Basin is not generally conducive to trapping natural gas and oil. Yet, as a result of natural folding of the bedrock veneers, some mini domes have formed and yield rewarding quantities of oil. The deposits are mostly found in the formations between the Mississippian and Ordovician Periods in pools of 3-10 mi^2. Deep well drilling may produce wells outside the historic ring of well site development which has taken place since the 1880's. New fields for drilling are increasingly identified with the use of GIS (Geographic Information System) mapping. Between 1988 and 1991 using Michigan Antrim Tracking System (MATS) as a part of GIS over 2200 natural gas wells were drilled into Devonian-Antrim shale making it one of the most active fields in the United States.[3]

Oil and Natural Gas Production

Ontario's first well "came in" at Lampton County and has remained in production for a century. In the lower Thames River in Mosa Township, natural gas is found and a few oil wells have been operated with insignificant yields. Today the Prairie Provinces account for 96 percent of the nation's production. Major refineries are located at Sarnia, Port Credit and Clarkson. Since the oil embargo of 1972, Michigan has enjoyed a significant increase in drilling and production activities which now place it in the top dozen states in yield. Money from oil and gas leases for drilling on public land has also resulted in millions of dollars for the Department of Natural Resources Trust Fund and Game and Fish Protection Fund. In addition to the Dundee, Monroe and Detroit River formations the Niagara Reef has been the major attraction for drilling. For a decade, "Texans in the north" have been quietly visible in the vicinity of Mecosta, Osceola and Isabella counties with Mount Pleasant as the "Oil Capital of Michigan." Ohio oil wells within the watershed have been relatively minor; however, that district's crude is refined into high-grade lubricants. Important Ohio refineries are located at Findlay, Lima and Toledo. Other significant Basin refinery complexes with their characteristic web of pipes with pungent odors, "the smell of money," are located at Duluth-Superior, Chicago, Milwaukee, Buffalo, Detroit, Trenton, Flat Rock, Bay City, Alma and West Branch, Michigan. The Marathon Oil Company plant at Melvindale, Michigan has the region's largest storage capacity. Natural gas wells are found in the area from the Niagara River to the Detroit River on both sides of Lake Erie, the central Lower Peninsula and south of Lake

---

[3]Robert Mecready, *et al*, "GIS Provides New Clues to Elusive Natural Gas Reservoirs," (*Geo Info Systems*, February 1992), pp. 42-45.

Ontario. Some natural gas wells have been brought into use on the bed of Lake Erie. The former coral patch reefs of the Basin may hold potential for limited oil and gas production in the presently unproductive Upper Peninsula and for expanded production in Ontario and Wisconsin (Fig 5-14).

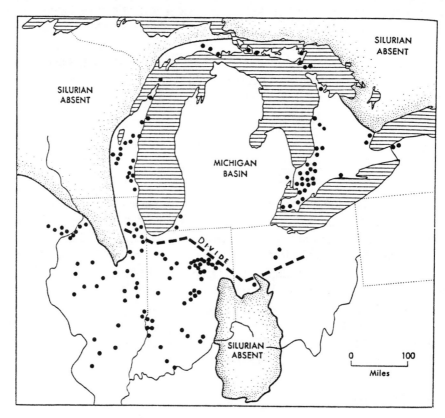

Figure 5-14. Distribution of middle Silurian patch reefs. Source: T. Clark and C. Stearn, *Geological Evolution of North America*, 2nd edition, The Ronald Press Co. Copyrighted by John Wiley & Sons, Inc., 1968. ©Reprinted by permission of John Wiley & Sons, Inc. (Divide added by author.)

Drilling into the Lakes Bottomland

The Great Lakes Bottomland -- the land underwater -- is public property which requires governmental (state/provincial) permits to fill or erect permanent structures on. The precedent of establishing successful natural gas drilling operations in the bottomlands (Lake Erie) has occurred. Now, if new bottomland drilling is licensed, the risks of blowouts, well head fires and oil spills would have to be accepted, especially in regard to the three middle lakes. In comparison to the oceans, where for years the risk and consequences of open sea drilling have been accepted, the Great Lakes present several contrasts worth discussion in relationship to drilling consequences.

Great Lakes - Ocean Drilling and Risk Contrasts

Great Lakes:	Oceans:
1. Fresh water	1. Salt water
2. Relatively limited resource	2. Extensive resource
3. Freezes for several weeks or months	3. No freezing or very limited period
4. No tides of significance	4. Tides which, when low, facilitate clean ups
5. Limited turbulence to dissipate spill residuals	5. Spill residuals somewhat dissipated by currents
6. Life recharge cycle decades long	6. Constant recharge
7. Lakes provide a major source of potable water for shoreline communities	7. Limited dependency on ocean for water

Crude Oil Drilling Options

a. Ban all drilling within waters of the entire watershed. The cooperation of eight states and Ontario would be needed.

b. Ban or allow drilling as a state/province option.

c. Establish jointly specific drilling areas with specific spill-blowout, fire standards.

d. Limit drilling to on-shore slant drilling.

e. Ban drilling for one century with review in late 21st Century.

f. Issue leases, but ban drilling until decision on allowances is made.

g. Direct human resources toward conservation of existing supplies of energy resources, stabilize population to help stabilize demand, institute and enforce rigorous conservation practices, support massive alternate energy research and development, especially solar.

Earthquakes in the Watershed

Most earthquake activity occurred in the Basin thousands of years ago when folding and faulting shifted the bedrock of the Precambrian and Paleozoic eras. The present-day geologic structure is not known for earthquakes because of its great distance from the active edges of the *tectonic plates*. Nevertheless, earthquakes still occur in the watershed causing minor damage, uncertainty, frantic phone calls to police and curious ones to newspaper offices, librarians,

119

geologists and geographers. Allegedly, the earliest recorded quake was one in 1636 described in the *Jesuit Relations*.

Michigan has been the epicenter for 22 earth tremors (Fig 5-15). The most notable earthquakes occurred in 1811, 1812, 1870, 1883 and 1906 which registered VIII on the Mercalli Scale. A VI tremor occurred in 1947, centered in Branch County, felling chimneys and whose effects were felt between Detroit and Chicago. In January, 1985, a 5.0 Richter Scale tremor was centered in Lake Erie, 40 km (25 mi) off-shore east of Cleveland, which rattled windows and glassware in the Detroit/Windsor area. Another quake, registering 4.2, which centered on St. Mary's, Ohio, at the edge of the Basin, occurred July 12, 1986. Faults from the ancient earthquakes have affected the topography and exposed valuable resources such as Keweenaw copper. In Ontario, scores of faults have been painstakingly identified for further study (Fig 5-16).

Figure 5-15. Epicenters of Michigan earthquakes recorded since 1872. Source: Michigan: *Natural Resource Register*, July 1986, p.19.

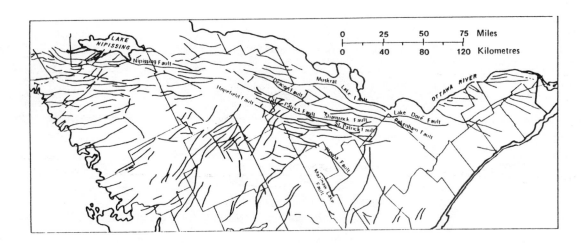

Figure 5-16. Location of faults in southern Ontario. Source: L. Chapman, D. Putnam, *The Physiography of Southern Ontario*, Ontario Geological Survey, Sp. Vol. 2, 1984.

In Summary.--The Great Lakes watershed, with the Michigan Basin as the primary structure, has an abundance of metallic and non-metallic resources dating from 2.5 billion to 220 years ago. All of these resources can be considered finite. Disquieting is the fact that in a span of two centuries, some of the resource deposits have been greatly depleted or exhausted. Further, given the present-day conditions of demography and social-industrial practices, extreme loss and total destruction of some resources is possible through misguided extraction and toxic-atomic waste disposal. Soul searching and tough disciplined decisions and actions -- not reactions, are needed now by citizens and leaders of the Basin and national/international governments in order to protect adequate resources for the immediate future and the people of distant millennia.

Reflections and Self-Learning: Chapter 5

1. Plan a route of travel from your home to the northern Lake Superior area include: highways, overnight stops, time to investigate wonders of the traverse, total distance and days to "Circle the Lake".

2. In what ways could operational perceptions be changed to both use and protect the mining areas as multiple-use areas?

3. Evaluate the concept of borrowing vs. inheritance in land-use.

4. Contrast geology and geomorphology -- use a dictionary if needed.

5. What are the primary metallic and/or non-metallic resources of your area?

6. What are some of the practices the mining industries are using to lessen negative land-use occurrences?

7. Categorize by geologic period the resources and products from the bedrock formations.

8. What new product or economic activity could be innovated from the geological resources of the Basin?

9. What will Lake Erie look like in 4500 AD?

10. Who do you think built the sandstone walls of the Jackson prison in the mid-1800's?

11. Discuss with others and determine a reasonable management plan for oil/gas drilling into the bottom lands of the Great Lakes.

12. Where is the best place to seek safety during an earthquake?

"When I tug at one thing in Nature I find it connected to everything else. "

John Muir

Chapter Six

THE GLACIER SHAPED LANDSCAPE AND RIVERS: SOURCE OF THE GREAT LAKES

The precious lakes, which form the core of the Basin, are a product of the glaciers. Today the lakes with varying levels are sustained by both direct precipitation and drainage from the land. In thinking holistically about the "Great Lakes" requires reaching into the complex web of the Basin's landscape features and scores of river watersheds. Thus, this chapter describes in modest detail (1) the glacial process, (2) the resulting landforms, (3) the inland lakes, (4) the Great Lakes, and (5) environmental concerns. Further listed are 185 intermediate and major river/watersheds which empty into the Great Lakes, including a summary of their unique physical or cultural characteristics.

The Glacial Process, Features and Resources

For nearly 220 million years after the Paleozoic Sea invasions, the uplifted surface was exposed to the weathering forces of searing sun, blasting wind, pelting rain, cutting streams and fracturing cold. It is surmised by geomorphologists that the modern-day Great Lakes depressions were drainage valleys of the post-Paleozoic river system. Further, based on well log records and computer-graphic modeling, it is theorized that several of the current inland lakes and rivers are held in former depressions of the pre-glacial topography (Fig 6-1).[1]

For reasons still being debated, about two million years ago the earth's atmosphere grew frigid, snow fell and accumulated, then compressed under its own weight and began to skid southward from the Hudson Bay area. In time, except for what is known as the "Driftless Area of Wisconsin", an ice sheet 1.6-3.2 km (1-2 mi) thick buried the northern part of the continent as far south as the margins of the Ohio and Missouri rivers and east to Long Island. Several times during the Cenozoic Era, Pleistocene Age glaciers advanced and receded over the Basin leaving distinctive deposits of drift or till. Of the four major stages of advance in North America the most recent was the Wisconsin. Even with the later land-healing growth of forests, evidence of glaciation is abundant and can be seen by both the casual and keen observers, including:

1. Rock minerals such as copper carried great distances from their bedrock source;

2. Soils unrelated to their underlying bedrock;

---

[1]R. L. Rieck, H .A. Winters, "Lake, Stream and Bedrock in South Central Michigan". *Annals of the Association of American Geographers* Vol. 69, pp. 276-288 (1979). "Glacially Buried Cuesta". *Ibid.* Vol. 72, pp. 482-494 (1982). J. W. Spencer, "Origins of the Basins of the Great Lakes". *American Geologist*, Vol. 7, pp. 86-97 (1891).

3. River valleys much wider than the present-day rivers even in their greatest flood stage;

4. Grooved, scratched, striated and highly polished rock surfaces in a constant direction and above river channels;

5. Hills/moraines containing a random mix of clay, sand, gravel and boulders without characteristics of water-layered deposition;

6. Distinctive plains with sorted materials (outwash, lacustrine) and unsorted deposits of till plain/ground moraines;

7. Unique shapes of hillocks such as drumlins, eskers, kames, kettles and beach ridges (Figs 6-2, 6-3).

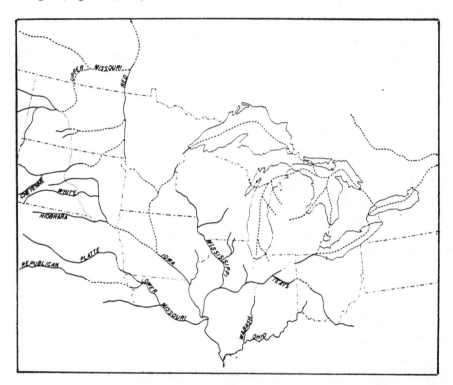

Figure 6-1. Theoretical pre-glacial drainage. From: *Great Lakes Basin*, American Association for the Advancement of Science, Pub. 71, H. J. Pincus (ed.). Copyrighted by AAAS 1962.

The Wisconsin Ice Lobes

Prior to its retreat, about ten thousand years ago, the Wisconsin ice sheet advanced across the peninsulas with an uneven front consisting of several principal lobes: the *Erie*, the *Saginaw-Huron* and *Michigan* lobes. The Wisconsin district was most affected by the *Chippewa-Michigan* and *Green Bay-Michigan* lobes while the *Rainy-Superior* Lobe covered the Arrowhead region of northeast Minnesota (Fig 6-4). In Ontario, the first land to appear from under the ice was the "Ontario Island" (Fig 6-5). The retreat of the *Mattawa* Lobe significantly affected the drainage at North Bay (Fig 6-6).

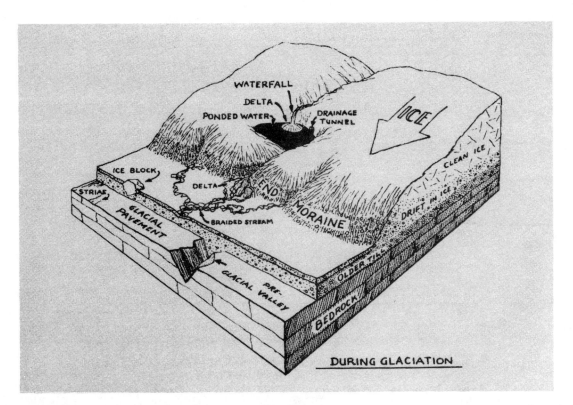

Figure 6-2. Glacial Landforms developed during glaciation. Source: Drawings by J. M. Campbell in, *The Glacial Lakes Around Us*, Michigan Geological Survey, Bulletin 4.

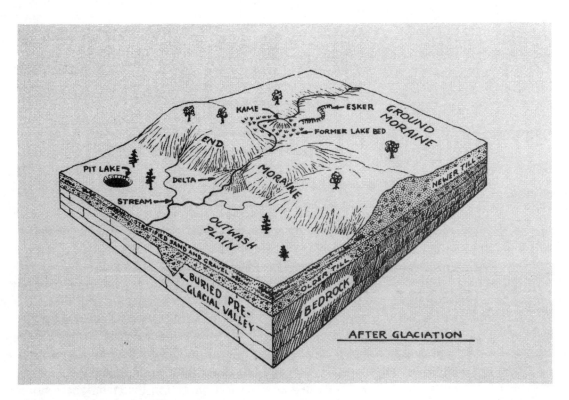

Figure 6-3. Typical post-glacial landforms. Source: J. M. Campbell in, *The Glacial Lakes Around Us*, Michigan Geological Survey, Bulletin 4.

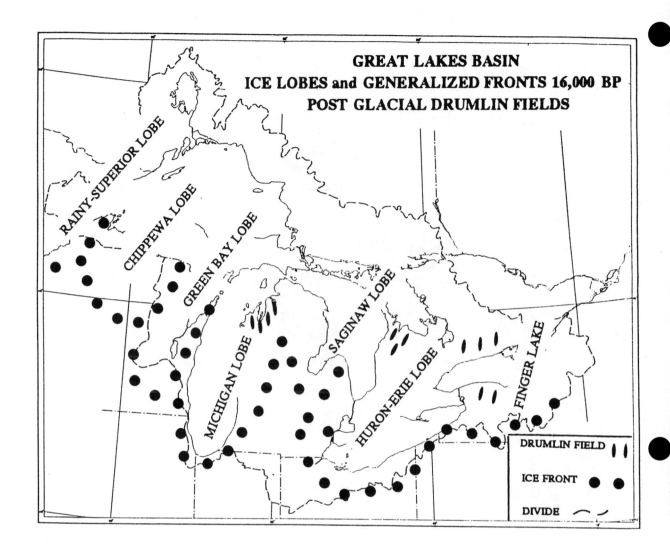

Figure 6-4. Base map: IJC.

Moraines and Till Plains

As the ice skidded forward exerting immense pressure on the top surface, material was ground and mixed forming a very abrasive rock-fragment ice under-surface which could more powerfully carve into exposed bedrock (Fig 6-7). When the lobe front melted due to reduced pressure and warmer weather, *hilly end moraines* were formed in a stationary situation. Today their hummocky belts of sand, gravel and boulders extend for hundreds of kilometers (Fig 6-8). *Ground moraines/till plains* were created when the ice stagnated and its surface area evaporated rapidly and somewhat evenly. In later years, the till plains usually became cultivated land while the steeper-sloped moraines were pastured or kept wooded. Today picturesque interlobate hilltop vistas are in great demand for skiing and housing sites. Although less dramatic than most interlobate areas, the original site of Detroit, was on the relatively higher ground of the Huron-Erie interlobate moraine.

128

Figure 6-5. Glacial Ontario Island, first province land to appear from under ice sheets. Source: L. Chapman, D. Putnam, *The Physiography of Southern Ontario*, Ontario Geological Survey, Sp. Vol. 2, 1984, p. 30.

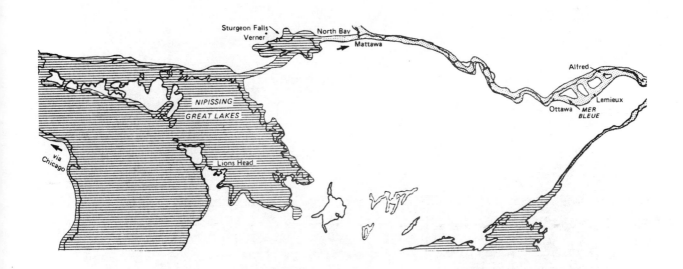

Figure 6-6. North Bay outlet and creation of Lake Nipissing terraces. Source: L. Chapman and D. Putnam, *The Physiography of Southern Ontario*, Ontario Geological Survey, Sp. Vol. 2, 1984, p. 30.

Figure 6-7. Glacial scratches left in bedrock near Shakespeare Point, Lake Nipigon. (Kelley's Island, Lake Erie have the most pronounced grooves.)

130

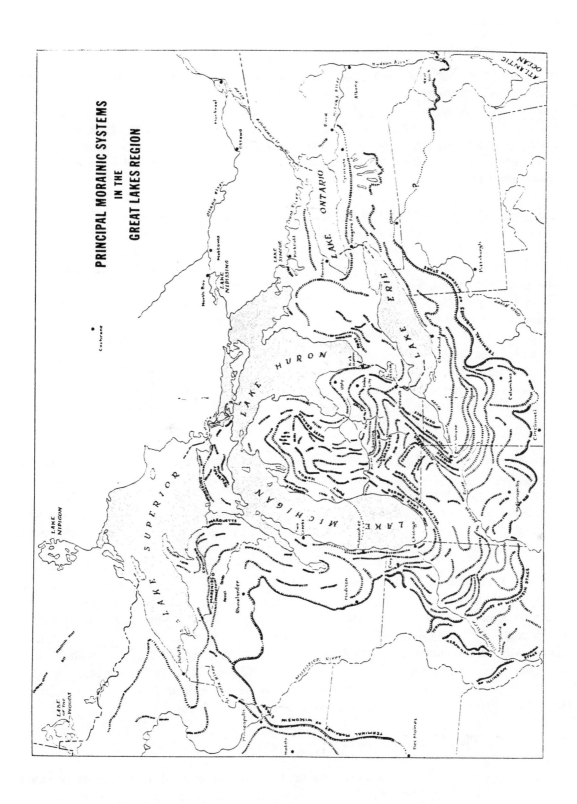

Figure 6-8. Principal end moraines in Basin. Source: J. M. Campbell in, *The Glacial Lakes Around Us*, Michigan Geological Survey, Bulletin 4.

131

Meltwater Features

Outwash plains were created when the glaciers melted rapidly providing a huge broad expanse of swiftly flowing water away from the ice front. In the rushing flow of water, sediments would be segregated with the heavier rocks being dropped first while gravel and sands were sorted and spread out. Narrow, fast-flowing glacial rivers hemmed in by steep-sloped moraines, created boulder-lined *valley trains* which provided an excellent source of heavy base material for construction projects. *Kettles, kettle lakes* and *pitted outwash plains* can be identified by the uniformly round or pit shapes. These "pot holes" were probably formed in till when blocks of ice broke away from the ice face.

Kames, Eskers and Drumlins.--Kames, eskers and drumlins are hills with smooth-sided profiles which formed in direct contact with the ice. When the lobes stagnated, small rivers would flow on top and in cracks of the ice sheets, washing out debris from the glacier and layering it in the channels. *Eskers* or "hog backs" were formed as the ice evaporated. The rubble in the meltwater river bottom would be laid down on the new till plain creating a hump above the plain. Eskers vary in length from a few meters to the Mason (MI) Esker whose profitable gravels, scenic parks and homesite vistas can be traced for nearly 50 km (30 mi). The Codrington Esker, north of Trenton, is the largest in southern Ontario. *Kames* have a conical hill shape which formed as the ice-channeled rivers flowed over the ice face at an indentation point or into a crevice where the till could be confined while being piled up. *Drumlins* were formed under the ice sheets and appear today as fields of inverted spoon-shaped low hills on the axis of the glaciers' retreat. Some drumlins may be 2,000 meters long and 400 meters wide at their face, then narrowing to a pointed tail (Fig 6-4).

Pleistocene Sand and Gravels.--While gravel excavators do not stimulate romantic tales, their seemingly mundane production contributes significantly to the well-being of people, especially in jobs, structures and highways. Most of the sand and gravel operations are excavations into outwash plains, eskers or kames. Deposits with clay, chert, shale, siltstone and ironstone which cause pitting in concrete are generally avoided. Initially, pits are opened at deposit sites nearest construction projects to reduce transportation costs.

Clay, Peat and Marl.--Clay materials deposited by the glaciers support over a dozen different types of fabrication operations including pottery, brick, tile and light-weight aggregates. Peat and marl, on the other hand, are used almost exclusively as soil conditioners and are declining in value because of the availability of chemical fertilizers. Michigan usually leads its nation in peat production with most coming from the Upper Peninsula. Ontario, in contrast, with a similar environment, surprisingly produces less. Perhaps the difference is related to distances to market and national population. Indiana and Ohio production of peat is estimated to be somewhat smaller than Ontario's. Wisconsin, though, has peat reserves equal to Michigan's one billion dry ton.

Safety Adjacent to Pit Operations: Costs

The necessary need to rent open the land to extract mineral resources is commonly understood and generally accepted by citizens. However, such operations have earned dangerous reputations for strip mines, quarries and gravel pits because of their high or unstable edges and ponded waters. In arriving at a consensus for safe economical excavation operations, two basic resource questions have to be re-evaluated: (1) What are fair operating standards?, and (2) What is a fair financial return to a private operator for the privilege, in the democracy, to extract for profit one or more of the Basin's finite resources? Rehabilitation of pits after aggregate removal may be one answer to the conflict in land-use between mining and agriculture. Another method to reduce conflict between citizens and developers may be active public participation to bring into the open reasonable options.

The Inland Lake Wonderland

Melt waters not only shaped the initial post-glacial topography, their flow also filled the depressions creating thousands of attractive inland lakes which provide an unmeasurable resource. Real estate appraisers may place a tax and sale value on a lakefront lot -- but what is the value to individuals' spirit surrounded in a mirrored reflection on calm waters in a morning sun (Fig 6-9)?

Natural Eutrophication Pattern

It is easy to assume that the inland lakes are a permanent landscape resource, especially after repeatedly driving by them. Yet, thousands of lakes, especially in the southern part of the Basin, have already disappeared through the process of *natural eutrophication*. In the process, the shallower inland lakes, warmed by the summer air, produce aquatic plant growth around their shores. When the plants die, they accumulate on the bottom. As the edges fill, nonaquatic vegetation takes root in the spongy organic matter. The rings of plants and soil, in time, fill a lake depression until a forest covering forms. People sometimes speed the process, causing cultural

Figure 6-9. Lake reflections -- what value?

eutrophication, by cutting water weeds and letting them drop to the bottom, or allowing nutrients of septic wastes and lawn fertilizer to drain into lakes.

Eutrophication Resources.--Former lakes filled with decaying matter provide valuable soils for muck land farming such as celery, tomatoes, onions and carrots, plus sod farms and peat mining operations. In some bogs of muck and peat, remains are found of ice-aged caribou, musk ox, wolves, mammoths and mastodons. The efforts of farmers in draining fields has led to disrupted water tables and to a bounty of food, which reversed the negative outlook held for Michigan in the 1815 Tiffin Report.

> ---so far as has been explored, and all appearances, together with the information received concerning the balance is as bad, there could not be more than one acre out of a hundred if there would be one of a thousand, that would in any case admit to cultivation.[2]

Lake Location Pattern and Economic Opportunities

As a result of the difference in time that the southern and northern portions of the Basin have been exposed to warm-drying air, the density of the inland lakes varies greatly by latitude. That contrast results in a significant intra-basin summer vacation travel migration to "the North" by people out of Ohio, Indiana and Illinois into northern Wisconsin, Michigan Ontario and the New York Finger Lakes, plus the "arrowhead" district of Minnesota. Martin's 1916 description is still timely:

> ...there are few parts of the world where so large a portion of the total area is occupied by lakes.[3]

The Arrowhead Lake District extends from Rice Portage Lake at the Fond du Lac Reservation into the international Boundary Waters Canoe Area. The Boundary Waters Canoe Area combines over 50 canoe routes which lead across the watershed divide, starting from the Sawbill, Brulè and Gunflint trails and McFarland Lake.

Michigan's auto license plates carry the message "Great Lakes State" or "Great Lakes" depending on the year. Both messages imply that the state is not only bound by four of the Great Lakes, but also holds more than 10,000 inland lakes. These lakes are widely distributed with only four of the state's 83 counties not having a recognized lake (Gratiot, Macomb, Sanilac and Shiawassee). Seven Michigan counties have more than three hundred lakes with all but two (Oakland and Barry) located in the Upper Peninsula: Marquette, 835; Luce, 571; Iron, 528; Gogebic, 498; Oakland, 447; Schoolcraft, 340; and Barry; 327. Yet, the largest lakes tend to be in the northern Lower Peninsula.

Major Inland Lakes and Areas

The Illinois and Pennsylvania districts, with their former glacial lakebottom sites, do not contain inland lakes. Northeast Indiana, centered on Angola, is that state's major area of lake-focused economic activities. Ohio's largest inland body of water is Grand Lake, 13 km by 4 km (8 mi by 2 mi), situated on the Mississippi Basin edge of the watershed.

[2]United States, *American State Papers, Public Lands, III*, pp. 164-65.
[3]Martin, *Physical Geography of Wisconsin, op. cit.*, p. 20.

In comparison, Lake Winnebago, Wisconsin's largest lake, is approximately 29 km (18 mi) long and 16 km (10 mi) wide. By far the largest inland lakes of the Basin are found in Ontario; however, the province's principal lakes are found outside the Great Lakes watershed.[4] Named for Upper Canada's first Lieutenant Governor and Commanding Officer of the Loyalist Queen's Rangers, is the Basin's largest inland water body --Lake Simcoe with an area of 743 km^2 (445 mi^2). The northern narrow segment of the lake on which the parks of Orillia front, carries the name Lake Couchiching. In comparison, Houghton Lake, Michigan's largest lake and named for the state's first geologist, is only 80 km^2 (31 mi^2) (Table 6-1).

TABLE 6-1

Major Inland Lakes of Michigan

Rank	Name	Area		County
		Km^2	Mi^2	
1	Houghton	80.0	30.8	Roscommon
2	Torch	74.1	28.5	Antrim
3	Burt	72.3	27.8	Cheboygan
4	Charlevoix	69.4	26.7	Charlevoix
5	Mullet	64.7	24.9	Cheboygan
6	Gogebic	52.0	20.0	Gogebic-Ontonagon
7	Portage	46.8	18.0	Houghton

SOURCE: Bert Hudgins, *Michigan: Geographic Backgrounds in the Development of the Commonwealth*, 4th ed. (Detroit, 1961) p. 29.

Ontario Lake Districts.--North of Lake Simcoe are situated several other major inland lakes including Joseph, Rosseau, Muskoka and Lakes of Bays. Route 169 along the western edge of the first three listed lakes is especially pleasant if one does not have to cope with the flow of weekend traffic. Near Peterborough are a series of northeast-southwest trending long, narrow lakes which probably are a result of disrupted drainage of the Kawartha ice front. The Kawartha Lake District includes: Chemong, Buckham, Pigeon, Story and Sturgeon lakes. To the south are Rice Lake and Lake Scugog. In these areas are found the highest density of cottages. The Kawartha Lakes drain into Rice Lake via the Indian and Otonabee rivers. In this section of lakes and rivers, the Otonabee River falls 48 m (140 ft) in the 16 km (10 mi) between Lake Katchiwano to Little Lake in Peterborough. Here the world's largest hydraulic lift lock, 22 m (65 ft), was opened in 1904 as part of the historic Trent-Severn Canal (Fig 6-10). At the lock site is a relatively new Canadian National Park and Interpretive Center.

[4]Ontario's principal non-Great Lakes Basin inland lakes: Lake of the Woods, 3149 km^2; Seul, 1658 km^2; Big Trout, 660 km^2; Lake St. Joseph, 492 km^2; Abitibi, 932 km^2, Rainy, 741 km^2; and Sandy, 526 km^2.

The New York Finger Lakes District.

There are several world-class places of natural beauty in the Great Lakes Basin; the Finger Lakes District is one of them. The scenic landscape situated between Rochester and Syracuse includes remnants of gently rolling low upland mountains, interspersed with deep trough valleys, some of which are occupied by eleven major "finger lakes" (Table 6-2). Picturesque *glens* have been carved into narrow canyons by post-glacial small streams with falls which flow as tributaries to the great troughs. Adding to the natural attractiveness of the district are pastoral fields and patches of uniformly-rowed vineyards.

Figure 6-10. Peterborough lift-lock on the Trent-Severn Canal.

TABLE 6-2

Finger Lakes Size Data

Name	Length		Depth		Elevation	
	Km	Mi	Meters	Feet	Meters	Feet
Canadice	4.8	3	27	91	330	1099
Canandaigua	25.6	16	79	262	206	686
Cayuga	64.0	40	130	435	115	384
Conesus	14.4	9	18	59	245	818
Hemlock	12.8	8	29	96	271	905
Honeoyo	8.0	5	9	30	245	818
Keuka	35.2	22	56	187	213	709
Otisco	9.6	6	20	66	235	784
Owasco	17.6	11	53	177	213	710
Seneca	57.6	36	190	632	133	444
Skaneateles	24.0	15	105	350	260	867

Adapted from: *Finger Lakes Region: 1985*, Finger Lakes Association Penn Yan, New York (a folder).

Because the Valley Heads Moraine blocks drainage to the south, people in western New York use the phrase in traveling from Lake Ontario towards Pennsylvania as going "up South" which also necessitates crossing the Portage Escarpment.

An unobstructed awesome view of Lake Cayuga and vicinity can be seen from the Cornell University Library tower in Ithaca. From bridges over the local waterways, deep gorges and tranquil waterfalls can be observed. Beginning about 3 km (2 mi) southwest of Ithaca, the Valley Heads Moraine and outwash deposits can be traced for about 19 km (12 mi) to North Spencer on NY. Highway 34-96. There the moraine forms the edge of the watershed with hummocky deposits of sand and gravel with pit lakes and marshes. When one pauses at a vista on the divide, enthralled by the glorious scenery of lakes in broad valleys, with elongated ridges, confining hollows and glens, one can ponder what inspiration they may have provided Carl Sagen as he evolved his exuberant notions about the *Cosmos*, his deep concerns about a nuclear disaster and the survival of Homo sapiens. Surely from the cutting edge heights of the Finger Lakes District watershed-divide can come more inspirational ideas for relating wisely with the universe.

Historic Uses and Duplicate Names

During the 19th Century, the inland lakes provided strategic floating collection points for rafts of timber cut and removed from surrounding forests. Other times, logs were boomed through lake outlets to mills further downstream. The early cottage era recreationalist found the lakes not only pleasant places to swim and fish, but also a pure source of drinking water and ice. Because of delivery of public service problems some counties have acted in recent decades with state/province and federal Boards of Geographic Names to adopt new names to eliminate historic duplications.

The Rivers and Watersheds: Source of the Great Lakes

The hundreds of watersheds of the brooks, creeks, and rivers which drain into the Great Lakes are significant to the water quality of the lakes because they are the source of the majority of replenishing water, major contributor to water levels, and primary carriers of the industrial-technical age toxic wastes. Thus, it is suggested that by emphasizing knowledge about the Basin's rivers and their watersheds, a more sturdy foundation can be laid to help maintain, improve and protect the Great Lakes and the overall quality of the Basin. This section is an attempt towards that goal by organizing here a basic inventory of rivers of the Great Lakes with a variety of summary data which it is hoped will stimulate more specific comprehensive writings and illustrated reports, either video or printed. DeBorah Kaplan, in a *Detroit Free Press* Sunday supplement, provides an initial sobering example of watershed reporting, in "What Have We Done to the Rouge?" (July 27, 1986).   Illustrating progress, Robert Ankeny in the *Detroit News* of February 12, 1993 (B-1) reported the beginning of a $46 million US-EPA funded national model program for treating urban area polluted rivers including rainfall, sewage overflow, road salt and industrial waste. Involved are forty-eight communities in the total River Rouge watershed.

River Characteristics

The rivers of the Basin tend to be short and drain relatively modest-sized areas because of the compact shape of the Basin and the huge lakes in its center (Figs 6-11 to 6-14). Although *major rivers* can be identified within the Basin, none are classified as *principal rivers* of either the United States or Canada. Some rivers are check shaped which indicates a reversal in direction. In the south most flow slowly over till and lacustrine plains which contrast with northern rivers. Extended mouthed rivers are common where sand dunes interrupt exit to the lakes. In urban places some have disappeared under concrete. Similar to human land needs, aquatic life requires a variety of habitats for their survival.   For their safe use in the food chain, needed are: (1) nearly uncontaminated water, (2) rubbled bottoms for fish spawning beds, (3) silt control, (4) variety of temperatures, and (5) hiding places.

The Rivers of the Basin

Table 6-3 lists by name and categorizes by Great Lake, 185 intermediate and major water course/watersheds of the Basin and provides a variety of information associated with the river or watershed. This table may provide a key for more specific work on wisely managing the lakes, reducing use conflicts (canoe/fishing) and to stimulate ideas for further economic development or preservation. It can be anticipated that several reviews and ponderings of the table will be necessary to gain its full benefit (Table 6-3).

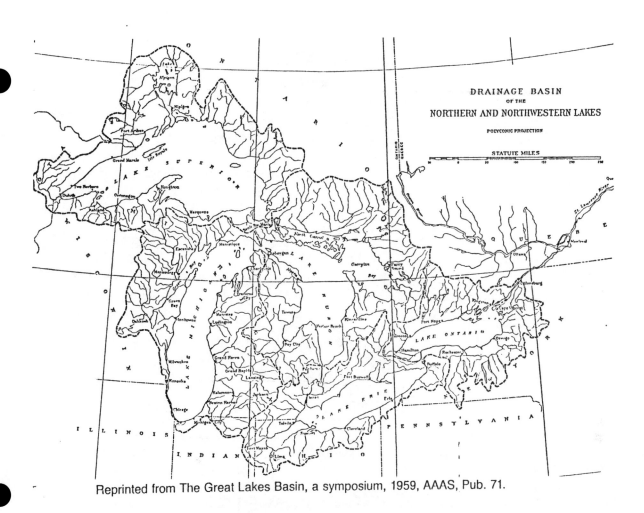

Reprinted from The Great Lakes Basin, a symposium, 1959, AAAS, Pub. 71.

Figure 6-11. Rivers of the Great lakes Basin. Source: International Joint Commission. Citing: *The Great lakes Basin* a Symposium, 1959, Pub. 71. ☉

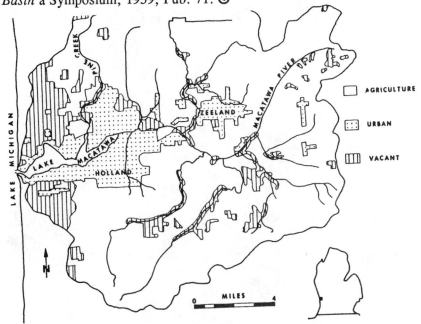

Figure 6-12. Sand dune extended river mouth and lake impoundment typical of Lake Michigan rivers. Source: R. H. Drake, R. L. Reinking, *Michigan Academician*, Vol. X, No. 3 (Winter 1978).

Rouge River Watershed

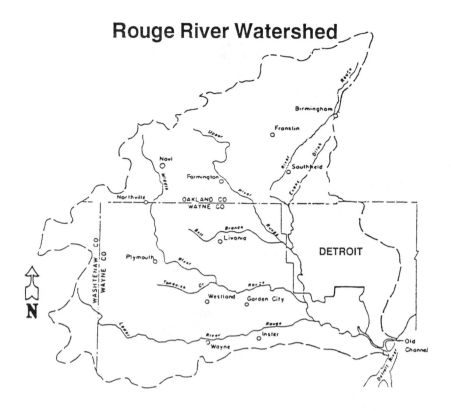

Figure 6-13. Rouge River watershed/basin. Source: Michigan: *Natural Resources Register*, July 1986.

River Flow Reversal
on the Divide:
Maumee-Wabash

Figure 6-14. Rivers at the Indiana divide (Wabash-Maumee) illustrating flow reversal. after B. Hudgins.

TABLE 6-3

Selected Watercourses Directly Flowing into the
Great Lakes by State/Province and Lake

Water Course (*Major River)	Summary Comment
LAKE SUPERIOR	
<u>Minnesota</u> (east to west)	
*Pigeon	International boundary; Grand Portage National Monument.
Brulè	Grand Portage S.F.; Devils Kettle.
Cascade	S.P.; falls; Pat Boyle S.F.
Devil Track	Canyon; falls.
Poplar	Lookout posts; skiing.
Onion	Ray Berglund S.P.
Temperance	S.P.; falls; Sawbill Trail.
Two Island	Taconite Harbor development.
Manitou	Finland S.P.
Baptism	Finland S.P.; campgrounds.
Beaver	Beaver Bay hamlet -- unincorporated.
Split Rock	Lighthouse; 765 ft elv.
Gooseberry	S.P.; falls.
Silver Creek	Two Harbors taconite development.
Knife	Airport.
Sucker	Rest Area.
French	Rest Area; 696 ft elv.
Lester	North Duluth; fine residential.
*St. Louis	Bong Bridge; Duluth-Superior; Fond du Lac Ind. Res.; slow current--2286 ft^3 p.s. flow.
<u>Wisconsin</u> (west to east)	
Nemadji	Highest fall in state at escarpment on Black R. tributary; Pattison S.P.
Amnicon	S.P.; falls; camping.
Poplar	Headwaters Brulè R. S.F.
Bois Brulè	Rapids; historic portages; Brulè R. S.F.
Iron	Roadside Park.
Flag	Headwaters in Chequamegon N.F.
Sand	Red Cliff Ind. Res.
Sioux	Name of aboriginal tribe and language family at edge of Basin.
White	Headwaters in weak shale; first rate trout stream; 14,000 ac. Bibon swamp.
Bad	Bad R. Ind. Res.; Copper and Tyler Forks Falls; S.P.
Montreal	State border; original name-- Kawasiji-Wangsepi=whitefalls river.
<u>Michigan</u> (west to east)	
Black	Dark flowing water from tannic acid.

TABLE 6-3 (Cont'd)

Selected Watercourses Directly Flowing into the
Great Lakes by State/Province and Lake

Water Course (*Major River)	Summary Comment
Presque Isle	"Almost an island" at mouth.
Carp	Very short; named for sucker=namebin.
Iron (Cold, Elk)	R. el Original on 1744 Bellin map of Canada.
Cranberry	Headwaters in Ottawa N.F.
Potato	Short meandering river without tributaries.
Ontonagon	Retains Amerind name, "place of abundant sturgeon."
Flint (Steel)	Source of flint for fire making.
Fire Steel	An Amerind nighttime hunting place by torch light.
Sleeping	Slow moving river at mouth; Nibawin=sleeping.
Misery	"A place of starvation" aka Carver R. for early surveyor.
Graveraet	Named for man killed there in 1791-- jealousy over woman.
Elm	Agate beach; Stanton Twp. P.; camping.
Salmon Trout	Red ridge at mouth; Amerind name Majamegoss=brook trout.
Perch-Sturgeon	Portage Shipping Canal across Keweenaw Peninsula.
Ogemaw (Falls)	Trellis of tributaries; falls 1 1/2 mi inland.
Silver	Headwaters at base of Mt. Curwood-- elv. 1980 ft.
Ravine	Enters Huron Bay; headwaters in Copper Country S.F.
Huron	Flows west of Huron Mountains.
Salmon Trout	Brook Trout R.
Yellow Dog	Flows through Independence Lake; Pinnicale Falls; Bushy Creek Falls.
Dead	Flows through largest city of Upper Peninsula.
Carp	Named for sucker prior to introduction of carp into Basin.
AuTrain	French name; sand beach at mouth; popular swimming place.
Sucker	Flows into Grand Marais east of Pictured Rocks N.L.P.
Two Hearted	Managed in part under Natural Rivers Act.
Betsy	Mouth at Shelldrake--a lumber town on Whitefish Bay.
Tahquamenon	S.P.; falls 16 m (48 ft); 100,000 annual visitors.
Waiska	Bay Mills Ind. Res.

TABLE 6-3 (Cont'd)

Selected Watercourses Directly Flowing into the
Great Lakes by State/Province and Lake

Water Course (*Major River)	Summary Comment
Ontario (east to west)	
Goulais	Moose habitat-swampy; rare to L. Superior orchids and Queen lady slipper.
Batchawana	Prov. P.; enters bay with shallow warmer water.
Montreal	Largest R. between White R. and the Soo; hydroelectric dams; spawning beds for lake trout; flows in eroded dike (not a fault).
Agawa	Prov. P.; steep walled valley; rugged hiking; R.R. tours; pictographs.
Magpie	Falls; rugged--last section of Trans-Canada Hwy. to be constructed.
Pakaskaw	N.P.; sand dunes; boreal forest; shield topography.
White	Prov. P.; dams; eskers; historic logging.
Black	One of duplicate named rivers based on color.
Pic	Modern Amerind school; Heron Bay hamlet.
Little Pic	Muddy bottom from clay of former lake.
Steel	Flows through Sartoy L.; off-shore Slate Island holds a herd of 100 woodland caribou.
Aguasabon	Magnificent scenery; enters at Terrance Bay.
Nipigon (strait?)	Arctic waters diverted into it since 1941 from Ogoki R.
Black Sturgeon	Headwaters Black Sturgeon L.
Kaministiquia	Thunder Bay--regional center of the north; world grain port; spectacular Kakabeka Falls 39 m (128 ft); park.

LAKE MICHIGAN

Michigan UP (east to west)	
Manistique	Seney N.W.R.; trellised tributaries reach within 16 km (10 mi) of L. Superior.
Fishdam	Short R. within Hiawatha N.F.
Sturgeon	Headwaters near Wheelbarrow L. in central Alger Co.
Whitefish	Flows into well protected bay.
Rapid River	Town of same name at mouth;
Days	Headwaters in Escanaba S.F. T43N R24W Section 24.
Escanaba	Trellis headwater creeks reach north of Marquette.
Ford	Flows basically east from Channing S. F., auto pioneer linkage.

TABLE 6-3 (Cont'd)

**Selected Watercourses Directly Flowing into the
Great Lakes by State/Province and Lake**

Water Course (*Major River)	Summary Comment
Bark	Potawatomi Ind. Res.
Big Cedar	J. W. Wells S.P. at mouth.
*Menominee	State border; all islands below Quinnesee Falls Wisconsin territory, above Falls Michigan islands; 4 bridges link twin cities Menominee-Marinette; 4000 mi^2 watershed.

Wisconsin (north to south)

Peshtigo	500 Sioux & Chippewa died in 1806 fighting over wildrice harvest canoes; 1871 forest fire killed 800+ people--town burned; 1123 mi^2 W.S.
Oconto	Copper culture historic site--burials date from 7500 BP.
Pensaukee	Short R. flows into Green Bay.
Duck Creek	Oneida Ind. Res.
*Fox-Wolf	Probable source of contaminants leading to deformities of bills of double-crested cormorants; 6400 mi^2 Fox W.S.; 3600 mi^2 Wolf W.S.
Kewaunee	Flows over dipslope of Niagara escarpment.
Twin	Hidden Valley P.; small port.
Manitowoc	May be pre-glacial riverbed; cross lake boat connections; off-shore reef.
Sheboygan (Onion-Mullet)	Near Elkhart flows in 15 mi^2 swamp in former lake--45 ft deep with muck and peat.
Milwaukee	Well protected modern international harbor at mouth; largest city of Wisconsin; German culture impact; pro sports; cross lake boat connections; 840 mi^2 W.S.
Racine	Racine reef off-shore--1/2 mile wide 1 mile long, 7-11 ft. underwater with 25-30 ft. drop-offs.

Illinois (west to east)

Calumet	Flow reversed into Mississippi Basin; harbor inland.
*Chicago	Flow reversed for sanitation purposes; water diverted into Mississippi Basin; largest city on Great Lakes; urban boat tours; lock at mouth; raft-laker-freighter inter modal connections to Gulf and Atlantic ports.

TABLE 6-3 (Cont'd)

**Selected Watercourses Directly Flowing into the
Great Lakes by State/Province and Lake**

Water Course (*Major River)	Summary Comment
Indiana (west to east)	
St. Joseph	Elkhart R. major Indiana tributary; complex glacial disrupted drainage pattern reaching east of Hillsdale, MI.
Michigan (south to north)	
Black	South Haven at mouth--peaches; waterfowl flooding; headwaters in Allegan State Game Area.
Kalamazoo	Dams; paper mills; mid-section in Allegan S.G.A.; Saugatuck S.P.; sand dunes buried hamlet of Singapore.
Macatawa	Characteristic extended river mouth-lake behind entrance to L. Michigan; Holland S.P.
*Grand	Longest R. in Michigan--225 mi; headwaters in Jackson Co.; Grand Haven S.P.
Black Creek	P.J. Hoffmaster S.P.; characteristic L. Michigan sand dunes beached by watercourse with at times mouth blocked by sand, high water and waves; interpretive center; walkways; viewing platform.
White	Toxic waste problem at Montague.
Muskegon	Unique land-sited wastewater treatment system; S.P.; headwater in state's largest lake; small metro-city at mouth; cross lake boat connection; dams--historic world's largest earth dam.
Pentwater	Mears S.P.; destabilized sand dunes.
*Pere Marquette	Cross lake boat connection; modern development activity.
Big Sable	Ludington S.P.; salmon fishing typical of L. Michigan.
Manistee	Popular canoe-fishing river; Manistee S.G.A.
Betsie	Commercial harbor; cross lake boat connection.
Platte	Historic site of introduction of salmon into L. Michigan and Basin.
Boardman	Traverse City-community spirit developing to control and limit growth in lower part of watershed; enters Grand Traverse Bay; harbor.
LAKE HURON	
Michigan UP (south to north)	
Carp (Gorman)	Many meanders; Hiawatha N.F.

TABLE 6-3 (Cont'd)

**Selected Watercourses Directly Flowing into the
Great Lakes by State/Province and Lake**

Water Course (*Major River)	Summary Comment
Pine	Trellis headwaters area; mouth at St. Martin Bay.
St. Mary's (strait?)	Route to locks; International boundary; rapids-falls (20 ft); lower part lakes, bays, channels.
Michigan LP (north to south)	
Black (Cheboygan)	Headwaters in Mackinac S.F.
Ocqueoc	Falls, drains between two large eskers of Presque Co.
Trout	Flows through private land in the Mackinac S.F.; cuts through eskers.
*Thunder Bay	Sport fishing center; dams headwater tributaries--Gilchrist and Hunt creeks, drains through Hunt Creek Fisheries Research Area.
AuSable	Annual canoe race; large delta built behind glacial Lake Warren; mouth penetrates ground moraine.
Saginaw Bay	
AuGres	Modern boat launch facilities for waterfowl and fishing use.
Rifle	Notable trout fishing; AuSable S.F.
Pine	Wigwam Bay Wildlife area.
Kawlawlin	Small watershed; bisects waterlaid moraine behind glacial Lake Nipissing.
*Saginaw	Largest watershed in Michigan--6000+ mi^2; drains lacustrine plain with scores of tributaries.
Pigeon	Recreation harbor; campground; DNR Field Office.
Pinebog	At mouth Port Crescent S.P.
Willow Creek	Lighthouse.
Black	Port Huron S.G.A.; flows south behind P.H. moraine of Huron ice lobe.
Ontario (south to north)	
AuSable	Pinery Prov. P.; flood control dam at Exeter; 160 mi^2 W.S.
Bayfield	High level terraces; oxbows-meanders; 100 ft deep - 1/2 mile wide valley; 200 mi^2 W.S.
*Matland	Goderich harbor; flows on clay plain with strong summer current; 981 mi^2 W.S.

TABLE 6-3 (Cont'd)

**Selected Watercourses Directly Flowing into the
Great Lakes by State/Province and Lake**

Water Course (*Major River)	Summary Comment
Saugeen	Flows out of highest land of S. Ontario, 1700 ft elv.; Southhampton resort harbor; 1565 mi^2 W.S.
Sauble	Sauble Falls Prov. P.; flows under drumlin in Arran Twp., Gray Co.; 300 mi^2 W.S.
Big Head (GB)	Drains wooded upland; flows over Niagara cuesta; 120 mi^2 W.S.
Beaver (GB)	Hoggs Falls; flows in pre-glacial valley; Epping Terrace development conflict; 225 mi^2 W.S.
Nottawasaga (GB)	Rugged; flows in deep cut cuesta valley-- dropping in places 100 ft per mile; 1145 mi^2 W.S.
*Severn (GB)	Georgian Bay Island N.P.; part of Trent-Severn waterway; drains Lake Simcoe-Couchiching; 1/3 in Shield; 2250 mi^2 W.S.
Muskoka	Three power plants, headwaters in Algonquian Prov. P.; many upstream falls; mouth at Parry Sound.
Magnetawan	Meanders from Algonquian Prov. P.-- descends 400 ft in 10 miles, no falls just rapids.
French (strait?)	Historic canoe route; flows from L. Nipissing.
French Wanapitei	Flows across Shield from Wanapitei L. north of Sudbury.
Spanish	Whitefish Falls at MacGregor Bay; former island now in dry lake bed; Pioneer Museum at Massey with logging and Amerind displays.
Mississagi	Prov. P.; Thessalon at mouth; Wakami Prov. P.
Garden	Sea lamprey spawning ground; Garden R. Ind. Res.

LAKE ST. CLAIR, ST. CLAIR RIVER, DETROIT RIVER (STRAIT)

<u>Michigan</u> (north to south)

Belle	Headwaters in lake bed ponded waters of Lapeer Co.; mouth north of Marine City; I-94 crosses at Adair.
Clinton	Metropolitan Parkway; historic canal; extended mouth; fan of tributaries behind glacial Lake Elton shoreline.
Rouge	Major industrial development; underground R.R. route; pollution control efforts still needed; local parks.

TABLE 6-3 (Cont'd)

**Selected Watercourses Directly Flowing into the
Great Lakes by State/Province and Lake**

Water Course (*Major River)	Summary Comment
Ontario (south to north)	
Thames	Flood control dams at Fanshawe, Mitchell, Stratford, Woodstock, St. Mary's; history of flooding in London, crosses lake plain; 125 mi. long; 2200 mi^2 W.S.
Sydenham	McKeough Dam and diversion 1984; navigable to Wallaceburg; low gradient over clay plains; 1000 mi^2 W.S.
LAKE ERIE	
Michigan (north to south)	
Huron	Headwaters in a spoke of inland lakes northeast of Milford in Oakland Co. circles around Ann Arbor and flows through a great glacial-age delta below Ypsilanti and a boulder belt above Rockwood; parks mixed with dense use.
Raisin	Untapped recreation potential; major thermal electric plant at mouth in Monroe; diversity of tributaries above beach ridge of glacial Lake Maumee; historic French long-lots.
Ohio (west to east)	
*Maumee	Principal watershed in Basin; natural reversal of flow from Mississippi Basin; Ft. Defiance key to USA land survey's in Basin; Ft. Wayne west metro city; Toledo capital city-port.
Portage	Port Clinton at mouth; flows through ground moraines and lake bed deposits.
Sandusky	Muddy from agricultural land erosion; Cedar Point city and park; Kelley Island S. P. offshore.
Vermilion	Short north flowing; Great Lakes Historical Museum at mouth.
Cuyahoga	Outstanding reduction in pollution; former description "fire hazard."
Grand	Headlands Beach S.P.
Pennsylvania	
Elk	Small W.S.; upper part flows west in front of uplift; lower part flows over lake bed clay deposits.

TABLE 6-3 (Cont'd)

Selected Watercourses Directly Flowing into the
Great Lakes by State/Province and Lake

Water Course (*Major River)	Summary Comment
New York	
Cattaraugus	Cattaraugus Ind. Res.; gorges of notable beauty cut 300-400 ft into Devonian rock; headwaters near Java Center.
Ontario (east to west)	
*Grand	Major river of southern Ontario; Six Nation Ind. Res.; 525,00 people in W.S.; 180 mi long; variation in flowage may limit development 1225 CFS mean, August 434 CFS; Luther flood control dam; scenic Elora Gorge; 2600 mi^2 W.S.
Big Creek	Descends 400 ft in 55 mi,; small flowage; enters at Long Point Bay.
Big Otter Creek	Port Burwell; upstream historic mill sites.
Catfish Creek	Port Bruce Prov. P.; irrigation water for tobacco land.
Kettle Creek	At Port Stanley bluffs 125 ft high; deep upstream cuts; relatively recent dam at St. Thomas.
LAKE ONTARIO	
Ontario (west to east)	
Niagara (strait?)	Most dramatic feature Niagara Falls; 32 mi. long; toxic chemicals entering flow; power plants; dams; intense development.
Welland	No longer flows into Niagara--last four miles are intake for power canal; descends 200 ft in first 15 mi.
Credit	Quiet canoeing and wintertime open air skating; deep cut in Niagara escarpment at Cataract; dam at Grangeville; 328 mi^2 W.S.
Humber-Don	Two small rivers of Toronto; flood plain loss of life in 1954; parks; 2 dams.
Ganaraska	Flood problems; 11,000 ac reforested for flood control aid; dam.
*Trent	Trent-Severn waterway; dams-locks; boating; linkage L. Ontario-L. Huron; 4780 mi^2 W.S.
Moira	Flood problem to Belleville; heavily forested upstream; 2 dams; 1090 mi^2 W.S.
Salmon	Mouth at Bay of Quinte; headwaters well into Shield; flow diverted by glaciation from Moira.

TABLE 6-3 (Cont'd)

**Selected Watercourses Directly Flowing into the
Great Lakes by State/Province and Lake**

Water Course (*Major River)	Summary Comment
Napanee	Flows in pre-glacial valley; dam Depot L.
New York (east to west)	
Perch	Flows into Sackets Harbor from Perch L.; recreational boating replacing naval use; historic park.
Black	Watertown; rafting rides; Science-Technology Museum.
Sandy	Short; direct flow; Southwick S.P.
Salmon	Port Ontario at mouth; Selkirk Shores S.P.; dam-reservoir at Osceola; State Fiddlers Hall of Fame.
Little Salmon	Texas at mouth; small W.S.; flows out of Adirondack Mt. Battle Island S.P.;
Oswego	Battle Island S.P.; federal port since 1799; linked to NYSBC-Erie Canal; sport fishing coho, chinook, lake trout.
Ironquoit	Rochester third largest city in NY; first indoor mall USA; photography; falls; atomic power plants; lower valley of former Genesee R.
*Genesee	Agricultural and natural beauty; Letchworth Gorge "Grand Canyon of East"; flows from south of Genesee, PA. north across entire state; flood problems reduced by Mt. Harris dam.
Johnson	Beach S.P. at mouth; headwaters near Iroquois N.W.R.
Tonawanda	T. Ind. Res.; industrialized; state prison at Attica; headwaters near North Java; historic major late 19th Century lumber river Erie Canal terminal

TABLE 6-3 (Cont'd)

Selected Watercourses Directly Flowing into the Great Lakes by State/Province and Lake

Summary of Watercourses Listed	Number
Lake Superior	74
Lake Michigan	39
Lake Huron	33
Lake St. Clair, St. Clair River, Detroit River	5
Lake Erie	15
Lake Ontario	19
Total	185
*Major	15

ABBREVIATIONS USED: aka=also known as; Ck. = creek; Co. = county; elv. = elevation; G.B. = Georgian Bay; ft = feet; hwy = highway; Ind. Res. = Indian Reservation; L. = lake; N.F. = national forest; N.W.R. = National Wildlife Refuge; Prov. P. = provincial park; R.R. = railroad; R. = river; S.F. = state forest; S.G.A. = state game area; S.P. = state park; Twp. = township; W.S. = watershed

FIELD SOURCES: R. Santer, Field Traverses 1985-1986. R. McNeill, G. Telfer, R. Santer, Air Photography of the Michigan Shoreline 1980-1981, (Ferris State University, 1980-1981).

PRINTED SOURCES: J. R. Borchart and N. C. Gustafson, *Atlas of Minnesota: Resources and Settlement*, 3rd ed., (Minneapolis: Center of Urban and Regional Affairs, University of Minnesota and Minnesota State Planning Agency, 1980). L. J. Chapman and D. F. Putnam, *The Physiography of Southern Ontario*, 3rd ed., (Toronto: Ministry of Natural Resources, 1984). *Ecotour*: Thunder Bay - White River - Sault Ste. Marie - North Bay, (Forest Service; Environment Canada, 1976-1979) 3 pamphlets. L Martin, *The Physical Geography of Wisconsin, op. cit..* Helen Martin, *Map: Surface Formations of the Southern Peninsula of Michigan*, Pub. 49, (Lansing: Michigan Geological Survey, 1955). B. Peters, "The Origin of Meaning of Place Names Along the Lake Superior Shoreline between Keweenaw, Portage and Montreal River," unpublished paper (Michigan Academy Science Arts and Letters, March 1985). Official State/Province Transportation Maps.

Further Comments on Use of Table 6-3

Reading, plodding through or pondering the list of 185 rivers and watersheds with comments takes time, energy and discipline; yet, much value, it is anticipated, can come from such effort. It can be expected that not all readers will have similar responses to the detailed and eclectic summary. Comments might vary from: (1) "The list is like reading a telephone book or dictionary -- boring," (2) "Gee! I didn't realize that -- that was interesting," (3) "Whew -- wow, this gives me an idea." To the latter, encouragement is now given to *pursue the idea*; be it one of academic research, free lance journalism, photography, an entrepreneurial business activity, environmental protection, forming a watershed council, or leisure-time activity.

The Natural Rivers Act

The designations for natural rivers in the United States are:

1. *Wilderness River*, a river in an extensive wilderness or primitive setting, with qualities associated with undeveloped settings.

2. *Wild Scenic River*, a river with wild or forested borders or backlands, in close proximity to man-made development.

3. *Country Scenic River*, a river generally in an agricultural setting with narrow bands of woods or pastoral borders, often with farms and other developments viewable from the river.

Under the Natural Rivers Act, local zoning is encouraged for carrying out proposals in a river management plan developed by a local planning body with active citizen participation. Property along a designated segment of a natural river, if private, remains private and any use of it *must* have the owner's permission. Under the act, provisions for setback of structures and maintenance of natural vegetation strips are included; however, persons with vested rights cannot be prohibited from making reasonable use of their private property or be required to relocate existing houses.

Dams and Fish Ladders

The practice of building dams for water power was introduced extensively by the founders of the pioneer villages. Later, generally after the timber harvest was completed, high earthen and reinforced concrete dams to produce hydroelectric power became a common sight along the rivers. Many of these dams, due to the silting of their impoundments and maintenance costs, in less than a century have become unsightly relics. On the other hand, well-designed and maintained dams can provide many advantages for flood control, scenic views, plus locally produced electric energy. Perhaps, in time, a few well-selected river sites will again witness a resurgence in the development for hydroelectric plants whose energy is renewed with each rainfall and melt of snow in its upstream watershed. In meeting the needs for both a dam and spawning salmon, the city of Grand Rapids became a pacesetting community by constructing a successful and attractive fish ladder which combined the efforts of biologists, artists and government administrators, with a blending of community pride and support. (Figs 6-15, 6-16).

Figure 6-15. Grand Rapids fish ladder.

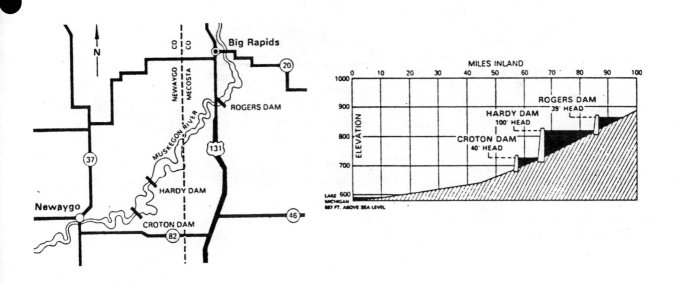

Figure 6-16. Dams of the Muskegon River -- Hardy Dam formerly the world's largest earth dam, is now the Lower Peninsula's largest impoundment: 2 miles across, 50 mile shoreline, 4000 acres of water surface; dam: 1000 feet wide, 3000 feet long, 100 feet head. Source: *Michigan Holiday News*, May 1986 (original Sources: U.S. Army Corps of Engineers - Milwaukee Muskegon River, sheets 1-6, April 3, 1931).

Formation of the Great Lakes

A description of the evolution of the Great Lakes begins with the drainage and ponding of the glacial meltwaters in pre-glacial river channels between the ice front and the moraines which constricted their outlet to the Mississippi River. Only a summary of the basic ice stages can be presented in this comprehensive description of the Basin. However, detailed accounts can be found in Hough's 1958 *Geology of the Great Lakes* and in Leverett and Taylor's 1915 *Pleistocene of Indiana and Michigan and the History of the Great Lakes.* In the summary which follows, with illustrations by James Campbell, the Kelley and Farrand Geological Survey publication of 1967, *The Glacial Lakes around Michigan* has been a primary resource. The series of drawings depict the formation of the immediate post-glacial Great Lakes and the earlier outlets. The *outlets*, Chicago, Ubly-Imlay, North Bay-French River and the glacial Lake Duluth-Lake Algonquian front, are of particular significance because they provide potential modern-day canal routes (Figs 6-17, 6-18, 6-19).

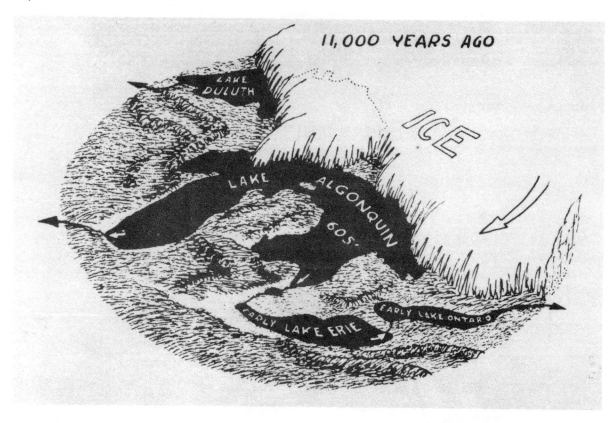

Figure 6-17. Glacial lakes 11,000 B.P. Source: Drawing by J. M. Campbell, *The Glacial Lakes Around Us*, Michigan Geological Survey Bulletin 4.

Table 6-4 summarizes the basic contemporary natural and cultural features of the Great Lakes. Especially notable are the several national land holdings and the recent bottomland parks. From a pollution management point of view, the holding periods are extremely important. If the Upper Lakes are allowed to be polluted to the extent of Lake Erie in the 1960's, a rapid recovery *cannot* be expected.

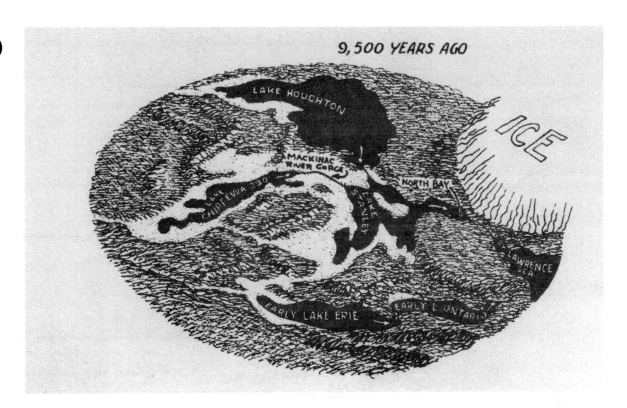

Figure 6-18. Glacial lakes at lowest elevation (black shading) 9,500 B.P. Former lake bottoms in white. Source: Drawing by J. M. Campbell, *The Glacial Lakes Around Us*, Michigan Geological Survey Bulletin 4.

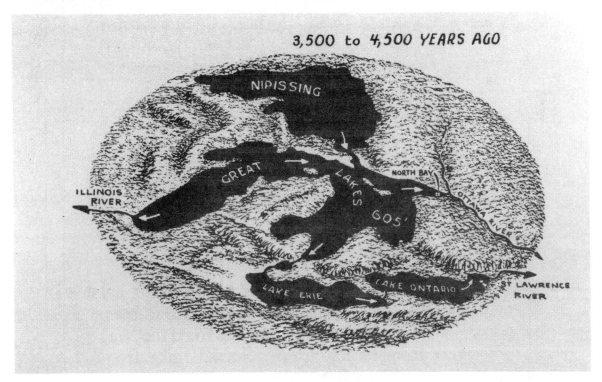

Figure 6-19. Glacial lake at highest elevation 3,500-4,500 B.P. Source: Drawing by J. M. Campbell, *The Glacial Lakes Around Us*, Michigan Geological Survey Bulletin 4.

TABLE 6-4

A Summary of Characteristics of the Great Lakes

	Lake Superior	Lake Michigan	Lake Huron	Lake Erie	Lake Ontario
Length	563 km 350 mi	491 km 307 mi	331 km 206 mi	388 km 210 mi	311 km 193 mi
Width	259 km 160 mi	190 km 118 mi	294 km 183 mi	92 km 57 mi	85 km 53 mi
Depth Maximum	407 m 1335 ft	282 m 925 ft	228 m 748 ft	64 m 210 ft	245 m 804 ft
Volume	12,230 cu km 2934 cu mi	4920 cu km 1180 cu mi	3537 cu km 849 cu mi	483 cu km 116 cu mi	1637 cu km 393 cu mi
Surface	82,100 km² 31,699 mi²	57,750 km² 22,278 mi²	59,500 km² 22,973 mi²	25,657 km² 9906 mi²	19,000 km² 7336 mi²
Watershed Area	127,700 km² 49,307 mi²	118,100 km² 45,598 mi²	133,900 km² 51,699 mi²	58,800 km² 22,703 mi²	70,700 km² 27,297 mi²
Shoreline w/Is	4795 km 2980 mi	2670 km 1659 mi	5120 km 3181 mi	1377 km 856 mi	1168 km 726 mi
Elevation	183 m 602 ft	177 m 581 ft	177 m 581 ft	174 m 571 ft	75 m 246 ft
Connected Inland Lake	Lake Nipigon Ogoki Reservoir	Lake Winnebago Houghton Lake	Lake Nipissing Lake Simcoe	Luther Lake Conestogo Lake	Finger Lakes Rice Lake
Outlet	St. Mary's River	St. Mackinac Chicago	St. Clair River	Niagara River	St. Lawrence River
Holding Period	191 years	99 years	22 years	2.6 years	6 years
Natl. Park/Forest	Pukoskwa NP Superior NF Apostle's Is NLP Chequamegon NF Ottawa NF Hiawatha NF Pictured Rock NLP Isle Royale NP	Ind. Dunes DLP Manistee NF Sleeping Bear NLP Hiawatha NF Nicolet NF Chicago Portage NHS	Georgian Bay Is NP Huron NF	Point Pelee NP Cuyahoga NRA Cedar Point NWR S. Sister IS NWR	St. Lawrence Is NP Iroquois NWR
Bottomland Parks	2	2	3		1
Watershed Uses:					
Agriculture	3% use	44%	27%	67%	39%
Resid/Indus	1% use	9%	9%	10%	7%
Forest	91% use	41%	68%	21%	49%
Other	5% use	6%	3%	2%	5%

Key: NF = National Forest NHS = National Historic Site
NP = National Park NRA = National Recreation Area
NLP = National Lakeshore Park NWR = National Wildlife Refuge

Source: The Marine Advisory Service, Michigan Sea Grant College Program, Cooperative Extension Service, Michigan State University, 1985. Field Traverse: Santer 1985.

Glacial Lakes and Contemporary Shoreline Features

The several stages of the glacial lakes; Lakes Maumee and Whittlesey (L. Erie), Lakes Chicago and Chippewa (L. Michigan), Lakes Duluth, Houghton and Nipissing (L. Superior), Lakes Algonquian and Stanley (L. Huron), each left their evidence on the contemporary landscape. Especially recognizable today are their former shoreline features of wave cut cliffs (Pictured Rocks N.P.) beach ridges (Ridge Rd., Lenawee Co., Mich.), lake terraces (Terrace Rd., North Bay, Ont.), and lake bed *lacustrine plains* (Saginaw Lowland US-27) (Figs 6-20, 6-21).

Lacustrine plains are found wherever the Great Lakes invaded the land. Most of these plains are extensively used for food production and are subject to flooding. In spite of mining, some ancient beach ridges of sand and gravel are preserved in local parks, old homestead sites and cemeteries. Douglas Houghton, unknowingly identified in his journal a beach ridge of glacial Lake Whittlesey lacustrine plain:

> Left Detroit for Kent Co. via the Grand River Rd....No rain having fallen for 4 to 6 weeks the consequence of which the road is exceedingly dry and dusty -- 12 miles from Detroit is a ridge of yellow sand at right angles with the Grand River road & elevated 12 to 14 ft. West from this country became more rolling although it still continued flat. --
>
> September 18, 1838[5] (Fig 6-22).

Place names and publications sometimes hold an accurate record of former physiographic features such as *The Sand Hill Monthly,* a publication of the Redford (ford of the red river, i.e. today's *River Rouge,* French for "red river") Masonic Lodge, formerly located on Lasher Road, north of Grand River Avenue (Fig 6-23).

Fluctuation of Lake Levels and Contemporary Shoreline Erosion Problems

During the post-glacial period, the lake surface elevations, it is judged, varied from a low of 54 m (180 ft) to a high of 240 m (800 ft) of elevation above sea level. As early as 1749 Lotbiniere recorded observations of French inhabitants at Fort Michilimackinac who stated that the lake levels rose and fell about equal amounts in 10-12 year cycles.[6] Ninety years later the Michigan topographer, S. W. Higgins, again confirmed the periodic fluctuation in levels. "The flood of the century" in 1839 which inundated the orchards along the Detroit and St. Clair rivers plus caused additional destruction, prompted early calculations on how to best manage the shoreline to reduce recurring community hardships due to high water.[7]

In the early 1950's, high water levels again caused millions of dollars of damage. Spurred by population, economic and technologic changes, in conjunction with a cycle of low water levels, many homes were built too close to the lakes to assure their survival. When high lake levels returned in the late 1960's through the 1980's, the cost in damages to structures continued the increasing cost spiral. By 1976, over 800 homes in Michigan alone, had been

[5]1838 Field Notes of Douglas Houghton, Journal 7 @ 4 x 7 inches, Clarke Historical Library, Central Michigan University, Mt. Pleasant, Michigan.

[6]"Fort Michilimackinac in 1749," *Mackinac History*, Vol. II Leaflet No. 5 (1976), p. 10. ("Lotbiniere's Plan and Description," translated by Marie Gerin-Lajoie).

[7]*Geological Reports of Douglas Houghton* (Lansing: Michigan Historical Commission, 1928), pp. 263-66.

Figure 6-20. Beach ridge, glacial Lake Whittlesey (Lake Erie 12,000 B.P.) at Ridgeway, Michigan on Ridge Road.

Figure 6-21. Terrace Road Lake Nipissing, North Bay.

Figure 6-22. Beach ridge remnant of Grassmere Lake stage of glacial Lake Whitlesey, Mt. Hazel Cemetery, old Redford neighborhood Detroit. Sand mining has remove ridge to edge of cemetery.

The Sand Hill Monthly

Published by Redford Lodge No. 152, F. & A. M.
"A Lodge of True Friendship"
17405 Lahser Road
DETROIT, MICHIGAN

NORMAN A. PAELKE, *Editor* — VE. 5-1949
12947 Rutland (27)

GEORGE R. REVAIT, Bus. Mgr.

| Vol. XVII | October, 1954 | No. 9 |

Figure 6-23. Sand Hill Monthly, Redford Lodge, provides a clue to the historic natural and cultural landscape of its area: sand hill = glacial beach ridge, redford = Amerind ford of the French named River Rouge - Upper Branch.

identified as being in immediate danger of severe damage or destruction due to shoreline erosion. By the mid-1980's, several of the structures had fallen into Lake Michigan, especially at Grand Haven (Figs 6-24, 6-25).

It can be asserted that the levels of the lakes have been relatively stable during the last century and a quarter. In that time, the variation in level has been about 2 meters (6 ft), a minor fluctuation in comparison to ocean tides or pre-historic Great lake changes. Media stories and photos, focused on homes and cottages collapsing over embankments, which in places receded up to 12 m (39 ft) in storms, have led to conferences and landowner hues and cries for the government, civil engineers, power companies or navigation leaders to "do something" to lower the levels by structural controls or existing diversions. At times of low water the clamor is to raise the level. Unfortunately, no easy or inexpensive relief solution exists.

Common and Seasonal Fluctuations

Lake levels fluctuate in three ways: short-term hours and days, an annual seasonal cycle and long-term over decades. In short-term, meteorological changes such as storms with high wind and barometric pressure changes cause the greatest fluctuations. Notable *seiches* or oscillations of water in the lakes have been recorded in relationship to barometric pressure: most recently in December, 1985, Lake Erie rose 2.6 m (8 ft) in a few hours causing a 5 m (16 ft) differential between Toledo and Buffalo.

In the yearly seasonal cycle, winter has the lowest levels when much water is frozen into ice. Mid-summer, after the spring thaw and before hot weather evaporation, results in the highest levels. An ice jam in spring can temporarily dam the flow and raise the lake levels 2 or 3 inches. The dredging of the St. Clair channel has, it is estimated, lowered the level of Lakes Michigan-Huron 3 inches. The man-made out diversions at Chicago (3200 CFS) and consumptive uses, when balanced against the in-diversions through Long Lac and Ogoki (5600 CFS), have an estimated 2.5 inches lowering effect on Lake Michigan.

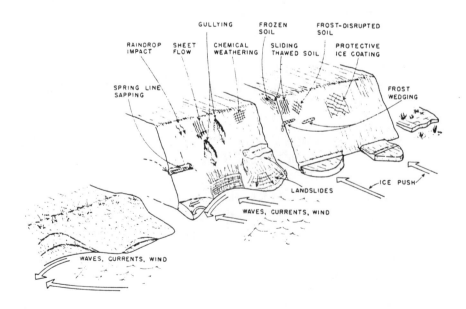

Figure 6-24. Recession Great Lakes shoreline factors -- diagram. From: *Great lakes Basin*, American Association for the Advancement of Science, Pub. 71, H. J. Pincus (ed.). Copyrighted by AAAS 1962.

Figure 6-25. Bluff erosion undermines a lakeshore home. Laketon Township, Muskegon County, Michigan. Source: B. Mills photo, Michigan Land Resources Division, July 1976.

The United States Coastal Barriers Act (1988) discourages development on shoreline holdings that have no other protected status. This is done by shutting off federal assistance such as flood insurance, grants, loans and disaster relief. The Act targets areas with less than one building per five acres. Affected are 25,283 ha. (63,209 ac) at 117 sites in Michigan (47,175 ac., 79 sites), New York, Ohio, Wisconsin and Minnesota. In 1993 in an effort to better manage the watershed run-offs, the US-EPA released a 1,500 page guideline. Directly affected are landowners including farmers and raparians. Targeted are past practices of lawncare, pesticide and fertilizer uses, improved animal waste and erosion control plus catch basin installation.

The International Joint Commission after years of intense study and public involvement is implementing forty-two recommended actions of its Levels Reference Study Board. Critical guiding principles include:

- Shared costs of 1/3 federal, 1/3 state/provincial, 1/3 local for an annual budget for lakes level control;
- Coordinated management and communications clearing house for Great Lakes - St. Lawrence River System;
- Discourage construction in areas subject to damage from fluctuating water levels;
- Remove some of the fill in the Niagara River;
- The making of no further consideration for three or five lake regulation;
- Erosion and flood setbacks plus real estate disclosure requirements of seller to buyer;
- Denial of subsidized flood insurance to new development in hazard zone;
- Improved GIS and hazards mapping, use with better distribution;
- Refinement of Global Climate Models to improve prediction capability and;
- Continued and expanded citizen involvement.

The report concludes that,

> "regardless of whether lake levels and flows are regulated, damage to shoreline properties, public infrastructure and water dependent businesses will continue without land-based action to curb such damage."[8]

Chemical Properties and Toxic Concerns

The Great Lakes water like rain or melted snow is commonly referred to as "soft" water which has many use advantages (Table 6-5). The industrial revolution has contributed much to improving the quality of life for people. Unfortunately, with the good has come the not so good chemicals which are, when misplaced in the environment, a threat to flora, fauna and human life. The International Joint Commission, "Pollution Hot Spots on the Great Lakes" map illustrates areas of primary concern which require concerted cooperative efforts to resolve (Fig 6-26, Table 6-6).

[8]"Final Report: 42 Recommendations for Actions," (*UPDATE: Levels Reference Study Board* Ottawa and Washington, DC: IJC, March 31, 1993) pp. 1-6 and *Levels Reference Study: Great Lakes - St. Lawrence River Basin*, (IJC, March 31, 1993) pp. 1-108.

TABLE 6-5

Analyses of the Great Lakes (parts per million)

	Lake Superior	Lake Huron	Lake Michigan	Lake Ontario	Lake Erie
Turbidity	Trace	Trace	Trace	4.50	41.00
Silica	7.40	12.00	10.00	6.60	5.90
Iron	0.06	0.04	0.04	0.05	0.07
Calcium	13.00	24.00	26.00	31.00	31.00
Magnesium	3.10	7.00	8.20	7.20	7.60
Sodium plus potassium	3.20	4.40	4.70	6.30	6.50
Carbonate	0.00	1.80	2.90	2.90	3.10
Bicarbonate	56.00	100.00	112.00	116.00	114.00
Sulfate	2.10	6.20	7.20	12.00	13.00
Nitrate	0.50	0.40	0.30	0.30	0.30
Chloride	1.10	2.60	2.70	7.70	8.70
Total solids	60.00	108.00	118.00	134.00	133.00

SOURCE: Howard J. Pincus (ed.), *Great Lakes Basin*, Pub. 71 (Washington, DC.: American Association for the Advancement of Science, 1962), p. 86.

The Sand Dunes -- Lake/Land Interface

The sand dunes of Michigan, Indiana and Ontario, which sparkle as if sprinkled with diamonds in the summer sun and rise as lofty lakeshore hills, are another of the Basin's attractive landscape features. They are also prized for industrial product manufacturing castings. The wind-piled sand mounds are so young as landscape features that in many places they are still moving and soil has not evolved on them. The sand dune building process generally follows a three-step *saltation* process: (1) the wind carries dry sand which skips, jumps and bounces against an object, usually vegetation, which can trap and hold the sand grains, (2) the pile of trapped sand forms a foundation and obstruction which forces the wind to change its speed which continues to pile more sand on the original obstruction, and (3) dune stability with a gentle windward slope and steep lee slope is reached when vegetation establishes itself and covers the exposed sand.

Dune Features.--Within the shoreline margins where dunes are found, several distinctive dune features are observable including:
1. *Fore dunes*, low 9-15 m (30-50 ft) dunes parallel to beaches;

2. *Blowouts*, dune areas which have been reexposed to the wind due to the vegetative cover's injury or removal by natural or human occurrences such as cottage development, walking paths, the operation of trail bikes and dune buggies. They generally have saddle-shaped depressions;

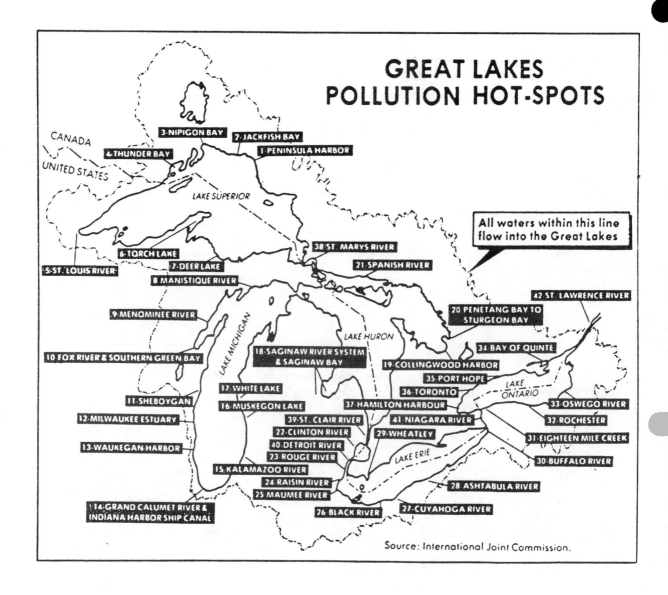

Figure 6-26. Areas of serious pollution concern. Source: IJC.

3. *Dune ridges*, a further extension of blowouts with pronounced "U"-shaped topography, unlike anything observable in arid lands. Along southern Lake Michigan they may rise over 75 m (250 ft) and stretch inland a thousand meters;

4. *Migratory dunes*, in their classic desert form, a rare development in Michigan; however, evidence of some dune migration includes the re-exposure of dune-buried forests and the building of backslopes at the rate of 1.5-3 m (5-10 ft) per year.

TABLE 6-6

Toxic Contamination Places -- Class A and B

Most Polluted Class A	Exhibits Degradation Class B	
Fox River	Lake Superior:	Lower Straits:
Milwaukee Estuary	Marathon	Lake St. Clair
Waukegan Harbor	Jackfish Bay	Thames River
Indian Harbor	Peninsula Harbor	Wyandotte
St. Mary's River	Nipigon Bay	
Saginaw Bay	Thunder Bay	Lake Erie:
Saginaw River System	Silver Bay	Rocky River
St. Clair River	St. Louis River	Grand River, OH
Detroit River	Upper Portage Entry	Port Colbourne
River Rouge		Grand River, Ont.
Raisin River	Lake Michigan:	Wheatley
Maumee River	Manistique River	
Black River, Oh.	Menominee River	Lake Ontario:
Cuyahoga River	Sheboygan River	St. Catherines
Ashtabula River	Great Lakes N.T.C.	Mississauga
Buffalo River	Muskegon	Toronto
Niagara River	Montague	Port Hope
Hamilton Harbor		Cobourg
	Lake Huron:	Bay of Quinte
	Alpena	Kingston
	Serpent Harbor	Sacketts Harbor
	Spanish River	Oswego Harbor
	Penetary Bay	Rochester Harbor
	Sturgeon Bay	Niagara Falls
	Sarnia	
	Collingwood Harbor	

N.T.C. = Naval Training Center

SOURCES: *Toxic Substances in the Great Lakes*, (Washington, DC., Environment Protection Agency, June 1980). Great Lakes Water Quality Board (Windsor: International Joint Commission, 1983). cited in "The Great Toxic Lakes," *Environmental Action*, (June, 1985). "IJC Areas of Concern," *The Bulletin of the Midwest Cleanwater Campaign*, Vol. 2 No. 2 June 1984. *TEF data*, No. 17, Feb. 1985, p.1.

The Michigan dune sand is usually found to be about 90 percent quartz grains from glacial drift mixed with magnetite, hornblende, calcite, tourmaline and other materials (Fig 6-27).

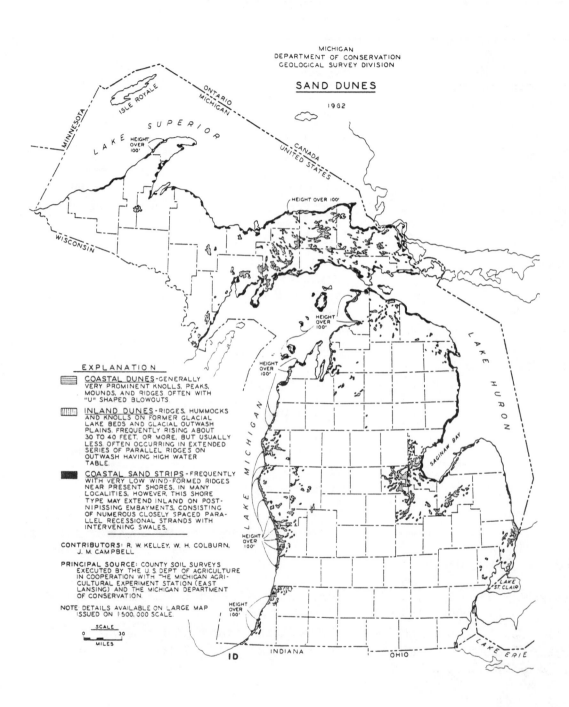

Figure 6-27. Michigan Sand Dunes. ID indicates the Indiana dunes formerly a part of Michigan Territory. Source: Michigan Department of Conservation.

166

The Sleeping Bear Dune has gained international acclaim and is the central feature of the Sleeping Bear Dune National Lakeshore Park area. The spectacular dune reaches 135 m (450 ft) above Lake Michigan; however, because its foundation is a moraine plateau, it is not strictly a sand dune. Other notable Michigan dunes are Grand Sable, 115 m (380 ft) and Silver Lake, of 100 m (300 ft). Ontario dunes are at Wiaton, Sauble Beach, the Bruce Peninsula, Grand Bend of the AuSable plus Crystal Beach and on the Prince Edward County shoreline of Lake Erie. In the Pukaskwa National Park on Lake Superior, there are a group of minor dunes mixed with the rocky shoreline trail which provides a delightful variety to a hiking experience.

Dune Protection

For several decades mining of the dune sands has been an important economic industrial activity. Especially threatened have been the Indiana dunes which, if the remnants were not protected as the Indiana Dunes National Lakeshore Park and Indiana Dunes State Park, could have been totally mined and disappeared from the earth. With protection, the Indiana dunes are a treasured unique niche of the Basin adjacent to the modern major Indiana port, Burns Harbor. The Nordhouse Dune area of 1360 ha (3400 ac) near Ludington, is a near wilderness area which has been targeted for oil drilling. With rare exception, it appears that the unique dunes remain threatened by mining, oil exploration and real estate development activities. A most fundamental question in regard to dune conservation and preservation is, can a democracy act effectively to protect its unique resources in a post-industrial society and global economy?

Underwater Preserves and Shipwrecks

As the economy of the region evolves in part more toward leisure time services activities and more ways to utilize the resources of the Basin, it is not surprising that the bottomlands of the lakes have begun to witness greater appreciation. Nearly 6000 shipwrecks, many well preserved in the cold water, are found in a few concentrated places while others are widely distributed on the lakes bottoms. MI PA 184-80 and MI PA 452-88 provide for protection and preservation of property on the Great Lakes bottomlands. Michigan has nine bottomland/underwater parks. Ontario has a National Marine Park, while New York, Ohio, Illinois, Wisconsin, and Minnesota are in the developmental stages of establishing underwater preserves.

Sport diving has become a well established activity. Michigan's bottomland preserves include: Whitefish Point, Alger at Munising (L. Superior), Thunder Bay at Alpena, Straits Area at Mackinac, Thumb Area at Port Austin, Sanilac Shores at Port Sanilac (L. Huron) and Manitou Passage (L. Michigan). The ship disasters which lead to the greatest losses of life include the: Eastland 825 lives (Chicago Harbor, July 24, 1915), Lady Elgin 297 lives (Lake Michigan, September 8, 1860), G. P. Griffith 275 lives est. (Lake Erie, June 17, 1850), Phoenix 230 lives est. (Lake Michigan, November 21, 1847), and Atlantic 200 est. (Lake Erie, August 20, 1852). Causes of the disasters are associated with fire, storms, floundering/capsizing, and collisions. Historic sites and museums can be found at Beaver Island, Dossin Great Lakes Museum - Detroit, South Haven, S. S. Keewatin - Douglas, S. S. Valley Camp - Sault Ste. Marie, Whitefish Point and the S. S. Silverside a submarine - Muskegon.

Summary

This chapter described, in varying detail, the Pleistocene glacial process, the diversity of resulting geomorphic land features, as well as, the inland lakes and watersheds whose rivers replenish the Great Lakes. Together these features comprise a major part of the natural eco-system of the Basin as a basis for a holistic understanding of the entire watershed. As an initial foundation for continued study, most important is the listing which identifies 185 of the water courses and watersheds which flow into the Great Lakes. Shoreline erosion and pollution concerns have been outlined to help guide reasonable economic development and individual actions which will allow sustained life.

Reflections and Self-Learning: Chapter 6

1. Recall or list the major physiographic sections of the chapter -- on which one would you like to gain even more information?

2. Contrast Paleozoic and Pleistocene.

3. Which glacially formed landscape features can you observe in your area -- list and cite specific or relative location.

4. Contrast lobe, moraine, drumlin, esker, kame, outwash and lacustrine plain.

5. How can gravel pits be made safer and more attractive -- at what cost?

6. Contrast natural and cultural eutrophication - how can cultural eutrophication be slowed?

7. What are the major inland lakes of the Basin? How many have you seen? Which one do you want to visit? What route would you use to get to it?

8. Contrast the shape of the Finger Lakes with other lakes of the Basin. What caused their shape?

9. How can lesser known waterfalls be both protected and used for economic value?

10. For whom or what are the major inland lakes and rivers named? Are there duplicate lake names in your area? Who would you name or rename a place for -- why?

11. Why or why not would you like to boat the Trent-Severn Canal?

12. In what ways are duplicate lake names a problem for rapid communication or delivery of services?

13. Contrast three river flow patterns. Why are the patterns different?

14. What did you learn from the summary of 185 watercourses which flow into the Great Lakes? How can the list of rivers be used?

15. Which river(s) in your area is/are designated under the Natural Rivers Act? What river would you designate? Why?

16. Describe the fluctuation of lake levels. Why do they change? What are the problems associated with their rise and fall?

17. Evaluate recent actions to protect the quality of the Great Lakes water. What other actions may have to be taken? What is fair-just water/land regulations in a democracy?

18. Are there and if so where are hazardous zones or wastes in your community?

19. What are the locations and value of sand dunes?

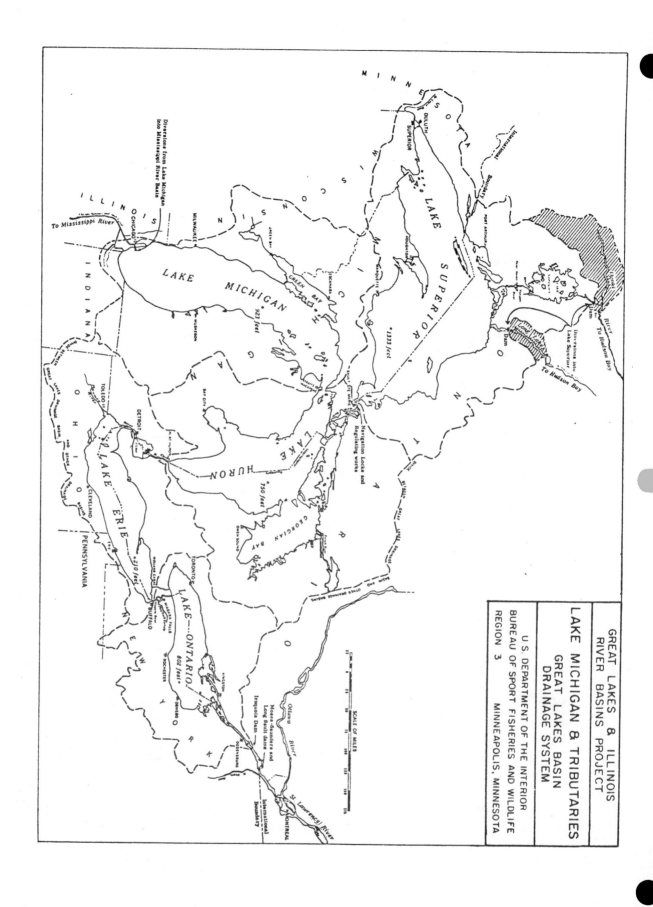

GREAT LAKES & ILLINOIS
RIVER BASINS PROJECT

LAKE MICHIGAN & TRIBUTARIES
GREAT LAKES BASIN
DRAINAGE SYSTEM

U.S. DEPARTMENT OF THE INTERIOR
BUREAU OF SPORT FISHERIES AND WILDLIFE
REGION 3   MINNEAPOLIS, MINNESOTA

*The city is one of society's permanent
institutions. Nevertheless, a full orbed human
being can not be evolved without free access to
the earth, oceans, bays, lakes, rivers and brooks
without the companionship of the birds of the
forest and beasts of the fields, without having
a daily vision of the sun, moon and stars in the
firmament.*

Woodbridge N. Ferris

Chapter Seven

PATTERNS AND RELATIONSHIPS OF THE
ATMOSPHERE, SOIL AND FAUNA

"We missed the four seasons," is a common reply to the question, "Why did you come back?" put to people who have returned to the Great Lakes area after extended stays in other climate regions. Yet in spite of the importance of weather and climate in decisions people make or the historic writing of environmental determinists, the atmospheric conditions, the related natural flora, fauna, and soil elements which will be described in this chapter influence; but do not determine or control the way of life of people. As evidence, note that the Basin's culture, including housing, clothing, food, marriage arrangement, transportation, religion, political system and economy, are all much different today than the way of life of the Amerind or Pioneers, even though the climate throughout the recent centuries has been similar. The basis for the difference is best linked to human inventions and diffusion of technical and economic/social innovations. Natural conditions only place *selective limitations* on how people choose to live. In short, in spite of the great importance of nature to life, a people's culture is chosen by the people and is changed by the people, both deliberately and unconsciously. In the foreseeable future, it will be humans who will pollute the environment to the point of uninhabitability or choose to protect it from toxic hazards.

Climate Change and Crucial Questions

Although the Basin's climate has remained relatively stable the last few centuries, given the geologic and glacial evidence it can be concluded the Basin's climate patterns have changed throughout the last two billion years. It is also safe to assume that very long-term climate patterns will remain in transition. Given the impermanence of climate patterns, it might be interesting to ponder the following questions:

1.   How would people and governments respond to the readvance of glaciers
      from their Arctic remnants?

2.   Could peace be maintained in the Basin and outside it if its tens of million
      inhabitants found it necessary to relocate south of the four former terminal
      lines of the glacial age ice sheets?

3.   As a hedge against a future readvance of the glaciers, should individuals or communities acquire and hold in trust a land reserve beyond the previous glaciated areas?

4.   Should the proposed schemes of freshwater transfer from the lakes to drought regions outside the Basin be linked to compensation for a "Glacier Readvance Trust Land Reserve"?

Climate Regions

Climate is usually described and mapped as separate regions based on an average of at least 25 years of recorded weather data. *Weather* is the daily condition of the local atmosphere. The weather forecasts report daily air temperature, precipitation by fall type (rain, snow, sleet, ice, hail), held moisture -- relative humidity, barometric pressure, wind speed and direction. Time of sunrise and sunset are solar system figures sometimes provided as useful complementary data. Helpful in the fostering of a cooperative Basin geocentricism spirit based on travel and common interests are the growing number of cross-border weather reports by television and radio stations.

The Basin is sited within three of the dozen world climate regions identified under the Köppen-Trewartha system (Fig 7-1). South to north these regions are the: (1) Humid Continental Long/Warm Summer, Daf; (2) Humid Continental/Short/Cool Summer, Dbf; and (3) Sub-Arctic, Dcf (Boreal Forest/Tiaga). The "Humid Continental" title and "Df" letters indicate that the region is a snow-forest area whose temperatures are affected by a large continental land mass with little direct ocean influence, but is moist enough by precipitation to support trees. The "a" signifies the area where the warmest summer month averages above 22°C (71.6°F) while the "b" indicates the area where the warmest month averages below 22°C (71.6°F). The "c" indicates less than four months over 10°C (50°F). Even though most maps use a precise line to demarcate the climate regions, in reality, only in some areas identifiable by sharp changes in physiography, are the *tension lines* as used by climatologists, more than *transition zones*.

Seasons and Climate Factors

The Basin's four distinct seasons (spring, summer, fall, winter) annually change in close association with a variety of climate factors other than by the precise dates of the earth-sun equinox-solstice cycle. This is apparent in relationship to the opening of the professional baseball season in the third week of spring, but not infrequently in cold and, sometimes, snowy weather. Similarly, the "fall" deer seasons of November are at least a month before the winter solstice, but commonly accompanied by "tracking snow."

The Basin's weather is influenced by several factors: (1) its mid-polar-equator latitude location, (2) its situation in a lowland corridor without high mountains which leaves it open to rapid exchanges of cold Arctic air and balmy subtropical air, (3) its 10 degrees of latitude range and 18 degrees of longitude extent interrupted by the varying shape and placement of the large lakes, (4) its situation in relationship to the jet stream, wind patterns and local topography, and (5) the sun. Figures 7-2, 7-3 and 7-4 illustrate the pattern of January and July temperatures plus the annual rate of precipitation. Tables 7-1 and 7-2 summarize average and record temperature occurrences for selected communities and a comparison of places located at the same latitude, illustrating land-water influence relationships.

172

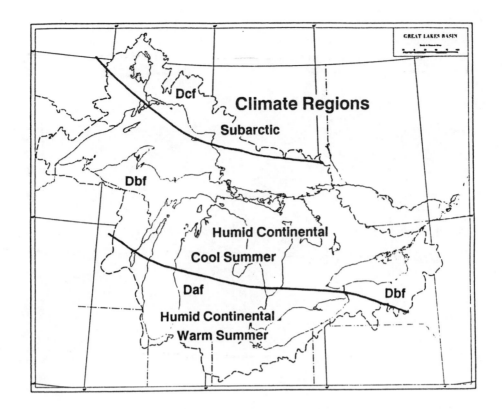

Figure 7-1. Basin climate regions after Glenn T. Trewartha/Köppen. Base map: IJC.

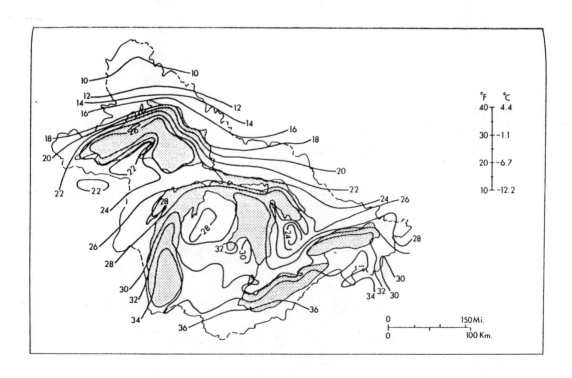

Figure 7-2. January mean daily maximum temperature. From: *Weather and Climate of the Great Lakes Region*, by Val Eichenlaub. Copyrighted 1979 by University of Notre Dame Press. Reprinted by permission. (Drawn by T. W. Holder).

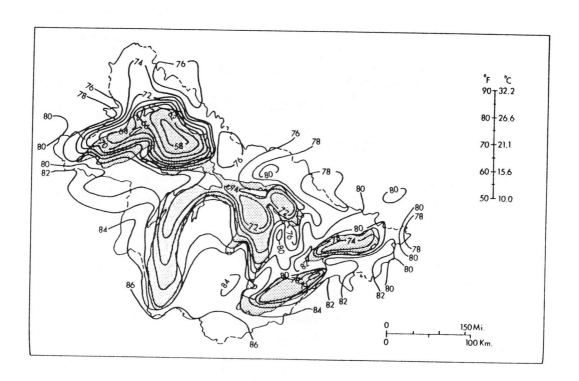

Figure 7-3. July mean daily maximum temperature. From: *Weather and Climate of the Great Lakes Region*, by Val Eichenlaub. Copyrighted 1979 by University of Notre Dame Press. Reprinted by permission. (Drawn by T. W. Holder).

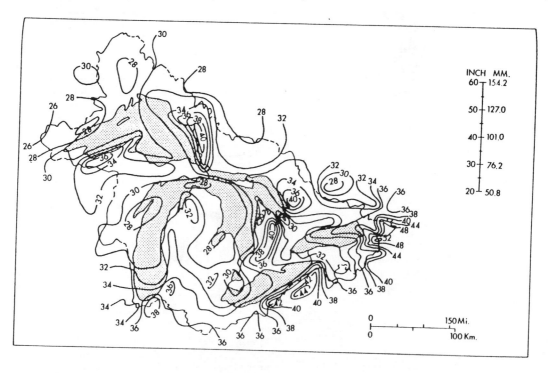

Figure 7-4. Mean annual precipitation (inches). From: *Weather and Climate of the Great Lakes Region*, by Val Eichenlaub. Copyrighted 1979 by University of Notre Dame Press. Reprinted by permission. (Drawn by T. W. Holder).

Climate and Weather Features

The Sun as a Source of Energy

If water is the key earth resource in the Basin, then the sun is the key energy resource for the Basin, for, without either, life could not be sustained. The Basin's environment, is affected by *oblique rays* rather than *direct rays* from the sun. With rays reaching the Basin at a non-vertical angle, the ray in effect heats a larger surface area (thus cooler) than the heat concentrating direct rays of the tropics. However, in relating the sun's energy to resource conservation, it can be argued that because the Basin has cooler temperatures and air heating is necessary to sustain health as opposed to the sub-tropics or tropics, solar heating devices are more energy conserving than in warmer climates (Fig 7-5). Further, Solar cells for lighting are also an important long-term energy potential which can be developed to complement utility systems (Fig 7-6).

TABLE 7-1

Selected Community Record and Mean Annual Temperatures

Community	Mean		Record	
	Jan. C/F	July C/F	Low C/F	High C/F
Chicago	-4.4/23.9	22.3/72.6	-30.2/-23	39.0/103
Detroit	-3.1/26.2	22.6/73.1	-30.8/-24	40.1/105
Duluth	-12.4/ 9.3	18.3/65.3	-40.1/-41	36.8/ 99
Green Bay	-9.0/15.6	20.5/70.1	-37.4/-36	37.9/101
Kingston	NL	NL	-32.8/-27	33.3/ 92
Lima, Ohio	-.4/31.2	22.6/73.1	NL	NL
S. St. Marie	-10.0/13.7	17.2/63.4	-37.9/-37	36.3/ 98
Sudbury	-12.2/10.0	19.7/67.4	-37.8/-37	38.3/101
Thunder Bay	-14.8/ 5.3	17.5/63.5	-41.1/-42	37.2/ 99
Toledo	-3.3/26.0	22.7/73.4	-26.4/-16	39.0/103
Toronto	-6.3/20.6	20.7/69.2	-32.8/-27	40.6/105
Wawa	NL	NL	-41.1/-42	31.1/ 88
White River(Ont.)	-19.3/ 0.4	15.7/60.5	-50.6/-60	35.7/ 97

Note: Statistics vary between sources.

SOURCES: *Climate of Michigan by Stations*, 1st and 2nd rev. eds., (E. Lansing: Michigan Weather Service, 1965 and 1971). *Climate Atlas - Canada*, Map Series I, Temperature and Degree Days, (Ottawa: Atmospheric Environment Service, Environment Canada, 1984). *Ohio Almanac*, (Lorain: The Lorain Journal Company, undated @ 1979). *Ontario Statistics 1984*, p. 10. *Statistical Abstract of the United States 1985*, pp. 206-218.

Figure 7-5. Solar panels for cool weather space heating.

Figure 7-6. Experimental solar cell for woodshed lighting. B. Trese, Michigan/California.

TABLE 7-2

Mean Temperature Comparisons:
Similar Latitude Communities

Community	January		July	
	C	F	C	F
Madison	-8.0	17.5	21.6	71.0
Milwaukee	-9.4	18.5	21.4	69.3
Muskegon	3.8	26.0	21.0	69.9
Flint	-4.8	23.2	21.4	71.0
Port Huron	-3.7	25.2	21.6	71.3
London	-6.0	21.2	20.5	68.9
Buffalo	-3.9	24.9	19.6	69.7
Syracuse	-1.4	29.4	21.8	71.7

SOURCES: *Ibid.* (Table 7-1) and *Weather Almanac*, 2nd ed., (Detroit: Gale Research Co., 1977).

The Jet Streams

The jet streams are strong currents of air which circulate at 30 to 35 thousand feet altitude. These currents are useful for long-distance air flight into and out of the Basin. The polar front jet stream, which is most closely associated with the Basin, somewhat guides the lower air masses, both warm and cold fronts, from the west to the east across the continent. As a result, the prevailing winds which people on the ground sense are from the west. In winter, the jet winds flow on a southerly path and guide frigid Arctic-polar air into the Basin. The summer jet wind flow is located to the north and pumps moist hot tropical air into even the most northern parts of the Basin. The jet stream is probably the agent by which DDT and other toxins enter the Basin from Latin America. In 1991 under provisions of the Clean Air Act - USA and actions by Environment Canada, 5 of 35 international Air Monitoring Stations were established in the Basin to check 11 pollutants targeted in the Great Lakes Water Quality Agreement (Eagle Harbor, MI; Burnt Island, Ont.; Sleeping Bear Dunes, MI; Point Petre, Ont.; and Sturgeon Point, NY).

Fronts, Air Masses and Daily Weather

Within the four seasons, the warm and cold lower altitude air masses move across the continent in what are called *fronts* which produce *cyclonic storms* of changeable daily weather which leads to the often heard remark "if you don't like the weather, wait a while -- it will change"! The Basin is usually affected by three dominant air masses: (1) the cold-dry polar, 60 percent; (2) the Pacific, 25 percent; and (3) the warm, moist maritime tropical, 15 percent of the year. Most typical fronts of air mass winds circulate around a low pressure cell and move 320-3200 km (200-2000 mi) per day. *Stationary fronts* move much slower or "hang on" for several hours or a day or two. Forecasts, even for a few hours ahead, are very difficult because of the lakes which cause unexpected movements of the cyclone-fronts. In spite of numerous ground stations and orbiting satellites supporting professional weather reports and forecasts, they cannot replace individual responsibility in becoming somewhat adept at weather watching and wisely responding to local weather signs. The household barometer is a useful instrument for indicating a rapid decline in air pressure -- a reliable sign of an approaching storm front-cyclone. A front with a wind shifting to the east is a strong sign of bad weather. An ethical question is: If a boat operator scoffs at watercraft warnings or makes alcohol-drug relaxing careless choices to challenge a storm, at what level of risk should public safety employees risk their lives to affect a rescue?

Severe Local Storms

Storms of November

Fall appears in the Basin, in brilliant hues of red, yellow, gold and brown leaves. Delight comes to many from nature's seasonal painting of the landscape especially those who take time to enjoy the beauty and to businesses that support color tour activities. Unfortunately for sailors on the Big Lakes, the yellow leaves warn of possible danger. All too often the November shift of the world system of jet streams, air masses and pressure cells leads to ships sinking and death to sailors.

The list of losses in the storms of November is enough to raise serious economic, technological and social questions related to lessening the heartache and toll. In the pioneer era, on November 18, 1842, fifty ships were wrecked. Three years later, Douglas Houghton perished in Lake Superior off Eagle Harbor. On November 10, 1913, eleven ore boats with all hands aboard were lost (Fig 7-7). During the 1940 Armistice Day storm, the toll was less than in 1913, even

Figure 7-7. Storm of November Memorial Plaque, Goderich.

though the gale force winds were more intense. More recently, the SS Carl Bradley sank with 35 lives lost in Lake Michigan on November 18, 1953. Eight years later, the SS Daniel J. Morrell was sunk in Lake Huron. On November 10, 1975, one of the newest, largest and well-equipped lakers broke in two just short of calmer waters of Whitefish Bay carrying 23 men to their death.

Tornadoes

In comparison to the tornado belt states to the southwest, the Basin has relatively few tornadoes. Historic Basin data concerning the number of tornadoes, however, is unreliable because of unreporting and low population densities. Thus, the increases now being recorded may not indicate an actual change in tornado occurrences -- just more people to sight them. About 12 tornadoes annually swirl through the Basin with devastating black funnel cloud winds of over 160 KPH (100 MPH) which sometimes bounce like a pogo stick out of the southwest sky, then hold to the ground and lay waste buildings, trees, crops and autos in its relatively narrow (1/2 mile) path while also causing injuries and death from blowing debris (Fig 7-8). In 1953, 116 people were killed, mostly in the Flint. The Palm Sunday, April 11, 1965, tornado caused few deaths but devastated a long path out of Indiana, Ohio and into Michigan. The April 3-4, 1974, storm resulted in multiple funnels and affected an extensive area of the southern part of the Basin costing millions of dollars of damage. The July, 1985 tornado in Barrie, Ontario, on Lake Simcoe, was one of the Basin's most northerly major occurrences.

Blizzards and Wind Chill

Frozen death can be the end for individuals unprepared to meet the harsh challenge of blizzards which periodically happen in the Basin. Blizzards last about one day, characterized by dropping temperatures, heavy accumulations of dry powdery snow and a steady sharp drop in pressure, followed immediately by high winds when the barometer indicates the passage of the front with rising air pressure. It is in this critical period of rising pressure and high winds that "makes" the blizzard which drifts snow to car and home rooftop heights, disorients walkers in blowing clouds of snow and "wind chills" the body seemingly below the registered air temperature. It is in the windy period that most people are killed by the storm itself; however, more people die from "digging out" from the drifts the following days.

Ice Storms

Ice storms occur throughout the Basin with, at times, significant economic losses and disruptions. Hailstorms occur with about 5 percent of the annual 20-50 (north to south) thunderstorms which usually just pelt driving rain on the landscape (Fig 7-9). The hailstones are especially damaging to fruit, field grains and window glass. Hailstones are formed around ice particles and enlarge in ice layers around the core through contact with super cooled droplets of water as they descend or ascend through thick clouds in down or updrafts.

Sleet and ice coatings, are common nuisances during the Basin's winter season and early spring. With society becoming more dependent upon electrical power, ice storms especially with modest winds are an increasing danger to health and welfare; thus portable electric generator sales are becoming a larger part of the economy. In March, 1976, over 600,000 Michigan residents were without electricity for several days when lines and poles were broken by wind and ice. Perhaps the time has come when power companies, community governments and educators cooperatively take action to elevate the level of awareness of the danger of ice storms and to develop coping skills needed to deal with cold weather power failures. Greater knowledge needed

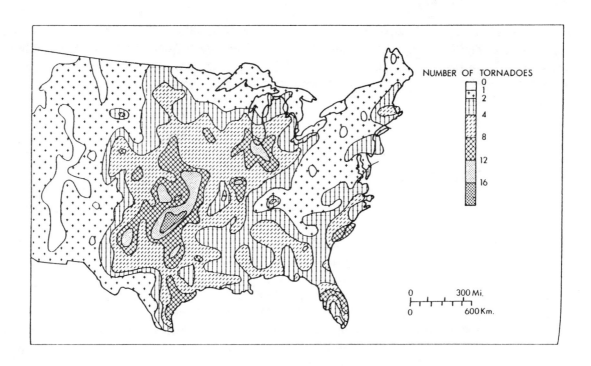

Figure 7-8. Tornado occurrences annually per 10,000 square miles. From: *Weather and Climate of the Great lakes Region*, by Val Eichenlaub. Copyrighted 1979 by University of Notre Dame Press. Reprinted by permission. (Drawn by T. W. Holder).

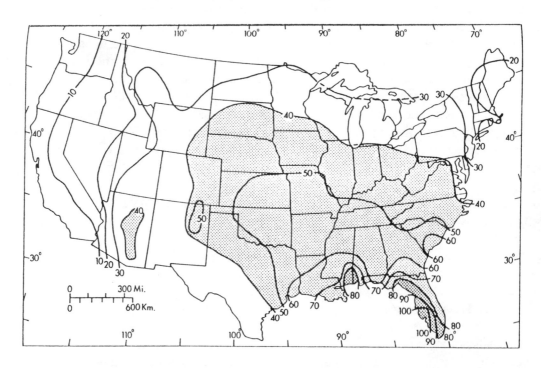

Figure 7-9. Mean Annual Thunderstorm Days. From: *Weather and Climate of the Great Lakes Region*, by Val Eichenlaub. Copyrighted 1979 by University of Notre Dame Press. Reprinted by permission. (Drawn by T. W. Holder).

includes: information about furnace operations, water line freeze protection, door openings, how to prepare a home for temporary abandonment if one is advised to go to a community shelter and how to report live down lines without a functioning telephone.

Thunder and Lightning

Hot humid/muggy summer days are a part of life in the Basin. However beautiful cumulo-nimbus clouds are, they become dangerous when accompanied by high winds and electrically charged lightning strikes from rapidly rising thunderheads (Fig 7-10). Improved record keeping indicates that during this century, lightning accounts for more deaths annually than tornadoes. Based on records since 1897, June through August are the most dangerous months. Seventy-five percent of the fatalities happen between noon and midnight. With the increase in out-of-doors summertime activities, plus Daylight Saving Time, there may be a need for increasing educational efforts on the dangers of lightning and precautions to exercise during an electrical storm.

Figure 7-10. Thundershower cloud formation with thunderhead building and black storm cloud line.

Common Weather Features

Lake Effect Snow and Snow

The Basin receives the heaviest snowfalls east of the Rocky Mountains. The pattern of the snowfall varies, however, because of the effects of the lakes. In general, the accumulation is greater to the north, but the lee sides of the lakes and the areas with higher elevations also tend to receive more snow than inland locations (Fig 7-11). To illustrate the influence of the lakes and elevation, the east shore of Lake Erie and western New York usually has a greater amount of snowfall than Thunder Bay on the north side of Lake Superior. Yet, because of latitude, western

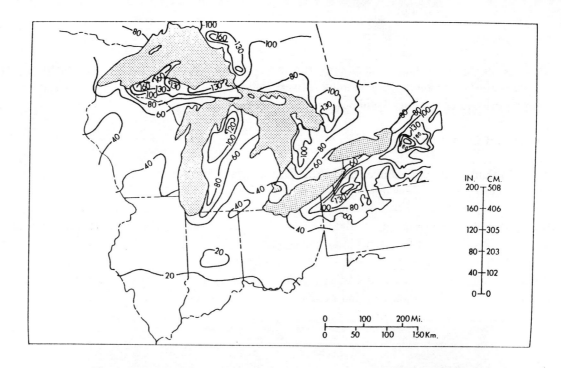

Figure 7-11. Mean Annual Snowfall -- Great Lakes Basin. From: *Weather and Climate of the Great lakes Region*, by Val Eichenlaub. Copyrighted 1979 by University of Notre Dame Press. Reprinted by permission. (Drawn by T. W. Holder).

New York, frequently has ground baring thaws and spring flowers emerge earlier than in Thunder Bay. Upper Peninsula communities take pride in "Copper Country Sunshine" and in jovial betting as to which settlement will claim the annual "snowfall sweepstakes." Herman recorded over 762 cm (300 in) in 1975-76, just short of the 802 cm (316 in) which fell in Calumet. The community of Beardmore, east of Lake Nipigon near the divide, in a positive action has adopted the snowman as their symbol of welcome to visitors to town (Fig 7-12).

The Amerinds also developed a rich vocabulary of terms to relate to snow conditions as the following Chippewa-Ojibway words attest:

1. Bisipon -- the snow is fine, tiny flakes,

2. Nokagonago -- the snow is very large clusters of flakes,

3. Zhakagonago -- the falling snow is soft,

4. Gawagonaga -- frozen ice pellets,

5. Biwan -- snow flurries,

6. Madjipo -- wind driven snow (blizzard).[1]

---

[1]Bruce F. Watson, *Minnesota and Environs Weather Almanac*, (Navarre, Minnesota: Freshwater Biological Research Foundation, 1974), pp. 5-7. Cited in Entine, *Our Great Lakes Connection, op. cit.*, p. 148.

Figure 7-12. Snow sculpture, Beardmore near Lake Nipigon.

At the eastern edge of the watershed, New York communities on Tug Hill Plateau, an elevation of about 600 m (2000 ft), make sensible claims as being "Snow Capitals." At Bennett Bridge, 48 km (30 mi) east of Oswego, a blanket of snow 130 cm (51 in) thick fell in a 16-hour period on January 17, 1959. At Hooker, New York, southeast of Watertown, a Basin record of 1185.9 cm (466.9 in) was measured. In comparison, Detroit's average snowfall rate of 78.9 cm (31.1 in), is very attractive for individuals who desire to avoid great accumulations.

Total Precipitation Patterns and Extremes

Total Basin precipitation varies between 132 cm (52 in), at the east end of the watershed in Lewis County New York, to a low of 66 cm (26 in) on the west edge of the divide in the vicinity of Swan River, Wisconsin and Hibbing, Minnesota (Fig 7-4). About 55 to 60 percent of all precipitation falls during the growing season which reduces the need for widespread rainmaking and irrigation activities. However, in some years drought causes severe crop damage.

Wind and Wind Generators

The greatest potentials for wind-powered electric generation are found in other areas of North America. However, on the east shores of the lakes, the average wind speeds of 19 KPH (12 MPH) are enough to economically support the installation of large NASA-type windmills. The modern wind generator near Buffalo, at Hamburg, is an example of a pioneering attempt to demonstrate the potential for wind generation in the Basin (Fig 7-13).

Figure 7-13. Windmill at Hamburg, New York.

Fog

Usually, fog is localized to a 1/2 kilometer belt along the lake shorelines and in river lowlands. Along the shore *advection fog* is formed by southern warm moist air flowing over the cooler lake air. The warmer air can hold more moisture than cold air, thus a water vapor of fog forms above the water surface. Technically, fog is recorded when visibility is reduced to less than 1 km (.6 mi). Severe fogs with less visibility are very disorienting. Fortunately, such springtime and early summer fogs do not last long, being dissipated by a change in wind direction or temperature. Wintertime fogs on the Great Lakes are generally not observed by tourists because they form over sections of open water away from the shoreline. These fogs are known as "Arctic sea smoke", steam fog and steam devils. The fogs are formed when frigid air from the north flows over the warmer unfrozen water (Fig 7-14).

Lake Freezing Pattern

The Great Lakes rarely form a total covering of ice except at the several straits, channels between islands and shallow water areas (Fig 7-15). Unfortunately, in late winter and early spring, Coast Guard, law enforcement personnel and citizens are called upon to risk their lives to rescue individuals who are carried into open water on dislodged ice sheets when warming trends, wind and shore currents combine to open a water gap at the shore.

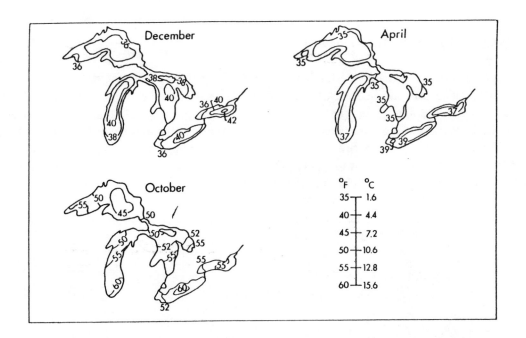

Figure 7-14. Mean Great Lakes Water Surface Temperatures. From: *Weather and Climate of the Great lakes Region*, by Val Eichenlaub. Copyrighted 1979 by University of Notre Dame Press. Reprinted by permission. (Drawn by T. W. Holder).

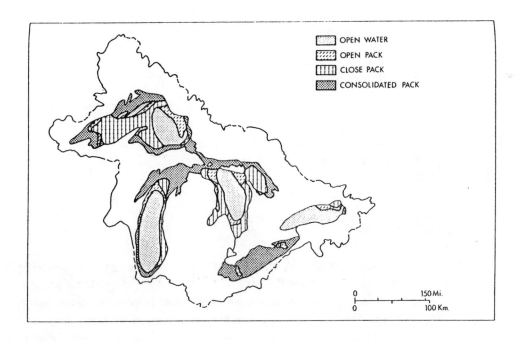

Figure 7-15. Mean Maximum Ice Extent. From: *Weather and Climate of the Great lakes Region* by Val Eichenlaub. Copyrighted 1979 by University of Notre Dame Press. Reprinted by permission. (Drawn by T. W. Holder).

Lake Effect Delayed Frost: The Fruit Belts

If spring brings danger to ice fishing people from drift ice, a balancing benefit comes to orchardists who raise fruit along the east sides of the lakes. Their benefit is related to the time differential between the spring and fall water warming and cooling. Budding of fruit trees is delayed in the belts of land near the lakes by the cool offshore water and west winds until there is little late spring frost danger. In reverse, in fall, the warmer lake water and west winds delay early fall frosts which allow the fruit to ripen. The environmentally valuable land affected extends, depending on topography with suitable relief for air drainage, about a dozen miles inland. With increased population and leisure-time, plus the attractiveness of the near shore areas for cottage and home development, these belts of land with delayed frost are being taken out of fruit production which pose serious zoning decisions (Fig 7-16).

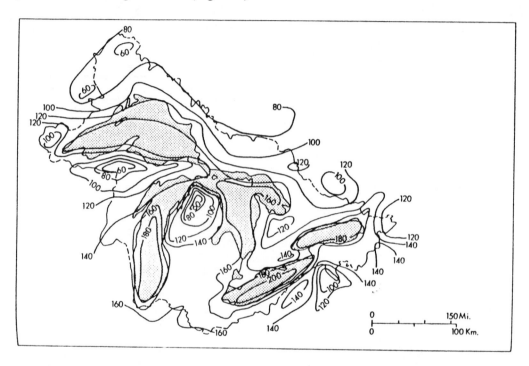

Figure 7-16. Frost-Free Days. From *Weather and Climate of the Great Lakes Region* by Val Eichenlaub. Copyrighted 1979 by University Notre Dame Press. Reprinted by permission. (Drawn by T. W. Holder).

Frost-Free Days Growing Season

The frost-free period, the fifth season or *growing season* is the Basin's most important food producing time. Unlike the four uniform length solar seasons, the growing season varies greatly in length based on locality because it is measured by the number of days between the average dates of the last and first plant-killing frost of spring and fall. What plant and tree species are found naturally in the environment and cultivated is directly linked to the varying lengths of the frost-free period. Also linked to the alternating freezing and thawing of the soil is frost heave or "growing boulders". Stones rise to the surface by a suction action due to different ground temperatures.

186

The frost-free season can vary greatly one year to the next and locally. In northwest Mecosta County, Michigan, which usually has more than 110 frost-free days with the average dates of last and first frost set at May 18 and September 29, ice formed the night of June 12, 1978, in gardens that had been sprinkled. Some home gardeners were dismayed on August 16, 1979, when a mid-summer frost killed their ripening beans and tomatoes. This is only a 64 day period. In comparison, Detroit, in 1946, recorded 218 days consecutively without frost -- a season long enough to grow cotton. In analysis to destroy the food growing capabilities of the Basin's areas with the longest, most productive frost-free periods seems imprudent, or in the words of a second-grader, "dumb."

Unintentional Weather Change

LaPorte, Indiana is frequently cited as an example of unintentional weather change. An analysis of precipitation records since 1925, when the South Chicago-Gary steel making complex was developed, and the present indicate about a one-third higher annual rate of fall. Additionally, more hail and thunderstorms are also observed. The increase has led to the conclusion that airborne dust and heat given off by the industrial processes provide nuclei and more favorable temperatures to cause the increased precipitation which is measured up to 24 km (15 mi) away. Areas of such occurrence are referred to as *heat islands* and *dust domes*.

Another Ice Age? -- Global Warming/Greenhouse Effect

Global warming or "greenhouse effect" does not seem to be occurring in the center of the Basin. Carl Ojala and Robert Ferrett of Eastern Michigan University analyzed the 1898 to 1988 temperature data from 45 National Weather Service Stations in Michigan. They found that between 1898-1955, 38 stations had an increase in annual temperature. However, between 1956 and 1988, the most reliable data years, 33 stations had a decline in annual temperature. Even urbanized areas such as Detroit, Flint and Jackson it was found had inconclusive temperature trends. Other studies indicate that cutting the original forest and its replacement with young plants is not effective in reducing carbon dioxide if forests are a major factor in reducing the greenhouse effect.

While evidence continues to be accumulated on artificial weather changes a frequent question put to earth scientists is, "Are we going into another ice age?". The best answer is, "I or we don't know for sure." However, because there is a scientific record of several ice advances and retreats with related climate changes, the possibility exists.

Val L. Eichenlaub, in *Weather and Climate of the Great Lakes Region*, University of Notre Dame Press, 1979, concludes:

---the probability of the present interglacial ending soon is higher than we might
like, at least if past climatic behavior is an indication---[2]

William Least Heat Moon in *Blue Highways* points in the same direction:

---the great ice sheets had gone away only to get more rock. "They'll be back.
They always come back. What's to stop them?"[3]

[2]Val L. Eichenlaub, *Weather and Climate of the Great Lakes Region*, (Notre Dame: University of Notre Dame Press, 1979), pp. 227-237, (This publication has been the authoritative aid for this section). "Global Warming", (Big Rapids, MI: *The Pioneer*, November 19, 1990), p. 1.

[3]William Least Heat Moon, *Blue Highways: A Journey into America* (New York: Fawcett Crest-Ballantine Books, 1982), p. 283.

Soil Types and Regions

Given the bountiful gardens observable in the Basin the attachment to the soil remains compelling even with the development of an urbanized citizenry. While the dependency of agriculture on soil is obvious, the success of much of industrial society is also inseparably tied to the basic knowledge of soils. Commonplace highways, sidewalks, water-septic systems, building foundations and power poles are all dependent for smooth operation on the soil in which they are installed. At construction sites the need to minimize vegetation removal and maximize its re-establishment to thwart soil erosion is important to help prevent the clogging of public sewers and ecosimplication. Preparation of Environmental Impact Statements (EIS) for construction projects is a promising step toward reducing losses.

Soil and Its Classification

Soil is the collection of natural elements, either organic, inorganic, gas or chemical, in the earth's crust which supports the growing of vegetation. The horizons or profile of a soil is used for classification based on various characteristics, i.e., texture, structure, thickness, color and chemical composition. The "A" horizon includes the surface layers to which organic matter has been added by plants, plus fine mineral particles and soluble materials. The "B" or subsoil horizon includes some of the fine particles and less soluble materials which have been deposited by percolating water. The "C" horizon is slightly weathered material beneath the subsoil. "D" horizon is bedrock material. Most Great Lakes Basin soils are classified as *transported soils* as a result of being carried to their place of deposition (Fig 7-17).

Characteristics of Poor Drainage.--"A" and "B" horizons appearing gray or splotched with gray flecks have been mottled by moisture and indicate poor drainage. Such soils are generally unsuited for installation of septic systems or require specially designed systems to make them work safely. Most landowners in the Basin would benefit, both their later peace of mind and pocketbooks, if they would seek assistance (prior to land purchase or development) from qualified earth scientists, health departments, agricultural agencies or civil engineers in evaluating soils (Fig 7-18).

Basic Soil Knowledge for Nonprofessionals.--The lack of uniformity in soil classification systems has thwarted education and the sharing of soils knowledge throughout the world and between fields of specialization. Two systems of soil classification are generally used by United States engineers. Highway engineers use a system approved by the American Association of State Highway Officials (AASHO) while most other engineers use the *unified system* adopted by the U.S. Army Corps of Engineers. Both systems differ from the classification system used by the United States Department of Agriculture that is based on the percentage of sand, silt, and clay-sized particles in soil texture. The AASHO soil classification system is divided into seven principal groups according to gradation, liquid limit and plasticity index. In the unified system, soils are identified according to performance as a construction material, their plasticity and texture.

Soil Types and Causes of Differences.--Soils in general acquire their distinct qualities from six natural factors: climate, vegetation, parent material, slope, drainage and time. In the traditional world regionalization of soils, Great Lakes soils are classified in the: (1) podzol, (2)

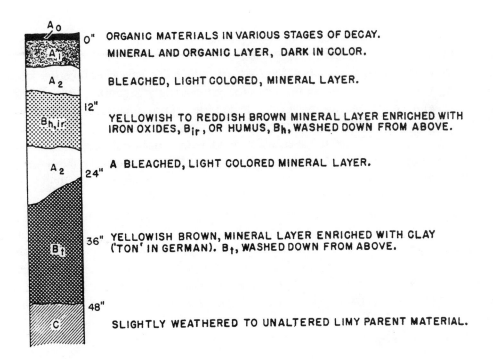

0"	ORGANIC MATERIALS IN VARIOUS STAGES OF DECAY.
	MINERAL AND ORGANIC LAYER, DARK IN COLOR.
	BLEACHED, LIGHT COLORED, MINERAL LAYER.
12"	YELLOWISH TO REDDISH BROWN MINERAL LAYER ENRICHED WITH IRON OXIDES, B_{ir}, OR HUMUS, B_h, WASHED DOWN FROM ABOVE.
24"	A BLEACHED, LIGHT COLORED MINERAL LAYER.
36"	YELLOWISH BROWN, MINERAL LAYER ENRICHED WITH CLAY ('TON' IN GERMAN). B_t, WASHED DOWN FROM ABOVE.
48"	SLIGHTLY WEATHERED TO UNALTERED LIMY PARENT MATERIAL.

Figure 7-17. Typical soil profile indicating horizons (Marlette loam). Source: E. P. Whiteside, *et. al.*, *Soils of Michigan*, Agriculture Experiment Station, Sp. Bul. 402, 1956.

Figure 7-18. Broken sidewalk typically laid over clay soil.

189

gray-brown podzolic, and (3) mixed organic-bog soils groups which are concentrated in north Eurasia, New England and the Great Lakes Regions.[3]

In recent years, the world's soil scientists have adopted a new classification known as the 7th Approximation. The orders and sub-orders are systematically organized by soil elements and named by using both Greek and Latin words. In the 7th Approximation, Great Lakes soils are regionalized as: Spodosols, Alfisols, Mollisols and Inceptisols (Fig 7-19).

Spodosols are soils of mixed materials covered with a light colored leached sandy layer, generally found in high latitudes. *Boralfs* and *Udalfs* are *Alfisols* which are the more commonly known, most agriculturally productive podzolic soils of the mid-latitudes. These tend to be gray or brown in color with a sub-surface clay accumulation horizon. Boralfs are found in places with cool to cold temperatures and free drainage. Udalfs are soils located where there are warmer conditions with moisture commonly held within the soil particle texture. *Udolls* is a *Mollisoil* which is a modest warm soil associated with the grassy steppe or commonly known prairie lands. The *Ochrepts* is an *Inceptisol* which is a developing soil with little organic matter, light in color and usually moist. In unraveling the complexity of the Great Lakes Basin soils, both air photos and satellite imagery along with field boring checks are being used to delimit the intricate distribution patterns (Fig 7-20).

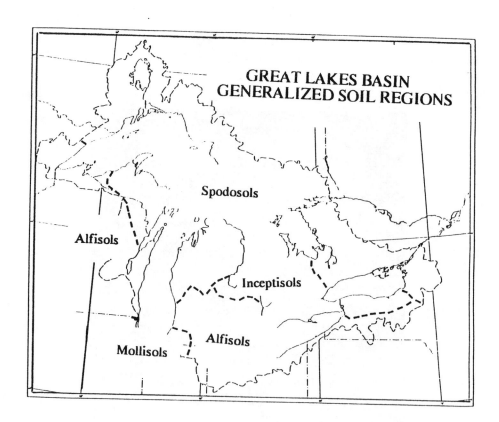

Figure 7-19. Principal soil orders of the Great Lakes Basin -- 7th Approximation. Base map IJC.

[3] *Goode's World Atlas*, 14th ed. (Chicago: Rand-McNally & Co, 1974), pp. 20-21. *Canada: a regional analysis* (Canada: J. M. Dent and Sons Limited, 1979), p. 197.

Animals: Fauna of the Land

Unlike the early 1600's when only one type of wildlife was observed -- natural, today there are four categories: (1) natural, (2) re-introduced, (3) introduced and (4) hybrid. However, today as a result of the untiring efforts of conservationists and preservationists, the alert traveler can observe animals ranging in size between the small scampering field mice to the relatively huge moose. The most commonly sighted animals include: white-tailed deer, red fox, raccoon, skunk, porcupine, cottontail rabbit, woodchuck. opossum, squirrel, urban rats and muskrats. Less often seen animals, especially common to the northern wilderness and rural areas, are: black bear, cougar, timber wolves, coyotes, beaver, badger, varying hare or snowshoe rabbit, otter, mink and weasel. The black bear is most easily seen at community dumps and have thus become local minor tourist attractions. Research by Richard Dukelow indicates that over 90 percent of the people-bear attacks are associated with garbage or people food and usually occur while individuals are hiking or camping.

Reintroduced Elk -- Wapiti

The combined results of logging and pioneer settlement plus overhunting, led to the demise of the Basin's American elk, which the Shawnee called *wapiti*. A relatively large, quiet, wooded area with openings, habitat is needed to support the animal which stands 1.6 m (5 ft) high at the shoulder and weighs between 315-400 kg (700-1000 lbs). Since restocking in the 1930's with a few animals from the Rocky Mountain remnant herd, the Pigeon River Country State Forest herd has grown to controlled hunting size and is the largest east of the Mississippi River.

In the 1970's a lingering conflict between oil well development interests and the elk herd advocates came to a somewhat forced settlement in the aftermath of the OPEC embargo. Under Mi PA 61-1939 and amended in 1973, the controversy was resolved by limiting drilling, roads, oil storage and pump sites to specific areas of the 37,800 ha (94,000 ac) forest which occupies parts of three counties in northwestern Lower Michigan. There are still objections to noise, dust and odor, in pumping while adjacent farmers are concerned about crop damage by the elk.

Moose: Residual Range and Reintroduction

In Europe, the animal called the American elk or *wapiti* is known as "the moose." The North American Moose is the largest animal in the deer family [2.3 m (7.5 ft) at the shoulders 825 kg (1800 lbs.)] and males possess a characteristic palmated set of antlers (Fig 7-21). The moose range has shifted somewhat northward in historic time and is closely associated with a few key browse species for its food supply including: balsam fir, white birch, trembling aspen, willow, Juneberry, dogwood, highland maple, mountain ash and cherry (Fig 7-22).   In 1985 and 1987, in a cooperative effort between agencies, a few dozen Michigan wild turkey were exchanged for Ontario moose. Previous attempts to reintroduce moose in the Upper Peninsula have failed because of poaching or brainworm disease. Poaching a moose is now a highly penalized activity, if convicted, but brainworm still easily spreads through the droppings of white-tailed deer. White-tailed deer continue to expand their range northward (Fig 7-23).

Bison/Buffalo, Pine Martin and Wolf

The bison or buffalo once grazed freely on grasses in a range which extended across the entire southern half of the watershed. Today, no remnant free roaming herds exist; however, in a few places, such as near Traverse City and L'Anse, ranch herds are raised primarily for tourism,

Figure 7-20. Modern soil map on air photo illustrates complexity of agricultural soil types in a small area. Source: U.S. Soil Conservation Service, Soil Survey of Mecosta County, Michigan, 1984. Note: Number 20 indicates gravel pit.

Figure 7-21.

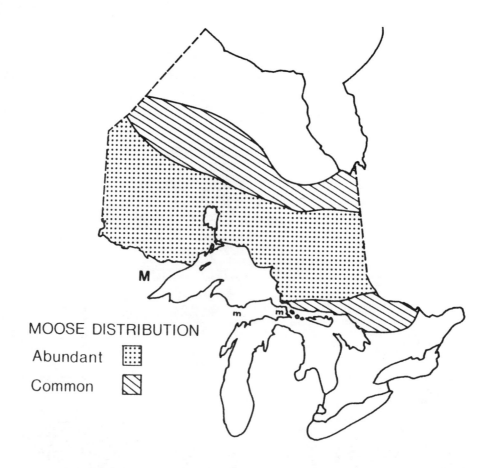

MOOSE DISTRIBUTION

Abundant

Common

Figure 7-22. Moose distribution in Ontario. m indicates reintroduction area in Upper Michigan and Minnesota range. Source: H. G. Cumming, *The Moose in Ontario*, Ontario Ministry of Natural Resources, 1972. Cited in *Boreal Mixedwood Symposium*, Canadian Forestry Service and Ontario Ministry of Natural Resources, 1981. (Letters added by author.)

private sport hunting and meat marketing. On a small scale with limited tourist interest, but important to the gene pool; Ontario pine martens, members of the weasel family, were released in northern Michigan in the mid-1980's in an attempt to replace the species which disappeared during the logging days. The Eastern timber wolf, or gray wolf, was openly hunted and destroyed into the 1960's throughout the Basin. In spite of their reputation, there is no documented incident of a wolf, killing a human in North America. Remnant packs remain in Ontario, Wisconsin and Minnesota, but none in the Lower Peninsula. In 1949 a small pack (12 wolves) became established on Isle Royale. Twenty wolves in ten counties are established in the Upper Peninsula. In comparison to wolves, is the huge and growing number of abandoned or stray cats and dogs which challenge animal control officials. Of continuing interest to those who study the fauna of the Basin is the relationship between the "animal rights movement" fur trapping and animal numbers or distributions.

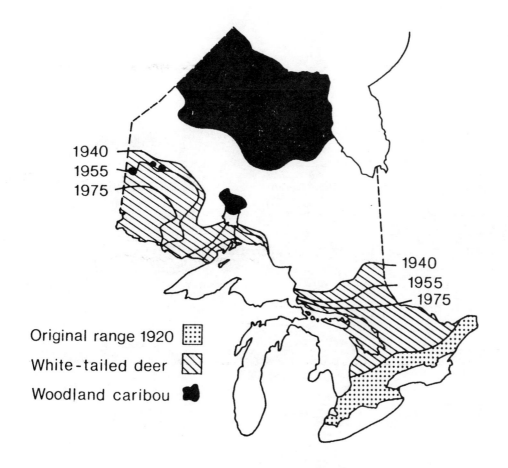

1940
1955
1975

1940
1955
1975

Original range 1920
White-tailed deer
Woodland caribou

Figure 7-23. Changing north limit of white-tailed deer range. source: *Boreal Mixedwood Symposium*, Canadian Forestry Service and Ontario Ministry of Natural Resources, 1981. Citing A. T. Bergerud, "Caribou," in *Big Game of North America*, 1978. Plus, P. Smith and E. Borczon, "Managing for Deer and Timber," *Your Forest*, Vol. 10, No. 1, 1977.

Fish: Fauna of the Waters

In spite of water pollution, natural eutrophication and technological/electronic advancements in fishing gear, fish of many species thrive in aquatic habitats related to the present-day climate (Fig 7-24). To offset environmental problems and to improve fish yields, several fish species have been introduced, including: salmon, carp, German brown trout and steelhead. Commercial fishing, now most active in Canadian waters, has undergone drastic changes but still is an important economic activity. Remnant U.S. operations may be found on Saginaw Bay and Bay De Noc.

Salmon in the Big Lakes and Rivers

The story of the introduction of Pacific (coho, chinook, pink and king) and, later, Atlantic salmon into the Great Lakes and rivers can be attributed to several complementary factors: (1) research and testing commitment, (2) diligent leadership by a few individuals in academic centers and natural resource government agencies, (3) lobbying by a well-organized group of fishermen

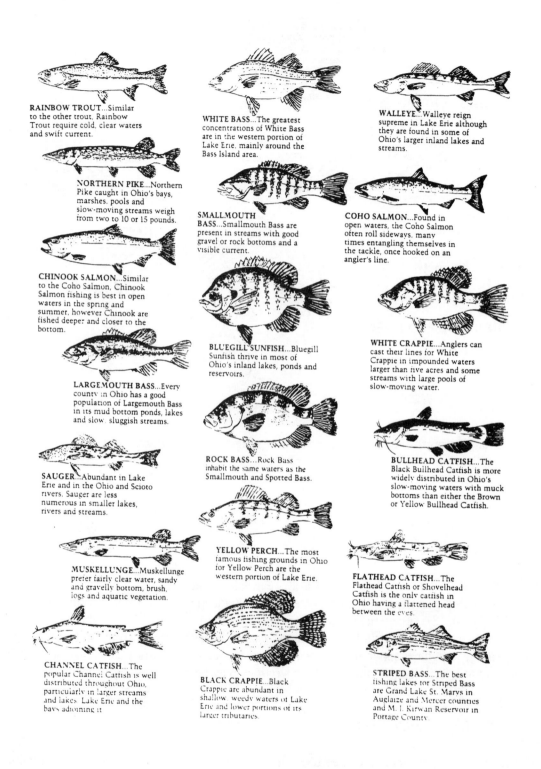

RAINBOW TROUT...Similar to the other trout, Rainbow Trout require cold, clear waters and swift current.

NORTHERN PIKE...Northern Pike caught in Ohio's bays, marshes, pools and slow-moving streams weigh from two to 10 or 15 pounds.

CHINOOK SALMON...Similar to the Coho Salmon, Chinook Salmon fishing is best in open waters in the spring and summer, however Chinook are fished deeper and closer to the bottom.

LARGEMOUTH BASS...Every county in Ohio has a good population of Largemouth Bass in its mud bottom ponds, lakes and slow, sluggish streams.

SAUGER...Abundant in Lake Erie and in the Ohio and Scioto rivers, Sauger are less numerous in smaller lakes, rivers and streams.

MUSKELLUNGE...Muskellunge prefer fairly clear water, sandy and gravelly bottom, brush, logs and aquatic vegetation.

CHANNEL CATFISH...The popular Channel Catfish is well distributed throughout Ohio, particularly in larger streams and lakes Lake Erie and the bays adjoining it.

WHITE BASS...The greatest concentrations of White Bass are in the western portion of Lake Erie, mainly around the Bass Island area.

SMALLMOUTH BASS...Smallmouth Bass are present in streams with good gravel or rock bottoms and a visible current.

BLUEGILL SUNFISH...Bluegill Sunfish thrive in most of Ohio's inland lakes, ponds and reservoirs.

ROCK BASS...Rock Bass inhabit the same waters as the Smallmouth and Spotted Bass.

YELLOW PERCH...The most famous fishing grounds in Ohio for Yellow Perch are the western portion of Lake Erie.

BLACK CRAPPIE...Black Crappie are abundant in shallow, weedy waters of Lake Erie and lower portions of its larger tributaries.

WALLEYE...Walleye reign supreme in Lake Erie although they are found in some of Ohio's larger inland lakes and streams.

COHO SALMON...Found in open waters, the Coho Salmon often roll sideways, many times entangling themselves in the tackle, once hooked on an angler's line.

WHITE CRAPPIE...Anglers can cast their lines for White Crappie in impounded waters larger than five acres and some streams with large pools of slow-moving water.

BULLHEAD CATFISH...The Black Bullhead Catfish is more widely distributed in Ohio's slow-moving waters with muck bottoms than either the Brown or Yellow Bullhead Catfish.

FLATHEAD CATFISH...The Flathead Catfish or Shovelhead Catfish is the only catfish in Ohio having a flattened head between the eyes.

STRIPED BASS...The best fishing lakes for Striped Bass are Grand Lake St. Marys in Auglaize and Mercer counties and M. J. Kirwan Reservoir in Portage County.

Figure 7-24. Common fish of the Great lakes Basin. Source: Ohio is the Greatest. Ohio Government, undated.

196

with support from shoreline beach owners, (4) the modestly fragmented status of the Great Lakes with one state, Michigan, having a disproportionate area of responsibility and (5) the easily visible large scale economic impact of "big fish" sport fishing. Yet, the underlying key to starting a non-native fish program in the Great Lakes was the result of the sea lamprey entering the ecosystem from the Atlantic, especially after the opening of the Erie Canal and the Welland Canal. The lamprey attached themselves to a large host fish usually lake trout, white fish or walleye, which led to their die-off. Further reduction of those species is also related to commercial fishing and World War II pollution of streams. Without abundant large fish of prey, the alewife rapidly increased in numbers and then, in the summer at the peak beach-using season, died off which littered the sandy shores with wind-wave rows of putrid odors.

The reversal of the problem began on the Platte River when coho fingerlings were released in 1967 which used the alewife as a food source. Simultaneously, a lampricide (trifluoro; ethyl-4-nitrophenol (TFM) was developed and released into rivers with lamprey spawning beds. Although an estimated hundreds of thousand lamprey are still in the lakes, within a few years, a huge sport salmon fisheries complex developed (charter boat sales/service of 14-35-foot craft, docks, gas, maps, motels, supplies, plus development of harbors of refuge) centered on rivers to harvest the salmon during the spawning runs, and on the Big Lakes during late summer when the fish were mature, 20-40 inches long. Super salmon are being developed by delaying the spawning runs for six or seven years, thus allowing the fish to grown larger. However, with the decrease in alewives standard salmonoids are averaging smaller sizes and the average annual catch has been down sixty percent since 1986. In contrast perch have increased their numbers and walleye have somewhat unexpectedly regained attention because of their rewarding schools in Saginaw Bay and Lake Erie. However, walleye have also decreased since 1989.

So far, sport fishing projects have overwhelmingly benefited males. This situation relates to the traditional pattern of Euro-American culture in which men have been deep water, big fish oriented, while women and families at leisure have been oriented to inland lakes with more modest-sized bass, pike, perch, bluegill -- panfish.[4] Improvement of the success rate and size of catch in the potentially more productive warmer water inland lakes are fundamentally more difficult than the salmon introduction story. People who fish the inland lakes tend to be less dedicated to their sport than trout/salmon fishermen, plus less organized or vocal. Further, the fragmented political nature of inland lakes, their distribution between hundreds of counties and townships, and the thousands of inland lakes tending to need unique management, are limiting factors of easy inland fishing expansion. Yet, fishing excitement for women can come quickly by joining men on the "Big Water". An example:

> In the fall of 1985, a senior citizen, wife of a former naval Lt. Commander and college department head, described in excited tones that she had gone fishing -- Really Fishing! In response to, "What is 'really fishing'?" she replied, "John took me onto the lake miles from shore, with water hundreds of feet deep, and we caught Big Fish! It was exciting!!"

[4]The potential for nurturing large inland lake fish is possible as pike and bass have been taken over 40 and 24 inches respectively in lakes with low fishing pressure.

To overcome the problem of non-reproducing lake trout in the lakes one hope is to reintroduce descendants of Lake Michigan Trout (from the original gene pool) which were used nearly a century ago to stock lakes in Yellowstone National Park. Another example of attempts to repair the genetic network is the reintroduction of grayling from Wyoming to a dozen river sites in Michigan. Sturgeon, the Basin's oldest and largest fish (8 ft., 300 lbs., 14-22 years to sexual maturity) and despised for net fouling by commercial fishermen, continues to be a threatened species. Natural breeding and restocked sturgeon are concentrated in Lake Winnebago/Fox River, the Menominee, Sturgeon and St. Mary's rivers (Michigan) plus the northwest Lower Peninsula. Given less polluted waters, another option to sport fishing may be a reinvestment in Great Lakes commercial fishing which could provide a source of protein for export and a source of a non-cholesterol main dish for the modifying American diet.

Non-native Species

In addition to the sea lamprey and alewife, a spiny-tailed water flea (zooplankton), quagga and zebra mussels (mollusks), and the goby species have become established since 1960 in the Basin lakes, harbors and rivers. Their origins are probably from bilge water emptied into the shipping system by ocean vessels. Zebra mussels and goby -- a five-inch, green whiskered fish are native to the Black and Caspian seas. Each of these species have had a changing influence on the Basin's water. The zebra mussels and its cold, deeper water niched relative, the quagga, are both prolific breeders. The zebra mussels have notably clogged community water intake pipes. Reduced catches of walleye may be linked to the mollusks' spread as they also notably clean the waters of algae, plankton other plants and sediment. Because of clearer water bass and pike numbers may increase and boaters will be able to view greater water depths.

Birds - Fauna of the Atmosphere

Birds, in addition to contributing to the balance of nature, perhaps are most important as visible sentinels in the struggle against debilitating pollution. Historically, caged canaries were used by miners to detect harmful trapped mine gases. Now, in the open atmosphere, by their grotesque mutations and reproductive disorders, they constantly provide warnings that the environment, in places, is unsafe for living. The bald eagle and its niche companions, osprey and kingfisher, as well as herring gulls, pheasants, sharp-tailed grouse, prairie chicken, passenger pigeon, and double crested cormorants, have all suffered and died of somewhat well-publicized disorders. Yet, to ignore nature's continuing "sentinel" alarms is to callously risk the demise of the fragile inter-connected community of species including Homo sapiens.

Relatively easily observable non-game birds, whose songs also can be heard, include: blackbird, robin, bluejay, sparrows, chickadee, warblers, wrens, mourning dove, bluejay, goldfinch, crow, owls, woodpeckers, cardinal, junco, Baltimore oriole, swallows, chimney swift, catbird, cowbird, flicker, green and great blue heron, bittern, killdeer, sandpiper, common tern, hawks (coopers, red-tailed, sparrow), pigeon, hummingbird, kingbird, least and great flycatcher, phoebe, horned lark, purple martin, nuthatch, thrasher, bluebird, cedar waxwing, meadowlark, grackles, scarlet tanager, grosbeak and indigo bunting. Common game birds include: several species of duck, Canada goose, ruffed grouse (partridge), quail, turkey and woodcock. Selected protected birds include: eagles, great blue heron, mute and trumpeter swan, snow geese, hawks, loon, sand hill crane and prairie chicken. Depending on jurisdiction, sometimes the quail and mourning dove are protected from hunting. Both the Atlantic (Lakes Erie-Ontario) and Mississippi (Lakes Superior-Michigan-Huron) Flyways are migration routes for Basin birds. Bird migrations are especially rewarding sights in the Boundary Waters Canoe Area and at Whitefish Point Bird Observatory where over 2,275 species have been tabulated. The native wild turkey with intra-Basin exchanges have significantly increased their population to hunting numbers especially in Indiana and Michigan ranges.

One of the most endangered species in the central district of the Basin is the piping plover which breeds and nests on beaches. Dogs on beaches in the plover nesting areas are a particularly bad problem because they drive the parents off their eggs who then do not return.

The Kirtland's warbler is an endangered species which is found in burned over jack pine stands of a specific height and age. This species reached its lowest numbers in Michigan in 1987. Sometimes military exercises at Camp Grayling, Michigan are adjusted to reduce nesting period disturbances. Both the common tern and Caspian tern are threatened in Michigan with only about 1200 nesting pairs of each species remaining in the state and water border areas. On balance, the once threatened cormorant population has grown to such numbers that they prompt "nuisance" claims by fishing enthusiasts. At Little Galloo island in Lake Ontario 100,000 of the birds have been reported. Other flocks have been reported at Les Cheneaux, Thunder Bay, Green Bay, Saginaw Bay and Apostle Islands. Some success is viewable by sighting the increased numbers of bald eagles. Once on the endangered list they are now on the threatened list in Michigan, Wisconsin, and Minnesota unlike the rest of the continent were they are still endangered.

Research in Ontario has identified the relationship of tree harvesting and birds' responses to the altered forest conditions. Age of a forest stand of trees appears to be directly associated with the bird species found in the forest (Fig 7-25). Research in Grand Traverse County, Michigan indicates an association of increases in spring temperature with butterfly observation. Such research is important to both managing the forests and protecting genetic pool resources.

Introduced Bird Species

People have mixed opinions about the starling which was introduced from Europe into New York in 1890. Since that time, the attractive black colored bird, which reflects many hues in the sunlight, has spread across the continent. The ring-necked pheasant, has been a very popular game bird introduced into the Basin a century ago from China. To replace in some areas, supplement and establish or cross-breed with the ring-necked species, the Michigan Department of Natural Resources, in a cooperative program with the Peoples Republic of China and its Sichuan Province, starting in the mid-1980's has brought to the state several hundred black pheasant species eggs for hatching and rearing. It is hoped that the Sichuan-blackhead, of which over 75,000 have been released in 25 counties, which roosts off the ground will thrive better in the present-day mixed cultural-natural environment.

Beyond the Atmosphere

There is admittedly not a seemingly close ecosystem linkage between the earth's soil, its animals, fish and birds with the stars and meteors of the earth. However, to see birds in flight or to enjoy the wonder of the vee of Canada geese in migratory flight at dusk and dawn over a farm field or lake, one must look into the sky. Then, by chance, in the background light, the stars or the occasional blazing trail of a meteor penetrating the atmosphere to the earth's environment from the universe can be seen. On college and university campuses of the watershed, planetariums and observatories are common against the skylines with their characteristic shapes. Ranked as one of the best of its kind in the nation is the Abrahms Planetarium at Michigan State University, named in honor of the founder of one of the world's largest air photo service companies located in

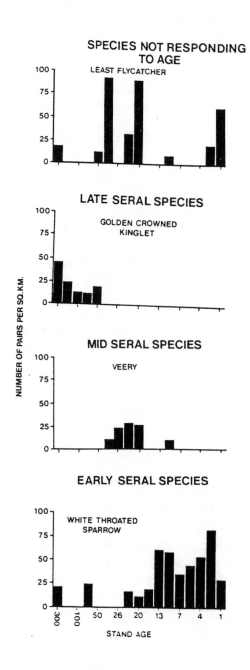

Figure 7-25. Bird species relating to age of forest stand. Source: D. A. Walsh, "Impact on Bird Populations," in *Boreal Mixed Hardwood Symposium*, Canadian Forestry Service and Ontario Ministry of National Resources, 1981.

Lansing. The University of Michigan has proven to be a fertile environment in which to educate pioneer astronauts. Space explorer James McDivitt has had a close association with the development of the Michigan Space Center at Jackson (Fig 7-26). The Chaffee Planetarium in the

Figure 7-26. Space shuttle logo created by artist Paul Collins, an African-American from Grand Rapids, Michigan. The crew included Sally Ride, the USA first woman into space, and Marc Gareau, Canada's first man into space.

Grand Rapids Historical Museum both stimulates people into further space exploration and keeps alive the memory of a native son who perished in the quest.[5]

Meteorites

One of the most intriguing physical phenomena which occasionally occurs in the Great Lakes Basin is the passing or falling of a meteorite. A meteorite is a meteor which reaches the earth's surface without entirely burning up in the atmosphere. Witnesses to the passing of a meteor are treated to a brilliant fireball of yellow or orange which can even be traced by unaided eyesight in the daylight sky. The three most common meteorites found are: (1) iron or *siderites*, composed of mostly iron-nickel alloys; (2) stone or *aerolites*, composed mostly of ferromagnesian silicate minerals; and (3) stony-irons, *siderolites*, composed of metals and stone materials. Of the three types, aerolites are most numerous. The best time to see a meteor shower is after midnight about August 12, when the earth regularly passes through the comet debris of Perseids. The night provides about 60 sightings per hour. During travel through the atmosphere, the meteor reaches a temperature of 4000°F, thus if a meteorite strikes the earth, it has the potential of igniting a fire. Meteorites, because of their direct source in the universe, are potentially of great scientific value and should be brought to the attention of professional astronomers.

[5]On January 27, 1967, Roger B. Chaffee, Virgil I. Grissom and Edward H. White died when fire and smoke from an electrical fire killed them during a ground check. At the time a suitable door system had not been designed to accommodate rapid exits in ground test emergencies and protection from water emergencies during an actual ocean landing.

In the 1950's, Canadian scientists found in Ontario, two huge meteorite craters with their distinctive circular shape. The Brent crater measures 3.2 km (2 mi) wide and Holleford 2.4 km (1 1/1 mi) across. Between 1883 and 1947, eight small meteorite falls have been documented in Michigan (Grand Rapids, Allegan, Iron River, Reed City, Rose City, Seneca, and Kalkaska). One meteorite exploded over Southeast Michigan, December 7, 1990. Pieces of it may have landed in the vicinity of Chelsea.

Ultimately as the sun consumes itself, the surviving people of the land of fresh water must prepare to travel into the universe. Perhaps in the travel into the deep universe, a place will be found with a climate and environment which will allow, like Noah's experience, pairs of flora and fauna of the Basin to be taken to assure their perpetual life. In the transition out of this universe, what flora and fauna would be desirable to take to an artificially sustained climate of a planet such as Mars? A moose or a bird? In looking at the stars, visions of the future can unfold -- the mind can be stretched to its fullest extent. The sky's the limit? What's beyond the sky? Who will be the first from the Great Lakes Basin to reach another planet or universe?

Reflections and Self-Learning: Chapter 7

1. Contrast environmental determinism and selective limitation.

2. What would your response be to a beginning of a new ice age or year without summer?

3. Contrast weather and climate -- what climate and soil regions do you live in?

4. Contrast types of seasons: calendar, growing-frost free, hunting -- when does "summer" arrive in your district?

5. Evaluate the differences in temperatures of communities of the same latitude (Table 7-2) -- why the variations?

6. Why may solar energy be more economically important in the Basin than in the sun/drought belt?

7. Why is the Jet Stream associated with pollution?

8. Discuss: Should shipping be allowed on the Great lakes in November? Why yes? Why no?

9. Evaluate: Which is more dangerous to life -- tornadoes, lighting, blizzards or shoveling snow?

10. Where are the best potential sites for wind mills?

11. Why are there different soil classifications? What should you know about soils before constructing a building?

12. Evaluate global warming in the Basin. What is a "heat island - dust dome"?

13. When is the best day and time to see a meteor?

14. Evaluate the progress in restoring the genetic animal pool in the Basin.

15. What role do you play in the "Balance of Nature"?

16. Discuss and evaluate the role and number of dogs and cats in the Basin.

17. Why would you want or not want to colonize Mars or outer space? What animals would you take to a space colony? Why?

*"A tree is almost sacred. I have a strange feeling
when I cut one -- they've stood there so long. I
like to plant trees."*

Muck land sod farmer 1986

Chapter Eight

FLORA AS AESTHETIC AND INDUSTRIAL RESOURCES

"IT'S SO GREEN!" blurted out a seatmate -- a junior economics major of the University of California-Berkeley, on a mid-summer flight as the jet approached Grand Rapids, Michigan. Perhaps the spontaneous remark is not surprising, for the luxuriant ground cover of trees, bushes, grasses and flowers of the land of freshwater stunningly contrast with low precipitation regions. Since the glaciers, the Basin's flora has provided both inestimable aesthetic beauty and a rich resource for economic strength.

Linnaeus, the Swedish botanist who devised the modern system of naming plants and animals admonished, "If a tree dies plant another in its place."[1] What the scientist encouraged, perceptive country folk have known for ages -- that forests are a *renewable* resource. This chapter in addition to noting the Basin's flora as an aesthetic resource, will describe its vegetation regions, review the historic logging era and environmental effects plus summarize innovative efforts to assure a sustained forest products industry.

Overview

In Ontario, cut trees supports a multi-billion dollar resource base in comparison to $.75 billion in 1971.[2] Starting in 1905 with the distribution of about 10,000 trees and peaking in 1972 with a distribution of 18 million trees, Ontario, similar to other lake state governments, have placed in the hands of landowners hundreds of million trees for re-planting. Additional millions of trees have been sustained in Agreement Forests and in areas of Woodland Improvement Programs.[3] One of the major keys to the credible and wise management of the Basin's forests is directly connected to individual and teamwork efforts focused at university centers and special purpose institutions like the Great Lakes Forest Resource Centre (GLFRC) established in 1965 at Sault Ste. Marie, Ontario. The Centre personnel are charged simply with the goal to insure the forests will be sustained as a useful and significant part of the Basin's environment (Table 8-1). Forest protection advertisements in mass publications continue to bring to consciousness the importance of controlled use of fire and the basic value of tree resources (Fig 8-1).

[1]Benjamin D. Jones, biography of *Linnaeus*, Ch. 9. Cited in John Bartlett, *Familiar Quotes*, E. M. Beck, ed., 15th ed. and 125th anniversary ed., (Boston and Toronto: Little, Brown and Co., 1980), p. 350-10.

[2]*Ontario Statistics 1984, op. cit.*, Chart 18-1, 18-2, p. 428.

[3]Ontario Government, *Private Land Forest: A Public Resource*, (Toronto: Ministry of Natural Resources, 1985), Table 10, p. 30.

One tree can make
3,000,000 matches.

One match can burn
3,000,000 trees.

Figure 8-1. Forest fire prevention is a key to sustaining tree resources.

Trees in Art and as an Aesthetic Resource

Only a few features of nature surpass trees in contemporary culture's mindset. John Bartlett's *Familiar Quotations*, can be used to measure the culture's obsession with trees and other nature features in literature and as an aesthetic resource.[4] In the 601-page Index of the 125th Anniversary 15th edition, there are 1803 columns of entries. "Tree," "trees" or "woods" entries take up four columns. Only a few other earth relationships surpass trees in column entries: life, 11 and living, 7; world, 8; day, 7; death, 6 and die or died, 6; earth, 6; and night, 5. In comparison, tree quotes far exceed such venerable earth physical features as: air, hill, harvest, insect, iron, lake, meadow, moon, mud, rain, river, roots, rose, soil, snow, sand, shore, sky, spring, star, stone and universe. Only approaching a similar number of nature entries as trees are land, sea, water and wind. By far, dominating entries are enduring quotes relating to the subject of love, 17 and God, 12. Based on the

[4]Bartlett, *Familiar Quotes, op. cit.*, pp. 940-1540.

206

frequent use of trees in literature, it is not surprising that some professional foresters feel a great sense of responsibility and credibility in managing the tree resources of the Basin.[5]

TABLE 8-1

Percent Land in Forest by Great Lakes Watershed

Lake Watershed	Canada	U.S.A.	Total
Superior	98.7%	80%	91%
Michigan		41%	41%
Huron	75.0%	52%	68%
Erie	15.0%	23%	21%
Ontario	46.0%	53%	49%

SOURCE: The Marine Advisory Service of the Michigan Sea Grant Program, Cooperative Extension Service Michigan State University, 1985. Extension Bulletins E-1866-1870.

The Original Forest Regions

The early centuries of inhabitance by the Amerind and fur traders left essentially unchanged the original *climax forest*. Today the original and remnant vegetation covering is divided into three forest regions plus openings and prairies (Fig 8-2). The forest regions are: (1) coniferous -- cone bearing evergreens, sometimes referred to as "softwoods"; (2) deciduous -- leaf shedding to bare branches, sometimes referred to as "hardwoods"; and (3) mixed. The hardness or softness of a wood to work is best related to its density, not its leaf-holding character. A *second growth* forest is a woodland where trees have, through the natural process, reestablished themselves after cutting. The majority of the wooded areas today in the southern two-thirds of the Basin area are second growth. *Plantations* refers to areas of planted trees. Regionalization of the three basic forests is based on 75 percent or more of tree species (deciduous or coniferous) within a stand. A more equal distribution is classified as mixed forest.

Coniferous Forest -- Boreal Mixed Forest Location

The coniferous forest is generally found north of Lake Superior and consists of black and white spruce, balsam fir, tamarack and jack pine. Since 1980, because of the natural and general interspersing of hardwoods such as trembling aspen and white birch, the term Boreal Mixed Forest is being adopted as a management term.

[5]K. A. Armson, "The Spruce Budworm Problem in Ontario -- Real or Imaginary?", Proceedings (Sault Ste. Marie: Department of Environment, Canadian Forestry Service, Great Lakes Forest Research Centre, September 14-18, 1982), p. 5.

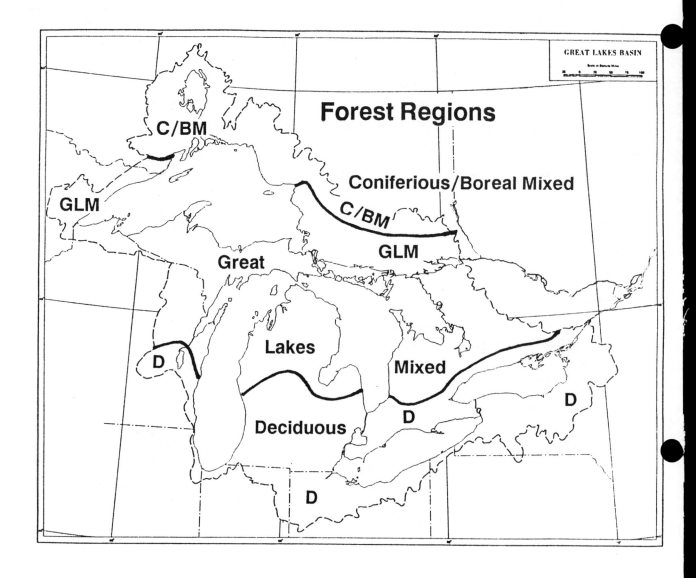

Figure 8-2. Great lakes Forest Regions. Base map: IJC.

Deciduous Forest and Woodlots

The Deciduous Forest has been for the most part cut. Remnants of this forest are found sustained in the fragmented private woodlots of the southern portion of the Basin. The hardwood timber species, such as black walnut, which may command over $20,000 as a single mature tree, are valuable for fabrications. Black cherry, white ash, the oaks, hickory, certain maples, beech, birch and elm also have significant value. With the increased use of wood burning for space heating, some of the most commercially desirable trees for value added by manufacturing, shade or wildlife habitat, have been burned. Tree theft has also significantly increased.

208

The Great Lakes Mixed Forest

The romantic era of logging is associated with the mid-19th and early 20th centuries Great Lakes Mixed Forest which covered the mid-section of the Basin from central and western New York to Minnesota. The lumber era is commonly linked to the fabulous stands of pine. After the huge white and red pine (sometimes called "cork pine" because the logs floated so high in water) were harvested, markets were developed for the white cedar and maple which were also abundantly mixed with the pine. Today, white cedar is prized for fence posts, white-tailed deer browse and protective winter shelter plus as a landscape shrub.

Oak Openings and Prairies

During the westward pioneer movement era and the farming settlement years in Ontario, some of the first desired areas for development were the oak openings and grassy prairies found in the deciduous forest from the Genesee River valley of New York through southern Ontario, Michigan and Wisconsin, plus northern Ohio, Indiana and into Illinois. Some early letter writers referred to the expansive open areas as being park like. Surveyors sometimes, depending on their background, referred to them as poor barren land very thinly timbered with oaks. Others would describe similar or the same land "splendid open forest free from underbrush."[6] It is argued that the use of the term barren, coupled with the "Tiffin Report," retarded the pioneer settlement into Michigan for well over a decade.[7] In contrast to the oak openings, the prairies had clearly recognizable tree margins, were treeless and basically covered with grasses. Prairie Ronde in Kalamazoo County, Michigan was 9.5-11 km (6-7 mi) across in 1830 and was described as, "...a great open green meadow" (Fig 8-3). In folk poetry it appeared as follows:

> And all about the prairie rim
> The circling forest grew,
> The bordering trees upon the Plain
> Their darking shadows threw.
> E. Larkin Brown[8]

In 1809, William Johnston, while traveling from Fort Wayne, Indiana to Fort Dearborn (Chicago), described a prairie with trees adjacent to the Elkhart River:

> ---a most delightful prospect is presented to view. There is scarcely a tree in an acre of ground for three miles...About a mile west of this prairie the road comes to the bank of the river...Here the timber is tall and thick on the ground principally white oak -- the soil is a white clay.[9]

[6]B. C. Peters, "The Remaking of an Image," *Geographical Survey*, Blue Earth Geographical Society, Mankato, Minnesota, Vol 3 No 1, (January, 1974), pp. 38-44.

[7]Similarly, settlement lagged in Essex County, Ontario until well after 1825. (Leo Johnson, "The State of Agricultural Development in the Western District to 1851," *The Western District* (Windsor: Essex County Historical Society, 1983), pp. 113-114.

[8]B. C. Peters, "No Trees on the Prairie: Persistence of Error in Landscape Terminology," *Michigan History*, Vol. 54 (Spring 1970) p. 26. Citing E. Larkin Brown, "A Poem for the Dedication of the Ladies Library Building at Schoolcraft, Michigan," Regional History Collection Western Michigan University Library.

[9]Shirley S. McCord (ed.), *Travel Accounts of Indiana 1679-1961* (Indianapolis: Indiana Historical Bureau, 1970), pp. 54-55.

Figure 8-3. Prairie Ronde Township, Kalamazoo County, Michigan, Section 23, W Avenue near 8th Street. Planted open flat land with wooded edge persists as a landscape feature.

After completing his traverse to Chicago, Johnston concluded that the territory,

> ---may be divided between swamps, ponds or lakes and prairies, the latter of which are by far the most extensive and would support immense herds of cattle...[10]

In addition to oak openings and prairies of grass, pioneer residents often selected first for settlement Amerind field clearings.[11]

Pioneer Perception of the Forest

After the Revolutionary/Loyalists War, especially in the U.S.A., the operational perception and government policies were directed toward widespread low density farm settlement which would facilitate holding the land and generate land sales revenue. These policies led to the widespread clearing of the land for extensive farming. Trees became of secondary importance, even a burden, especially after construction of the necessary farm buildings and setting aside a woodlot for heating fuel or for future construction materials. Usually the woodlot was sited on wetland or hilly upland.

[10]McCord, *ibid.*, p. 56.

[11]Author note: In 1968 when conducting graduate fieldwork in Barry County, Michigan on the Richland Prairie, several isolated huge bur oaks could be identified in fields and along fence lines. These trees then provided some supporting evidence to the pioneer descriptions which refer to prairies as having some isolated oak trees in the expanse of grass. Further, the main intersection of Jackson, Michigan is near an original Indian cornfield of 1828.

With such perceptions operating, the girdling, chopping, sawing, grubbing, burning, and stump pulling proceeded for the most part with minor concern for conservation, wildlife shelter, erosion or sustaining a wood fuel supply for town dwellers. In the mixed forest of central Michigan a pioneer girl observed in later life, practices of the 1860's in that area:

> They were city men or followers of trades which had no connection with farm life. They went straight into the thick timber-land, instead of going to the rich and waiting prairies, and they crowned this initial mistake by cutting down the splendid timber instead of letting it stand. Thus bird's-eye maple and other beautiful woods were used as fire-wood and in the construction of cabins, and the greatest asset of the pioneers was ignored.[12]

Today, "reading the landscape" is a valuable ability. Where attractive shady woodlots stand, a potential home buyer or developer would be advised to investigate for a high watertable. On farms where woods have survived as a resource reserve, its reproductive capacities can be interrupted when a hobby-farmer allows livestock pasturage in it, as the animals eliminate the new shoots of trees, leading to a weakened stand of homogeneous aged mature trees (Fig 8-4). Urban parks, cemeteries and public forests also hold for an observer a glimmer of the original forest-soil-topography-climate associations such as oak-hickory-walnut on well drained land, maple-beech-birch and elm-ash-bass or poplar-cottonwood-aspen on moist soils.

Figure 8-4. Pastured wood lot. Green Township, Mecosta County, Michigan.

[12]Anna H. Shaw, *Story of a Pioneer*, (New York: Harper & Row Pub., 1915; New York: Kraus Reprint Co., 1970), p. 20.

Cutting of the Northern Pine -- Hardwood Mixed Forest

In the mid-19th Century, a more orderly system of timber harvest and non-local marketing was developed. Leaders of successful commercial logging enterprises became known as lumber barons. Their homes in river mouth lakeshore communities testify to the wealth made from the Great Lakes Mixed Forest Region.

The historic removal of trees from the forest land did not require the efforts of the romantic and legendary giant Paul Bunyan -- what was necessary, was the arming with axes and saws of thousands of short, slightly-built men often desperate for money. This army of chore boys, cutters, teamsters, blacksmiths, cooks, top loaders, skidders and river hogs, led by a cadre of lumber barons, cruisers with an eye for a calculator, foremen, clerks, scalers and barn bosses, were more than equal to their forest adversary, the tree. In the century 1840-1940, billions of board feet of white pine were removed. Temporary logging camps were successively built, moved or abandoned, leaving relics of smoky dim-lit bunkhouses, dining halls, offices and barns. Small communities, which had sprung up along rivers and railroad lines to serve the activities of the men in the woods, soon found that agriculture could not support the local economy. Ghost towns began to dot the landscape and county government's tax delinquency lists lengthened as farmers abandoned their land rather than incur more losses in a disarrayed economy. In part, the land abandonment forced the issue of conservation and reforestation. At the Hartwick Pines State Forest in Michigan, a typical logging camp has been reconstructed to help preserve a few virgin pine and the exuberance of the time. The camps, except for cooks and official's wives, were occupied by males, whose rousting voices mixed with the snort of oxen, whinny of horses, incessant clangs, and creaks of big wheels and the logging railroad. The work in the woods lasted for six winter months which dovetailed nicely for young farmers trying to make capital improvements on their small farms. For some, bawdy houses and taverns became "banks of deposit" for their money.

Health Care for the Woodsmen.--Logging was not only accident-prone, it was also a threat to health as men labored wet with sweat and snow from dawn to dark. By the 1870's, less romantic but still heroic, women of the Sisters of Mercy began their extension of organized health care to the lumberjacks. St. Mary's Hospitals and Training Schools were eventually established in several logging centers such as at East Saginaw, 1872; Bay City, 1878; and Big Rapids, 1879. These were opened regardless of creed or nationality to woodsmen and others paying $5 for an annual hospitalization certificate which provided board, medicine, doctor's fee and care by the Sisters.

Northern Lumbercamp Woodstove to Florida Microwave Oven

In December, 1981, an 82-year-old former resident of Newberry, Michigan shared a story which compared a logging camp woodstove to the microwave oven:

In 1917 she joined her baker husband as a cook's assistant in a lumbercamp in the vicinity of Shelldrake on Whitefish Bay. Her chores included helping to bake scores of loaves of bread for breakfast and supper meals and lunch pail sandwiches, dozens of cookies and donuts daily for all meals, and pies. All cooking and baking was accomplished on large iron woodstoves with ovens. After reminiscing about all the stoves she had cooked over: wood, kerosene, bottled gas, natural gas and electric plus her new microwave oven which she uses in her Florida retirement home, she was asked which of all the stoves she liked best to cook with -- a flashing sparkle of the eye came and within a split-second she blurted out firmly, "Microwave!...is so fast and convenient."[13]

Origins of the Renewed Forest

The regeneration of the cutover mixed forest-pine lands, which now hold again a vast potential for economic development, innovative product manufacturing and stable employment may have had its beginnings in meetings held in 1882. In that year, many Canadian and U.S. foresters participated in the American Forestry Congress held in Montreal and a similar meeting held in Cincinnati. Following these conferences, R. W. Phipps of Toronto prepared a first of its kind Canadian government report titled, *Necessity of Preserving and Replacing Forests, 1883*. He firmly focused on the problem and potential solution.

> ---the settler here, in many cases cleared too much to his own injury, hill, swamp, sand, and hard pan which might well have been left untouched while there was at no great distance plenty of excellent land. That poor land left in forest would have; by its climatic influence, rendered much more easy and consequently, [have been] much more lucrative, [than] the production of crops on the other and would if fairly used, have continued an inexhaustible reserve of timber...[14]

In the American portion of the Basin, Bela Hubbard and others warned in 1887 of the excessive cost of rampaging cutting practices and voiced pleas to plan for the future.

> Michigan takes the lead..., the next cycle of ten years will find little white pine timber left in the State. Pennsylvania, New York, and Wisconsin follow not far behind....it will require less than half another century to leave us treeless unless planting on a large scale be resorted to. Wonderful progress indeed, but attended by what waste of this great natural store-house of wealth, and with how little provision of the future![15]

Contemporary Concerns and Forest Use

Finally, during the first third of the 20th century, several state/provincial, local and national forests were established. Table 6-4 lists the national forests and parks which are now operated within each of the lake watersheds. As early as 1909, Hiawatha and Huron National Forests were established in Michigan. In Ontario, in 1921, the Agreement Forest Program, came into operation. The County of Simcoe, in that year, initiated the replanting of 405 ha (1000 ac) of derelict land which became the Hendrie Forest (Fig 8-5). By the mid-1980's, there were 58 Agreement Forests under county, regional municipalities, townships, conservation authorities and national commission supervision. These forests cover 110,025 ha (272,000 ac) of Ontario land. In the United States in the mid-1930's, the federal Civilian Conservation Corps began its forest rehabilitation operations.

---

[13]Interview with Dorothy Thackham at Plymouth, Michigan, December 17, 1981.
[14]*Private Land Forests: A Public Resource*, op. cit., p. 1.
[15]Bela Hubbard, *Memorials of a Half Century*, (New York: G. P. Putnam's Sons, 1888; Reprint, Detroit: Gale Research Co., 1978), pp. 375-376.

Figure 8-5. Hendrie Forest historic marker noting Ontario's first Agreement Forest. Simcoe County, County Road 22 near Anten Mills.

That work now provides the mature resources of trees which is stimulating a resurgent forest products industry.

Contemporary Forest Management

Clearing and overcutting trees for short-term gains continues to be the most damaging practice to the land, soil and forest. In 1979, Ontario passed The Trees Act that restricts and regulates the destruction of trees. So far, 22 province counties have local bylaws which further attempt to protect woodlots. By the 1990's satellite images reveal huge areas of pine in northern Michigan which have been clear cut for wood-burning power plants and blast furnace operations. In the U.S.A. districts, where forests have given way to questionable clear cutting and agricultural pursuits, soil erosion remains a concern. Also, Christmas tree plantation management in relationship to pest control is a continuing problem. In Wisconsin, another set of forest/farmland development problems has been identified --toxic poisoning of the land and groundwater in Waushaua County.

> ---in 1984, wells in this farm neighborhood were tested for Aldicarb, an extremely toxic carbamate insecticide. Aldicarb has an oral toxicity index of one. ...malathion, a common organophosphate insecticide, has an oral toxicity index of 1375.[16]

The source of Aldicarb was probably aerial application of pesticide on pasture land. Aldicarb was found in 82 of 144 wells tested in six counties.

Multiple Uses of Forest Areas

The multiple-use concept of forest management has dominated the land rehabilitation era. In these years, national and state/provincial forests have been best known for recreation uses such as camping, hiking, hunting, fishing, trail bike riding, nature study and snowmobile riding, rather than for cut timber. Since the early 1970's, requests for fuelwood permits from government agencies have increased; however, in some urban vicinities they have decreased to the point of non-issuance because the supply of deadwood has been depleted. For the future, most indications are that more conflicts will arise between those most interested in the mature public forest being used for timber production and those interested in their recreational uses. Questions now are: What safeguards need to be in place to prevent the late 19th Century cycle of over-cutting? What is the role for public land in a democratic society?

Wood Products and Forest Specialty Products

Tens of thousands of people, primarily men, are again actively employed in the contemporary forest industries. Their occupations include: cutters, sophisticated specialized machinery operators, loaders, truckers, saw and paper mill operators, and pallet to fine furniture makers. The primary industrial wood products are paper (printing-computer-writing), paper-box boards, toilet and tissue paper, newsprint, wood pulp, lumber -- increasingly pressure-chemically treated lumber, veneer, plywood, chip and particle/oriented strand boards. The most significant export wood products are newsprint and lumber. Sawdust, once burned or dumped into lakes, is now processed into particle board, innovative products and molded into art objects. Worker safety and injury prevention are continuing challenges related to an orderly economic growth of the industry. Some of the most important specialty products, economically, are nuts, maple syrup, and mushrooms. Leading syrup production areas include New York, Michigan, Wisconsin, Ohio plus Ontario. Both Quebec and Vermont surpass each of the Basin's state/province districts. In recent years, some longtime morel mushroom gatherers have become concerned about over-picking, habitat disruption and trampling in certain of the most popular hunting places. The most valuable native nut species include: walnut, butternut, hickory and hazelnuts. The *filazel* a cross between the European filbert and the American

---

[16]Tom Lamm, "A Real Crisis in Real Country," *American Land Forum*, Vol V No 2, (Spring 1985), p. 11.

hazelnut shows promise. The hybrid fast growing Poplar can become a very energy and labor efficient (handcut or chipping) tree with high growth BTU yields as a heating fuel. A potential tourist curiosity in the Crystal Falls area is a 1,500 year old, 38 acre, 100 ton mushroom (armillaria bulbosa) detected in the late 1980's. An unharvested forest product, with increasing economic value, is fall color touring (Fig 8-6).

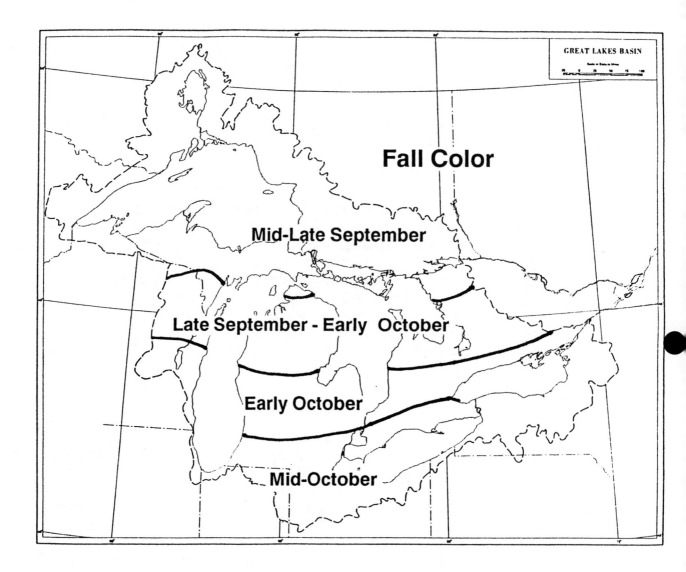

Figure 8-6. Generalized dates by latitude for fall color. Base map: IJC.

Wildflowers

One of the most delightful aspects of touring the Basin by motor vehicle is coming upon stretches of roadway clearings with a profusion of wildflowers. In Michigan alone, there are over 2100 plant species. Perhaps, more people will assume the role of Fort Wayne's Johnny Appleseed and quietly plant wildflower seeds, or lead community action to reevaluate mowing schedules (Fig 8-7, Table 8-2). On balance, the "beautiful" purple loose strife a wetland plant introduced from

Eurasia in the 1800's is now proving troublesome because it displaces native plants (sedges, cattails, canary grass) to the detriment of wildlife cover and waterflow rates.

The Toledo area's nine Metroparks system, which was formed in 1939 in Lucas County, is a lesser known, well-managed park system in the Basin. Within the system, 67 rare and endangered plant species are protected and being nurtured. Wildwood Preserve Metropark is a 184 ha (460 ac) hardwood upland forest area with open meadows and wildflowers in profusion. Oak Openings Park provides insights into the micro-habitats of the non-forested oak openings and wet prairies plus their altering by farm and park activities. Some communities to expand the appreciation of the urban landscape have created self-guided tree tour folders which identify species and largest specimen.

Figure 8-7. Roadside wildflowers.

Present-Day Timber Selling

E. F. Johnson, Timber Supervisor, Lake Erie District of the Ontario Ministry of Natural Resources, places the responsibility for wise management and sustained high quality timber on *both* the contemporary buyer and selling landowner. Further, to maintain the forests in a time of inflation, fair price adjustments are essential. Still other nefarious practices within the marketing system tend to reduce wise management including: loose scaling, unexplained grading rules, or unpaid for logs. Yet, Johnson concludes that:

> If the farmer had practiced good management and had received a fair price for his product, it could have been shown that forest crops compete favorably with agricultural crops and the woodlot owner would have held his trees in much higher regard (Fig 8-8).[17]

[17]Canadian Government, *The Management of Southwestern Ontario Hardwoods*, Proceedings (Sault Ste. Marie: Department of Environment, Canadian Forestry Service, Great Lakes Forest Research Centre, April, 1973), pp. 9-10.

TABLE 8-2

Selected Wildflowers of Michigan and Arctic Alpine
Plants of Pukaskwa National Park, Ontario

Common Michigan Wildflowers	Arctic Plants of Pukaskwa N.P.
Cardinal Flower	Hair Sedge
Wild Lupine	Northern Painted Cup
Yellow Lady's Slipper	Franklin's Lady-Slipper
Butterwort	Fragrant Cliff Fern
Lead Plant	Sea Lymegrass
Evening Primrose	Crowberry
Canada Dogwood	Eyebright
Michigan Lily	Shortleaved Brome
Black-Eyed Susan	Alpine Sweet vetch
Indian Paintbrush	Northern Tway Glade
Trout-Lily	Mountain Clubmoss
New England Aster	Butterwort
Marsh-Marigold	Glaucous Bluegrass
Dwarf Lake Iris	Bluegrass
Wild Bergamot	Alpine Bistwort
Fringed Gentian	* Bird's Eye Primrose
Butterfly Weed	Pearlwort
Fireweed	* Encrusted Saxifrage
Houghton's Goldenrod	Tufted Club-Rush
Trillium - protected	Spike Moss
	Least Asphodel
	Spiked Wild Oat
	Alpine-Bilberry
	Rock Cranberry
	Smooth Woodsia Fern
Total species about 2100 (200 endangered - threatened)	Total plant species in park 533 (282 herbarium)

* Plant found in park, then not again until Hudson Bay area.

SOURCES: "Wildflowers of Michigan," a poster, Michigan Department of Transportation and Department of Natural Resources, 1986. "Plant Checklist for Pukaskwa National Park," and Jean Mare, Park Geologist.

Aquatic Plants — Essential and Troublesome

Aquatic plants are vital to the ecosystem. They provide protection habitats, food and oxygen for aquatic animals. Surface flowers such as the pond lilly are often cited as attractive. Yet, in high densities, water plants are viewed as a nuisance by water craft users and people who fish. Common water weeds frequently targeted for control on eutriphicating lakes include: chara, coontail, curly leaf, floating-leaf pond weed, milfoil, sago pond weed, water weed and wild celery.

Forest Activities at the Basin Edge and Center
a Century Apart

Four contrasts in forestry activities can be shown when comparing activities a century apart and between the Basin's edge and center. Contemporary edge sites in Wisconsin, New York and Lake Nipigon area each have unique forest activities and they contrast with Big Rapids as a logging supply center in the 1880's and present.

Astride the watershed divide in north central Wisconsin and northwestern Michigan are three National Forests: Chequamegon, adjacent and south of the bay of the same name; Ottawa, a 609,016 ha (1.5 million ac) tract which adjoins the smaller Nicolet 262,000 ha (655,000 ac) National Forest. The Nicolet lies within a one day drive of Minneapolis and Chicago, but is situated as an intervening recreational site in comparison to both the Ottawa and Chequamegon National Forests. The Nicolet N.F. is a land of many lakes and streams and contains the headwaters of seven Wisconsin rivers. The forest itself is comprised of mixed species; especially oak, white birch, aspen, pine (jack, red, white), balsam fir, hemlock, white spruce and cedar. These are interspersed with upland openings, sedge meadows, marsh and shrub swamps, bogs and 1200 archeological sites. Table 8-3 illustrates an attempt to plan for both increased uses based on population and life-style changes with a multiple-use concept for the next half-century (Table 8-3). Within the plan it is expected that the timber "supply potential" will continue to be out of balance and exceed the "forest plan production" objectives by about 25 percent as recreational demands are expected to double. In comparison, with similar management goals, the Huron-Manistee National Forest (Michigan) sold 76,000,000 board feet (30% hardwoods) of a planned 82,200,000 in 1986 which indicates the uncertainty of planned goals and market place reality. Near Lake Nipigon, active block cutting of black spruce is occurring and white barked birch is stacked for cordwood fuel (Fig 8-8).

At the opposite edge of the Basin, in Tioga County, New York, the regenerated low mountain mixed forest has become attractive enough to draw some timber operators "back east" (Fig 8-9). A century ago Tioga County was the source of both pioneers and loggers who migrated to Mecosta County, Michigan, in the center of the Basin. Similar to other pioneers, they carried place names with them as "cultural baggage." Thus, Tioga Company appears on the Big Rapids map of 1879 in several locations, especially along the Muskegon River (Figs 8-10, 8-11). Today, the Tioga complex still exists (Fig 8-12). Located across the street from the former Tioga plant is a forestry cutting knife and tool operation which depends on specialty steel imported primarily from Sweden, West Germany and Austria. Swede Hill Park, adjacent to the river, is a memorial to the pioneer Swedish/Scandinavian woodworkers and families who came to the woods of the Basin in the 19th Century (Fig 8-13). Furniture production locally continues to be linked to Scandinavia.

TABLE 8-3

Nicolet National Forest Visitor Use and
Forest Production Plans 1980-2035

ACTIVITY/ Category	Units of Measure Per Year	Present Level 1980	1986 1995	1996 2005	2006 2015	2016 2025	2026 2035
DEVELOPED RECREATION	MRVD						
Current Management		314	364	482	568	612	647
Supply Potential			850	850	850	850	850
Demand Trends			435	560	656	748	844
Forest Plan Objectives			353	425	472	512	547
DISPERSED RECREATION (includes hunting and fishing)	MRVD						
Current Management		531	574	665	779	907	1019
Supply Potential			12000	12000	12000	12000	12000
Demand Trends			620	738	873	1010	1103
Forest Plan Objectives			592	698	830	951	1040
WILDERNESS	MRVD						
Current Management		14	15	17	20	22	25
Supply Potential			160	160	160	160	160
Demand Trends			15	17	20	22	25
Forest Plan Objectives			15	17	20	22	25
TIMBER	MMBF						
Current Management		63	72	97	106	127	133
Supply Potential			181	181	181	181	181
Demand Trends			97	115	123	130	138
Forest Plan Objectives			97	103	122	130	138

NOTES: Range is excluded due to the nonexistent demand for use of the Nicolet's forage resource.
MRVD -- 1000 Resident Visitor Days
MMBF -- Millions Board Feet

SOURCE: U.S. Department of Agriculture, Forest Service, *Proposed Land Resource Management Plan Nicolet National Forest*, (Washington, DC.: U.S. Government Printing Office, 1984, Table 1, p. 6.

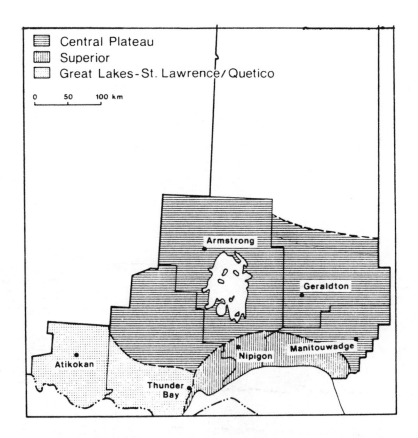

The three areas for FEC study in the North Central Region.

Figure 8-8. Forest Ecosystem classification study areas north of Lake Superior. Source: Canada Forestry Service, *Forestry Newsletter*, Summer 1984, p. 6.

Innovations

To sustain the forests, there are numerous natural, technical, political and economic challenges which silviculturists have to meet. Two notable ones, at opposite ends of the life cycle of trees, are breeding and premature death from insects. To nurture the regeneration, there are several breeding methods used. The traditional method is natural restocking from trees left in place during selective or block-cutting harvesting. Clear-cut areas may be regenerated from undisturbed root stock, such as aspen stands (Fig 8-14). On the other hand, much clear-cut and farmed land requires replanting (Fig 8-15). Planting of open land may be accomplished by seeding from an airplane, replanting of nursery stock by hand or mechanized planter.

Recent research, at several locations in the Basin, has focused on the most rewarding method of raising seed stock. In the 1930's, huge nursery beds were established to rear seedlings -- especially conifers. Nursery beds, however, allow intermingling of roots which then are disturbed when taken apart for transplanting. To overcome that disadvantage, several types of individual containers, such as tubs made of paperboard, rigid plastic, styrofoam, tarpaper and wooden boxes, have been experimented with -- especially for restocking deciduous trees. In spite of initial results from breeding experiments, the best data on cultivation method comes at harvest time, decades after initial planting.

221

Figure 8-9. Contemporary logging/sawmill activities Spencer Tioga County, New York, adjacent to the divide.

Figure 8-10. Historic 19th Century logging mark of Tioga Land Company (TLC) from Muskegon River, Big Rapids, Michigan.

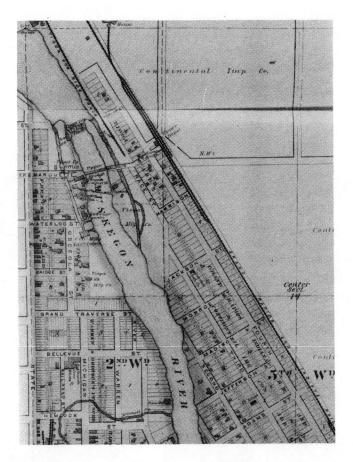

Figure 8-11. Tioga Land Company mill site, 1879, Big Rapids, Michigan. Source: E. L. Hayes, *Atlas of Mecosta County*, Philadelphia, C. O. Titus Co., 1879.

Other wood product industry innovations relate to heavy equipment. Today the woods resound with the roar of powerful engines, chain saws, skidders, loaders, chippers, trucks, debarkers and crushers. In contrast, a quiet innovative use for the public forests has cropped up since the 1960's -- the isolated small patch growing of marijuana. If one observes carefully while flying over the forests of the Basin, illegally cultivated plots can be seen. Similarly, when hiking along unfrequented two-track paths, warning indicators on the landscape suggest the presence of a nearby crop and the intent to protect it. Looking to the future, because of their rapid rate of loss, urgent and continuing innovative actions are needed to protect a wide diversity of wetland habitats with their rich variety of fauna and flora.[18] Given the scientific uncertainties of cloning an individual specimen of a tree species plus the mysteries of how best to breed and rear trees, it is not surprising that a woodlot owner has a pang of emotion when looking up into the first branches of an oak which are fifty feet above the ground -- reflecting, then saying quietly to the timber buyer, "Okay, mark it" (Fig 8-16).

[18]C. Nicholas Raphael, "Prehistoric and Historic Wetland Heritage of the Great Lakes." *Michigan Academician*, Michigan Academy of Science, Arts and Letters, Ann Arbor, Vol. XIX No. 3, (Summer 1987), pp. 331-365.

Figure 8-12. Contemporary site of Tioga Mill, now Hanchett's. In background Michigan Knife, a maker of logging cutter blades and the former Pine Shop, continental distributor of high quality furniture. Big Rapids, Michigan.

Figure 8-13. Swede Hill Park, Big Rapids, Michigan.

224

Figure 8-14. Clear-cut and second year growth of contemporary aspen forest. Pere Marquette State Forest, Austin Township, Mecosta County, Michigan, Section 9.

Figure 8-15. Former outwash plain farm field with no tree re-vegetation in over two decades. Green Township, Mecosta County, Michigan, Section 34.

Figure 8-16. "Wise utilization is the first step of conservation." Selectively cut, mature red oak. Note early stage of core rot on left side of stump. Austin Township, Mecosta County, Michigan.

Death Threats to Mature Trees

The spruce budworm is one of the most destructive forest insects in North America. Massive epidemics of the pest have led to millions of cubic meters of loss of spruce and mature balsam fir in Minnesota and Ontario. The mixed forest continues to be harmed by white pine blister rust and the westwarding invasion of gypsy moths which attack and strip the leaves of deciduous trees. In 1979 the gypsy moth became established on only 11 acres in four counties of Michigan. By 1992 over 700,000 acres in 40 counties were affected. It is debated by some whether the gypsy moth which feeds on 300 species of plants with oak trees the favored host, actually kills or weakens the plant to other killing stresses. How to control or turn to useful purposes, the spruce budworm and gypsy moth is a challenge for both the brain power of young and mature minds alike. In addition to a natural parasite, the budworm and gypsy moths have been attempted to be controlled by chemical insecticides, bacteria, viruses, chemical sterility and hormones to interrupt breeding. The microorganism *Bacillus thuringiensis* (Bt) may prove to be a rewarding alternative to chemicals.

Summary

During the last two centuries the flora of the Basin has been ruthlessly cut, burned and cleared, usually for private agricultural and timber purposes. Because of misperceptions, ignorance and greedy practices, much of the most valuable forest was lost. Realizing abuses and a need for the resources of a sustained forest, the late 19th and 20th centuries have witnessed mammoth efforts to regenerate parts of the three original climax forest regions (coniferous/boreal, mixed and deciduous). Management has been directed at sustaining yields with multiple-use recreation practices and control of forest pests. Within the southern deciduous forest were many treeless grass prairies and oak studded openings. Many challenges face society to assure fair marketing practices, minimum environmental damage and illegal activities. In spite of many concerns, the trees, grassland and wildflowers still are a primary source of aesthetic fascination and economic bounty.

Reflections and Self-Learning: Chapter 8

1. Contrast renewable and non-renewable resources -- list several in each category.

2. What are the origins of public forests in the Basin?

3. What is the purpose of the GLFRC?

4. How do you account for trees being a focus in memorable writings as catalogued in Bartlett's *Familiar Quotations*?

5. Contrast deciduous, coniferous, boreal mixed forest, oak opening and prairie.

6. Where were historic woodlots on farms located? Why? What are wetland tree associations?

7. Where might you observe remnants of the original forest in your community?

8. Evaluate multiple-use forest management with single-use. What are the potentials for conflict? What may be the first rule in forest conservation?

9. Of the historic logging jobs which one would you have liked to have or not have? Why?

10. Why did request for fuel wood collection permits increase after 1970?

11. Does your community have a wildflower planting program or a self-guiding tree tour folder?

12. When is the peak color season in your district?

13. What do you think will happen if one species of aquatic weed is killed off in a lake?

14. Contrast forest activities at the edge and center of the Basin?

15. What are the insect or other threats to mature trees?

16. What insect problems related to trees have you had in your area?

17. What can you do to help sustain woodlots, trees or forests in your district?

18. Map the tree species and sizes in your yard, block, playground, park or campus area. Is there a specific grouping or pattern? If so why or why not.

"He who will not economize will have to agonize."
Confucius

"Travel teaches toleration."
Disraeli

Chapter Nine

ECONOMIC ACTIVITIES AND TRANSPORTATION LINKS

It can be hypothesized that until there is a modern-era global economic evolution, there cannot be a wholesome environment to support life of the world community. From the time of the Greek influence in western government philosophy, economics has been known to be the key to shaping cultures of societies. Both economics and geography are words derived from Greece. Ancient Greek *oikos* has been modified into modern *eco* and translates as "house or home." The suffix *nomics* translates as "to manage." In extension, the earth is the home of Homo sapiens. Geographers (*geo* = earth, *graphy* = description) maintain academically the responsibility of describing both natural and cultural (human) features of the earth. Yet, geographers and ecologists (*ology* = study of) can describe and study the earth environment as an unhealthy, polluted, war torn, politically discomforting, nuclear, biologically and chemically threatened planet home of an alarmingly fast growing number of Homo sapiens; but their descriptions and study will not sustain life -- the world economic system manages the running of the earth home. As a result of the Great Lakes Basin economy being a sub-part of the contemporary world's economic systems which has life destroying occupational patterns, it can be expected that destructive influences will remain as threats to Basin residents into the foreseeable future. To counteract the various known threats to survival, it is suggested that significantly more of the Basin's and world's best brain power be educated and diverted into evolving an economic system which would allow for the *demos* -- the people of the Basin and earth -- to survive with a reasonable quality of life. On balance, not all bright college-age or other thinkers should flock to economic study, because it is in the political process that economic systems are established. Thus, what the world is to become also depends on a concurrent political (Latin: *politicus* = government) system evolution. To fail in wise economic and political innovations is to perish. Optimistically, humans have so far always chosen the pathway of survival.

The Great Lakes Basin Economy

The contemporary economy is dominated by urban industrial production of durable goods, concentrated in shoreline cities, but with the most extensive areas of land devoted to agriculture and forestry. To describe the Basin's economic system in detail is beyond the scope of this text. However, in general, it is composed of a hodge-podge of sometimes conflicting and incompatible set of national, state/provincial local laws, common practices and rules relating to: employment; piece, hourly, salary, barter and fringe benefit pay; property, inventory, small business, corporate, sale, value added and income taxes; tax and pollution credits; health, injury compensation and unemployment, life, dependent children, and burial insurances. In 1982, the University of Michigan published a monumental description and analysis of the *Michigan Fiscal and Economic Structure* edited by H. E. Brazier and D. S. Larsen. *The Great Lakes Economy: A Resource and*

Industry Profile of the Great Lakes, was prepared by the Federal Reserve Bank of Chicago in conjunction with the Great Lakes Commission in 1985. Both are major graphic and tabular compendiums which provide aid in the quest for understanding the region's economy.

Location of Economic Activities and Tax Rates

Location of economic activity has been a topic of frequent description and analysis by geographers.[1] It is not uncommon that many location decisions are made without analytical thinking. A new economic activity simply becomes established where the founder resided. Yet, the best economic thinking and location can be off-set and a firm with a marketable product or service can be driven to bankruptcy by poor business decisions. Never-the-less, location factors remain a key to development. Significant in location and marketing for life supporting occupations in the Basin in a global society include several traditional cost factors: real estate, labor, capital, construction, utilities, transportation, professional services, taxes, insurance, regulations and fees. Market size distance, education and skills of the work force are also notable factors to be considered. The Michigan Department of Commerce has created a point scale for evaluating and certifying local industrial parks of a minimum size of 16 ha. (40 ac.) to help guide economic expansion (Table 9-1).

TABLE 9-1

Criteria and Point Scale Used for Certifying Industrial Parks

Criteria	Maximum Points
Sanitary sewers	13
Community and auxiliary services	13
Municipal water service	10
Storm sewers	9
Paved streets	9
Protective covenants and restrictions	9
Soil characteristics	7
Highway accessibility	6
Airport facilities	6
Rail accessibility	5
Grading and clearing	4
Special park features	4
Harbor facilities	3
Natural gas service	2

SOURCE: Michigan Department of Commerce.

[1]C. L. and A. G. Vinge, *Economic Geography*, Totowa, NJ: Littlefield, Adams and Co., 1966, pp. 318-330.

Tax rates within the Basin indicate a *spatial* variation related to local and state/province governmental decisions. The variations also relate to intra-basin competition and differing ways of raising funds for government services. Sales Tax rates by percent and local maximum options are as follows: Michigan 4/0%, Indiana 5/0%, Wisconsin 5/.5%, Ohio 5/2%, Pennsylvania 6/0%, Minnesota 6/1% and Illinois 6.25/4%. Michigan has the lowest rate. However, when per capita property taxes are compared Ohio ranks lowest: $541, Indiana $571, Minnesota $718, Illinois $785, Wisconsin $798, Michigan $894 and the national average $666.[2] Canada has a Goods and Services Tax which appears to have resulted in increased cross-border shopping since its enactment. The concluding point of these examples is that isolated comparisons of a few tax rates in relationship to economic decision-making and location analysis can be misleading. What seems to be needed is a comprehensive holistic local to national gathering of data and analysis of the tax structure of the Basin to provide a basis for knowledgeable actions by citizens.

Past and Present Economic Transitions

The Basin economy has evolved through four major changes in historic times: (1) the Amerind barter-trade period (pre-1615), (2) the Amerind-Euro-American fur trade period (C. 1615-1815), (3) the pioneer agricultural-mining-logging period (C. 1815-1915), and (4) the industrial production period (C. 1915-present). Since World War II, much emphasis has been placed on diversifying the segments of the economy, especially between *basic* activities (agriculture, mining, forestry), *secondary* activities (industrial-value added by manufacturing) and *tertiary* activities (services; education, finance, leisure-time, health, government). The 1970's oil embargo and concurrent foreign automobile import surge perhaps in the long-run triggered a painful, but rewarding introduction to another evolution of the economy which is shifting to a greater emphasis on foreign trade, education, electronics, headquarters operations, information and other services.

The early 1900's witnessed the Basin's world pacesetting developments in perfecting the assembly line, the unique lake freighter and the motor vehicle industry. In time, the production of trucks, buses and automobiles became focused on and synonymous with Detroit and today extends into the mid-South and Canada (Table 9-2). By mid-century, the Basin's leadership in a varied range of durable consumer goods and capital equipment: food processing, furniture, chemicals, pharmaceuticals, machine tools, mobile homes and wood products seemingly assured dominating sales in domestic and foreign markets. Wages and benefits to workers and managers climbed well above world and U.S.A. averages. Although the economy is shifting into innovative activities, there appears to be still some difficulty in adjusting to inter-regional and international competition and no consensus among leaders in business, labor, government, education and religion has emerged. Table 9-3 summarizes what appears to be emerging in the late 20th century economy and perhaps may help to establish a consensus.

The Basin now is headquarters for well over 200 of the continent's 1000 largest corporations. It has an unusually well-educated population with several world-class institutions. The Basin's transportation networks are in place, being expanded selectively and maintained. Locationally, in relationship to world and domestic markets, the Basin still has a *central place* advantage.

[2]"Closing the Tax Gap." (*Grand Rapids Press*, May 1, 1993), p. C1 (Map: US Census Bureau); "The Going Rate." (*Detroit News*, April 15, 1993), p. 3BNE. Historic note: Michigan began a major tax/school financing restructuring in July, 1993.

TABLE 9-2

Automobile Assembly Cities of the Great Lakes Basin

Michigan
  Chrysler:
    Detroit
    Sterling Heights
  Ford:
    Dearborn
    Wayne
    Wixom
  General Motors:
    Flint
    Hamtramack
    Lake Orion
    Lansing
    Pontiac
  Mazda:
    Flat Rock

Ohio
  Chrysler:
    Toledo
  Ford:
    Avon Lake
    Lorain

Illinois
  Ford:
    Chicago

Ontario
  Chrysler:
    Windsor
  Ford:
    Oakville
    St. Thomas
  General Motors:
    Oshawa
    Scarborough

ADAPTED FROM: *Auto '93*, Consumer Guide, 1993.

Employment Trends

In spite of the fact that the landscape shows evidence of economic vitality, the landscape also provides evidence in abandoned buildings, unemployment offices and rusted railroad tracks that the economy is experiencing a period of great difficulty. Also visible on the landscape is the rapid expansion of child care-development centers which indicates not only a change in economy, but also employment opportunity gains by women, a decreasing family size and change in family structure. Tool rental service and household goods storage sheds also reflect a mobile life style with less family and neighbor interdependence.

There is ample evidence, just by looking at sources of goods, that foreign and domestic competitors can fill most local consumer needs. Thus, in part, to maintain Basin economic stability, reliable *quality* and *service*, has to be a part of the product for dollar transaction. Within the Basin, opportunities for new entrepreneurs bodes well because they can enter a field without investment in outmoded technologies. Further, with intra-regional bank reorganizations, venture capital for male or female risk takers is increasingly available. Also smaller new organizations can more easily target a specific need in the global marketplace. In time it appears, the Basin and global economy may have to adapt to a steady-state system which is in no way linked to growth or increased sales based on population increases, foreign sales or widely fluctuating national

TABLE 9-3

Transition Economy Summary Great Lakes Basin 1980-2000

Past Economy	Emerging Economy
Little foreign competition (war damage, tariffs, transport costs, technology)	Keen foreign competition
Moderate technology changes	Intensifying technical change
Sale of moderately complex products into somewhat unsophisticated, growing consumer market	Sale of complex products into increasingly sophisticated saturated, competitive markets
Growth in units sold and tons of production	Growth in value, but stable volume
Limited domestic competition	Accelerating domestic competition

ADAPTED FROM: *Choosing a Future*, Prepared for AmeriTrust Corporation, March 1984, p. 7.

currencies if an integrated world economy develops and population stabilizes. In transition authorized Foreign Trade Zones have been placed in: Duluth, Milwaukee, Chicago, Battle Creek, Detroit, Toledo, Cleveland, Buffalo, Niagara County, Syracuse and Watertown.

Transportation

Integral to a viable economy is a well-developed transportation system of roads, railroads, bridges, airports, canals, pipelines and water ports to agglomerate employees, raw materials and distribute products. Additionally, hiking trails are needed for recreation and transmission systems for utilities, including: water, sanitary and storm sewers, electric power, cablevision, and telephone-communication, are necessary in an advanced civil society. Politically, it is easier to get elected and re-elected when emphasis is focused on visible aspects of the transportation system; thus, roads and people movers are built and maintained more easily with public tax support than underground sewers and treatment facilities. Fundamental to all transportation networks, is access. Simply put, if there are no access lines or the system is used to capacity, growth is stifled. Thus, the water resource of the Great Lakes can only support shipping and manufacturing activities if there are adequate ports, water depths, water lines and treatment facilities.

Contemporary Main Streets

Table 9-4 identifies the several contemporary main and secondary highway routes which have evolved from the original animal path-Amerind trail network. These routes carry the primary long-distance truck and auto traffic which help to bind together the Basin's people and commerce. In the table of major highway routes in the Basin, the several "divide" communities underlined allows the reader to develop a more precise notion of the area and extent of the watershed. It is near these underlined headwater places where the genesis of the Great Lakes is found.

How the communities connected by the several highway corridors interact socially and economically within and outside the Basin still needs to be determined in order to better evaluate the overall economic functioning of the Basin. Billboard and radio advertising for Michindia businesses provide audio and visual evidence of the blurred nature of the Indiana-Michigan border near South Bend.

Highway Travel and Snow Removal

From the invention of the automobile until World War I, snow removal from the region's roadways was uncommon and many motorists stored their autos in winter time. The war brought demands for snow removal and with it the designation "all-weather road" came into being to facilitate the transport of war materials. In the present-day, priority is given to the *national defense expressways* (Interstate or Trans-Canada highways) and at the county level, weekday priority is given to opening school bus and milk truck routes. Frequently, these routes influence the selection of country home and business sites.

Highway Numbering and Costs

By the 1920's confusion, and waste of time and money were common when motorists could not follow directions and became lost (Table 9-5). As a result, governments co-operated in creating the U.S. highway numbering system which was not based on route financing. In the mid-1950's the National Defense Highway Act (NDHA) was passed which authorized the Interstate highway network. These expressways with uniform specifications by law, were designed to: (1) connect metropolitan-sized cities, (2) provide roadways to move heavy military equipment between cities and strategic sites such as the Soo Locks, and (3) facilitate evacuation of metro-city residents. The major cost (75%) of the defense highways was financed by the national government. Originally, the 73,600 km (46,000 mi) system cost an average of $1 million (U.S.) per mile. In the mid-1980's, freeway costs average $2 million (U.S.) per mile. In comparison, an asphalt paved rural primary road costs about $130,000 (U.S.) per mile and a paved bike path about $12,000 (U.S.) per mile. The Detroit (2.9 miles) and Scarborough (4.1 miles) people movers designed to guide development, cost $200 and $147 million (US) respectively.

The U.S. and Interstate systems are numbered with *even digits* (2-98) for east-west routes and *odd digits* (1-99) for north-south routes. The U.S. highways are numbered north to south and east to west which places US-2 in the Upper Peninsula and US-20 in the southerly part of the Basin. Complementary US-43 and 41 are located on the west edge of the Basin while US-23 and 25 are found to the east. The Interstate numbering is similar, but instead numbered south to north and west to east. Thus, I-94 is north of the east-west tending I-80, and I-81 is east of the north-south tending I-75. In the Ontario highway system, the three-digit numbers or letters indicate the most advanced freeways such as 400 through 405 and QEW (Queen Elizabeth Way). Over the years, perhaps due to lack of attention to detail, some inconsistency in numbering has been introduced into the system.

TABLE 9-4

Great Lakes Basin Main Streets

Route	Linkages
WEST-EAST ROUTES	
I-94	(Minneapolis, Madison) Milwaukee, <u>Chicago</u>, Kalamazoo, Ann Arbor, Detroit-Port Huron, Sarnia;
Tollways I-80, -90	Chicago Skyway, Indiana Toll Road, Ohio Turnpike, New York State Thruway, <u>Chicago</u>, Toledo, Cleveland, Erie, Buffalo, Syracuse, <u>Westmoreland</u> (Albany, Boston);
KH-401	Detroit, Windsor, London, Kitchener, Toronto, Belleville, Kingson, Landsdowne (Cornwall, Montreal via Rt. 20);
KH-17	Thunder Bay, Sault Ste. Marie, Sudbury, <u>North Bay</u>, connects with Duluth via Ont-61 and US-61, Trans-Canada Highway (Montreal-Vancouver).
Secondary Highways	
KH-11	Nipigon, <u>Jellicoe</u> (Gearldton), <u>North Bay</u>;
US-2	(Seattle), <u>Swan River</u>, Duluth, St. Ignace;
US-10	(St. Paul, MN.), <u>Custer</u>, Manitowac, Ludington, Detroit;
I-96	Grand Haven, Grand Rapids, Lansing, Detroit-Windsor;
US-6	Lansing, IL, to <u>Sauk Village</u> via I-394 (Nappanee), Bowling Green, Cleveland, <u>Andover</u>;
US-20, -5	Hammond, Michigan City, <u>South Bend</u>, Elkhart, Angola, Toledo, Norwalk, Cleveland, Erie, Buffalo, Geneva, Auburn, <u>Cardiff</u> (Boston);
US-12	<u>Chicago</u>, Gary, Ypsilanti, Detroit;
KH-402	Sarnia, London, Lambeth KH-401.
NORTH-SOUTH ROUTES	
I-75	Sault Ste. Marie, St. Ignace, Bay City, Saginaw, Flint, Detroit, Toledo, Findlay, Lima, <u>Wapakoneta</u> (Cincinnati, Atlanta, Tampa);
I-81	<u>Alexandria Bay</u>, Watertown, <u>Cortland</u> (Binghampton);
I-69	Port Huron/Sarnia, Flint, Lansing, Angola, <u>Fort Wayne</u>, (Indianapolis);
KH-400,-069 QEW	Sudbury, Orillia, Toronto, Hamilton, St. Catherines, Niagara Falls, Erie Beach.

TABLE 9-4 (Cont'd)

Great Lakes Basin Main Streets

Route	Linkages
Secondary Highways	
I-43, US-41	Copper Harbor, Escanaba, Green Bay, Milwaukee, <u>Chicago</u>;
US-131, -31	Mackinac City, Petoskey, Big Rapids, Grand Rapids, Kalamazoo, <u>South Bend</u>;
US-27, -127	Houghton Lake, Mt. Pleasant, Lansing, VanWert, <u>Mercer</u> (Cincinnati);
O-21	Sarnia, Goderich, Owen Sound.

(City) = Non-Basin connected city, <u>city</u> at or near edge of Basin.

In the U.S. system, the prefix 1 as in US-131 indicates a length of highway parallel to a long-distance U.S. route such as US-31. In the Interstate system, even numbered prefix digits indicate a *loop* of expressway into a city which reconnects with the main Interstate route such as I-496 in Lansing. Odd prefix digits indicate Interstate *spurs* which lead into a city or links with another roadway network, such as I-196 between Benton Harbor and Grand Rapids.

State/Province and County Roads

State/province and county highways are for the most part identified unsystematically. However, since the 1960's, most states, in cooperation with counties, have instituted a multi-county designated road letter-number system. In the Designated County Road System, a state is divided into letter areas. Within the lettered areas, geographic and direction awareness is developed for the "all-weather" inter-county roads by using the numbering system similar to the Interstate Highway system (Fig 9-1).

At the county level, nearly a dozen systems are in use in the Basin identifying the standard survey section or concession line roads. Most of these systems do not logically interface with adjacent county road identification systems. For instance, 19 Mile Road in Mecosta County (meaning 19 miles north of the county line) links into 13 Mile Road of Newaygo County (meaning 13 miles north of the center of the county). In Macomb County 19 Mile Road refers to 19 miles north of downtown Detroit (Fort Larned) and it extends west into Square Lake Road -- Commerce Road of Oakland County. As a result of uncoordinated local road identification systems, unnecessary traffic is increased on the better identified routes. The maps of survey system local roads in the vicinity of Appleton-Fox Cities (Wisconsin), Sarnia (Ontario) and Green Township (Michigan) illustrate three rural road numbering systems (Fig 9-2 to 9-4).

TABLE 9-5

Excerpt of 1916 Toledo Auto Club
Route 757 Grand Rapids to Cadillac
(Grand Rapids to Rockford Section)

Mileage		Directions
Total	Intermediate	Grand Rapids --->
0.0	0.0	GRAND RAPIDS; Monroe & Fulton Sts. at Soldiers' Monument. Start northwest with trolley on Monroe Street.
0.2	0.2	4-corners; bear diagonally right with branch trolley on Ottawa St. Keep straight ahead past City Hall 0.4.
1.4	1.2	Jog left and right with trolley, which leaves to right 1.5. Go under RRs. 2.0, now on Monroe Ave. Join trolley from right 4.1 and follow tracks across long iron bridge 4.3.
4.7	3.3	Fork; bear right around Fair Grounds, following trolley.
5.0	0.3	Where trolley goes right, bear slightly left across RR., curving right just beyond.
6.5	1.5	Fork; bear right with poles across RR. 8.4, following along the Grand River.
10.7	4.2	4-corners; turn left upgrade around Grand River Club House.
12.5	1.8	Left-hand road; turn left with travel.
13.0	0.5	End of road at yellow brick school; turn right and next left with the travel.
15.3	2.3	4-corners, foot of grade; turn left with poles.
15.5	0.2	End of road; turn right around brick school. Thru Rockford 15.7. End of road --->

(Similar directions continue to Cadillac)

Source: Auto Routes published by the Toledo Auto Club, 1916.

Figure 9-1. Road sign of U.S. evolving system of inter-county highways.

Bridges and Tunnels

In the "land of freshwater" with its numerous waterways, bridges and tunnels are significant landscape features in establishing and maintaining a cohesive society. The loss of one of the region's eight international bridges would cause immediate economic disruption (Table 9-6).

Hundreds of other bridges, ranging from aesthetically and historically beautiful covered bridges to complex civil engineering feats, also help to lace the Basin together. Perhaps it is not surprising that bridges have become places of fond memories and the subject of painters, photographers and poets. Maybe the sensitive artist is leading the way to a deeper understanding of technology as bridges seemingly have a psychic-spiritual quality, yet unmeasureable scientifically, which survives beyond the actual existence of a bridge.

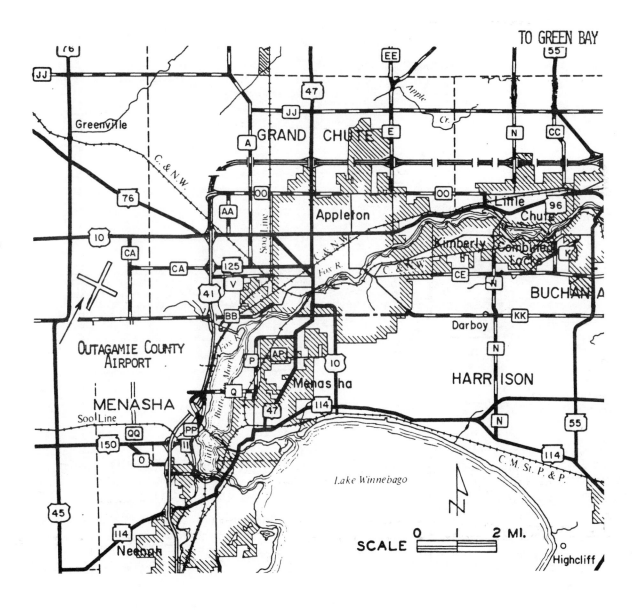

Figure 9-2. Letters and double letters county road identifications (non-systematic) Fox Cities, Wisconsin. Source: Fox Cities Chamber of Commerce, *Fox Cities Profile*, ca. 1985.

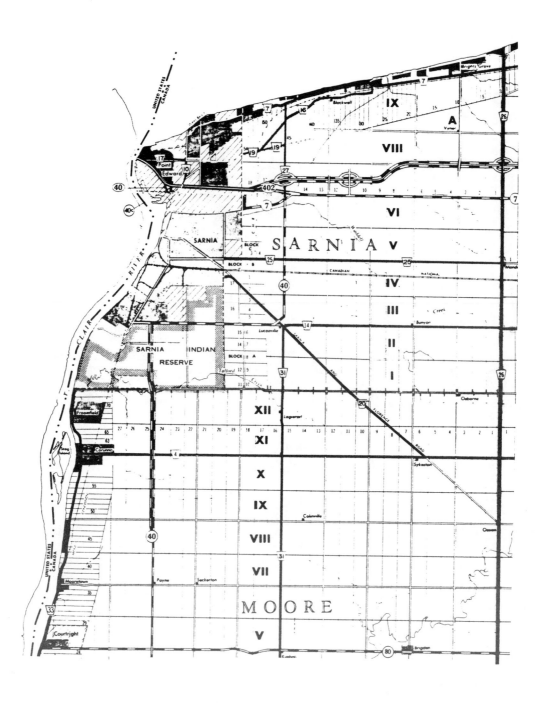

Figure 9-3. Roman number county road identification system (survey-concession system). Note French "ribbon farms" along shore. Source: County of Lambton, Ontario.

242

ROADS

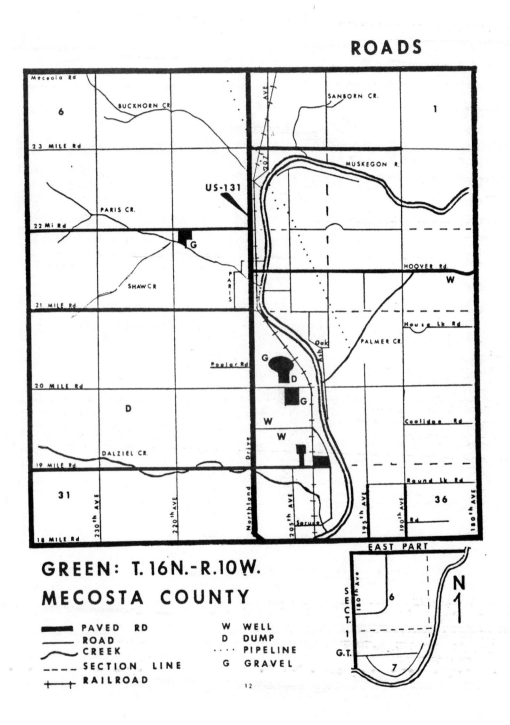

Figure 9-4. Road-avenue county road identification systems (systematic) based on Federal Survey. Numbers related to miles from south/east county borders (N-S avenues, E-W roads). Source: R. A. Santer, *Green Township Atlas 1974*, Ferris State University.

TABLE 9-6

Notable Great Lakes Basin Bridges

Bridge	Water Body Crossed	Communities Linked
International Bridges		
Pigeon River - Peace	Pigeon R	Grand Portage-Ont.
International	St. Mary's R.	Sault Ste. Marie M.-Ont.
Blue Water	St. Clair R.	Port Huron-Sarnia
Ambassador	Detroit R.	Detroit-Windsor
Peace	Niagara R.	Ft. Erie, Ont.-Buffalo
Rainbow	Niagara R.	Niagara Falls Ont.-NY
Whirlpool	Niagara R.	Niagara Falls Ont.-NY
Alexandria Bay	St. Lawrence R.	Ontario-New York
Other Notable Bridges		
"The Big Mac" (Mackinac)	Strait of Mackinac	St. Ignace - Mackinac City
The Bong	St. Louis R.	Duluth-Superior
The Thunder Bay Balanced Lift	Walsh St., Kaministiquia R.	Thunder Bay
The Zilwaukee	Saginaw R.	Saginaw
The Bay View Bay	Sandusky Bay	Sandusky
I-81 Syracuse	At I-90 NY Thruway	Syracuse
Hurley-Montreal	Montreal R.	Hurley-Ironwood
O-8 Akron	Little Cuyahoga	Akron
Lesser Known Pairs and Groups		
Grand Island N & S (2)	Goat Island, Niagara E. Channel	
Toledo (6+)	Maumee R.	
Fox Cities (6+)	Fox River, L. Brutte Les Morts	
Menominee - Marinette (3)	Menominee R.	Menominee - Marinette

The Singing Bridge*

We drove across a singing bridge,
A singing bridge today
A brook was tumbling underneath
Along its rocky way.

I listened to the singing bridge,
It hummed a special tune,
Over and over it sang to me,
"Come back soon,
Come back soon."

Leland B. Jacobs
<u>circa</u> 1920 used with permission copyrighted in
Just Around the Corner Holt, Rinehart, and
Winston, New York, Chicago, 1964

The Singing Bridge Remembered

Who says the singing bridge is gone --
That it's no more to see
Or hear it hum its welcoming,
Its special melody?
Not so. It still is there to sing
If but in memory!

Leland B. Jacobs
1985 (Source: Personal
letter to author.)

Tunnels

When built, the Basin's three modest length international tunnels were innovative feats of accomplishment. The Detroit-Windsor Tunnel is the region's best known and provides an alternate automobile route to that of the Ambassador Bridge. The tunnel's popularity is derived, in part, because it connects the Detroit Renaissance Center with the central business district of Windsor. Paralleling at a slight distance is a railroad tunnel which serves freight crossing needs.

First International Tunnel.--The world's first international submarine railway tunnel was opened between Port Huron and Sarnia in 1891. Up to that time, the St. Clair River was the only gap in a rail line that linked Toronto with Chicago. For years the Grand Trunk Railroad used barges to move up to 1,000 rail cars a day across the river. The cost to use the barge system was high as ice jams caused delays and loading-unloading the barges was also time consuming. After

---

*The site of the Singing Bridge and Park is on US 23, Michigan, Arenac County, Whitney Township (T20N R7E), Section line 12-13.

two years of innovative labor, the nearly 12,000 feet of tunneling (2,290 feet under water) was completed. Tunnel operations were electrified in 1908 and dieselized in 1958. A second tunnel is in the planning stages. In 1938 the Blue Water Bridge was opened, complementing the tunnel connection between Michigan and Ontario.

Aviation

At Greenfield Village millions pay homage to the Wright brothers by visiting their cycle shop which was formerly located in Dayton, Ohio. Less well-known are the 1890's controversial aviation exploits of Augustus Herring on the shores of Lake Michigan. In St. Joseph was built a powered, controlled, heavier than-air machine which is claimed to have been flown October 22, 1898.[2] In the contemporary era, several hundred airfields usually in towns of 7,000 people or more, comprise the aviation network. About two-thirds of the aircraft sites are licensed operations. Perhaps ten percent of the airfields handle commercial air service. About five percent have air control towers, while the majority have neither runway paving nor lights. About 100 airports have paved runways longer than 1200 m (4400 ft) which can accommodate jet planes, while others are located on water as seaplane bases (Fig 9-5).

Air Traffic Hubs and Metro Airports

Of North America's thirty large air traffic hubs, three are located in the Basin --Chicago having three airports, with O'Hare the super largest, is dominant (Fig 9-6). Toronto International and the smaller Detroit-Ann Arbor airports (Metropolitan and Willow Run) rank among the 10 busiest continent airports. O'Hare ranks as the world's busiest airport with an average of one take-off and landing per minute. It is being challenged by Dallas/Ft. Worth and Atlanta. In comparison, Detroit Metro's flights average about one every six minutes. In recent years manufacturing and service activities have been sited near the major airports to gain access advantages, resulting in congestion. To facilitate both traffic flow and passenger/visitor use of airport facilities, detailed route and terminal maps and atlases could be marketed or integrated into existing highway i.e. transportation maps. Similarly, regional shopping centers could be added to highway maps to assist customers of the Basin economy.

In spite of the huge Basin market, the majority of the evolving air express collection-sorting-rerouting process has been developed outside the region, especially in Memphis, Tennessee. Perhaps this is another indication of the hyper-congestion, limited space and over-population conditions in the historic dominant metro centers and the slowness of other Basin metro-centers to compete with a visionary outlook. Now the local economic development challenge is to consolidate and cooperatively well-equip sub-regional airports with rapid ground connections.

Airports' Environmental Impact

To gain the economic benefits which airports contribute to communities and lessen the human impact, an extensive amount of land is usually idled for airport buffer zones. For instance, Ontario has 20,015 ha (50,039 ac) of Canada's 98,765 ha (246,912 ac) devoted to airports -- 1/3 more land area than any other province. To minimize noise conflicts, planners use the Canada

---

[2]Leslie W. Flott, "Augustus Herring...Aviation Pioneer," *Chronicle*, Historical Society of Michigan, Vol. 10, No. 3 (1974), pp. 2-8.

noise exposure forecast (NEF), a measure that reflects human sensitivity to noise. The diagram of the Harry W. Browne International Airport at Saginaw illustrates the (1) built-up areas around the field perimeter, (2) the limited space for expansion, and (3) the proximity of utility poles to the runways (Fig 9-7). A frustrating situation for airport managers occurred in Chatham, Ontario, where the runway is adjacent to private farmland, but the landowner built an isolated silo 112 m (123 ft) from its end. Obviously conflicts in use and rights in the public-private landowner zone adjacent to airports, while maintaining human safety, remains a challenge.

DETROIT, METROPOLITAN WAYNE COUNTY

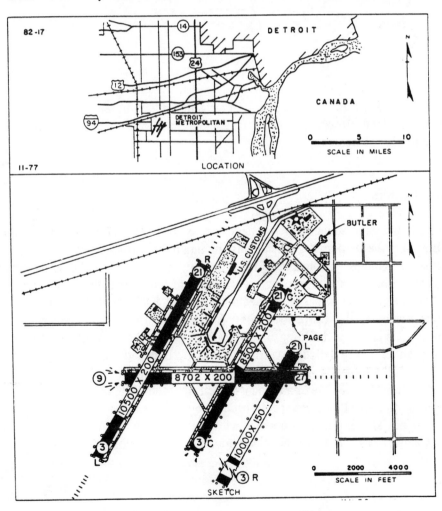

Figure 9-5. Detroit Metropolitan Airport. Source: Michigan Bureau of Aeronautics, *Airport Directory*, 1986.

247

Figure 9-6. Great lakes Basin airport hubs. (Ontario hub added by author.) Source: Great Lakes Commission and Federal Reserve Bank of Chicago, *The Great lakes Economy*, Harbor House Publishers, Boyne City, Michigan, 1985.

Mail Handling Centers

The economy and social cohesiveness are closely related to swift delivery of postal materials. Both of the national governments maintain extensive mail services which assure deliveries into the remotest hamlets and to ships on the lakes. Similarly, both countries use geographically oriented ZIP (zone improvement) codes to aid in the electronic sorting of mail. In the U.S., the five digit code is based on Sectional Center Facilities (SCF), the first three digits, and post office numbers, the last two digits. Using the ZIP + 4, a geographic area can be identified electronically to a building or *blockface* (a single side of a street between two intersections) thus facilitating delivery, editing of mailing lists and marketing demographic studies. In addition to 32 SCFs in the Basin, the U.S. Postal Service operates, with steady employment, 7 airport mail facilities, 29 vehicle maintenance facilities and 3 bulk mail centers (Table 9-7). Canada's postal code also allows electronic processing and location to a blockface or buildings. The system combines six letters and numbers with the first letter identifying a region: K = East Ontario, L = Central, M = Toronto, N = Southwest, and P = North Ontario.

Railroads

Since the 1840's, the railroad network steadily expanded and became both a reliable and dominant form of transportation. Huge centers for servicing passengers and freight became landmarks of architecture at several locations; however, Chicago and Toronto developed into unrivaled national rail hubs. In Ontario railroads continue to be a powerful segment of the

SAGINAW, HARRY W. BROWNE INT'L.

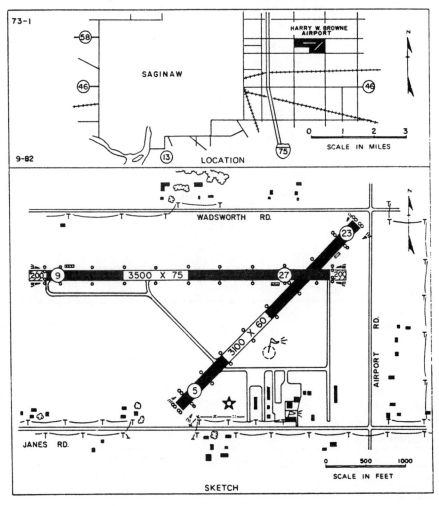

Figure 9-7. Harry W. Browne International Airport, Saginaw, Michigan. source: Michigan Bureau Aeronautics, *Airport Directory*, 1986.

TABLE 9-7

Selected U.S. Postal Service Facilities in the
Great Lakes Basin 1986

Sectional Center Facilities (SCF)	Zip Numbers	Sectional Center Facilities (SCF)	Zip Numbers
Illinois		New York	
Chicago	606	Buffalo	140-143
N. Suburban	600-603	Rochester	144-146
		Syracuse	130-132
Indiana		Utica	133-135
Ft. Wayne	467-468	Watertown	136
Gary	463-464		
South Bend	465-466	Ohio	
		Akron	442-443
Michigan		Cleveland	440-441
Detroit	481-482	Lima	458
Flint	484-485	Toledo	434-436
Gaylord	497		
Grand Rapids	493-495	Pennsylvania	
Iron Mt.	498-499	Erie	164-165
Jackson	492		
Kalamazoo	490-491	Wisconsin	
Lansing	488-489	Green Bay	541-543
Royal Oak	480, 483	Milwaukee	530-532, 534
Saginaw	486-487	Oshkosh	549
Traverse City	496	Portage	539
		Rhinelander	545
Minnesota			
Duluth	556-558		

Airport Mail Facilities	Bulk Mail Centers
Eastern Region:	
Greater Buffalo International Airport	Chicago (Forest Park)
Rochester	Detroit (Allen Park)
Syracuse-Monroe County Airport	Buffalo
Central Region:	
Chicago - O'Hare Airport	
Cleveland - Hopkins Airport	
Detroit - Metropolitan Airport	
Milwaukee Gen. Mitchell Field	

Vehicle Maintenance Facilities

Erie	Flint	Saginaw
Chicago (6)	Livonia	Warren
Ft. Wayne	Grand Rapids	Duluth
Gary	Kalamazoo	Akron
South Bend	Lansing	Cleveland
Ann Arbor	Muskegon	Green Bay
Dearborn	Pontiac	Milwaukee
Detroit (2)	Royal Oak	

SOURCE: US Postal Service, *1986 National Five-Digit Zip Code and Post Office Directory*, Washington DC.

economy in product hauling and especially passenger service which is impressive to most U.S. travelers to the Province. Toronto also maintains an exceptional rail-subway system which interfaces with the primary rail-passenger lines at Union Station (Fig 9-8). Since World War II and the paving of the interstate system, rail use in the U.S. has greatly diminished or ceased even though the lines frequently remain on rail maps. Why people in the U.S. have abandoned the use of trains is complex; however, one can observe that the lure of the rails draws thousands of U.S. citizens to the Soo, Ontario by automobile only to board the rail cars of the Algoma Central Railroad for a pleasure ride to Agawa Canyon. At the Soo, as in other Ontario metro-centres, the

DOWNTOWN TORONTO

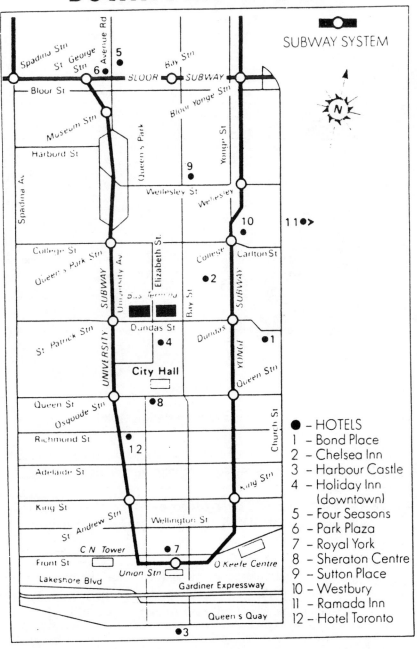

Figure 9-8. Downtown Toronto Subway System.

rail station is located within an easy, clean, safe walk to modern hotels, restaurants and spacious contemporary indoor shopping malls. Inter-modal transportation, such as taxis and buses, complement the network.

In contrast, in the U.S.A., rusting rails, weed growth and views down the right-of-ways with no sight of a train give evidence of the lack of train use in the Basin. Small, temporary, appearing hastily constructed and often closed, passenger railway stations dot the tracks along traditional east-west corridors and suggest a feeble attempt to regenerate passenger service in the 1970's (Fig 9-9 to 9-11). In trade-off, appearing somewhat out of place on the highways, are truck rigs which look like trains with a tractor cab with one, two or three trailers attached which in total weigh up to 40 ton.

Figure 9-9. Grand Rapids, Michigan passenger railway station, 1986, built 1975.

Richard C. Noble of the Booth News Service, described the truck-auto safety concern after noting that 4500 people annually die from crashes involving big trucks.

> The adrenaline keeps pumping until the rig roars by hammering down the highway to terrorize another motorist. If you ask the general public, all have horror stories about big trucks.[4]

To lessen stress, stimulate the recreational economy and hold for future use many rail right of ways are being converted into linear parks. Research reported by the University of Wisconsin Sea Grant Program confirms the fuel advantage of rail over truck transportation (Table 9-8).

[4]"Those Big Trucks Do Make Roadways More Hazardous," *Grand Rapids Press*, February 23, 1986, p. D11.

Figure 9-10. Jackson, Michigan passenger railway station 1986, constructed 1873. Largest station building between Detroit and Chicago.

Figure 9-11. Holloway, Lenawee County, Michigan railway station 1986, converted to a residence.

TABLE 9-8

Relative Energy Efficiency
by Mode and City

Mode	BTU's per Ton Mile	Ton Miles per Gallon
Airplane	63,000	3.7
Truck	2,400	58.0
Railroad	750	200.0
Pipeline	NA	300.0
Lake Vessel	NA	600.0
Barge (Tow)	500	250.0

City	Gasoline Used Per Capita		% of Population Commuting by Auto
	Gallons	Liters	
Houston	546	2075	94
Detroit	482	1832	93
Los Angeles	428	1626	88
Chicago	353	1341	76
New York	323	1227	64
Toronto	248	942	NL
Australian Cities	218	828	NL

SOURCE: *The Great Lakes Transportation System*, University of Wisconsin Sea Grant Program Technical Report 230, 1976, pp. 121-3. L. R. Brown and J. L. Jacobson, *The Future of Urbanization*, Worldwatch Paper 77, Worldwatch Institute, May, 1987, pp. 17-18.

In writing about North Bay, an historic regional rail centre of Ontario, Michael Barnes observed,

> Rails made North Bay and they will do so again as energy resources need to be husbanded.[5]

To regain rail advantages, a high speed passenger train, constructed with foreign technology, is being considered to link Detroit and Chicago. However, the independence of travel and flexibility of use of cars and small trucks are also equally important mobility needs.

Looking into the Short-Term Future

What would the economic, social/family, safety and employment impacts be if the transportation system matured in the 21st Century to include: (1) widely available auto-trains with

[5]Barnes, *Gateway City the North Bay Story, op. cit.*, p. 125.

rapid side loading drive-on/drive-off capabilities, and (2) inter-modal yards for transferring rapidly train freight into small and medium-sized trucks for urban deliveries? Further, how should land and lake transportation interface, plus canals be developed?

Now another probing question. In a democracy, how accessible, with what exclusive space and at what cost to individuals in taxes, should local community transportation be developed and maintained? Evidence that this question remains unanswered is the mishmash of continuing experiments operating at different levels of support relating to sidewalks, bike paths, school and large bus systems plus a light sprinkling of county area transportation systems (CATS) and Dial-a-Ride transportation (DART). If Toronto has earned the best reputation for developing an integrated intermodal system of moderate direct cost trains, buses, subways, autos, bike lanes and sidewalks which are clean and efficient, perhaps then the Big Rapids, Michigan bus services can provide a clue to a typical U.S. immature transportation system. This college town/county seat community of 15,000 people is linked by eight (8) public bus systems and one (1) private company. Each system is independent and vehicle maintenance is performed separate from each other (Table 9-9). In answering locally related transportation questions, decision-makers could reevaluate: (1) whether school districts belong in the transportation business, (2) whether school bus systems should be allowed to carry, on-demand or by contract, non-student individuals, (3) the economic advantages of bus system consolidation.

Pipeline Systems

Less often seen on the landscape and under the Great Lakes waterways are oil and natural gas pipelines which, since mid-century, have become vital in transporting energy for industrial production, indoor space heating and most transportation modes. Where air temperatures for sustained lengths of time dip below $18^{0}C$ ($65^{0}F$), the human comfort level, body protection is needed. When temperatures reach and hold at $4^{0}C$ ($40^{0}F$) and lower -- refrigeration storage temperature, energy is needed for space heating in order to sustain health. In the past, wood and coal met the need in spite of their production and atmospheric pollution risks.

In comparison to the extensive network of electric power and telephone lines, the natural gas and oil pipeline system is somewhat modest in accessibility as hundreds of inhabited township-sized areas lie outside the pipeline grid. As a result, LP (liquid propane) gas or "bottled gas" is trucked into those townships for residential/commercial use. Fuel oil and wood are especially popular as heating fuels in the northwest district of the Basin.

The steel pipelines used to carry natural gas from the fields to the major storage and distribution points range in size from between 10 cm (4 in) well head lines to 105 cm (42 in) leading short distances into the storage fields. The greatest convergence of pipelines are at Duluth, Chicago, Sarnia-Port Huron, Detroit-Toledo and Toronto. Other significant concentration points include Buffalo, Syracuse, Thunder Bay and the Austin Gas Storage Field of Mecosta County, Michigan (Fig 9-12). The Austin Fields originally produced gas; however, since its depletion, gas is pumped under pressure into its sedimentary-Paleozoic bedrock formation in the summer months from sources in the Gulf of Mexico, Texas, Louisiana, Oklahoma and Canada, for redistribution into the metro-Detroit area during the cold months. Most of the former Michigan-owned pipeline system has been merged with Texas petroleum capital interests. The Trans-Canada pipeline brings natural gas from Alberta to Montreal. Enroute are served Thunder Bay, Sudbury, North Bay and Toronto. The Great Lakes Transmission Company operates a 90 cm (36 in) line from Minnesota to Sarnia to carry natural gas from the Canadian Prairie Field to southern Ontario.

TABLE 9-9

Bus Systems Interacting with Big Rapids

System	Users and Comments
Indian Trails Motorcoach (private)	Headquarters in Owosso; long-distance inter-city; all ages, daily service.
Big Rapids Dial-A-Ride	Headquarters in Big Rapids; intra-city service only; all ages; weekdays and Saturday service.
M-CAT	Headquarters in Big Rapids Township, county area service plus by contract inter-county service limited to one county north and to Intermediate School District for servicing handicapped students (originally buses could not legally cross county line); all ages, weekday and Saturday service.
Big Rapids Public Schools	Headquarters Big Rapids, limited to school district and school children only, weekdays - school year.
Morley-Stanwood Public Schools	Headquarters Stanwood, limited to school district plus daily trips in school year to Vocational Center in Big Rapids, vocational students only.
Reed City Public Schools	Headquarters Reed City, limited to school district plus daily trips in school year to Vocational Center in Big Rapids, vocational students only.
Evart Public Schools	Headquarters Evart, limited to school district plus daily trips in school year to Vocational Center in Big Rapids, vocational students only.
Chippewa Hills Public Schools	Headquarters in Remus, limited to school district plus daily trips in school year to Vocational Center in Big Rapids, vocational students only.

TABLE 9-12 (Cont'd)

Bus Systems Interacting with Big Rapids

System	Users and Comments
Pineview Public Schools	Headquarters in Woodville (Newaygo Co.), limited to school district, high school-age students only, daily trips to Big Rapids in school year.
Big Jackson Public Schools	Headquarters in Parks (Newaygo Co.), limited to school district, high school-age students only, daily trips to Big Rapids in school year.
Ferris State University	Headquarters in Big Rapids, limited to teams, coaches, classes, employees and spouses for scheduled out-of-town events.

Pipelines and the Environment

From an environmental management point of view, the desire to control vegetation growth within the thousands of kilometers of pipeline easements and right-of-ways continues to cause concern. At odds are the opponents of the use of chemical sprays and those who advocate machine or hand chopping. In some locations planning and zoning commissions have to make decisions relating to new subdivision developments which are proposed over or near existing lines. In such situations, commonly debated topics are house set-off distances and how much soil should remain over a pipe after landscaping to reduce accidental puncturing. One advantage of pipeline route clearing on public land is their near ideal use for snowmobiling. Additionally, in forested areas, huge amounts of cut edge are created which favor many species of wildlife.

Summary

Economics, or home management, from the days of Greek civilization, is one of the most dominant processes which affect the lives of people and environment. Without the economic system evolving into a coherent global system, ecologists and geographers will continue to describe an unhealthy earth. The major economic activities of the Basin's people are in transition; however, durable goods, agriculture, forestry and tourism are still dominant. Increasingly, tertiary services are replacing primary and secondary industries. Given the Basin's location and access to world places, entrepreneurial initiatives, supported by bank reorganizations, have a fertile region in which to succeed, especially when quality and service to users remain at high levels.

Complementary transportation modes, with well placed bridge and tunnels, plus snow removal are primary needs for a viable economy to agglomerate people and materials for production and distribution to users. About two dozen "main street" freeways with logical

Figure 9-12. Austin gas field complex, Mecosta County, Michigan.

identification systems serve the Basin, but local roads with non-standard identifications thwart efficient road use at the county level. Contemporary maps are needed to assist in the access of periodic visitors and users of regional shopping centers and the congested airport complexes. The role of railroads and long-distance trucking for the 21st Century is not yet clear. Ultimately, as brain power is devoted to understanding the hodgepodge of laws, rules and elements of local, regional, national and global economic and transportation systems it is judged that the making of wise holistic inter-related decisions, will follow and support the transition into a healthier economic age.

Geography results from a blending of the descriptive skills of the physiographer, cartographer, demographer, historiographer and photographer.

Photo Essay C

The Changing Landscape

1. Abandoned Automobile Drive-In Theater
2. Tool/Video Rental
3. Group Child Care
4. Household Goods Storage
5. Tourist Information - Copying Service
6. Underground Utilities
7. Above Ground Utilities
8. Flood Damaged Road
9. Terry Fox Memorial, Trans-Canada Highway

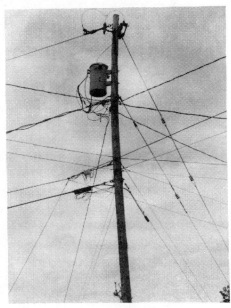

262

Reflections and Self-Learning: Chapter 9 and Photo Essay C

1. Why are economic activities important in shaping the landscape?

2. Evaluate economics and government versus geography and ecology in shaping the landscape.

3. Translate: *oikos, nomics, graphy, ology, demos.*

4. Why is the Basin economic system difficult to describe with certainty?

5. Do you have an area set aside for an industrial park? How would you rate its potential for attracting a new enterprise?

6. Why are analysis of tax rates alone unreliable in the potential to attract or hold economic activities?

7. Evaluate the stage of economic activity in your community: basic, secondary, tertiary.

8. Map the location of automobile assembly plants: Is metropolitan Detroit the hub of production? How long would it take to drive between Detroit and the outlying plants? What may be the reason for the distance?

9. Why are quality and service important to sustaining economic activities?

10. What are the advantages and disadvantages to converting railroad rights of ways into linear parks?

11. Based on the looking into the short-term future section and Table 9-9, how can local U.S.A. transportation systems be improved?

12. Describe several of the highway numbering systems.

13. What is a French long-lot or "ribbon farm"?

14. Write a poem or song about the work, life or cultural feature of your area.

15. What are human conflicts which may be linked to airport development?

16. What are some of the advantages of zip codes?

17. Evaluate energy costs by mode of transportation.

18. Based on the photos in Essay C, describe changes in lifestyles during the last fifty years. What new inventions are related to the changes?

19. Who is Terry Fox? Why a monument to him?

Chapter Ten

THE ST. LAWRENCE SEAWAY, PORTS AND IN-LAND COMMUNITIES

When LaSalle guided the building of the Griffon in the late 1600's, he envisioned a necklace of ports linked to each other and the world by ship. Two and a half centuries later, proponents touted that, "The Great Lakes-St. Lawrence Waterway will be the greatest transportation improvement of the age."[1] If food for export is a major measure of greatness, then the grain ports at Thunder Bay, Duluth-Superior and Toledo, which are among the largest on earth, are evidence that the 1927 touters were not off the mark. Along the shoreline, distinctions can be made between three types of communities: (1) communities with harborage only for leisure-time watercraft, (2) commercial ports which can only accommodate Great Lakes vessels, and (3) international commercial ports which serve standard ocean vessels. Margaret Bogue and Virginia Palmer's historical guide to Lake Superior and Doris Scharfenberg's vacation guides to the shorelines of Michigan and Ontario provide detailed information on the parks and harbors along the water edges. In this chapter the emphasis will be on the significant features of the St. Lawrence Seaway and a brief synopsis of both the shoreline and inland communities (Fig 10-1).

The St. Lawrence Seaway

The complement of channels, canals and locks of the St. Lawrence Seaway system, dedicated in 1959, are the key engineering feats which have allowed over a score of Great Lakes cities to become true inter-continental ports. The first major engineering project of the Seaway was the Welland Canal, located in Canada, which links Lakes Ontario and Erie as a bypass around the Niagara Falls. The original canal and locks were opened to shipping in 1829. In 1932 the current canal became operational for the 42 km (26 mi) long system with eight locks (3 twined) each 23 m (76 ft) wide and 219 m (730 ft) long which sets the size for the most recently built ships operating in the middle and lower lakes. In 1985 Seaway shipping and the Basin's economic activity were severely disrupted when a large concrete section of one of the locks collapsed forcing an untimely halt to shipping. That disruption, plus other accidents in the shipping narrows, and winter-season closings, constantly lead to challenges from truck, train and port cities on the other three coasts.

---

[1] Clyde L. Newnom, *Michigan's Thirty-Seven Million Acres of Diamonds*, Detroit: The Book Company of Michigan, 1927, p. 61.

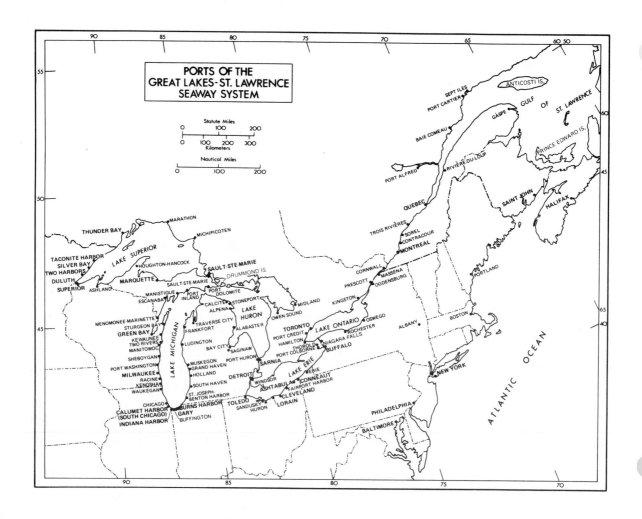

Figure 10-1. Principal ports of the Great Lakes - Seaway System. Source: University of Wisconsin Sea Grant College Program, Technical Report No. 230, 1976.

The Soo Locks

At the falls of the St. Mary's River, in 1855, the State of Michigan built the first "Soo" lock and established a user toll. Later improvements were made, especially to meet the iron-copper shipping needs in 1881 with the addition of two larger locks. At that time, the state donated the locks to the federal government which placed the complex under the control of the Army Engineers who then removed the toll fee. On the Ontario side, in 1895, a lock with wooden gates was sliced through the red sedimentary rock. That lock remained in commercial operation until 1978. Parks Canada now operates that lock and grounds for recreational uses.

The present-day four commercial locks, which also serve recreational boats, are all located in Michigan. The Davis and North Canal opened in 1914 and the Sabin Lock in 1919 (Fig 10-2). The demand to move huge quantities of iron and wheat during World War II stimulated the completion of the MacArthur Lock in mid-1943. The fourth and largest lock, the Poe, was opened in 1969. Its length, 360 m (1200 ft), and width of 33 m (110 ft) was the catalyst for the design of the distinctive long lake freighters which link middle and upper lake ports. The largest vessel operating on the lakes is the 1981 William J. DeLancey, with a length of 304 m (1013.5 ft) which

266

can hold over 60,000 ton of pelletized iron ore. Grain shipments in the other "super freighters" are similar in weight. In the smaller high-sided ocean vessels, loads of 27,000 ton or 1 million bushel of wheat are common consignments for direct shipment. Depending on railroad competition and the situation of the economy, especially the demand for grain and iron, shipments through the Soo Locks vary; however, bulk cargo totals usually ranks it among the world's leading canals. Yet, since the mid-1980's tonnage figures have declined considerably.

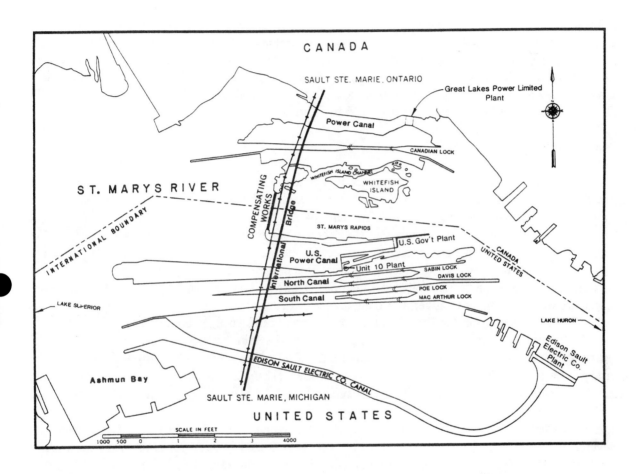

Figure 10-2. Soo Locks and Lake Superior water regulatory works. Source: U.S. Army Corps of Engineers -- Detroit District, *Great lakes Water Level Facts*, 1986.

Milestones in the Completion of the Seaway

In 1909 the Boundary Waters Treaty assured that the U.S.-Canada boundary waters "... shall forever continue to be free and open for the purposes of commerce." The International Joint Commission (IJC) was empowered by the treaty to approve projects which might affect the levels or flow of the boundary waters. Some individuals contend that Lake Michigan should not be affected by the Boundary Waters Treaty. Observing Lake Michigan's natural connection to Lake Huron, most Basin political leaders consider Lake Michigan projects a legal concern of the IJC. Table 10-1 summarizes the chronology of the development of the Seaway and continued concern about tolls as a basis for fair national competition.

Great Lakes Shipping

At several lakeside locations can be found: ship repair services, vessel enlargement or conversions and the building of technologically advanced complex self-unloading freighters up to 1000 plus feet. Further, at times, military watercraft are built on contract. Major shipyards are located at Port Weller, Collingwood, Thunder Bay, Sturgeon Bay, Marinette and Toledo. In recent years large shipbuilding in Saginaw-Bay City has decreased. Freighter crew sizes have decreased 10-25 percent to an average of 22 people per vessel. The Canadian Bulk Fleet is expected to continue downsizing from 87 vessels in 1981, 49 in 1991 and 37 in 2001 AD. Similarly, US-flagged ships on the lakes have gone from 126 to 59 vessels.

Marketing with Foreign Ports

The basic purpose of the Seaway is to enhance the possibilities of trade with non-Basin areas. Since the completion of the Seaway, Great Lakes trade has been established with at least 60 nations and 110 foreign ports (Table 10-2). One of the marketing conditions faced by the several Great Lakes port directors, which tends to slow the development of trade, is that most maps used to plot routes and locations are Mercator projection maps. Such maps are good for direction navigation, but extremely poor in illustrating area, shape and distance. For example, in comparison to water and land shipping, Detroit and Liverpool, United Kingdom are by water, 5920 km (3700 mi) apart while Baltimore to Liverpool the distance is 6296 km (3935 mi). The water difference is only 375 km (235 mi), but the Detroit-Baltimore overland difference is about 960 km (600 mi).

In spite of foreign trade developed, entrepreneurs still have a highly fertile area of the economy in which to enter the export-import field. Two sectors of the economy that appear to be ready to be lifted to a higher level of development are: (1) the connection of hinterland production to Basin and foreign ports, and (2) diversifying from raw material (colonial like) shipments to value-added exports (Table 10-3).

To assist local communities in the expansion of commerce and trade within North America, several formerly somewhat competing organizations were joined in 1983 for combined action under the Great Lakes Maritime Forum. The initial coordinating organizations included:

Ontario Ministry of Transportation
   and Communication,
St. Lawrence Task Force,
Government of Quebec,
Great Lakes Cargo Marketing Corporation,
Great Lakes Commission (U.S.) representing 8 states,
St. Lawrence Seaway Development Corporation (U.S.),
St. Lawrence Seaway Authority (Canada),

International Joint Commission,
Lake Carriers Association,
Wisconsin Ports Council,
Dominion Marine Association,
Great Lakes Task Force,
L'Association des operateurs de Navires du St.-
   Laurent,
Seaway Review magazine.[2]

---

[2]Jacques LesStrang, *The Great Lakes/St. Lawrence System*, (Maple City, Mich.: Harbor House Publishers, Inc., 1984), p. 6.

TABLE 10-1

**Summary of Important Dates Relating to
St. Lawrence Seaway Construction**

Date	Activity
1892	Minnesota Congressman Lind's resolution for joint route study to connect Atlantic to head of Lake Superior.
1909	Boundary Waters Treaty -- International Joint Commission (IJC) established.
1921	IJC recommends U.S.-Canada treaty to improve St. Lawrence River between Montreal and Lake Ontario.
1932	Hoover-Bennett Treaty signed agreeing to 27-foot depth waterway from St. Lawrence River to Lake Superior.
1934	U.S. Senate defended Treaty (opposition from railroad, private utilities, coal mining, East and Gulf Coast ports).
1940 and 1943	U.S. Senate reviewed and defeated treaty.
1951	U.S. Congress defeats enabling act, "Canada Seaway" continues to gain support.
1954	With President Eisenhower's support, the Wiley (WI) - Dondero (MI) Seaway Act passed stating U.S. would share cost of construction of international sections.
1955-1959	Construction activities focused between Massena, NY and Lake Ontario.
1958	Seaway Corporation (U.S.) control transferred from Department of Defense to Department of Commerce.
1959	Joint U.S.-Canada agreement on tolls to be levied on St. Lawrence River Locks and Welland Canal, 29-71% U.S.-Canada split.
April, 1959	First ship (iron ore) sailed through to test system.
1966	Seaway Corporation (U.S.) transferred to Department of Transportation.
1970	Seaway relieved of construction debt and system designated by Merchant Marine Act - 1970 as a seacoast moving system to more equal status with other U.S. coastal regions.
1990's	Tolls, pilotage reform, railroad deregulation, tax incentives for barge construction and ocean freight rates continue to be issues concerning fair competition with other coast ports.

SOURCE: United States Department of Transportation, adapted from, *The St. Lawrence Seaway* (Washington, DC.: St. Lawrence Seaway Development Corporation, undated ca. 1982), pp. 10-12. *Transport of Thunder Bay* (Port Authority Thunder Bay Harbour Commission, Fall 1992 and Spring 1993).

TABLE 10-2

The St. Lawrence Seaway
Foreign Ports of Call

Africa (South, East and West)	Mediterranean, Black Sea, Red Sea	Europe, Continent, U.K.	CHILE
CAMEROUN	ALGERIA	BELGIUM	Antofagasta
Douala	Algiers	Antwerp	Africa
CONGO REPUBLIC	Ghazaouet	DENMARK	San Antonio
Pointe Noire	EGYPT	Copenhagen	Talcahuano
GHANA	Alexandria	FINLAND	Valparaiso
Tema	Port Said	Helsinki	DOMINICAN
GUINEA	ETHIOPIA	FRANCE	REPUBLIC
Conakry	Assab	LeHavre	Rio Haina
IVORY COAST	ISRAEL	IRELAND	Santo Domingo
Abidjan	Ashdod	Dublin	ECUADOR
KENYA	Haifa	NETHERLANDS	Guayaquil
Mombasa	ITALY	Amsterdam	El Salvador
NAMIBIA (Southwest	Genoa	Ghent	Acajutla
Africa)	Leghorn (Livorno)	Rotterdam	JAMAICA
Walvis Bay	Marghera	NORWAY	Kingston
NIGERIA	Naples	Oslo	PERU
Lagos	Trieste	POLAND	Callao
Port Harcourt	MALTA	Gdynia	Matarani
SENEGAL	Malta	ROMANIA	
Dakar	MOROCCO	Constanta	**Far East**
SIERRA LEONE	Agadir	SCOTLAND	JAPAN
Freetown	Casablanca	Greenock	Kobe
SOUTH AFRICA	Safi	SWEDEN	Lokura
Cape Town	Tangier	Stockholm	Moji
Durban	PORTUGAL	UNITED KINGDOM	Osaka
East London	Lisbon	Liverpool	Shimizu
Port Elizabeth	SPAIN	U.S.S.R.	Tokyo
TANZANIA	Barccelona	Leningrad	Yokkaichi
Dar Es Salaam	Valencia	Riga	Yokohama
Tanga	SUDAN	WEST GERMANY	KOREA
	Port Sudan	Bremen	Pusan
India-Bangladesh	TUNISIA	Bremerhaven	HONG KONG
BANGLADESH	Lagoulette	Hamburg	Hong Kong
Chittagong	Sfax		PEOPLES REPUBLIC
INDIA	Tunis	**South America-Caribbean**	OF CHINA
Bombay	TURKEY		Shanghai
Calcutta	Iskenderum	BRAZIL	Tientsin
Cochin	U.S.S.R.	Paranagua	PHILIPPINES
Jamnagar	Odessa	Rio de Janeiro	Manila
Madras	YEMEN	Salvador (Bahia)	SAUDI ARABIA
Paradip	Hodeidah	Santos	Jeddah
SRI LANKA	YUGOSLAVIA	COLOMBIA	SINGAPORE
Colombo	Rijeka	Barranquilla	Singapore
		Buenaventura	TAIWAN
		Cartagena	Kaohsiung
			Keelung

Source: USA D of T, St. Lawrence Seaway Development Corp. 1983.

TABLE 10-3

Twenty-Five Years of Shipping Totals on the Seaway
1959-1983

Total Metric Tons	990,051,345
Total Cargo Vessels Locked	142,577
Shipment Composition	Percent
Grain (wheat, barley, rye, soybean, oats, flax)	39%
Iron Ore	28%
Industrial Goods (steel, iron products)	7%
Other materials and products	26%

SOURCE: J. LesStrang. *The Great Lakes/St. Lawrence System*, p. 9. For a yearly categorization, see: *The St. Lawrence Seaway Traffic Report for the....Navigation Season*, The St. Lawrence Seaway Authority, Washington, DC. and Ottawa, LC #HE630.S17523, 1984, pp. 52-56.

Port Communities

Within Ontario's portion of the Basin there are over 55 ports. Of these, nine have notable intercontinental shipping activities. On the U.S. side of the Basin there are a similar number of ports with about a dozen having significant international trade linkages (Tables 10-4, 10-5).

Box 1

Cargo Definitions

<u>Bulk Cargo</u> - the tonnes of bulk cargo assessed at the Bulk rate of tolls as defined in the St. Lawrence Seaway Tariff of Tolls.

<u>Cargo Tonnes</u> - the tonnes of cargo carried by a vessel on each or any transit.

<u>Commodity</u> - the classification of commodities is based on that prescribed by the Canadian Transport Commission and the Interstate Commerce Commission of the United States.

<u>Container Cargo</u> - the tonnes of containerized cargo assessed at the Containers rate of tolls as defined in the St. Lawrence Seaway Tariff of Tolls.

<u>Government Aid Cargo</u> - the tonnes of cargo assessed at the Government Aid rate of tolls as defined in the St. Lawrence Seaway Tariff of Tolls.

<u>Gross Registered Tonnage</u> - the gross registered tonnage of a vessel according to the country of registry.

SOURCE: St. Lawrence Seaway Authority and St. Lawrence Seaway Development Corporation.

TABLE 10-4

Notable Basin Trade Ports

Port City	Comment
ONTARIO	
Oshawa	(North central Lake Ontario, city 5 km inland) auto materials and parts, sugar, fuel oil, salt, steel; trucks 100%.
Toronto	(Northwest Lake Ontario - Ontario's largest concentration of industry) POL*, grain, scrap metal, liquid chemicals, molasses, cement, vegetable oil, soybeans, containerized general cargo; rail 80%, trucking 20%, province capital city functions, tallest free standing structure in world.
Hamilton	(West - head of Lake Ontario, fine natural harbor, center Golden Horseshoe) iron, steel, agricultural products, construction materials, POL, phosphate, soybeans, salt, sand, stone, gypsum, fluorspar, machinery, motor vehicles, cotton, glass, lumber, nickel products, twine; rail, trucking; 2nd largest city in Ontario.
Port Stanley	(North central Lake Erie at Kettle Creek) cement, wheat, corn, soybeans, oil, asphalt; trucking; only privately owned rail passenger train service in Canada.
Windsor	(Detroit River - major auto production center) packaged freight, grain, steel, salt, fluorspar, crushed stone, coal, vehicles, vegetable oils, POL; railroad, trucking, 2 tunnels and bridge links.
Sarnia	(Head of St. Clair River - major petro-chemical center, POL, varied chemicals, grain; rail, trucking, tunnel and bridge link to Port Huron only Canadian city with Indian Reservation within city limits.
Goderich	(Southeast Lake Huron - North American grain port since 1886) grain mainly wheat, salt; rail, largely trucking - can handle 200 per 13-hour day; historic goal.
Collingwood	(South Georgian Bay - Nottawassaga Bay - major shipbuilding and ship service center) steel, grain; rail, trucking; ski centre.
Thunder Bay	(North central Lake Superior - world's largest grain handling port) grain - 60% of Canada's total export, mainly wheat, barley, flax, rapeseed, malt, oats, and birdseed, coal, iron ore, potash, general and special cargo, paper, POL, ore, potash, general and special cargo, paper, caustic soda, wood; rail ro-ro, trucking; port boat tours.
Other grain ports:	Georgian Bay-Midland, Port McNicoll, Owen Sound, Kingston.
UNITED STATES	
Oswego	(East south shore Lake Ontario - link to NYSBC) grain, general cargo, aluminum; Conrail, trucking - 25 firms. $6.3 billion nuclear plant.

TABLE 10-4 (Cont'd.)

Notable Basin Trade Ports

Port City	Comment
Buffalo	(Foot of Lake Erie at Niagara River - second largest city in New York) coke, gypsum, salt, chrome ore, iron ore, foundry sand, rutile and zircon sand, china clay, machinery, graphite electrodes, specialty steel, fertilizers; rail, trucking; Empire State games.
Erie	(South central Lake Erie - Pennsylvania's 3rd largest city) machinery, specialty ores, pig iron, chemicals, coal and steel scrap; rail, trucking; state park.
Cleveland	(South central Lake Erie - largest port on Lake Erie) unfinished steel, bulk materials - wire rods, rolled steel, iron ore pellets, potash, food stuffs, chemicals, glassware, machinery; rail, trucking; restored swimming beaches.
Toledo	(Head of Lake Erie - significant university) bulk coal, iron ore, grain, general cargo, cement, liquid products, news - print, POL, agricultural products, steel, machinery; rail - 8 rail lines, trucking - 100 carriers, Glass Museum, Zoo.
Detroit	(Detroit River - Automobile Center). coal, iron ore, POL, cement - 80% tonnage, steel, scrap metal, agricultural products, machinery, general manufactured goods - container shipping; rail, trucking, Riverfront redevelopment.
Indiana	(South head of Lake Michigan at Burns Harbor - established 1973 specifically for Seaway traffic) refrigerator items, bulk liquids, POL, grain, general cargo, coal, coke, slag, pig iron, steel, scrap, potash, salt, machinery; rail, trucking, barge; Indiana dunes.
Chicago	(Southwest head of Lake Michigan - well sited to serve hinterland of the continent); iron, steel, grain, general and bulk cargo, wheat, corn, soybean, sunflower seeds, prepared feeds, cornfluten pellets, POL, diverse chemicals; exceptional rail and trucking, barge; major cultural center.
Kenosha	(Southwest Lake Michigan - "reefer" port) refrigerated products, general and bulk cargo, steel; rail, trucking.
Milwaukee	(West central Lake Michigan - cross lake port with hinterland to the Rocky Mountains; rubber, veneers, diversity of grains, flour, powdered milk, butter, cheese, canned goods, refrigerated cargo, chemicals, POL, scrap pig iron, coal, liquid chemicals; rail, trucking; German cultural activities.
Green Bay/ Gills Rock	(Head of Green Bay, - well protected harbor) foodstuffs, refrigerated cargoes, tallow, bulgur, rolled oats, powdered milk, malt, paper products, pitch, machinery; rail, trucking, gateway to Door County and boat connection to Fayette (Mich.).

TABLE 10-4 (Cont'd.)

Notable Basin Trade Ports

Port City	Comment
Duluth-Superior	Head of Lake Superior - 2300 water mi (3702 km) from Atlantic Ocean), iron ore, grain, coal, bentonite, limestone, salt, cement, POL; rail trucking, the twin ports are one of the U.S. top ten tonnage ports serving the mid-continent hinterland, iron ore production decline = surplus power, trend to diversification, electronic and information services.
Other export coal ports:	OHIO: Ashtabula, Conneaut, Sandusky, Lorain; MICHIGAN: Monroe.

Comment order: (Location - Notable feature) materials shipped; transportation modes; unique community feature.

* POL = petroleum, oils, lubricants.

REFERENCE SOURCE: J. LesStrand, *The Great Lakes/St. Lawrence System*, pp. 28-61.

Erie: Pennsylvania's Toe in the Great Lakes

Erie County is Pennsylvania's only county with a shoreline on a Great Lake. It also is the only area of the "Keystone State" which was not a part of William Penn's grant from Charles II. When the survey of Pennsylvania's northern boundary was made between 1785 and 1787, it was found that the state had only 6.4 km (4 mi) of Lake Erie waterfront and it was without a harbor. Then federal land acquisition of the present-day triangular-shaped parcel was delayed until overlapping claims by New York, Connecticut, Massachusetts and Virginia were quieted by those states ceding "their" interior lands to the federal government. Finally in 1788, Pennsylvania gained control of 80,874 ha (202,187 ac) for $151,640. In time the historic City of Erie, grew into Pennsylvania's third largest community somewhat in isolation from the rest of the state and county because of the low mountain divide which extends east-west, south of I-90.

Fort Presque Isle, which is the name of a small low projecting peninsula which juts out into Lake Erie, was established in 1753 by the French as a stronghold to extend their influence into Pennsylvania. George Washington, in his early public service to the Crown, carried a letter to Fort LeBoeuf (just over the divide at Waterford) whose contents gave notice to the French that they were "trespassing on British Territory." The letter was rejected which in part led to the French and Indian War. With the lasting defeat of the French, the British, in 1764, gained control of Ontario and most of the rest of Canada which established the common language and cultural heritage for the Basin into its modern era.

TABLE 10-5

A Great Circle of Selected Domestic and Local
District Ports

Ports and Lakes	Activities and Historic Comments
ONTARIO	
Kingston (Ontario)	Historic capital and farmers' market, Royal Military College, Armed Forces Center, national and provincial male-female prisons, Olympic sail training site, International Ice Hockey Hall of Fame (ice hockey innovated by Lord Stanley of Preston in 1855).
Belleville (Ontario)	Yacht harbor, flying club with air tours.
St. Catherines (Ontario)	Fruit belt and wine centre, historic underground railroad terminal, 1st electric streetcar in North America.
Leamington (Erie)	"Tomato capital," vegetable processing, Point Pelee N.P. - birds, southern most point in Canada.
Owen Sound (Georgian Bay-Huron)	Sailing, Tommy Thompson Art Gallery, Harrison Park Sunday band concerts, Inglis Falls.
Parry Sound (Georgian Bay-Huron)	Boat cruises, 30,000 Islands, world class Festival of Sound, Firetower Park -- grounds maintained by handicappers.
Schreiber (Superior)	Gateway to "Magnificent 100 Kilometers," RR centre, recreation services.
MINNESOTA	
Grand Marais (Superior)	U.S. Coast Guard Station, boat link to Isle Royale N.P., trading post founded 1859 by surveyors, fine harbor.
Taconite Harbor (Superior)	Iron ore/pellet port facilities developed in 1950's.
Silver Bay (Superior)	Historic iron tailing dumping in water controversy, herring gull colony, world's 1st large-scale iron pellet plant.
Two Harbors (Superior)	1st Minnesota iron port 1884, mid-1980's adaptation to tourist services.
WISCONSIN	
Ashland (Superior)	Historic mining and military explosives production, wood processing, RR center, transition to outdoor recreation economy Chequamegon Bay - Apostles Island Nat'l. Lakeshore Park.

TABLE 10-5 (Cont'd.)

A Great Circle of Selected Domestic and Local District Ports

Ports and Lakes	Activities and Historic Comments
Kewaunee (Michigan)	Cross lake RR-auto link, platted 1836, underutilized waterfront buildings, means "prairie hen" in Chippewa.
Manitowac (Michigan)	Cross lake RR link, underutilized marina, platted 1836, settled by Germans, Irish, Norwegian lumber men.
Sheboygan (Michigan)	City of nearly 50,000, diversifying from lumber, RR, agriculture.
Racine-Kenosha (Michigan)	Recreational marina and cargo port.
ILLINOIS Waukegon-N. Chicago (Michigan)	Industrial suburbs, post-World War II rapid growth, RR linkages, waterfront pollution concerns, Great Lakes Naval Training Center.
Kenilworth-Glencoe (Michigan)	Highest waterfront per capita income rate.
Evanston (Michigan)	Largest N. Chicago suburb on waterfront, mixed-transitional economy, outstanding education center, balanced with retail and industrial activities, non-local (Old Orchard) shopping impacting balance.
INDIANA Gary (Michigan)	3rd largest Indiana city, first-ranking U.S. steel center.
Michigan City (Michigan)	State Prison, Tri-State Labor Day yacht race (Chicago, Michigan City, Benton Harbor/St. Joseph).
MICHIGAN Bridgeman (Michigan)	Cook nuclear plant.
Benton Harbor/ St. Joseph (Michigan)	Twin city, economic imbalance with some progress, electronics, fruit processing, amateur golf championship, Blossom Festival.
Holland (Michigan)	Tulip Festival, 3rd largest in U.S., center of Christian Reformed Church, Dutch ethnic district, wooden shoes, Delft ware, windmills.

TABLE 10-5 (Cont'd.)

A Great Circle of Selected Domestic and Local
District Ports

Ports and Lakes	Activities and Historic Comments
Muskegon/Grand Haven (Michigan)	Historic center of "47 sawmills and 40 millionaires, "innovative waste water treatment and spray irrigation-cropland facility, paper, heavy engines, communication center, cross lake linkage, innovative municipal solid waste recycling, dune park.
Ludington (Michigan)	Chemicals, innovative site pump-storage electric production, strong local history support - White Pine Village, salmon derby, RR-cross lake linkage.
Manistee (Michigan)	Wood processing, chemicals, Ramsdell Opera House - National Register Historic Places, invention site of logging Big Wheels.
Traverse City (Michigan)	Regional services center for northwest Lower Peninsula and east Upper Peninsula, specialized hospitals, Northport artist colony, recreational services, Cherry Festival and processing, Sleeping Bear Nat'l. Lakeshore Park.
Petoskey (Michigan)	Specialized hospital services, golf courses of national merit, up-scale recreational services.
Harbor Springs (Michigan)	Historic wealthy recreation center, 19 buildings on Michigan Community Historical Preservation list, invention site of Shay logging engine.
Escanaba (Michigan)	3rd largest city in Upper Peninsula, site of strategic RR iron loading dock, U.P. State Fair.
Ontonagon (Superior)	Wood processing, paper, recreation services.
Houghton/Hancock (Portage L., Superior)	Wood products innovations, unique lift bridge, boat air links to Isle Royale N.P., snow sculpture, retail, medical, mining, recreation services center.
Marquette (Superior)	"Capital of U.P.," iron pellet shipping, state prison, retail-recreation-university-government services.
Munising (Superior)	Recreation services, boat rides to Pictured Rocks Nat'l. Lakeshore Park.
Rogers City (Huron)	Support services activities for world's largest limestone quarry.
Alpena (Huron)	Minor regional center, Jesse Besser Museum.

TABLE 10-5 (Cont'd.)

**A Great Circle of Selected Domestic and Local
District Ports**

Ports and Lakes	Activities and Historic Comments
Bay City (Saginaw Bay-Huron)	Secondary seaway port - some years 2nd to Detroit in activity, auto parts, packing boxes, sugar, cheese, salt, electrical fabrications.
Port Huron (Huron)	Retail trade area large for size of city population (80 mi north, 35 mi west, 30 mi south), strong CBD, extensive marina (6) developments, major yacht race, exchange rate affecting Canada to U.S. retail trade, boyhood home of Thomas Edison (born Milan, Ohio) holder of most patents, bridge-tunnel link.
Wyandotte (Detroit R.)	Tradition of independent local government ownership of utilities, chemical products industry, Bob-Lo boat dock service to island amusement park, ethnic festivals, claim state's 2nd largest air fair, Polish, Irish, old stock America, world's 1st Bessemer steel mill.
Monroe (Erie)	Most historical markers per capita, rich history relating to French, War of 1812, Gen. George Custer, largest coal fired electric plant, French long-lot survey.
OHIO Port Clinton/ Marblehead/Put-in-Bay/Sandusky (Erie)	1812-15 Peace Monument - joint U.S. - British officer burial site, F. T. Stone hydrobiology center, Marblehead light -- treacherous waters, ordinance depot, recreation services, regional amusement - theme park, Toledo strip originally Michigan Territory (Figs 10-3, 10-4).
Ashtabula (Erie)	Major coal port with RR links, major Great Lakes Basin hardwood and products center with export trade, covered bridge area, high church density (Fig 10-5).
Conneaut (Erie)	Grape and wine production, small fishing center, N.E. origin of historic Connecticut-Western Reserve -- surveyed in townships of 25 mi^2 vs. standard 36 mi^2 (Fig 10-6).
PENNSYLVANIA (Erie)	3rd largest Pennsylvania city, a Great Lakes community in mind-set linked most closely with Cleveland and Buffalo -- not Pittsburgh or Harrisburg, electrical equipment and paper products, diversified small industries, historic fort, water and peninsula recreation center (Fig 10-7).

TABLE 10-5 (Cont'd.)

A Great Circle of Selected Domestic and Local District Ports

Ports and Lakes	Activities and Historic Comments
NEW YORK Dunkirk (Erie)	Basin community with a "fight back spirit" in the economic transitions of 1970-'90's, historic county seat of famous Chattauqua Co., grape belt district, 85% harbor use by non-Dunkirk inhabitants, history of solid waste dumping in lake, new waste treatment plant doubling capacity, expanding water plant for industry, non-"smoke stack" expansion, innovative electric generation for municipal heating and cooling, 400 new boat slips constructed in mid-1980's, ice cream, aluminum products and printing ink production, steel finishing activities, out-migration impacts.
Rochester (Ontario)	Innovative photography site, 3rd largest city in NY., major retail sales center and malls, 1st U.S.A. urban indoor mall, art & music center, medical center -- deaf, Susan B. Anthony Home, International Museum of Photography, science-planetarium center, historic public market.
Sackets Harbor (Ontario)	Settled 1801, pre-War 1812 timber and potash trade with Canada -- after 1807 embargo act citizens resorted to smuggling, historic naval shipyard and battlefield of 1812-15 war, military base until post-World War II, oil storage, recreational boat center and services, burial place of Zebulon Pike.

Pioneer settlement in the area began after General Wayne's victory at Fallen Timbers-Toledo and concurrently with Amerind Treaty of Greenville land purchases. Most of the early settlers came from New England, New Jersey, New York and Pennsylvania -- a pattern which continued through northern Ohio, Michigan and into Wisconsin.

The current Erie employment pattern illustrates a diversified economy with a shift from durable goods production to services and government employment. A central business district (CBD) has undergone revitalization and historic-economic consciousness raising.

Hinterland Economic Centers

The individual identification of the score of notable trade ports, on which there have been numerous books written, and four dozen selected local district ports illustrates a variety of economic activities, both historically and contemporarily, within the Basin. This section will focus on several hinterland communities and their economic activities. Perhaps by transferring some of the economic focus away from the large port-shoreline cities, the basis for additional,

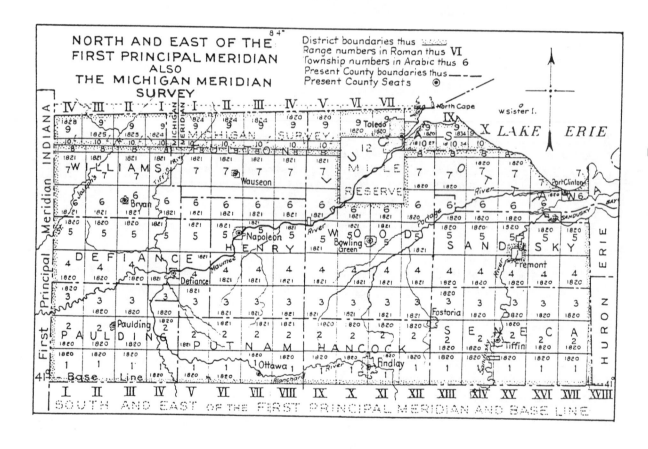

Figure 10-3. Survey of Michigan-Ohio boundary showing the "Toledo Strip" -- Michigan Territory, which ultimately became a part of Ohio. Source: J. V. Bergen, "Sources of Ohio Maps,: *Journal of Geography*, Vol. 81, No. 1 (1982).

Figure 10-4. Michigan-Ohio boundary marker established in 1915 based on a joint cooperative survey with team members including Federal-Michigan-Ohio surveyors. Mile post 71 Point Place -- Lost Peninsula. Only monument in Basin citing a "geographer" by name. (Note: 1915 spelling has been corrected.)

more balanced economic growth and international trade can emerge within the Basin. Each of the port communities are dependent to a great extent on the production of thousands of *hinterland* hamlets, villages, towns and cities. Without reliable production and transportation interlinkage of rural food, forest products, mined ores, quarried stone and out-of-doors open recreation space plus the continual infusion of rural educated people and their ideas into the city, the economic sense of agglomerating people in large cities or ports disappears. The fact is that neither urban nor rural communities can comfortably survive without the other. Perhaps the wars in Vietnam and Afghanistan illustrate the point that to either control militarily the countryside or the cities does not bring harmony to the whole. J. H. Thompson, in the *Geography of New York State*, graphically portrayed urban-rural interdependency using the nodal region concept.

Contemporary Place Descriptions

Place descriptions of communities of the Basin generally can be divided into one of two categories: (1) academic geographies, or (2) traveler guides. Most academic geographies have focused on large cities such as: *Chicago* by Irving Cutler, and Detroit in Lawrence Sommers' *Michigan*. Since the 1930's depression era guides of the Federal Writers Project, several brief summaries of communities have been published. While each of these works brings together in one document useful economic and travel information, the United States published works appear to fall short of the Canadian-Ontario counterparts. The primary weakness is that the USA focus is too narrow, being either biased to water front communities, community history or general county history without linkage to the present, plus frequently, the maps are unreadable. The *Traveler's Encyclopedia: The Maps, The Highlights, The Discovery Guide to Ontario* by the Ontario

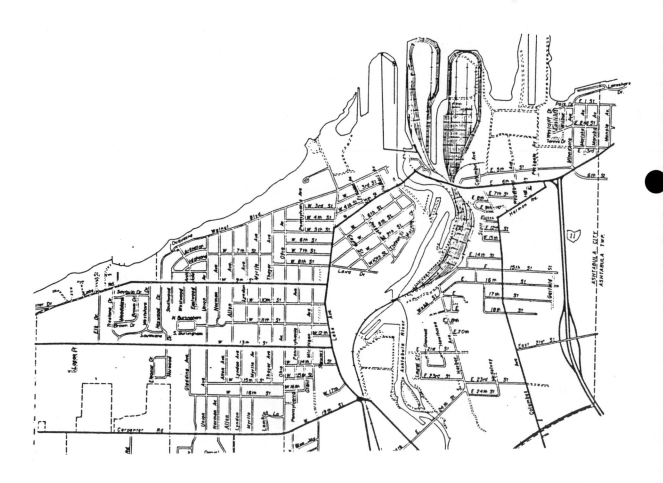

Figure 10-5. Ashtabula, Ohio coal harbor and railroad pattern. Source: Ashtabula Chamber of Commerce.

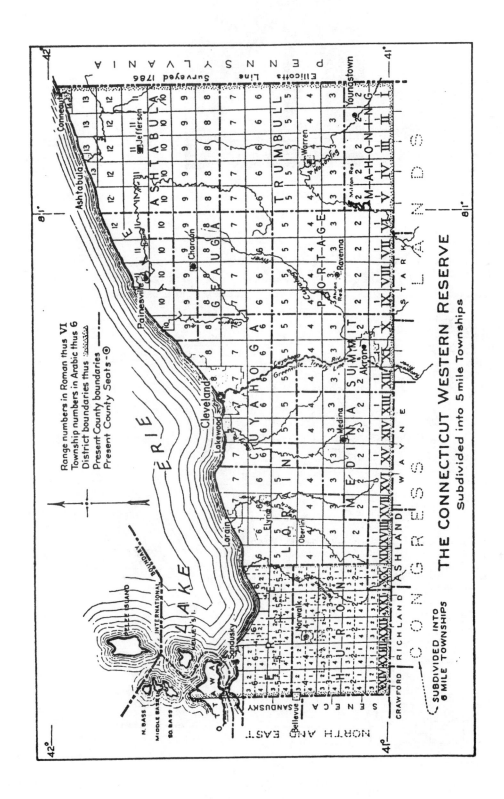

Figure 10-6. The Connecticut Western Reserve with 25 square mile Townships. Note river pattern for divide-portages. Source: J. V. Bergen, "Source of Ohio Maps," *Journal of Geography,* Vol. 81, No. 1 (1982)).

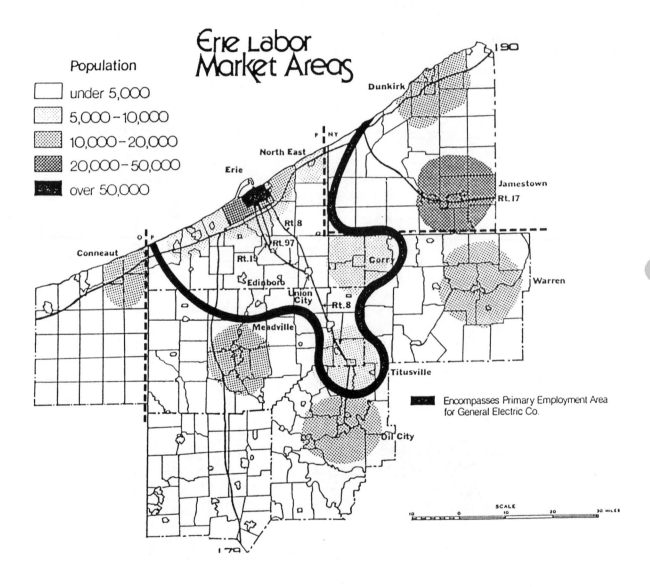

Erie Labor Market Areas

Population

- [ ] under 5,000
- 5,000 – 10,000
- 10,000 – 20,000
- 20,000 – 50,000
- over 50,000

Encompasses Primary Employment Area for General Electric Co.

Dunkirk
North East
Erie
Jamestown Rt. 17
Conneaut
Rt. 8
Rt. 97
Rt. 19
Corry
Warren
Edinboro
Union City
Rt. 8
Meadville
Titusville
Oil City

SCALE
10   0   10   20   30 MILES

Figure 10-7. Example of simple market area map -- Erie County, Pennsylvania, illustrating cross divide interaction. Source: *The Erie labor market Profile*, ca. 1985.

284

Ministry of Tourism and Recreation plus the *Ecotour of the Trans-Canada Highway*, published by the Forestry Service of Environment Canada, can be trend setting examples for fostering comprehensive brief highlight awareness of both historic <u>and</u> contemporary activities of most communities in the Basin.

Advantages of Comprehensive Hinterland Community Survey

Knowledge of what and where people are doing things is fundamental in linking innovations together in a place for economic advancement. Further, what has been previously accomplished at a place can provide inspiration to others in taking a reasonable risk to achieve. If leaders, residents and students are to become more informed on the activities of the Basin and further develop the potential which it holds, time and publishing resources will once again have to be allocated to individually describe the contemporary communities' functions in the present-day and historically. Lacking such information on the "building blocks" of the Basin, the full economic benefits which it holds probably, then, cannot be reached in the transition to the information-service-global village age.

Henry Ford is often quoted as saying: "History is bunk." Yet, it was his vision which established the tourist-education mecca of Greenfield Village which grosses millions of dollars annually based on preservation and interpretation of relatively recent history. Unlike Ford's fabricated Greenfield Village, each Basin community has a life of its own, a uniqueness, an importance in the world scheme of things, or it has potential of becoming an innovative site or significant place beyond its present self. The responsibility for maintaining and preserving a community's heritage rests with the local citizens; however, other levels of government, plus higher education, can assist the tapping of local community potentials. In the preparation of contemporary *historical geographies*, topics such as land-use changes, maps, photography, people with skills who labored to accomplish tasks, and women's roles in the economy can be balanced with those often emphasized --Pioneer era, wars, forts and prominent males. Tenterden, Kent County, England produced a 117-page 8 1/2 by 14 inch booklet in 1967 *Tenterden Explored: An Architectural and Townscape Analysis* which included photographs, a preservation ranking and analysis of *every* home and business plus maps and air photos covering several centuries. The simple black and white volume, with sensitive artist sketches, is available inexpensively to both citizens and travelers plus government planners, to assist in gaining comprehensive knowledge of a community with a sense of place on earth and a vision of its role into the future.[3]

As one traverses the Basin, the landscape reveals a transition towards equality and the worth of a greater diversity of people. For example, the Terry Fox Memorial on the Trans-Canada Highway and the Woman, Man and Child sculptures in the Toledo Portside Park, are lakeshore examples of realistic and symbolized art being used to stimulate thought which also have economic value by making places "nice to visit and -- spend money." In the hinterland, Seneca Falls, New York has become the site of the Women's Hall of Fame which helps to provide international recognition for a seemingly isolated place. At Gaylord, Michigan, Alpine architecture is used to lure people and business to the community. Belding, Michigan has built an international reputation for its 3 on 3 basketball festival -- the Gus Macker.

In analysis, by combining entrepreneurial risk-taking, art, historical geography along with adaptive or traditional industrial-commercial enterprises, a strengthened, expanded Basin economy

[3]Frederick MacManus and Partners, *Tenterden Explored: An Architectural and Townscape Analysis*, (Maidstone, Kent Co., U.K.: Kent County Council, 1967), 117 pp.

can emerge in hinterland communities which can act as a population safety valve to relieve demographic pressures on metropolitan centers.

Table 10-6 selectively illustrates the diversity of important and unique ways the people of the hinterland communities are employed and attempts to stimulate ideas or action for continued development. The selection includes communities ranging in size from hamlets to metropolitan fragmented cities. An attempt has been made to include settlement activities at the edge of the Basin. Institutions of higher education significant in local economies and development are identified separately (Appendix 1).

TABLE 10-6

Selected Hinterland-Inland Communities with
Uniqueness, Historic Note or Economic Comment

Community	Comment
ILLINOIS (Statehood nine years before opening of Erie Canal)	
Sauk Village*	Historic Amerind Sauk Trail, neighborhood shopping center, Plum Creek Forest Preserve.
Chicago Heights*	Industrial suburb (black - Latino), satellite RR terminals, CBD decline related to non-local shopping mall.
WISCONSIN (Part of Michigan Territory 1818-1837)	
Oshkosh	Experimental Aircraft Association air museum and air show.
Appleton/Fox Cities	Fox River combined locks adapted for recreational use, world's 1st hydroelectric plant -- 1882, state's 1st homestead, world's 1st electric lighted home, 1000 Island Environmental Center.
Ripon	Claims birthplace of Republican political party, Wisconsin's largest cookie factory and independent bakery in U.S.A.
Custer/ Nelsonville*	Outstanding view of divide from hill on US-10, Tomorrow R. and millpond site-portage area.
East Central District	See Figure 10-8.
Rhinelander- Oneida County	1st rural comprehensive zoning ordinance in U.S.A. - 1933 (to manage rural settlement and control school bussing costs), town named for RR president not German River.
Hurley	Formerly notorious "Sin City," now licit human services center, a "muck-raked" iron mining town with 29 saloons in 1926 now transforming its image and economy based on tourism.
MINNESOTA (Statehood 1858)	
Floodwood/Swan River*	Historic portage area with several parks, trucking (US-2), dairying, road maintenance, natural resource services.

TABLE 10-6 (Cont'd.)

**Selected Hinterland-Inland Communities with
Uniqueness, Historic Note or Economic Comment**

Community	Comment
Hibbing/Eveleth*	Mining centers, U.S. Hockey Hall of Fame, chop stick manufacturing, peat processing, recreation services.

ONTARIO (Quebec 1774-1791, Upper Canada 1791-1840)

Community	Comment
Beardmore*	Heavy equipment repair, fly-in services, hospital, world's largest snowman, logging, recreation services.
White River	Fly-in services, recreation services.
Sudbury, RMC	Metropolitan centre: retail, education, government industry, and recreation services, Science North, world's tallest chimney, major mining: nickel-copper.
North Bay*	Headquarters Ontario Trappers' Association, major world fur processing centre, lumbering, RR centre, metropolitan area services, military activities, performing arts, theater, boat tours to Dokis Res., Champlain Trail Park, historic entry point into Basin.
Orillia	Resort centre, parks: monument and sculpture (Champlain, Somebody's Mother), Stephen Leacock home (Canada humorist), Trent-Severn Canal lock.
Waterloo/ Kitchener/ Cambridge	Secondary banking and insurance centre, expanding consolidated metro-city services, distilled liquor, shoes, furniture, sausage production, optometry education, sports museum.
Stratford	Shakespeare Festival Theater, art and tourist centre.
London	Model inland community, insurance and banking centre, retail, arts, communications centre, motor vehicle, locomotive, brewing, electrical appliances, light bulb production, food processing, printing household distribution, urban parks, Canada's oldest regular infantry regiment - Wolseley Barracks, two largest employers: University of Western Ontario (4415) and Victoria Hospital (4200).
Peterborough	Trent-Severn Canal lift-lock (1/4 million served annually), recreation services, well-mapped historic route tours, Karartha Downs, serpent mounds, 31% of labor force in manufacturing vs. 20% national average: electrical items, time pieces, outboard marine items, grain processing (oats), Waterspout Park.
Madoc	Contemporary and historic mining centre (gold, iron, marble, talc), agricultural activities, cheese making, cottage district-recreational services.

TABLE 10-6 (Cont'd.)

Selected Hinterland-Inland Communities with
Uniqueness, Historic Note or Economic Comment

Community	Comment
NEW YORK	
Watertown*	RR center for north NY., Fort Drum, 2 hospitals with 924 beds, 50-mile service area, trucking, dairy center, industries: paper goods, thermometers, snow-removal equipment, ski lifts, aircraft parts, optical goods; cross border cable-TV subscription marketing (over 75,000 subscribers in nine Ontario counties).
Syracuse	Events center, state offices of Baptist, Congregational churches, seat of Roman Catholic Diocese, capital of Iroquois Confederacy, American art center, regional medical facilities, retail malls, state fair, production of: machinery, air conditioning, auto parts, pharmaceuticals, and chemicals, average city for test marketing.
NEW YORK (Named for Duke of York)	
Ithaca	South terminus NYSBC, recreation services, 7 falls, agriculture marketing and innovations, business machines, research instruments, largest inland marina in NY, newspaper established 1815.
North Spencer*	Gravel mining, logging, church, and outdoor recreation, UFO landing site (?).
Watkins Glen	Motor vehicle racing and museum, laser images historical drama.
Seneca Falls/ Waterloo	National Women's Hall of Fame, wine making, NYSBC, army depot, world supplier of liquid pumps, knitting mills, chemicals, bronze, TV picture tubes.
Phelps/Palmyra	Sauerkraut processing, Revolution-Pioneer cemetery, silted dam site, agricultural experiment station, founding site and annual Pageant of Church of Jesus Christ Latter Day Saints, NYSBC.
Batavia	Large farm-agribusiness area, insect sprayer equipment production, earth-movers, residual area of draft-horse use, largest dairy herds in NY, adapted large abandoned factory to new small businesses.
PENNSYLVANIA (Headwaters of Genesee River)	
Genesee/Hickox/ West Bingham/ Gold/Ulysses* (N. Potter Co.)	Low capital economic base, agriculture: dairy and potatoes, hunting-fishing (deer, bear, turkey, trout), bedroom communities: linked to Wellsville and Friendship, NY, concerns about road conditions.
Albion*	U.S.A. only manufacturer of 16-foot wood lifeboat and whitewater rapids oars, low bed truck-trailers.

TABLE 10-6 (Cont'd.)

Selected Hinterland-Inland Communities with
Uniqueness, Historic Note or Economic Comment

Community	Comment
OHIO (core area Northwest Territory 1787-1803)	
Akron/Hiram/ Kent*	Historic rubber products center, transportation equipment, non-electrical machinery ordinances, greenhouse plants. Akron means "high" in Greek as in height of land, home of President James Garfield and Great Lakes Tomorrow, Hywet Hall and Gardens.
Bucyrus*	Bratwurst Festival, farm vacation enterprises, hog farming, machinery, transportation equipment, rubber, plastic goods, florescent lamps, hoses.
Tiffin	Highest value diversified crop and livestock area in state, vitreous china bathroom fixtures, clay shooting targets, stone, abrasives, appliances, forging machines, named for Surveyor General and Ohio's 1st state governor.
Findlay	One of last areas to be settled in Ohio Black Swamp, leader in oil gas refining, robotics, beer/pop cans, reclaimed rubber, coated metals, photographic processing, waterbeds, plastic goods.
Lima	Highway travel services, transportation equipment, auto and aero-space parts, machinery, motors, cranes, agriculture-food products, named for quinine from Lima, Peru which aided pioneer settlement.
St. Mary's/ Wapakoneta*	Space exploration museum, home of Neil Armstrong -- 1st on the moon, German ethnic heritage, dam-reservoir, processed meats, vegetables, machinery, presses, rubber products, floor tile, recreation services -- wall of history.
Defiance	Pivotal historic fort remains and park for which it is named, survey point of origin and legal descriptions -- Michigan Meridian, only city in county.
INDIANA (Statehood 1816)	
Ft. Wayne*	1st ranked tourist county in state, world's largest private collection of Abraham Lincoln materials, Johnny Appleseed Park, genealogy center for nation, N.E. Indiana medical services, food processing and distribution, communications -- telephone center, auto parts, truck production, aero-space/optical, magnets, wire, RR, moving vans, insurance Headwaters Pk. planned.
Angola (MT)	Recreation services, courthouse -- jail National Register of Hist. Places, Soldiers' Monument, named for Angola, NY.
Shipshawana (MT)	Major flea market-auction center -- horses, Amish district and newspaper published, agricultural services, pharmaceutical goods packaging, village name means in Potowatomi "vision of a lion."

TABLE 10-6 (Cont'd.)

Selected Hinterland-Inland Communities with
Uniqueness, Historic Note or Economic Comment

Community	Comment
Napanee	Amish and tourist center, recreation-travel vehicles, woodcrafts.
Elkhart (MT)	World center musical instruments, mobile home and recreation vehicles -- 160 companies, Midwest Museum of American Art, pharmaceuticals, electronic components, metal window casings, fire-fighting equipment, RR classification yard.
South Bend/ Mishawaka- "Michiana" (MT)	Adapted millrace to white water recreation and training site, industrial plants: electrical, agricultural, machine tool and construction materials, machine tool and construction materials, government, professional, financial, art, services center, RR., 2nd county in state for tourism -- football, average U.S. city for test marketing.
LaPorte (MT)	World center for washing appliance parts distribution, comfort foam production -- rugs and furniture, cast iron foundry, world class firearms collection, name means in French "The Door" -- to the open forest.

MICHIGAN (New France < 1760, Quebec Province -- Dep't. of Hesse 1774-1791, Upper Canada -- Counties of Kent and Essex 1791-1796, British occupied Territory of Michigan 1812-1814)

Community	Comment
West Bloomfield	Holocaust Memorial Center opened 1984.
Ann Arbor	Headquarters; Historical Soc. of Mich, Mich. Acad. Sci. Arts and Letters, center for manufacturing evolution, continent's largest sports stadium rail passenger service, world class research center.
Lansing/East Lansing	State capital government functions, USA 3rd largest state library, regional retail, medical center, auto production, rail passenger service, cyclotron research, world center for agricultural innovations.
Jackson	Michigan Space Center, auto parts, electronic equipment, largest RR station between Detroit-Chicago, artificial cascades, harness raceway, world's largest walled prison, regional public library, historic innovations hearth, claims birthplace of Republican political party.
Kalamazoo/ Battle Creek	Pharmaceutical products, wine district, muck land farm produce, antique car museum, summer theater, world class hot air balloon meets, world center for cereal production and distribution, innovative community annexation, CBD revitalization.
Grand Rapids	Convention center -- 2nd in Michigan, acculturated core area of Dutch ethnic settlement, G. R. Ford Presidential Museum -- only non-publicly elected US President, diversified economy: industry, finance, medical, government, retail and art, garden bedding plants -- home products production and distribution; symphony orchestra (world's 1st major female music director).

TABLE 10-6 (Cont'd.)

Selected Hinterland-Inland Communities with
Uniqueness, Historic Note or Economic Comment

Community	Comment
Flint	Least diversified SMSA in U.S.A. -- automobile manufacturing dominant.
Big Rapids/Paris	Evolving center for outdoor sculpture, wood products and machinery, extractive resources, regional medical and field utility services, health care innovations hearth, outdoor recreation -- tubing, historic fish hatchery.
Gaylord/Grayling	Attractive Alpine architecture community theme, wood products, quest for "clean industry," recreational services, state military training center, virgin white pine forest park, canoe racing and National Hall of Fame.
Newberry	State mental health center, wood products, recreational services.
Iron Mountain/ Kingsford/ Quinnesec Niagara, WI.	Transitional economy from iron ore and charcoal to paper and wood products with cross state line linkages, part of Green Bay market area, friendly border settlement of legal island ownership in Menominee R. -- all islands above Quinnesec Falls belong to Michigan, below to Wisconsin.
Calumet/Quincy	Sites of deveolping Keweenaw National Historic Park.
Bergland	Outdoor recreation -- hunting/fishing, serves 4 states (MI, MN, WI, IL), small logging activity, elementary school, 4 churches, 8 bars, -- "a quiet place to live."

* indicates community located near edge of Basin/watershed
(MT) = Michigan Territory 1805-1818

SOURCES: Table summaries based on data observed and from offices of regional or local planning and development, chambers of commerce and Sea Grant Programs.

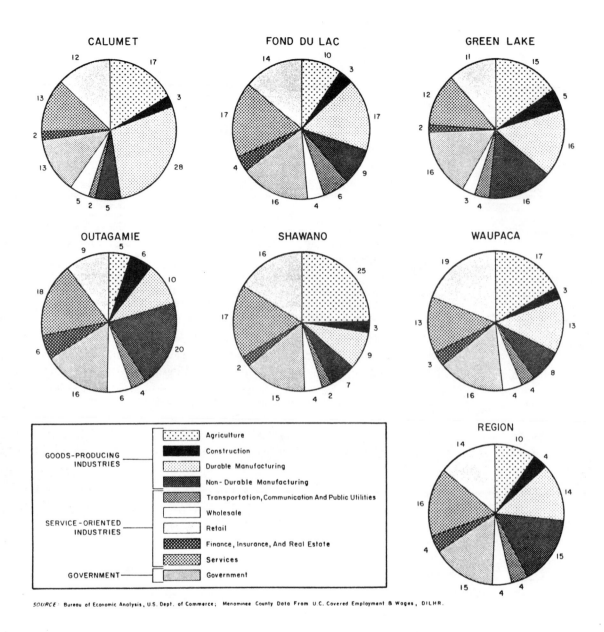

Figure 10-8. East Central Wisconsin economic structure -- employment by activities 1981.
Source: East Central Wisconsin Regional Planning Commission, **OEDP**, April 1981, graphing US Department of Commerce data.

Figure 10-9. Lake freighter repair yard, Sturgeon Bay, Wisconsin.

Summary of Community Tables and Questions

The listing of the 20 notable port cities plus over 100 other shoreline and hinterland communities in the previous three tables could seem to be just another random compilation of places and comments. In spite of the complexity of data, one can gain several insights relating to the people of the Basin, their economic activities, possible transportation links, opportunities for further development and confidence to risk launching an innovative idea or expand media coverage. Based on Tables 10-5 and 10-6, it should be evident that many smaller communities have been successful in developing ideas or have taken advantage of nearby cultural-natural resources to advance them to world leadership ranking. The several publications referred to and the graphic illustrations in the chapter when analyzed, may provide a model for communities in presenting economic and travel data.

Although the data in the listings can stimulate inspiration for further cooperative and world marketing activities, many questions can be raised and reflected upon the future of the St. Lawrence Seaway and how to use it to advance the Basin economy.

1. How important is quality to economic development?

2. How many ports and types should be maintained?

3. What ideas, new products, festivals or economic development activities should be launched in the next year, five years or the decade?

4. How important is it to reduce political-geographic community fragmentation to better compete in a global economy?

5. How much waterfront land in a community should be allocated to port docks, marinas, industry, parks, residential and retail uses?

6. How important is the St. Lawrence Seaway to the Basin economy?

7. How important is the maintenance of the several modes of transportation in the Basin to hinterland- port city interaction?

8. What is the potential value of a written historical geography to a community?

9. Diagram your community and indicate its primary economic activity sites -- if it is a port city list its hinterland communities -- if it is an inland community list its port city and regional center city.

10. Contrast: hamlet, village, town, city and metropolitan city.

11. Select a product or service you would like to market -- where would you locate your activity and why?

12. What actions can be taken to set aside "Intra-regional rivalries?

13. How can the past investments in the development of the St. Lawrence Seaway be protected?

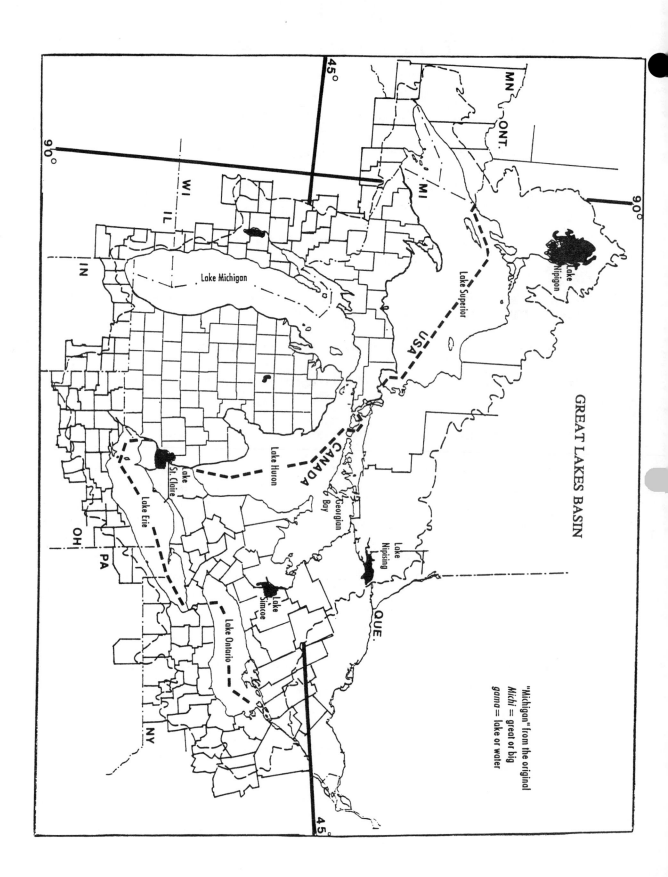

GREAT LAKES BASIN

"Michigan" from the original
Michi = great or big
gama = lake or water

Lake Michigan
Lake Superior
Lake Huron
Lake Erie
Lake Ontario
Lake St. Claire
Lake Simcoe
Lake Nipigon
Lake Nipising
Georgian Bay

MN
ONT.
WI
IL
IN
MI
OH
PA
NY
QUE.
USA
CANADA

45°
90°

296

Far down in the valley the wheat grows deep,
And the reapers are making the cradles sweep...
McGuffey's Second
Electic Reader, 1879

Chapter Eleven

FOOD AND AGRICULTURE IN THE ECONOMY

Without food people starve. Simply put, food is fundamental within an economy and for human survival. To assure support for a sustained population locally and in other places of the world, constant unselfish evaluation of the food land resources is needed by each generation. The critical concerns today, and for the future, appear to be: (1) population growth and relocations in relationship to agricultural land loss which turns food land into unyielding artificial deserts (Fig 11-1), (2) in production, the contamination of the food chain by toxic chemicals, (3) loss of skilled farm operators through political policies with a concurrent concentration of food production into fewer large agribusiness operations.

The Vanishing Farmland: Examples and Comparisons

Economically in the Basin, agricultural activities rank second after industrial production, but ahead of leisure-time services and basic forest and mining activities. Ontario and Michigan comprise the Basin's agricultural heartland. Michigan agriculture ranks as the state's second leading economic activity with an estimated 12-15 billion dollars in total related activities involving nearly a half-million employees. In spite of the high rank and huge financial value, the state has like in other parts of the Basin, become dependent on foods imported from other states and nations. In 1972 Donald Isleib of the Michigan Department of Agriculture (MDA), estimated that Michigan imported about half of its food.[1] By 1982 imported food costs in Michigan rose to an average of nearly 20 million dollars per day.[2] In contrast, as recently as the horse to tractor evolution, the state was self-sufficient in foods except for sub-tropical and tropical spices, condiments, drinks and fruit, which led Clyde Newnon to this 1927 assessment:

> Even though Michigan consumes almost all her agricultural products, the State is
> not only growing her share as compared with other states, but much more than that
> of practically every northern crop...[3]

It was further predicted that "...there are four million acres that can and will be brought under cultivation and made to produce sustenance for a rapidly increasing permanent urban population."[4]

---

[1]*Michigan Agricultural Land Requirements*: A Projection to the Year 2000 A.D., (Lansing: Michigan Department of Agriculture, February 1973), Mimeograph, pp. 1-11.
[2]Richard Struthers and Rosemary Lewando, *The Michigan Food System: Increasing Dependence or Self-Reliance*, Emmaus, Pa.: The Cornucopia Project of Rodale Press, 1982), p. i.
[3]Clyde L. Newnon, *op. cit.*, p. 25.
[4]*Ibid.*, Newnon, p. 21.

Figure 11-1. Continuing apartment building construction on the food land. North edge of metropolitan Detroit, looking towards 19 Mile Road east of Hayes Road. Clinton Township, Macomb County, Michigan.

Unfortunately, the germ of economic weakness which would throw logic and intuition haywire was occurring at the same time. Again the year is 1927.

> Michigan is showing the world that the more we produce, the more we consume, and the more we consume, the richer we become...Michigan knows by experience that the ability to purchase will take care of itself. This has been proven, for is it not a fact that, despite all the yowling of calamity barkers that the American people were headed for the poorhouse because of their extravagance and waste, their wealth has, on the other hand, increased? (author's underlining)[5]

The well-documented Wall Street stock market crash came within two years. Afterwards, in the early 1930's, Michigan's bank failures and closings became turning points toward the national and world Great Depression.

Farmland Gain and Loss Trends

Temporarily, during the immediate decades following the "Roaring Twenties," there was an illusionary surplus of farmland. This was due to the fields, once used for pasture, hay and oats crops for horses, becoming quickly available for other uses. At the same time, crop yields were

[5]*Ibid.*, Newnon, p. 58.

increased by the diffusion of hybrid seed varieties, insecticides-pesticides-fungicides, and by greater plant populations whose rows no longer needed to be based on the width of a draft horse. As a consequence, farm acreage in Michigan declined between 1940 and 1992 by 45 percent.

In 1973 the Michigan Department of Agriculture (MDA) published a *baseline study* of farmland holdings, trends and requirements projections through the year 2000 A.D (Fig 11-2). It was concluded, that if food land losses continued to the year 2000 A.D., the state

> ---Will have 2.5 million acres of agricultural cropland. Were we to arrive at that acreage, our ratio then of four humans to one acre of agriculturally productive land would be substantially higher than the ratio of humans to crop acres in Taiwan today [1973].[6]

Following the release of the Land Requirement Report, the state enacted M.PA 116-1974, the Farmland and Open Space Preservation Act which provided tax rebates to approved landowners who agree not to sell or shift land into non-agricultural uses for a period of ten years. Since enactment, about 1.8 mil ha (4.5 mil ac) have been approved for protection and tax rebates. In analysis, the farmland protection under M.PA 116-1974 is meager even though the agreement period is renewable. Non-farm developers can in certain situations, where land prices are rising fast enough, induce owners to sell by offering to pay any tax penalty.[7] The actual statistical situation in farmland holdings in Michigan may not be fully known; however, losses are observable when one explores the rural-urban fringes. The MDA concluded that to support a population of 10.7 million in 2000 A.D., at least 3.2 mil ha (7.95 mil ac) of pasture and crop land is the minimum food land need. The MDA report bluntly ended with:

> The specific identity of the required minimum of 7,951,256 acres -- some of which must necessarily come from those categories of land acknowledged to be inferior must be performed quickly, and a statewide land-use plan must be adopted which will ensure the continued availability of these lands for agricultural production.[8]

No plan yet has been enacted.

Ontario Foodland Loss

The province has evolved further than any of the Basin's districts in administering local planning and zoning concepts for the overall health and welfare of communities. One of the milestone decisions involving preserving food land and providing for orderly expansion of urban development came in 1973. In that year, the Regional Municipality of Niagara designated several thousand acres of land within an urban development boundary. As a result, following public hearings, which brought out concerns about the planned loss of so much fertile land, 680 ha (1700 ac) were deleted from the proposed urban development area as unique farmland which should be

---

[6]*Michigan Agricultural Land Requirement, op. cit.*, p. 3.

[7]*Grand Rapids Press*, "The Vanishing Land: 3.9 Million Acres of Michigan Farmland Were Lost to Developers from 1959-1982," February 9, 1986, p. A-17; and "Land Act Aids Farmers," December 14, 1983, p. C1. See also Judy Blain "Anguish in Agland." *West Michigan Magazine* Vol. 16, No. 8, August 1987, pp. 28-33; Mike Magner, "West Michigan Farms Endangered", *Grand Rapids Press*, July 14, 1993, p. A1.

[8]*Michigan Agricultural Land Requirements, op. cit.*, p. 10. In 1979 the USDA and MDA definition of a farm was changed to a place which produces $1000 of agricultural sales in a year. Previously the definition was a place of 10 or more acres with 50 or more dollars in sales or a place less than 10 acres with $250 or more in sales.

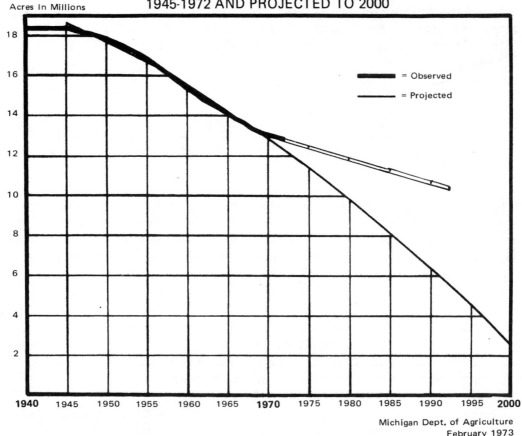

Michigan Dept. of Agriculture
February 1973

Figure 11-2. Trend of land in farms in Michigan 1945-1972 revised to 1992. Source: Michigan Department of Agriculture.

preserved for food-producing purposes. Finally, in a visionary judgment in 1979:

> The Ontario Municipal Board ruled that common sense and the public interest dictated that good agricultural lands should be preserved and only used for urban expansion when necessary and in the absence of poorer agricultural lands; natural justice requires that regard be given to existing development commitments while keeping in mind the common good, financial prudence requires consideration be given to the cost of municipal services existing or necessitated by urban expansion proposals and the burden on the community.[9]

This action provides a contemporary example of what people in the Basin can accomplish to thwart the continued destruction of food land resources (Table 11-1).[10]

[9]Ontario Municipal Board Reports. Re Niagara Planning Area Official Plan Partial Referral (Niagara Falls, Port Colborne, Thorold Urban Area Boundaries). Report 9, Feb. 9, 1979, p. 286.

[10]R. R. Krueger, D. M. Mitchell ed. *Managing Canada's Renewable Resources*, (Toronto: Methuen, 1977), pp. 132-148. R. R. Krueger, "The Struggle to Preserve Specialty Crop Land in the Rural-Urban Fringe of the Niagara Peninsula of Ontario," *Environment*, Vol. 14, No. 3, (1982).

TABLE 11-1

Loss of Niagara Fruit Land 1951-1971

Fruit Crops	Change Acres Lost	Percentage Change
Peaches	-4,800	-34
Pears	- 400	- 7
Cherries	-1,000	-24
Prunes and Plums	-2,600	-55
Apples	- 500	-13
Total Tree Fruits	-9,300	-30
Grapes	+1,500	+ 7
Small Fruits	-1,700	-85
All Fruit Crops	-95,00	-17

Note: Niagara here includes Lincoln, Welland and Wentworth counties.

More recently in a February, 1984, *Update*, "Ontario's Farmland in Perspective - Setting the Record Straight," it was reported that:

> Since 1978, over 70 percent of the municipalities in southern Ontario with agricultural land to look after have incorporated food land protection provisions when developing or revising official plans.

Further, the Ministry of Agriculture and Food (note emphasis on "food") has identified four areas, with unique combinations of soil and climate conditions that are especially important to the food base:

(1)   The Niagara fruit growing region,

(2)   An area south of KH-3 south of Blenheim in Kent County,

(3)   The Leamington & Harrow areas of Essex County, and

(4)   The Meaford to Thornbury area in Gray County.

Foodland Losses -- Vision of the Future

In spite of gains made in the preservation of specialty food land in Ontario and modest steps taken by state governments, it seems that during the foreseeable future there will be continued pressure and losses of critical agricultural-foodland. This observation and concern is based on the following points:

1. The world, nation and Basin population will continue to grow,

2. Stable population in the world is many decades into the future,

3. The freshwater and well-watered arable land of the Great Lakes Basin will become more attractive to people and entrepreneurs as dry land resources become more costly, thus competition for foodland uses will intensify,

4. The present economy based on a mix of free enterprise and government regulation, adapted to population growths, will continue (no stable economy will emerge for many decades),

5. The residents of the Basin will continue to be asked (taxed) disproportionately to support non Basin economic development in the world and other parts of the nations.

Assuming that no one else in the world has an obligation to feed people in a most favored agricultural area of the earth, such as the Great Lakes area; then, the people of the Basin have the greatest obligation for continued food production and preservation actions to feed itself.

Contemporary Record Productions in Perspective

In the present-day economic transformation process, another challenge is to keep in perspective agricultural record production, billions of dollars values and high product rankings. First, somewhat disquieting in analysis, is that "common knowledge" supports the notion that the agricultural section of the economy has relentless "record productions" of most foodstuffs which cause surpluses and economic dislocations. While record productions occur, if Michigan agricultural statistics are representative, they are limited to a very few products and over half (24 of 37) had their record production prior to 1970 (Table 11-2). In keeping dollar values and production ranks in perspective, the most important point is neither of those totals, but per capita yields and food delivery to people. In other words, how much food is there available, assuming an effective transportation and market system, per individual in the world? Seemingly, *the goal of agriculture is to feed people* -- not to be a manipulative value/ranking cog in a fragmented world economy or a hedge against inflation by buying speculatively food land as happened in the 1970's. Table 11-3 compares Michigan and Ontario agricultural systems. In most categories, Ontario agriculture is a larger part of the economy, especially in the Canadian gross national product. The significant difference of concern is in the dollars devoted to food imports where Michigan's dependency on non-local food is even more alarming.

Responding to smoking and health concerns, tobacco marketings in Canada have decreased significantly. Tobacco farms are being shifted to tomatoes and other vegetable production. In addition to the Michigan and Ontario heartland districts, several of the Basin's other districts have developed agricultural or horticultural products which hold high rankings on the continent (Table 11-4).

TABLE 11-2

Michigan Record Production Year and
National Rank for Selected Farm Products 1985 and 1992

	Record Year	Nat'l. Rank 1992	(1880)		Record Year	Nat'l. Rank 1992	(1880)
Field Crops				**Livestock**			
Sugar beets	1990	5		Cattle-calves/	1944/		
Wheat-W	1984	17	(4)	Feed	1973	--	(13)
Hay	1984	7		Turkeys	1968	11	
Corn-grain	1990	8	(12)	Milk-whole	1964	--	
Soybean	1990	10		Milk cows	1945	--	(11)
Dry beans (all)	1990	2		Hogs & pigs	1944	11	(18)
Oats	1946	13	(9)	Chickens	1944	--	
Rye	1919	10	(15)	Eggs	1944	16	
Barley	1918	--	(9)	Wool	1934	--	
Potatoes	1904	10		Sheep	1867	--	(4)
Buckwheat	--		(4)	Trout	--	4	
Hops			(4)	Mink	--	12	
Vegetables				**Fruit**			
Snap beans	1984	3		Apples	1982	3	
Carrots	1984	3		Sw. cherries	1978	4	
Tomatoes Fr.	1943	13		Plums/prunes	1971	3	
Tomatoes Proc	1982	4		Pears	1964	5	
Sw. Corn Fr.	1970	4		T. cherries	1964	1	
Lettuce	1967	9		Grapes	1932	5	
Onions	1965	9		Peaches	1918	6	
Cauliflower	1949	5		Strawberries	1940	5	
Spearmint	1948	6					
Celery	1941	3		**Floriculture**	--	5	
				Honey	--	8	

SOURCE: *Michigan Agricultural Statistics 1985* (record year), pp. 6-7, and *1992* (rank), p. 4, Michigan Department of Agriculture; *Michigan Manual*, 1887(?) (1880 ranking), p. 397; *Agriculture Across Michigan*, Nov. 15, 1989, MDA, p. 1, and Jan. 15, 1991, p. 1.

TABLE 11-3

Michigan-Ontario Agricultural System, early 1980's

	Michigan - USA $	Ontario - Canada $
Number of Farms	63,000	82,448
Acres in Production	7,939,000	11,165,587
Total Acres in Farms	11,400,000	14,923,280
Receipts of Total Crops	$1.8 billion	$1.8 billion
Receipts of Livestock	$1.2 billion	$3.1 billion
Receipts from Fruit	$68,634,000	$104.195,000
Total Cash Receipts	$3.0 billion	$5.0 billion
% National Cash Receipts	2.0%	26.8%
Food Imports	$7.5 billion	$2.5 billion
People Employed	490,000	500,000

Several Sources 1980-84

TABLE 11-4

State/Province and Agricultural Product
Usually in Top Three Rankings

Apples MI NY WI Ont.	Gladioli MI
Asparagus MI OH	Grapes MI OH Ont. NY
Bedding Plants MI Ont.	Mushrooms MI
Carrots MI OH	Plums MI
Celery MI OH	Potted Lilies MI
Cucumbers for Pickles MI OH	Red Kidney Beans MI
Dairy WI NY OH Ont.	Sweet Cherries MI NY Ont.
Dry Beans MI	Tart Cherries MI WI
Geraniums MI	Tomato proc. OH MI Ont.

Based on medical recommendations to lower the consumption of fatty red meat, poultry, lean venison and fish are becoming greater factors in the Basin's economy. To reduce Basin import costs, and shorten the food chain, many fruits and vegetables could be produced and packaged locally in the Basin at lower energy and marketing costs.

Foodland by State/Province District

The previous tables and comments on farmland loss and production comparison provide evidence of the importance and vitality of the Basin's agricultural economy. Attention now can be focused on *where* the key food lands are located and thereby identify the areas in which both rural and urban dwellers can work together cooperatively and democratically to insure the land's preservation for future generations. Each of the farm regions can usually be classified within one of six categories: (1) general -- mixed crops, livestock and poultry; (2) cash crop -- wheat, soybean, tobacco, potatoes, etc.; (3) livestock-poultry; (4) dairying; (5) fruits; and (6) specialty -- maple syrup, mushrooms, birdseed, certified seeds or horse raising (Fig 11-3).

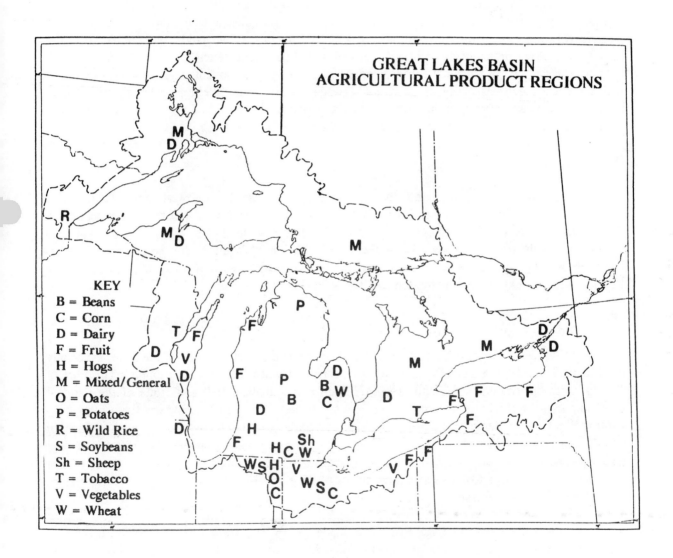

Figure 11-3.

New York

The Watertown Dairy Region, comprising three counties (St. Lawrence, Lewis and Jefferson) is situated on both sides of the divide. This market area annually produces more milk than all other three county areas in New York, New Jersey and Pennsylvania. Dairying yearly contributes about two-thirds of the total local farm market receipts. The Finger Lakes Region is a well-known part of the grape juice and wine making belt which extends west into northeastern Ohio. Today, 100 acre and larger units of grapes are planted by power hole drilling attachments to tractors and are harvested by mechanical pickers. Town names such as Naples and Vine Valley near Lake Canandaugua provide a hint to the origins of the district's people and the focus on the grapevine.

Interspersed within the belt are each of the five other categories of farm operations. Because of the shift in the use of horses for show or racing, and tax shelter write-offs, those engaged in "horsey" activities are frequently not considered agriculturists. Nevertheless, horse operations need feed and bedding, thus the "horse-set" provides a large market for fruit belt farmers who are essentially converting food land back to horse feed land. A century ago most horses were heavy draft breeds such as Clydesdales, Belgians and Percherons, now lighter breeds such as quarter horses, Arabians and standard-breds dominate. In comparison to horse racing which has expanded especially in Ontario (24 wagering tracks to Michigan's 9), the number of ponies has decreased reflecting the aging of the Baby Boom generation. Typically horse operations require an average of 5.1 ha (12.8 ac) of land used to support each horse.

Pennsylvania

Erie County is divided into two physiographic areas by the watershed ridge. The shorelands portion has a growing season only exceeded by the state's most southern counties. Within the Basin district, vineyards, orchards and vegetable farms are most evident and productive. This area has become Pennsylvania's leading market source for grapes and cherries. Dairying is found more often on the Mississippi watershed side of the divide. Overall, Erie County usually ranks among the top ten counties in agriculture receipts.

Ohio

Today Ohio's most important agricultural region is the northern part of the state, especially the Maumee Valley, the Sandusky area for soybeans and wheat plus the lake plain. The Port of Toledo, with the Andersons, Cargill and Mid-State's Terminals, has become one of the nation's most important agricultural marketing and shipment sites (Fig 11-4). As recently as the mid-1960's, eighty-three percent of the northern sub-region's total land area was farmed. Much of Ohio's vegetable production, even mid-winter yields, comes from about 280 ha (700 ac) of land under glass and plastic sheeting. Greenhouse operations are especially concentrated in the northeast lake shore in Cuyahoga County and represent about 25 percent of the U.S.A. total. Temperature control costs and tax pressures are threats to this food production which reduces transportation costs, delivery time and provides a diversity of jobs.

Grape viniculture, on Lake Erie islands and in six lake shore counties of the northeast, forms the western anchor of the grape-wine-juice belt. Muck land of the northwest counties, which was drained in the 1880's, has produced huge crops of tomatoes, onions, celery, sugar beets and other truck-to-market foodstuffs. Of these, tomatoes have the greatest value.

Figure 11-4. Toledo Harbor. Source: Toledo Port Authority.

Chardon, a small town located about 24 km (15 mi) south and 40 km (25 mi) east of Lake Erie and Cleveland, is the focal point of Ohio's maple syrup industry. It also is known as the "Buckle on the Snowbelt" which is formed by lake effect snow which averages 267 cm (107 in). The community also has a state police post --"the Yukon" -- which illustrates the traditional government policy of scattering people-oriented services into rural areas to help diversify and stabilize the economy.

Indiana

The Indiana district of the Basin is not noted within that state as a primary agricultural region. Nevertheless, within the Great Lakes watershed it holds some valuable farmland, especially when compared to the northern half of the Basin. Therefore, while in the state political-economic process the district may be perceived as being most suitable in the short-run for urban-industrial land uses, in the long-run it may well be most practical to protect it as a vital agricultural land area. Major crops of the district include: corn, oats, wheat and soybeans. Limited fruit, grapes and maple syrup activities balance the agriculture economy. The most easily observable contrasting farm landscape feature in the district relates to the picturesque, efficient, well-tended Amish farms. These non-electrified farms, operated with horse power and implements common to the late 19th and early 20th centuries, provide both high yields per acre and a baseline to compare with modern mechanized chemical agriculture (Fig 11-5).

Illinois

The Illinois-Chicago district was once highly productive with vegetable farming and dairying notable. Given urban sprawl, now only a faint residual of land based agriculture remains observable. Food transportation and processing have replaced food raising activities. Yet, on the northern rural-urban fringe, especially in Lake County, some agricultural activities persist, centered on dairying. The situation of near total conversion of a local sub-region to urban uses, as in Chicago, may occur in a broad band along the transportation corridors of the Great Lakes megalopolis, if the vision of Constantinos Doxiadis is realized, without accompanying food land protection (Fig 11-6). The following quote describes in part the conversion process.

> They come to the countryside for cheaper land and lower taxes, sunshine and open spaces, room to relax and enjoy outdoor living, a safe and healthy environment in which to raise their children, a place to grow a garden and perhaps a few chickens, refuge during misfortune, and a home in their declining years.
>
> The change in the rural scene often begins when a farmer sells off a front lot or two or perhaps a front tract of an acre or so. The price the farmer received was high compared with the value per acre of his farm as a whole. Because of this, other farmers are induced to sell off their frontages. More houses follow. Later, entire farms are broken up into tracts and subdivided. The change continues and as the years go by, country roads begin to look like residential streets. As the nonfarm population grows land is bought for gas stations and roadside stores and shops, then for other business and industrial uses.[11]

Wisconsin

The agricultural pattern of Wisconsin is similar to Ontario and Michigan in which the southern half is most favored in soils and climate. Similarly, it is in that part of the district, plus the Door Peninsula, where the greatest concerted efforts are needed to protect the prime food land.

When one drives into the Door Peninsula, where commercial orchards were first established a century ago, one can easily become caught in the web of beauty and exuberance for life which the people pursuing happiness display in the small farm and fishing villages that are converted into summer-tourist season lively art centers. In traversing the area, one can sense from both the pace of life and the orchards of cherry, plum, pear and apple, plus vineyards of grape and the wine cellars, that they are on the other side of Lake Michigan in the vicinity of the Old Mission Peninsula.

In contrast, as one ventures into the mid-section of the district, the robust essence of Wisconsin agriculture is found -- dairying. From the road the foreground is orderly with pasture grasses trimmed by herds of cows while adjoining hayfields have a uniform height of fragrant alfalfa. Periodically, 2-3-4 times a season, the fields are cut and huge 3/4 ton bales of hay dot the

---

[11]Irving Cutler, *Chicago*, (Dubuque: Kendall/Hunt 1973), p. 164 quoting: U.S. Department of Agriculture, *The Why and How of Local Zoning*, Ag. Info Bul. No. 196, Washington: Gov't. Print Off, p. 1.

Figure 11-5. Farmsteads of the 19th Century. Source: *Combination Atlas Map of Lenawee County*. Chicago: Events and Stewart, 1874.

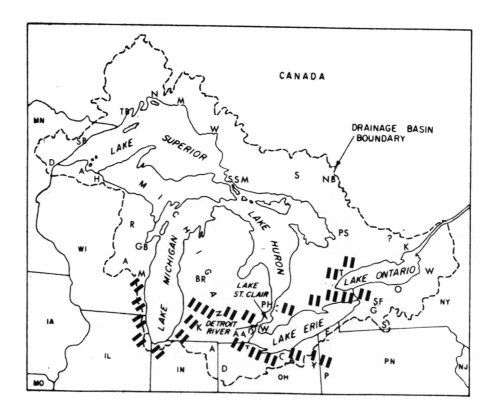

Figure 11-6. Great Lakes Megalopolis (hachured). Base map: Michigan Department of Natural Resources.

park-like meadows waiting to be hauled to farmstead barns or loafing areas. The farmsteads are signaled on the horizon by the lofty, circular, round-top shaft shapes of life-giving corn and haylage silos. Mounting health concerns about fat and cholesterol in diets are significant because nearly eighty percent of the district's agricultural cash receipts come from processing milk, cheeses, creams and butter. The average-sized farm has reached about 80 ha (200 ac) and is continuing to increase. In the post Vietnam war years about one-fifth of the district farms have gone out of operation. The co-operatives, which date from 1872, are also under enormous pressure to adapt to new processes and market demands. Specialty crops of the district include green peas and sweet corn for canning, cranberries and other small fruit plus tobacco which can occasionally be seen with characteristic drying barns. Barley, to support the alcoholic beverage industry, is an important cash crop.

Minnesota

The Minnesota district is primarily non-agricultural. That land that had been in production in 1954 decreased over 40 percent by the mid-1980's. The most important food product from this area is the harvesting of wild rice. Incidental appearances of hay, dairy and beef cattle, plus poultry can be seen on isolated plots of land. In short, the Minnesota district of the Basin and the area extending across northern Lake Superior is dependent on food imports.

Ontario

Southern Ontario is the agricultural heartland of Canada and with its extension into southern Lower Michigan, it comprises a significant part of the heartland of the Basin. Statistically, agriculture is about six percent of the Gross Provincial Product -- seemingly a small, easily overlooked and undervalued segment of the Ontario economy. Yet, that 6 percent is a critical 26 percent of the Canadian total agricultural production. Of further significance is that the 26 percent comes from a relatively small area which also is attractive to alternate economic use pressures. For the most part, Ontario avoids competing in the small grain markets because of the greater dollar reward in the specialized production of livestock, poultry, eggs, milk, tobacco, fruit and vegetables. The southern Ontario farm sub-region cash receipts far exceed the three times larger in area Saskatchewan grain land. Some agricultural production, especially livestock and wine, may shift to US regions of the Basin with the expansion of free trade.

Agriculture in the Canadian Shield

The vast area of the Canadian Shield, in spite of its low population densities and open space, holds a very poor land base for food production. On balance, there are some isolated pockets of rewarding production of dairy foods, cattle, poultry, eggs and root vegetables near Thunder Bay and especially east of Sault Ste. Marie to Sudbury. However, many farms are fragile economic units with an abundance of bare rock, thin soils, boulder erratics, interspersed with swamps and poorly drained land in addition to the short growing season. In analysis, it appears over the long-term the growth of the north will hinge on food from southern Ontario and grain from the prairie.

Michigan

Michigan's primary agricultural lands, like Ontario's heartland and Wisconsin's, are situated in the areas of greatest human concentration. With few exceptions, most of the leading counties in production are sited south of the Bay-Muskegon transition zone. In spite of a large urban population and shift to a greater reliance on imported food, it still ranks in the top 1/3 to 1/2 of dollar values of agricultural production in the nation. Seemingly contradictorily, in attempts to stabilize cherry prices some orchardists' have pulled up mature trees to reduce production. Such short-term actions do not lessen the need to protect fruit belt lands. In national government per capita payments to states and local government, Michigan ranks 30th -- below the national average. Such a payment flow of tax dollars perhaps reflects one of the problems in the Basin's economy, which reliable food production cannot overcome, i.e., in good economic years there is an excess of wealth which can easily be shared with the nation's developing regions. However, in periods of economic downturn and transition, the local capital which could equally well be used for economic recovery continues to flow outside the Basin. Retirement checks, which increasingly flow outside of the Basin, also contributes to a weakening of the Basin's economy which agricultural incomes cannot alone rebalance. Given free trade, export sales are expected to increase, especially with Mexico.

Summary

Agriculture in the Basin is a basic and significant part of the local-regional-national and international economy. Two primary problems in the long-term analysis challenge the brain power and discipline of citizens: (1) loss of high-quality food land to alternate economic uses, and (2) the transition to global food need situations. Of each of the state/province districts within the Basin, Ontario has so far developed the most mature policies for controlling urban sprawl and protecting food land. Imports of food have become increasingly large and divert in times of economic downturn, unnecessarily huge amounts of money from the Basin. Horses, except for Amish-Mennonite operations, are non-farm economic entities for pleasure time riding, racing and tax write-offs which, however, have a direct bearing on food land management. The long-term challenge and choices are in assuring an adequate foodland resource base forever.

1. Why are southern Michigan and Ontario considered the Basin's "agricultural heartland"?

2. What is the economic disadvantage of increasing food imports? How can the people of the Basin lessen the cost of imported food?

3. Why or how did the Basin change in a half-century from being nearly self-sufficient in food production to import dependent?

4. What do you think the reason is that "Food" is in the title of Ministry of Agriculture and Food rather than just "Agricultue"?

5. How can food production land be protected for future generations?

6. Contrast agricultural production in the several districts of the Basin -- especially Ontario and Michigan.

7. What is happening to tobacco land in Ontario -- why?

8. What are the leading agriculturally ranking products of the Basin?

9. How are horse numbers related to demographic changes and potential food production? How have horse breed and types changed in the last century? Why?

10. What are the implications of the similar location of the Basin's agricultural heartland and the "Great Lakes Megalopolis"?

11. What is happening to the food producing land in your area? Is action needed to protect it?

12. Why are the fruit growing areas located where they are?

13. Why is the relatively small area of southern Ontario a disproportionally large part of the Canadian agricultural economy?

14. What may be the combined effects of money flows out of the Basin for imported foods -- either to other states or nations and below average tax dollar returns plus pension check mailings to other places out of the Basin?

15. Contrast Amish farms of the present with typical farm operations of the 19th century.

16. Evaluate northern Indiana as an area which could be ranked high for agricultural/foodland protection within the Basin.

17. Who has the obligation to protect foodland?

"Human history becomes more and more a race between education and catastrophe."

Herbert G. Wells

Chapter Twelve

ECONOMIC RELATIONSHIPS OF THE MILITARY, MASS COMMUNICATION AND EDUCATION

Military, communication and education activities are other fundamental components of the economy, culture and landscape of the Basin and link directly to its people's survival. It is anticipated that the summary of these activities will provide a basis for future decision-making in relationship to both the evolving economy and education needs of the people.

Military Activities, Installations and Economic Relationships

The terms warrior, war chief, war club, and war party allude to the vast amount of human resources which were devoted to aboriginal military affairs and provide a reminder that warfare is not a cultural or racial exclusive. About the time of World War I the former animosities of the Revolutionists and Loyalists were put aside by their descendants to fight together the continual threats to democracy. Now, one can only reflect on the economic costs of wars while quietly reading the long lists of men's names on memorials in seemingly every county seat and on metal tablets at many college campuses. Increasingly now women meet the "call to arms" to risk their lives on the "home front" and, at times, in places where the battle site violence is indistinguishable from "non-combatant" zones. Notwithstanding the pain of global conflicts, wars have great economic stimulus which in the 1940's significantly contributed to ending the hardships of the 1930's depression. Between 1939 and 1945, Detroit became known as the "Arsenal of Democracy." Further, Michigan enjoyed the benefits of receiving the largest number of war contracts of all the states and provinces.

As an "Arsenal of Democracy" the men and women of the Motor City, with their scrap collecting and ration line standing children, produced prodigious amounts of wheeled vehicles and other armaments which poured out of the converted auto factories. Civilian car production ceased between 1942 and 1946. Further, it was not until 1950 that auto production again reached the 1929 level. In mid-World War II Henry Ford boldly established a bomber plant to assembly-line build aircraft at Willow Run. To support that project the Detroit Industrial Expressway (I-94) was hurriedly constructed as the region's first limited access multi-lane highway. That innovation was a major advancement over the USA's first concrete road laid in 1907 at Detroit on Woodward Avenue between 6 and 8 Mile Roads which was poured from hand pushed and lifted wheelbarrows. The extra newspaper editions with six-inch headlines which proclaimed the end of World War II did not include stories of the relocation of the German V-2 rocket scientists to the southern U.S.A.; however, their subsequent research would trigger the need for the Basin to adapt to space-age electronic technologies. During the Korean, Vietnam and isolated conflicts to the present, military spending locally has been the reverse of that of World War II while the proportion of individuals serving in the military from the Basin has remained the same.[1]

Military Installations

A few small and modest-sized military facilities are found at strategic and widely separated places in the Basin including: <u>Michigan</u> -- (1)Detroit: Arsenal, Coast Guard Air Station and Base, (2) Camp Grayling (formerly Ferris), the Army National Guard facility which also serves guard and reserve units of Illinois, Indiana and Ohio, (3) Traverse City Coast Guard Air Station, (4) Selfridge Field Air National Guard Base at Mt. Clemens, (5) Fort Custer Records Office and National Cemetery at Battle Creek, (6) Sault Ste. Marie Coast Guard Base, (7) Veterans Hospital at Allen Park; <u>Wisconsin</u> -- (8) Milwaukee Coast Guard Base: <u>Illinois</u> -- (9) Great Lakes Naval Training Center at North Chicago, (10) Fort Sheridan at Chicago, (11) Glenview Naval Air Station at Glenview and Coast Guard Air Station; <u>Ohio</u> -- (12) Camp Perry at Port Clinton, (13) Ravenna Ammunition Depot in Portage County; <u>New York</u> -- (14) Fort Drum at Watertown, (15) Griffiss Air Force Base at Rome, (16) Seneca Army Depot; <u>Ontario</u> -- (17) Windsor, Lambton, London, Toronto Army Barracks; the North Bay Military Complex; the Kingston Military Complex; and the Royal Military College at Kingston.

Fort Drum Economic Projections.--In 1984 it was announced that an Army Division would be stationed at the 42,906 ha (107,265 ac) fort. Originally, the military site was established in 1908 on land leased by the Chamber of Commerce. The refurbishing project provided modern facilities for troops, dependents and civilian support personnel. Economically, a garrison of 10,700 plus about 10,900 dependents and 2,250 civilian employees can stimulate an estimated economic impact of about one million dollars per day. In the 1990's Fort Drum troops served the Somalia food effort. On the Basin's west side the closing of K. I. Sawyer, the Upper Peninsulas largest employer, and P. B. Wurtsmith Air Force Bases along with the Coast Guard facilities at Muskegon and Grand Haven have caused local stress, as well as, opportunities to adapt to new activities. As military installations are recycled to other uses some toxic and aging ammunition concerns have been raised including sites at the: Muskegon Ordinance Plant, the National Guard Target Range in Grand Rapids, Camp Claybank AAA Range in New Era and the Big Rapids National Guard Range.

The Royal Military College: Bond of the Polar Bears

The Royal Military College at Kingston is the officer training center for Canada. The massive entry arch to the college holds memorial plaques of the fallen of World War I (Fig 12-1). It also holds a clue in the single digit "9" of a unique bond between the cold-weather young men of the Basin.

For decades, November 11th or the Monday closest to it, has been observed as Armistice Day (Veterans Day)/ Remembrance Day to commemorate the end of World War I in Western Europe (November 11, 1918). Yet, for several thousand troops from the Upper Great Lakes states who trained at Camp Custer near Battle Creek, and their combat experienced expert artillery comrades in arms from Ontario and other parts of Canada, the fighting, dying, sickness and

---

[1]"Living Veterans 1950-1983," *U.S. Statistical Abstract: 1985*, Table 576, p. 346, *USSA: 1992*, Table 553, p. 347. "Defense Contract Awards 1981-83", *U.S. Statistical Abstract: 1985*, Table 548 p. 335, *USSA: 1992*, Table 531, p. 338. Breandan O. hUallachain, "Regional and Technological Implications of Recent Build up in American Defense Spending," (Washington, DC: *Annals of the Association of American Geographers*), June 1987, p. 211.

Figure 12-1. Memorial Arch, Royal Military College, Kingston, Ontario. Designed by J. M. Syke. Material: Indiana limestone on a base of Quebec granite, foundation laid June 1923, unveiled June 1924 -- TRUTH DUTY VALOUR. Source: Office of Information Services, compliments of Royal Military College of Canada.

longing for home did not end until mid-1919. The men were the "Polar Bears" who "had to return to remind us that they had ever gone."[2] Formally, they were the American Expeditionary Force to North Russia comprised of about 5500 men of the 339th Infantry Regiment, 1st Battalion 310th Engineers, 337th Field Hospital and 337th Ambulance Company. The Canadian Expeditionary Force of 497 men were of the 67th and 68th Batteries of the 16th Canadian Field Artillery Brigade.

[2]E. M. Halliday, *The Ignorant Armies*, (New York: Harper and Brothers, Publishers, 1960), p. xi. For additional Polar Bear materials see List of Sources -- Polar Bears.

Specifically, the mission of the North Russian Expeditionary Forces remains confused. However, the units ended up fighting the embryo Soviet Army in an area south from the port of Archangel along the Dvina River to Shenkursk and Ust Pedenga before being evacuated. At times during the several skirmishes, only the daring and skill of the Canadian artillery men allowed the less experienced infantrymen and medical/support personnel to escape with their lives (Fig 12-2). In 1929 a commission was sent to the Soviet Union to supervise the recovery and return of the bodies of those men who died and sometimes were hastily buried. Not all the graves were found, but 86 remains were located and reburied in the Polar Bear Plot of White Chapel Memorial Cemetery in Troy, Michigan (Fig 12-3). During the last half-century many other veterans of the "forgotten conflict" have rejoined their youthful comrades in the special plot as a final place of peace and bond.

Figure 12-2. Troops of North Russian Expeditionary Force -- The Polar Bears. Source: Ferris State University Geography Section.

Print and Electronic Media: Ties That Bind

During the several decades of life following formal schooling, the products for continuing education are those of the mass media: newspapers, magazines, radio and television. In addition to being daily sources of information, they provide information outlets for retail marketing and for binding communities together socially (See Letter to Editor Box 2).

```
┌─────────────────────────────────────────────────────────────────────┐
│                              Box 2                                    │
│  ───────────────────────────────────────────────────────────────     │
│                                                                       │
│                        News from the North                           │
│                                                                       │
│  "Could we have some news about Canada in your newspaper?  We moved   │
│  here last summer from Canada and we, as well as hundreds of other    │
│  Canadian students who are studying in Grand Rapids, would love to    │
│  read about some action in Canada.                                    │
│                                                                       │
│  Did you know that people in Grand Rapids think that we Canadians      │
│  live in igloos and wonder if we have microwaves, computers or large   │
│  shopping malls? They think we have winter all year round.  Do they   │
│  know that we have a prime minister named Brian Mulroney?  They say,   │
│  "And who is your president?" The citizens of Grand Rapids would       │
│  benefit a great deal if you could assist in increasing their         │
│  intellect by informing them about a great country called Canada.      │
│  The U.S. is not the only country on the maps!                        │
│                                                                       │
│                                             Letter to Editor          │
│                                             Grand Rapids Press         │
│                                             March 27, 1987             │
│                                                                       │
└─────────────────────────────────────────────────────────────────────┘
```

Further, newspapers, radio and the instantaneous satellite sound and photographic coverage of events fills one of the critical requirements for the peaceful functioning of the emerging "global village."

Newspapers in the Basin

In spite of a long term trend of the loss or consolidation of local newspapers with the resulting lessening of the diversity of editorial content and competitive points of view in *nodal-regions* of the Basin, it can be an indication of a strength of survival and economic adaptation to compete internationally. Reassuringly, an examination of publications or community newspaper stands shows that a diversity of newspaper publication is being maintained. But, access to print publications because of their number, space limitations, mailing costs and library funding systems will continue to provide challenges for writers and purchasers to share knowledge (Table 12-1).

Newspapers on both sides of the international border appear similar in size, layout and variety in mastheads (Fig 12-4). However, two slight variations in distribution occur. In Ontario, weekly newspapers are distributed on Wednesday while Thursday is the usual delivery day in the states. Also in contrast is the printing of a large Saturday/weekend edition in the Province as opposed to a heavy Sunday issue.

TABLE 12-1

Selected Great Lakes Basin Newspapers,
Approximate Circulation (in thousands) 1993
and Change Trend From 1985

Established	Community	Newspaper	1993 Circulation	+ or - since 1985
MINNESOTA				
1892	Duluth	News Tribune Herald	D	60 -
			S	84
1891	Grand Maris	Cook Co. News-Herald	W-M	4 +
WISCONSIN				
1920	Appleton	Post-Crescent	D	55 +
			S	70 +
1915	Green Bay	Press Gazette	D	59 +
			S	85 +
1885	Hurley	Iron County Miner	W-Th	3
1882	Milwaukee	Journal	D	240
			S	490
1890	Superior	Telegram	D	15 -
ILLINOIS				
1847	Chicago	Tribune	*D	735 -
			S	1135 -
1890	Chicago Heights	Star	Th-S	70
INDIANA				
1889	Elkhart	Truth	D	28 -
			S	31 -
1863	Ft. Wayne	Journal Gazette	D	62 +
			S	139 +
1907	Gary	Post-Tribune	D	74 -
			S	87 -
1872	South Bend	Tribune	D	90 -
			S	130 +
OHIO				
1924	Bucyrus	Telegraph-Forum	D	7
1842	Cleveland	Plain Dealer	D	432 -
			S	561 +
1835	Toledo	Blade	D	153 -
			S	215
1905	Wapakoneta	News	D	5 -

TABLE 12-1 (Cont'd.)

**Selected Great Lakes Basin Newspapers,
Approximate Circulation (in thousands) 1993
and Change Trend from 1985**

Established	Community	Newspaper	1993 Circulation + or - since 1985	
PENNSYLVANIA				
1888	Erie	Times	D	40 -
		Times-News	S	83 -
NEW YORK				
1880	Buffalo	News	D	310 -
			S	383 +
1895	Geneva	Finger Lakes Times	D	20
*1815	Ithaca	Journal	D	20
	Rochester	Democrat and Chronicle	S	260 +
		Times-Union (Gannett)	D	83 -
1877	Syracuse	Herald and Journal	D	91 -
1861	Watertown	Daily Times	D	40 -
			S	43
ONTARIO				
1848	Goderich	Signal-Star	W-W	5 +
1846	Hamilton	Spectator	D	115 -
*1810	Kingston	Whig-Standard	D	35
1878	Kitchener	Kitchener-Waterloo Record	D	79 +
1845	London	Free Press	D	120 -
1907	North Bay	Nugget	D	23
1867	Orillia	Packet and Times	D	11 +
1853	Owen Sound	Sun Times	D	23 +
1884	Peterborough	Examiner	D	25
1853	Sarnia	Observer	D	24
1912	Sault Ste. Marie	Star	D	26
1908	Sudbury	Star	D	28
1903	Thunder Bay	Chronicle Journal	D	30 +
1892	Toronto	Star	D	523 +
			Sat	800 +
			S	527 +
1844		Globe & Mail	D	183 -
1918	Windsor	Star	D	86
MICHIGAN				
1835	Ann Arbor	News	D	54 +
			S	66 +

TABLE 12-1 (Cont'd.)

Selected Great Lakes Basin Newspapers, Approximate Circulation (in thousands) 1993 and Change Trend from 1985

Established	Community	Newspaper	1993 Circulation + or - since 1985	
1862	Big Rapids	Pioneer	D	6+
1831	Detroit	Free Press	D	622 -
1873		News	D	482 -
		News/Free Press	*S	1215
1876	Flint	Journal	D	106 -
			S	124+
1890	Grand Rapids	Press	D	147+
			S	191+
1837	Jackson	Citizen Patriot	D	38
			S	42
1837	Kalamazoo	Gazette	D	64
			S	81+
1855	Lansing	State Journal	D	70+
			S	93+
1846	Marquette	Mining Journal	D/S	18
1864	Menominee	Herald Leader	D	4
1857	Muskegon	Chronicle	D	47
			S	52+
1872	Port Huron	Times Herald	D	30+
			S	38+
1859	Saginaw	News	D	57
			S	66+

*Oldest/largest   D = daily   S = Sunday   W = weekly

SOURCE: Individual Newspapers and *The 1985 IMS/AYER Directory of Publications*, (Ft. Washington, Pa.: IMS Press, 1985). *Yale Directory of Publications and Broadcast Media* (formerly Ayer), (Detroit: Gale Research, Inc., 1993).

Radio and Television

During the three-quarters of a century since KDKA in Pittsburgh initiated reliable radio broadcasts, the home *ensemble* of outdoor features which support electronic communication has successively changed. By the 1950's, outdoor wire antennas for crystal sets and large vacuum tube radios were being replaced by multi-pronged housetop television antennas. Today, planning and zoning commissioners throughout the Basin debate the wisdom and content of ordinances to regulate the placement of earth-satellite dish antennas.

Figure 12-3. Polar Bear Monument, White Chapel Memorial Cemetery, Troy, Michigan.

Figure 12-4. Selected mastheads of Basin newspapers.

323

Perhaps the greatest potential that the earth-satellite dish antenna holds for the Basin is its use to facilitate the expansion of cross border *mean information fields*, i.e., areas in which an individual or group of people are aware of a new idea via communication. Scrambling signals which would enhance private corporate finances also limits the spread of knowledge in a democracy. Perhaps a noteworthy point is that taxpayers and governments provided the original risk capital to launch space-age communication. As cable TV and earth-satellite systems are increasingly used in the Basin, from a geographic point of view, there still is a lag, especially by advertisers, in pinpointing at least by community route number and prefix phone number area code, the location of business activity they tout. With modern communication and advertising, "where" continues as important as "what and when."

Education

One of the advantages of locating business activities in the Basin is its concentration of educated people and their continuing quest to advance the level of knowledge through research, schooling and innovative activities. The economic commitment to education is visible in the pattern, density, variety of institutions and libraries.

Education: An Historical Background

In 1787, the United States Northwest Ordinance, which governed all but the New York and Pennsylvania districts, stipulated that:

> Religion, morality and knowledge being necessary to good government and the happiness of mankind, schools and the means of education shall forever be encouraged.

Thus, public schools are common within the Basin and complement religious group affiliated schools. With some contrast, the descendants of the "Always Loyal" Ontarioans have also innovated an education system no less apparent on the landscape.

Ontario Education History.--As early as 1807 Ontario passed a public education act; however, until the mid-19th Century, schooling at the lower levels was provided by churches. Section 93 of the 1867 British North American Act (BNA) mandated education as a province responsibility. Since 1979 responsibility for all levels of schooling is placed in the Ministry of Education. Between the years 1966 and 1981, the number of local school boards was reduced from about 1600 to 193. In comparison, school district consolidation in Michigan decreased the number from 4532 in 1952 to the current 575. Attendance is compulsory in the Province between ages 6 and 16 and optional for 5 year olds. Until the last half century, higher education was nearly the exclusive domain of the universities. Now, community colleges and other institutions account for about forty percent of post-secondary student enrollments. In the first half of the 20th Century, women numbered only one out of four university students. Now there is a near balance between the sexes, but most are enrolled in the social and health sciences.

Funding and Costs

In Ontario, the public, nine Roman Catholic Separate School Boards and other church related schools receive grades K-12 funding through the local and provincial government. In the

USA private schools, including those operated by religious groups, are funded primarily by independent private sources; however, under U.S.A. law, school busing is provided to both public and private students. An unresolved legal question still exists concerning transportation of students between public and private schools for shared time instruction in, generally, math and science classes. Economically throughout the Basin, since school busing, hot meal programs, special entitlement programs and consolidations, the local school districts have become the largest employer of many communities. It remains to be researched how the variations in funding policies affect the number, density and types of schools plus home schooling found in the Basin.

Busing Costs

Locally transportation is usually the second ranked line item cost in a school budget. The following example illustrates the economic significance of lengthening a school bus route a half mile (.8 km). Thinking holistically, as a student of geography:

1. It costs about $1.75 (US) per mile to operate a school bus.

2. To operate a school bus one-half mile twice per day, such as to serve a new residence, costs $1.75 per day.

3. Figuring 180 days in a school year (180 x $1.75), $315 per school year is needed for an extra one-half mile of daily service.

4. As an alternative, at $10 per book, 31 books could be purchased -- enough to supply one classroom for 3-5 years.

In analysis, it may be concluded that the money to forever encourage education is available, but that it is tied up in meeting costs dictated by other land-management choices.

In the years after the post-World War II Baby Boom, massive school consolidation and specialized school transportation programs brought an end to the commonplace one-room schoolhouses which now appear on the landscape as churches, granaries, homes, museums or as decaying buildings (Figs 12-5 to 12-7). Replacing the pioneer schools are sprawling one-story flat-roofed brick and glass facilities located on central sites or outlying areas depending on community sentiment and available space. The land space demand, whether for a consolidated or urban school district, has also witnessed a dramatic change. Whereas less than 2 ha (5 ac) were adequate for a 500-pupil junior high building in 1918, the spatial needs to serve 500 pupils expanded to 12-16 ha (30-40 ac) in the 1960's. The Basin's newest school architecture shows a trend toward much less glass and natural ventilation to save on fuel costs. Undoubtedly, another evolution of school architecture is needed to blend openness and energy efficiency.

Public Schools and Religion Innovation

The answer to the question, how to provide religion instruction to public school children separate from the public school ground, but during the school day, has vexed many school community leaders and concerned parents. On the streets of Fort Wayne, Indiana, one can observe an innovative solution -- the Weekday Religious Education Mobile Classroom. In 1948 a decision of the U.S. Supreme Court triggered the Associated Churches of Ft. Wayne innovation of mobile classrooms to allow for religion instruction off public school grounds. Presently there are ten classrooms adapted from the shells of mobile homes in operation. They are moved to sites near

LITTLE RIVER SCHOOLHOUSE - SCHOOL SECTION LAKE PARK

Figure 12-5. Little River School, a post Civil War racially integrated school. Located in School Section Lake Park, Morton Township, Section 16, Mecosta County, Michigan. In the pioneer era, funds from land sales in Section 16 of all survey townships were used for elementary education -- thus the term "school section." Source: Tina Hartley, artist. Use with permission.

the public elementary schools and parked on the street. The sites have utility hook-ups and meters independent from the public schools. Students in the third through fifth grades, with written permission, may attend a half-hour religious education session, once per week. Participation averages 83 percent. The Ft. Wayne mobile religion classroom program is believed to be the largest and longest running program in the Central States.[3]

Higher Education

The people of the Great Lakes have created one of the richest treasuries of higher education institutions and libraries in existence on the earth. The summary table of 325 diverse and unique institutions by state/province and type of degrees granted only hints at the wealth which can be tapped or lost in making economic and education choices of the future (Table 12-2).

[3]Letter from Marie Boyce Goodrich, Religion Teacher, Ft. Wayne, January 24, 1986.

Figure 12-6. Amish school built 1986, Austin Township, Mecosta County, Michigan.

Figure 12-7. Centennial School, now residence -- built 1876 -- Section 2, Raisin Township, Lenawee County, Michigan. Exterior woodwork refashioned under direction of Henry Ford in 1934 one-room school restoration project.

TABLE 12-2

Summaries of Institutions of Higher Education in the Great Lakes Basin

ONTARIO:

13	Universities (Grant Doctorate)
1	Military College (Grants Master's Degree)
19	Colleges of Applied Arts and Technology (Grant Master's Degree)
4	Agriculture Colleges (Grant Master's Degree)
21	Pre-University, Community and Other Colleges/ Institutes (Grant Associate's Degree)
58	Total

MINNESOTA:

1	University (Grants Master's Degree)
1	College (Grants Master's Degree)
1	Community College (Grants Associate's Degree)
3	Total

WISCONSIN:

4	Institutes, Colleges and Universities (Grant Doctorate)
8	Schools, Colleges and Universities (Grant Master's Degree)
11	Institutes and Colleges (Grant Baccalaureate Degree)
7	Institutes and Colleges (Grant Associate's Degree)
30	Total

ILLINOIS:

9	Schools, Institutes and Universities (Grant Doctorate)
6	Seminaries and Colleges (Grant Doctorate or 1st Professional Degree)
13	Institutes, Colleges and Universities (Grant Master's Degree)
5	Colleges and Universities (Grant Baccalaureate Degree)
12	Colleges (Grant Associate's Degree, includes 8 campuses of City Colleges of Chicago)
1	Other
46	Total

INDIANA:

1	University (Grants Doctorate)
2	Seminaries (Grant Master's and 1st Professional Degree)
4	Universities (Grant Master's Degree)
6	Institutes, Colleges and Universities (Grant Baccalaureate Degree)
7	Colleges and Universities (Grant Associate's Degree)
20	Total

OHIO:

7	Colleges and Universities (Grant Doctorate)
3	Seminaries and Colleges (Grant Master's Degree)
4	Universities and Colleges (Grant Master's Degree)
11	Institutes, Colleges and Universities (Grant Baccalaureate Degree)

TABLE 12-2 (Cont'd.)

Summaries of Institutions of Higher Education in the
Great Lakes Basin

11	Colleges and Universities (Grant Associate's Degree)
2	Others
38	Total

PENNSYLVANIA:

2	Universities (Grant Master's Degree)
1	College (Grants Master's Degree)
3	Total

NEW YORK:

7	Universities (Grant Doctorate)
2	Seminaries (Grant Master's or Doctorate)
13	Institutes, Colleges and Universities (Grant Master's Degree)
5	Colleges (Grant Baccalaureate Degree)
16	Institutes and Colleges (Grant Associate's Degree)
43	Total

MICHIGAN:

9	Colleges and Universities (Grant Doctorate)
18	Colleges, Academy, Center and Universities (Grant Master's Degree)
3	Seminaries and Bible Schools (Grant Master's Degree or 1st Professional Degree)
19	Colleges (Grant Baccalaureate Degree)
29	Public Community or Junior Colleges (Grant Associate's Degree)
5	Business or Church Related Colleges (Grant Associate's Degree)
1	Private Law School (Grants 1st Professional Degree)
84	Total

SUMMARY

50	Institutions: Doctorate (non-Seminary)
66	Institutions: Master's Degree (non-Seminary)
16	Seminaries: Master's Degree, 1st Professional Degree, Doctorate
80	Institutions: Baccalaureate Degree*
109	Institutions -- Pre-University, Junior, Community College: Associate's Degree**
4	Other
325	Total

* degree based on four or five years of study
** certificates and degrees based on at least two, but less than four year of study

Appendix 1 provides a listing of the institutions and location. That listing may prove valuable because it includes only institutions which are actually located in the Basin and by that situation have a vested interest in the Great Lakes watershed.

Analysis of Types and Names of Institutions

The names of many institutions of higher education clearly convey their mission such as: Alfred College of Agriculture and Food Technology, Illinois College of Optometry, Goshen Biblical Seminary, Bellin College of Nursing, Medical College of Ohio-Toledo, Canada Memorial Chiropractic College, Lutheran School of Theology, Davenport College of Business and Milwaukee School of Engineering. However, especially in the United States, the use of the terms university-college-school-institute less reliably convey missions and levels of educational development. Regardless of naming confusion, the Basin supports and benefits from several well-known, highly respected world-class universities including: Chicago, Cornell, Michigan, Michigan State, Northwestern, Notre Dame, Queen's, Rochester, Syracuse, Toronto, Wayne State and York. Important now and for the future, is that each institution holds a potential to become *world class* in some attribute.

Libraries, Maps and Equality

To gain the full potential benefits of education requires an extensive system of libraries to store and retrieve previously acquired knowledge. The Great Lakes Basin has within it some of the largest and finest libraries and map collections within the world.

Higher Education Libraries

In 1844, two years after Father Edward F. Sorin established in a small log structure the embryo University of Notre Dame at South Bend, Indiana, he declared:

> When this school, Our Lady's School, grows a bit more, I shall raise her aloft so that, without asking, all men shall know why we succeeded here. To that lovely lady, raised high on a dome, a Golden Dome men may look and find the answer.[4]

Indeed the University has succeeded and the "Golden Dome" dream has become a distinctive and identifying landmark of the campus. The dome rises 61.7 m (206 ft) and is topped with a 198 kg (440 lbs) cast iron gold leaf gilded 5.6 m (19 ft) statue of "Our Lady." In comparison, the gold cross of the Sacred Heart Church steeple rises to 68.9 m (230 ft) as the campus' highest man-made structure. These *iconographic* symbols well denote the Judeo-Christian dominant religious culture of the contemporary society of the Basin. The 14-story Memorial Library, 63 m (210 ft) high with 38,000 m^2 (430,000 ft^2) of air-conditioned space with seating for 3,000, is the third highest structure on the campus and one of the tallest college libraries on the continent. Especially important is the library's archives which is comprised of four million documents pertaining to the study of American Catholicism. In bound volumes and book titles, it ranks about eighth in comparison to other Basin universities (Table 12-3, Fig 12-8). In addition to the unique holdings of the Notre Dame Library archives, the Indiana district of the Basin possesses one of the foremost genealogy collections in the Fort Wayne Public Library. In a step towards non-violent conflict

---

[4]"The Murals of Luigi Fregori (1819-1896)," Dept. of Info. Services University of Notre Dame @ 1985, 1 sheet 2 pages typed mimeographed. See also Thomas J. Schlereth, *The University of Notre Dame: A Pictorial History*, 2nd ed., (Notre Dame: University of Notre Dame Press, 1977), p. 60.

Figure 12-8. University of Notre Dame Memorial Library. The mural "Words of Life" is 39.6 m (132 ft) high and 19.4 m (65 ft) wide. It consists of 7000 pieces of granite of 81 varieties from 16 nations with 171 different finishes. The library is exceeded in height on campus by the cross of Sacred Heart Church and the Golden Dome statue of Our Lady atop the Administration Building. Source: Public Information, University of Notre Dame.

TABLE 12-3

Major Great Lakes Basin Libraries

University of Toronto*	University of Michigan*	Cornell University*
University of Chicago*	Northwestern University	Center for Research Library
Wayne State University	Michigan State University	State University of NY - Buffalo
University of Western Ontario*	University of Notre Dame	York University
University of IL at Chicago	University of Rochester	Syracuse University
Queen's University	Kent State University	University of Waterloo
University of Guelph	Case Western Reserve	Newberry Library

* Major map collections.

Source: *The Chronicle of Higher Education*. August 26, 1992, citing the Association of Research Libraries.

resolution, an Institute for International Peace Studies has been established at Notre Dame. About eighteen carefully selected students, three each from the former Soviet Union, United States, China, France, United Kingdom and Japan, study together focusing on the question, "What kind of world do you want to live in?".[5]

Map Collections

The University of Western Ontario, located in London, typifies the traditional public regional university with picturesque durable stone buildings which has quietly developed into an internationally important center for learning and research (Fig 12-9). Also in the tradition of great universities, the library is a prominent, accessible, treasure of the campus. What sets the University of Western Ontario's library apart from others is its huge cartographic holdings. The 1977 World Directory of Map Collections described it as "the largest university map collection in Canada." The collection, administered by the Department of Geography, holds over 175,000 map sheets, 1300 atlases and more than 20,000 other special items. There is a complete set of 10,000 topographical maps of Canada of all scales and 40,000 topographical sheets of the United States Geological Survey plus navigational charts for both nations. Twenty percent of the map collection users are from outside the university.[6]

[5]"Focus with J. P. McCarthy and Father Hesberg," WJR 760-AM Radio, Detroit, April 22, 1986.
[6]Interview with Serge Sauer, Map Curator-Geographer, summer 1985; "A LaCarte -- A Look at Western's Map Library," N. L. Nicholson, *Alumni Gazette*, Vol. 57 No. 3, 1981, pp. 6-8.

Figure 12-9. Middlesex College -- University of Western Ontario. The similarity of architecture to the Christian church maintains a symbolic link to its antecedent pre-1881 Huron College which was a training site for Anglican evangelical holy orders. One of the university's 40 charter signers included Isaac Barefoot, a full-blooded Mohawk. Source: University of Western Ontario, University Relations and Information.

Equality Between the Sexes in Education

Representative of the Basin's well-established, liberal arts, church affiliated, traditionally academically selective, small city located, compact campus colleges with a world vision and spirit, is Heidelberg College, located in Tiffin, Ohio, 160 km (100 mi) south of Detroit (Fig 12-10). The college's earliest history is atypical because its first graduating class, after being funded in 1850 by the Reformed Church of the U.S., included a female. Another of its students, but not a graduate, was the first female admitted to the Ohio Bar of Law. Thus, Heidelberg College is one of the earliest non-sex discriminating institutions in the U.S.A. and is the third oldest higher education institution in Ohio. Heidelberg also illustrates the coalescing of Protestant religious denominations. In 1934 the Reformed Church in the United States merged with the Evangelical Synod of North America to form the Evangelical and Reformed Church. In 1957 those churches merged with the Congregational Christian Churches as the United Church of Christ (UCC), the denomination which presently administers the college. UCC in Ontario refers to the United Church of Canada which came into being in the mid-1920's as a result of the merger of segments of Methodist, Presbyterian and Congregational denominations.

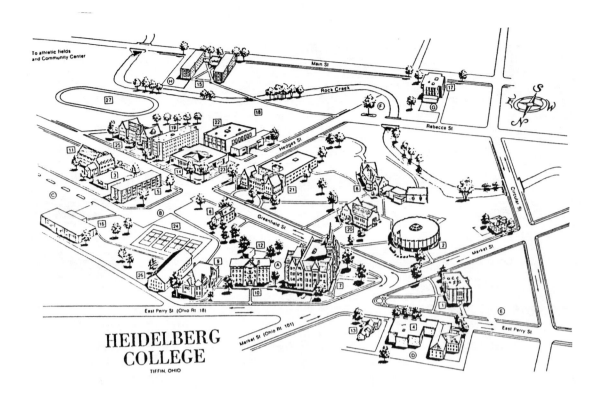

Figure 12-10. Heidelberg College, Tiffin, Ohio -- note the library (circular building) at flag pole dominates the entrance to campus. Source: Heidelberg College Resource Book 1985, 1986.

Summary

Necessary elements of the contemporary economy include military activities, print and electronic communication, and educational pursuits. The Basin has located within it a variety of Army, Coast Guard, Navy and Air Force installations; however, economically more money flows out of the Basin in support of military activities in other parts of the USA than is generated in production and employment within the Basin. The Royal Military College is the major institution devoted to the development of leadership training. In military history, the Basin troops that fought together in the North Russian Expeditionary Force (1918-1919) created a little-known bond between some of the men of the region. Because of extensive cross border and intra-basin linkages so far developed, advertisements need to be more specific in identifying codes, road locations and community names. Perhaps the greatest recent historical and potential strength of the Basin rests with the 325 higher education institutions, several of which have reached world-class status. The Basin's potential is further strengthened by its several major libraries, specialized map collections, archives and diversity of art institutions. The Basin has been a leader in the development of community based, opportunity, technical-professional education accessible to most, regardless of sex, age or race. The notable opportunities to further develop the higher education programs in the Basin exist, especially related to international relationships, watershed management and peace maintenance or conflict resolution.

Reflections and Self-Learning: Chapter 12

1. Map the military installations in the Basin. What are their economic contribution to the Region?

2. How do the national/continental patterns of defense spending effect the Basin's economy? -- How has the pattern of spending changed since 1940?

3. Describe the "Polar Bears".

4. Evaluate the Letter to the Editor of the Grand Rapids Press.

5. Why is "Where" important in advertising?

6. Evaluate the "Religion, morality and knowledge" stipulation in the 1787 Northwest Ordinance to the present.

7. Investigate how school consolidation has affected where children in your area go to school and their community loyalties.

8. What is the relationship of increased land needs for school sites and bussing to schooling costs?

9. Write a story on what it would be like to go to school in an Amish community or at the turn of the last century.

10. Evaluate the present-day make-up of higher education institutions in the Basin. How can inter-institution communication and pooling of Great Lakes Basin knowledge be further developed. Which institution would you like to visit? -- Why?

11. Map the location of the major Basin libraries and centers for map holdings, or gather additional data to rank the libraries by size of holdings.

12. What education problems or concerns need to be further researched and possible suggestions for solutions made?

13. Compare the campus map, the library photo and college building to your campus.

14. If you sat on a local zoning commission -- what standard(s) would you set for neighborhood installation of TV dish antennas? Consider: size, set backs, painting and lettering.

*"We in Michigan are confronting a great challenge.
We hold in trust a resource that has become the envy
of the world."*

*James J. Blanchard
Governor of Michigan
State of the Great Lakes 1985*

Chapter Thirteen

CHALLENGES AND CHOICES NOW

Near the core of the region's culture is the quest to make life more comfortable and an ethic to organize society to enable the coming generation to have a less rugged life than the parent one. In the process of attaining technological advancements, a comparatively high standard of living, higher per capita incomes and more leisure time; the number of people in the Basin has increased at a higher rate than the world as a whole. As a result, the natural environment has been significantly altered and its quality has deteriorated in places to the point of being life threatening.[1]

The challenge and choice now, if the traditional ethic is to be adhered to, is to become knowledgeable concerning the conditions of the Basin's culture and environment. Then, make educated choices -- sometimes boldly at great risk -- to assure the future well being for ourselves and yet unborn generations while at the same time preserving Truth, Goodness, Beauty, Liberty, Equality and Justice.

The focus of this chapter is to describe (1) several conditions which are contributing to environmental stress, (2) the relationship of women in shaping the landscape, (3) crime, as an important economic and environment factor, plus (4) to illustrate the complexity of local service regions.

Contemporary Environmental Stresses

Barbara Walker in her 1983 comprehensive one-volume work, *The Woman's Encyclopedia of Myths and Secrets* cites the need for a re-examination of Western religious beliefs and impacts on nature in resolving the challenges of environmental stress.

> ---the traditional Christian attitude toward nature has given sanction to exploitation
> of the environment by science and technology and thus contributed to air and water
> pollution, over-population and other ecological threats.[2]

In examining Judeo-Christian traditions associated with the environment of the Basin, Genesis 1:28 is a critical passage which relates to choices made within the culture. Salient in analysis is that the passage does not direct humans to over-fill or over-replenish its population nor in taking "dominion," for humans to deplete flora and fauna to extinction. The Land's Directorate of

---

[1] *The Detroit Free Press*, Nickie McWinter, "Some Community Needs Can't Wait for the Future," June 6, 1986, p. B1. *Los Angeles Times*, M. N. Schaaf, "Dreaming About Lost Orange Groves," March 27, 1986, Part V, p. 2.

[2] Barbara G. Walker, *The Woman's Encyclopedia of Myths and Secrets*, (San Francisco: Harper and Row Publishers, 1983), p. 849.

Environment Canada *Stress on Land*, is a profusely illustrated comprehensive study on the long-term implications of "... what Canadians are doing to their land resource."[3] In most cases the stresses described are cause for concern in all districts of the Basin. Environmental stress may be defined as any adverse impact on people, the earth's resources which affects land or water use, property value or land/water capability.

Acid Rain: Origins, Affected Areas and Remedial Actions

The Ontario research facility at Dorset has received world-wide attention for its innovative investigations of acid precipitation and testing of over 3000 Ontario lakes for acid sensitivity. Similar concerns about acid in rain and lakes are found in New York, Wisconsin, Minnesota and Michigan. Acid rain's major detrimental effect appears to be the increasing lake acid levels to the point at which usually desirable forms of aquatic life cannot survive (Table 13-1).

Forests and other plant life are also affected directly through their leaves and the soil. The major economic concern, especially for the northern part of the Basin, is the harm to the leisure-time fishing industry. Much of the acid rain, although it is contested, is from high-sulphur coal and long-range air transportation of pollutants across state and the international borders. To monitor such relationships, in 1978, the Canada-United States Research Consultation Group on Long Range Transportation of Air Pollutants (LRTAP) was established. The area most sensitive to acid precipitation lies not only within the Great Lakes Basin but also in the Arctic watershed, the southeastern and northwestern U.S.A. plus many other areas of the world. In New York, Sweden and Ontario experimental liming, 22.5 kg (50 lbs) per surface acre annually, is being tested to determine if an artificial method of acid buffering can be successful.[4] By the mid-'80's, Michigan thermal electric production had shifted 103 of 107 plants to using low sulphur coal from the Great Plains. Ontario has instituted a Least Emissions Dispatch Systems (LEDS) whereby Ontario Hydro generates power from its cleanest plants first. When one looks beyond the Basin edge for contemporary long-term solutions, it is disquieting. While copper smelters in the U.S.A. are required by the Clear Air Act to reduce emissions of sulphur, new smelters are being located in Mexico near the border. The Environmental Defense Fund organization scientists predict that emissions, if uncontrolled, will exceed the reductions made at the smelters in the western states.[5]

Discussion Point.--In the post-Chernobyl atomic plant/radioactive cloud wind-drift era, it is advocated that the time has come for international regulation of toxic substances. In the 1960's and '70's, uniform national standards were legislated at the federal level, now trans-national standardized laws are needed to assure global and local survival. How can international toxic pollution safety standards be developed and enforced?

[3]Canadian Government, *Stress on Land*, Folio 6, (Ottawa: Lands Directorate, Environment Canada, Ottawa, 1983), 323 pp.
[4]Ontario Government, *The Case Against Acid Rain: A Report on Acidic Precipitation and Ontario Programs for Remedial Action*, (Ontario: Ministry of the Environment, October 1980 with 1982 Supplement) p. 20.
[5]"Science Magazine Reports of Acid Rain," *The Woodlands Forum*, Vol. 2 No. 2 (Fall 1985) and Vol. 3, No. 2 (Summer 1986), The Woodlands, Texas: The Woodland Center for Growth Studies, p. 18 and p. 3.

TABLE 13-1

Biological Effects on Fish of Low pH Waters

pH	Effect
6.5 or less	Continued exposure results in significant reductions in egg hatchability and growth in brook trout. -- *Menendez, 1976*
6.0	Coupled with high CO_2 concentrations pH's below 6.0 can adversely affect certain trout species. -- *Lloyd and Jordan, 1964*
5.5-6.0	Rainbow trout do not occur. Small populations of relatively few fish species found. Fathead minnow spawning reduced. Molluscs rare. -- *EPA, 1972*
5.5	Declines in a salmonid fishery can be expected. -- *Jensen and Snekvik, 1972*
5.0-5.5	Very restricted fish populations but not lethal unless CO_2 is high. May be lethal to eggs and larvae. Prevents spawning of fathead minnow. Lethal to some mayflies. Bacterial species diversity reduced. -- *EPA, 1972, Scheider et al, 1975*
5.0	Tolerable lower limit for most fish. -- *Doudoroff and Katz, 1950, McKee and Wolf, 1963*
4.5-5.0	No viable fishery can be maintained. Lethal to eggs and fry of salmonids. Benthic fauna restricted. -- *EPA, 1972*
4.5	Flagfish reproduction inhibited and general activity of adults reduced. -- *EPA, 1972*
4.0-4.5	Fish population limited -- only a few species survive (pike). Flora restricted. -- *EPA, 1972*

SOURCE: Ontario Ministry of the Environment, Extensive Monitoring of Lakes in the Greater Sudbury Area 1974-76, Ministry of the Environment (Ontario), 1978, p. 20. References shown in italic. Cited in: *The Case Against Acid Rain*, (Ontario: Ministry of the Environment, 1980 and 1982 Supplement), p. 20.

Radioactive Waste The residents of the Basin are challenged with making choices on how to dispose of both low and high levels of radioactive materials. These wastes, which can vary from slightly traceable radioactivity to those with hazardous lifetimes of a few hours to 24,000 years, can threaten both human life and the food chain. In the years since Hiroshima no agreeable solution has emerged on how to store the waste, partly out of fear, and proven hazard. However, five options generally are scientifically and politically discussed:

1.   Place wastes in a "suitable" container and dump them into the ocean,

2.   Bury wastes in a shallow landfill, mark with signs and fencing,

3.   Bury wastes in a general sanitary landfill,

4.   Place wastes in inactive mines,

5.   Reprocess waste into a less hazardous form.

At present, the Elliot Lake area holds the bulk of uranium tailings. Temporary storage of radioactive wastes usually occur at plant production sites. So far Ashland, Wisconsin has been the most active sub-region in taking local action to establish nuclear-freeze zones.

Perhaps another option to reduce and eliminate long-term atomic wastes could be the halting of nuclear production with a massive unprecedented effort -- the social equivalent to world war --to innovate and diffuse an environmentally safe energy supply or to rebalance population to a survival level not requiring extensive pollution.

Trash Disposal--Landfills

Regardless of what it is called, an average 1-3 kg (2-6 lb) per person of throw away material is produced each day. The rate varies depending on the size of a community, per capita income and commercial activities. Small cities tend to generate about half as much waste as a large metropolitan city (Table 13-2).

TABLE 13-2

Average Waste Produced Per Person in 38 Communities
Ontario: 1980*

Population	Number of Municipalities	Average Waste Generation Per Person	
		kg	lbs
>250,000	8	1.04	2.28
100,000-250,000	8	1.09	2.39
50,000-100,000	8	0.95	2.09
25,000-50,000	8	0.95	2.09
<25,000	6	0.86	1.89

* Based on sample survey for residential and light commercial solid wastes only.

SOURCE: Michael Hare, *Municipal Solid Waste Generation for Ontario*, (Toronto: Ontario Waste Management Advisory Board, 1982), 1982. Cited in *Stress on Land*, (Environment Canada), p. 37.

Very early in time communities established open dumps which were common until after World War II. Their associated features were unattractive such as: rats, scavenger birds, bears, blowing debris, smoldering fires, stench, uncontrolled run-off or leachate which contaminated ground and surface water and wasted land. Because dumps were commonly located close to the edge of town on the east or downwind side, as community populations increased, and zoning was weak, dumps were leveled and converted to residential uses. Home-owners of such sites subsequently have had to contend with cracked foundations and lowered property values. Michigan's hazardous wastes may average about one million tons yearly. Milwaukee has long been a leader in recycling sanitary waste as fertilizer.

Most communities in the Basin continue to view trash as waste rather than a resource. Therefore, comprehensive systems of recycling have not been institutionalized. The one notable exception is the beer and soda bottle deposit laws of Michigan and New York. However, with the increased sales of wine coolers and non-carbonated boxed drinks, litter has proliferated at the expense of recycling.

Sanitary landfills, when managed wisely, can provide community recreation areas including picnic, tennis and ball fields such as at the huge Kodak plant complex in Rochester. By adapting fill methods to above ground refuse cells, "Mt. Trashmores" on plains can be created for wintertime sliding "hills" and local vistas such as at Riverview, Michigan. On the other hand, in addition to the food chain disruption, landfills associated with Michigan's 1973-1974 PBB (poly brominated biphenyl) episode have had prolonged adverse impacts both on scattered farm sites and at those professionally prepared in Gratiot and Kalkaska counties.[6]

Women and the Landscape

Mary E. Mazey and David R. Lee in their monograph, *Her Space Her Place: A Geography of Women*, ask in the title of Chapter One, "Where is She?".[7] In the case of the Great Lakes Basin the answer is "nearly everywhere" -- the home-highway-CBD, running the Chamber of Commerce or a real estate office and as presidents of universities. The leadership role of women is especially apparent in New York with the preserved homes of Susan B. Anthony of Rochester, and Elizabeth Cady Stanton plus the National Women's Hall of Fame in Seneca Falls. Community sculptures also reveal respect for women (Figs 13-1 to 13-3).

How the landscape of the Basin would be different had sex roles been other than they were during the last three centuries is difficult to conclude. For instance, flowers and other yard plantings in suburban and upper-class neighborhoods or planter boxes in lower-class areas are usually explained by women on the American side of the Basin as female attempts to "soften" the landscape of men -- especially "harsh straight lines," "uniform colors" and "hard building materials." On the other hand, Ontario business districts and parks, no less designed by males, tend to have significantly more trees, strips of well-manicured grass and flowers carefully tended by male gardeners. More cross border research is needed to determine whether flowers and landscaping are most determined by culture or sex (Fig 13-4).

---

[6]Joyce Egginton, *The Poisoning of Michigan*, (New York: W. W. Norton and Co., 1980). Wayne Kiefer, Central Michigan University, Mt. Pleasant, "Gratiot County Landfill Michigan's Foremost Toxic Waste Site," (unpublished manuscript) Michigan Academy of Science Arts and Letters (Kalamazoo: March 26, 1982).

[7]M. E. Mazey and D. R. Lee, *Her Space Her Place: A Geography of Women*, (Washington, DC.: Association of American Geography, 1983, 84 pp. with bibliography.

Figure 13-1. Susan B. Anthony home -- Rochester, New York.

Figure 13-2. Somebody's Mother - Orillia, Ontario.

342

Figure 13-3. Sculpture Laura Smith Haviland, Adrian, Michigan. Pioneer in slave freedom, education and health care.

Figure 13-4. Windsor park with profusion of flowers typical of Ontario.

Female Place Names and Maps

Throughout the Basin place names are predominantly male (Steven Court or Tecumseh), gender neutral (Plymouth or Sarnia) or physiographic terms (Detroit, Redford or Thunder Bay) rather than female names such as Elizabeth Court, St. Mary's River, Notre Dame or Bertha Goodison Hall. Even when a female gains prominence, maps may not perpetuate her family name. Ann Arbor and Anna Howard Shaw provide an example. Ann Arbor, named for the wives of its two founders, has endured as a place name, while Shaw Creek has not.

Why No Shaw Creek?.--The Reverend Anna Howard Shaw, M.D. has a background similar to many pioneer Americans. As a child she migrated with her family from Great Britain to Massachusetts and subsequently joined the great mid-19th Century westwarding flow of people into the interior of North America. Shaw came to the wilderness of Green Township, Mecosta County, Michigan, in 1859, as a girl of twelve with two older sisters, two brothers age 20 and 8, and her mother. However, her father and other brothers remained in Lawrence, Massachusetts to earn and send money to the female led younger part of the family. Shortly after the six Shaws arrived at their rude log cabin (no door, windows, chinking or floor) which was laid-up the previous summer by her father and brother, the 20-year old brother became ill and returned to Massachusetts, leaving the young women and lad to fend alone among the wolves and bear. Water at first was drawn from a nearby creek. Later, Anna dug the family well as one of her outside of the house chores.

By the time of her death in 1919, she distinguished herself in many ways: (1) at age 15 she was a two dollar per week one-room school teacher, (2) in 1880 she became the first woman ordained as a Methodist Protestant Church minister after graduation from Boston Theological Seminary in 1878, (3) in 1885 she received a Doctorate in Medicine from Boston University, (4) in 1888 she joined Susan B. Anthony as a close associate and Chautauqua lecturer for the National Women's Suffrage Association (NWSA), (5) she was a vice-president at-large of the NWSA from 1892-1904 and served as president 1904-1915, (6) she lectured with former U.S. President W. H. Taft in Europe in support of world peace and the League of Nations, (7) in 1919, near death, she became the first living woman to receive the highest U.S. Civilian presidential citation -- the Distinguished Service Medal. Prior to her death she became assured of the passage of the 19th Amendment (Women's Suffrage) to the U.S. Constitution. In 1983 she was one of thirty women initially selected for recognition in the Michigan Women's Hall of Fame, Lansing[8].

In spite of her record of service, leadership and international recognition, Shaw Creek, near her pioneer homestead, a 3rd order stream of the Muskegon River and Paris Creek tributary, no longer appears on contemporary maps to honor her or her family name (Figs 13-5, 13-16).[9]

Criminal Activity and a Quality Environment

Crime has become a major factor in the daily and financial lives of the people of the Basin. The total cost of crime is not known and estimates vary. Some estimates suggest that it is

[8]In 1988 as part of its Bicentennial of the United States Constitution observances, the Big Rapids, Mecosta County community raised a life-size statue of Anna Howard Shaw on its Community Library grounds within the original plat of the city.

[9]Shaw. *op. cit.*, 338 pp. Fran Harris, *Focus Michigan Women 1701-1977*, (Lansing: Coordinating Committee of the National Commission on Observance of Women's Year, 1977), pp. 38-40. Nancy Crawley, *Grand Rapids Press*, "Big Rapids Remembers," February 13, 1986, p. C4.

equal to the open economy. It is estimated that the cocaine addicts of metro-Detroit with other drug abusers, contribute to fifty percent of the state's homicides, eighty percent of burglaries and property crime, plus up to 10 billion dollars in economic losses to businesses, schools, and government through untimely death, thefts, inept job performance, absenteeism and drug rehabilitation programs[10]. An initial analysis of the statistical crime data confirms citizen feelings that Ontario is a safer place to live and travel. Several factors contribute to a less violent situation in Ontario including: (1) gun control, (2) a tradition of respect for authority, (3) a court system which tends to be more consistent in punishing crime, (4) a justice system which functions more speedily, and (5) organization of police units (Table 13-3).

TABLE 13-3

Major Index Criminal Offenses for Michigan and Ontario
1966, 1976 and 1982

Offense		1966		1976		1982	
		Total	Per 100,000	Total	Per 100,000	Total	Per 100,000
Murder	M	365	4	1,001	11	870	9
	O	70		182		184	2
Rape	M	1,844	22	3,281	36	4,083	44
	O	177		474		614	7
Robbery	M	12,423	145	30,241	332	24,470	264
	O	1,316		4,323		5,646	65
Assaults	M	10,641	125	24,154	265	28,952	313
	O					46,362	532
Burglary	M	72,333	850	51,207	1,661	162,457	1,759
	O	35,520		83,976		108,940	1,250
Theft Motor Vehicle	M	27,612	324	55,688	612	61,252	663
	O					24,866	285
Larceny	M	153,895	1,808	321,192	3,528	326,283	3,531
	O					98,527	1,130
Total Crime Index	M	279,113	3,279	586,764	6,445	615,423	6,661
	O					764,461*	8,771*

*Ontario Total includes: attempted murder, arson, weapons offenses, prostitution, other sex offenses, theft under $200, possession stolen goods, fraud.

SOURCES: *Michigan Statistical Abstract 1984*, pp. 269-270; *Ontario Statistical Abstract 1984*, pp. 722-723.

[10]*Detroit Free Press*, "Power Keg," July 1, 1986, pp. A1, 16. *The Grand Rapids Press*, "20 Years After the Great Riot," July 12, 1987, p. A 18.

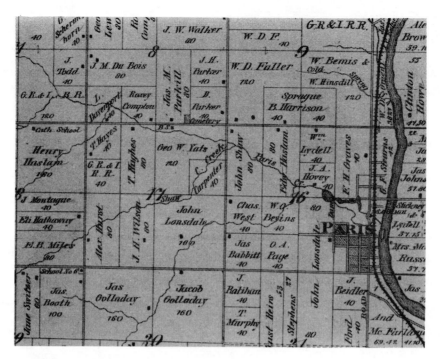

Figure 13-5. 1879 County Atlas -- map showing Shaw Creek. Source: E. L. Hayes, *Atlas of Mecosta County*, Philadelphia, C. O. Titus Co., 1879.

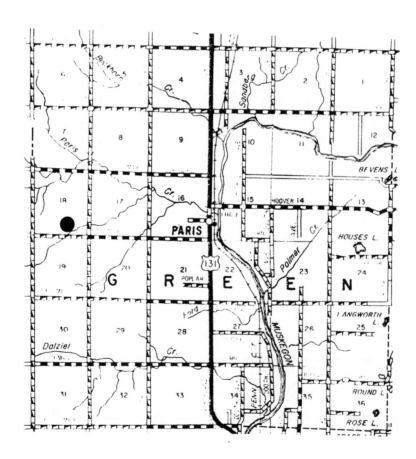

Figure 13-6. Present-day county map without Shaw name. Source: Michigan Department of Transportation.

Police Forces and Unit Organization

One of the significant differences between the United States and Canada in crime fighting and delivery of police services is in the division of forces into units. Michigan, alone, has about 510 police reporting agencies including sixty-seven State Police post units (Table 13-4).

TABLE 13-4

Number of Michigan State Police Posts and Police Reporting Agencies by Regions

Police Area	Number of State Police Posts	Type of Reporting Agency	Number of Police Agencies
Detroit Area	9	Michigan:	
East Michigan	11	Cities/Villages	361
South Michigan	11	County Sheriffs	83
West Michigan	11	Townships	56
North Michigan	12	Special	9
Upper Peninsula	13	State Police	1
Total	67	Total	510
		Ontario:	
		Ontario Provincial Police (OPP)	17
		Metro-Region Police	36
		Village/Town Police	91
		Total	144

SOURCE: 1976 Uniform Crime Report, (Lansing, Michigan: Department of State Police), p. 7. Michigan Official Transportation Map. (undated ca. 1992). Ontario Government, ministry of the Solicitor General, Annual Report, 1981.

In comparison, Ontario has 144 reporting units, even though the total Michigan (23,500) and Ontario forces are somewhat similar in size. Between 1962 and 1981, through unit consolidation, Ontario reduced its municipal police units from 278 to 127. The total units for the United Kingdom, the *cultural hearth* for both countries, is less than fifty.

Pattern of Crime

In actual numbers of crimes committed, large urban cities and areas along the major highway corridors account for the greatest number because of the greater population and mobility which freeways offer. However, the highest percent growth in total index crime in recent years has occurred in the central and north parts of the Basin. Regardless of area or sex, most deviant activity is concentrated in the 15-30 age group (Fig 13-7).

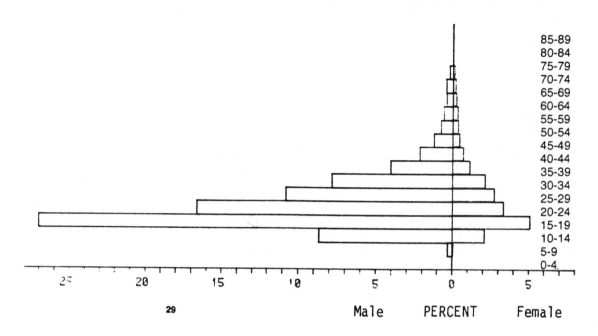

Figure 13-7. Total index crime (murder, rape, robbery, assault, burglary, larceny, motor vehicle theft and arson) arrests by age/sex 1984 -- Michigan. Source: Michigan Uniform Crime Report.

Prisons and Correction

One of the end results of the criminal justice system is the sentencing of individuals to prison. In recent years, the concept of isolation has been to both protect society from criminals and to reform their behavior. As a result, now there are only two prisons by name in the Basin: the State Prison of Southern Michigan (the largest walled criminal institution on the continent) and the Ontario Prison for Women (Table 13-5). To support the corrections effort, about 13 people per 10,000 population are employed in comparison to about 25 per 10,000 engaged in community protection and apprehension of criminals (Tables 13-6 and 13-7).

In comparison to other state/province districts of the Basin, Illinois and Ontario have concentrated the serious criminal facilities in Chicago and Kingston respectively. Contrary to some emotional concern, neither city has seemingly suffered economic stifling as a consequence of criminal facilities. Similarly, Jackson, Michigan, in 1986, was able to gain "All-America City" status. In Kingston, a university campus is within a short walk to the Women's Prison and the Kingston Penitentiary is adjacent to the Canadian Olympic water craft training harbor (Fig 13-8). Where to site criminal facilities, which costs frequently over $22,000 per inmate annually to operate, continues to be debated in many localities. Similarly, how to prevent crime and correct it remains a challenge. Perhaps closer analysis of the entire Basin system would be beneficial.

TABLE 13-5

Prisons and Correctional Facilities
Great Lakes Basin -- 1985

ILLINOIS
Crossroads Community Correctional Center (CCC)   Chicago
Jessie Ma Houston CCC   Chicago
Metro CCC   Chicago
Salvation Army CCC (Male, Female)   Chicago

INDIANA
Indiana State Prison   Michigan City
Westville Correctional Center   Westville

MICHIGAN
Federal Correction Institution   Milan
Huron Valley Facility (Male, Female)   Ypsilanti
Kinross Correction Facility   Kinross
Marquette Branch Prison   Marquette
Michigan Dunes Facility   Holland
Michigan Reformatory   Ionia
Muskegon Correctional Facility   Muskegon
Phoenix Correctional Facility   Northville
Riverside Correctional Facility   Ionia
State Prison Southern Michigan   Jackson

MINNESOTA
Federal Prison Camp   Duluth

NEW YORK
Albion Correctional Facility   Albion
Attica Correctional Facility   Attica
Auburn Correctional Facility   Auburn
Orleans Correctional Facility   Albion
Rochester Correctional Facility   Rochester
Watertown Correctional Facility   Watertown
Wende Correctional Facility   Alden

OHIO
Lima Correctional Facility   Lima

ONTARIO
Collinsboy Institution   Kingston
Joyceville Institution   Kingston
Kingston Penitentiary   Kingston
Prison for Women   Kingston
Regional Treatment Center   Kingston
Montgomery Center   Toronto
Warkworth Institution   Campbellford

PENNSYLVANIA
None

TABLE 13-5 (Cont'd.)

Prisons and Correctional Facilities
Great Lakes Basin -- 1985

WISCONSIN	
Federal Correctional Institution (CI)	Oxford (Adams Co.)
Green Bay CI	Green Bay
Oshkosh CI	Oshkosh

SOURCES: National Directory Law Enforcement Administrators; Canadian Almanac and Directory 1986.

TABLE 13-6

State and Local Police and Corrections Employment
Per 10,000 Population: 1983 and 1988

State	Police		Corrections	
	1985	1988	1985	1988
Indiana	21.0	22.1	9.5	12.2
Illinois	33.0	33.2	10.1	13.7
Michigan	22.8	25.4	10.6	17.3
Minnesota	18.8	19.9	8.9	10.2
New York	34.3	37.0	19.9	29.1
Ohio	22.4	23.0	8.8	12.4
Pennsylvania	24.0	23.9	8.6	12.3
Wisconsin	24.7	26.6	9.5	10.8
East North Central	25.5	26.6	9.7	13.6
Mid-West	24.7	25.6	9.5	13.2

SOURCE: *Statistical Abstract of the United States 1985*, p. 176 and 1992, p. 191.

Service Regions: The Complexity Explosion

The two decades after World War II have usually been named the "Baby Boom" period. Perhaps just as fitting for those years could be the "complexity explosion" based on the rapid changes technologically and socially, plus the change needed in conflict resolution as a result of atomic power. Nonetheless, people of all ages of the past also found themselves living in stressful situations and under demeaning social-political systems including unstable food supplies, rampant diseases, witch-hunts, inquisitions, slavery, fluctuation in climate, forced migrations, conscription to fight in barbaric wars, corrupt political and justice systems, uncertain employment, unscientific explanations of nature and the universe, inequality and inaccessible education systems. Thus, to longingly peer into the past does not seem realistic nor reveal a simple, tranquil haven to wish for its return. Rather, now seems to be the very best of times to be alive, in spite of present-day

TABLE 13-7

Crime Rate by Type for Selected Large Cities: 1990
(per 100,000)

City	Crime Index Total	Violent Crime*	Property Crime**
Chicago	---	---	8,220
Detroit	12,132	2,699	9,493
Milwaukee	9,299	1,000	8,299
Cleveland	9,115	1,818	7,297
Toledo	9,610	1,064	8,546
Buffalo	8,893	1,608	7,286
Rochester	11,039	1,237	9,802
Akron	7,845	1,159	6,686

*Violent crime = murder, forcible rape, robbery, aggravated assault.
**Property crime = burglary, larceny, vehicle theft.

SOURCE: *United States Statistical Abstract*, 1992, p. 182.

Figure 13-8. Women's Prison with College of Education of St. Lawrence University in background -- Kingston, Ontario.

stress. Even though these may be the "best of times," the apparent need and demand for mental-social-human services has increased rather than decreased during the "age of invention." Social complexity can be seen on the landscape of the Basin in artists' attempts to turn "junk" into valuable pieces of art and in the variety of buildings staffed to deliver human services to: the physically and mentally handicapped, senior citizens, dependent children/families, abusers of controlled substances, the unemployed, those desiring birth control information or devices, probationees/parolees, plus children's services for those abused, orphaned, needing foster care, or day care, as well as 24-hour "hot lines" for emergency psychiatric intervention, detoxification and other services such as unmarked safe houses.

Proliferation of Non-Uniform Service Regions

In the quest to provide human services, there has been created throughout the Basin a profusion of non-uniform, seemingly randomly bound service regions (Figs 13-9 and 13-10). Sometimes service area boundaries are found to be the same, such as in Wisconsin where Health and Social Services Regions plus Vocational Rehabilitation Regions coincide. Some states identify a county area by a number derived from their alphabetical listing. None-the-less, a problem of place orientation exists beyond the constantly varying ways of identifying counties or of bounding local regions. In the Michigan-Wisconsin border area, there are varying sub-region names given to the same county. For example, Florence County or county number 19 in Wisconsin, is in the *Northern Region* for Health and Social Service/Vocational Rehabilitation, *Bay-Lake Region* for Planning, *District Seven* of the Division of Highways, *Rothchild Unit Area 80* of the Department of Revenue-Manufacturing Division, *Lake Michigan District* of the Department of Natural Resources and *Area One* for Soil Conservation Service Personnel.

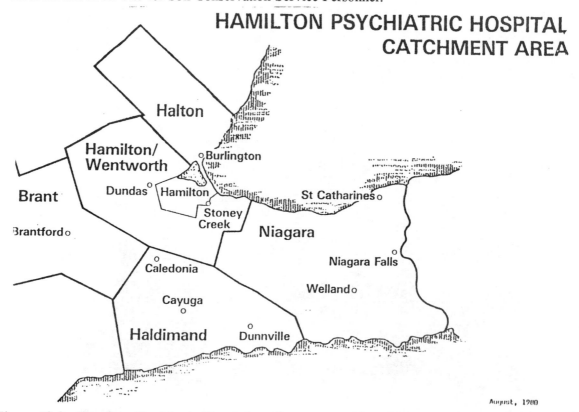

Figure 13-9. Hamilton Psychiatric Hospital catchment area 1985. Source: Ontario Ministry of Health.

352

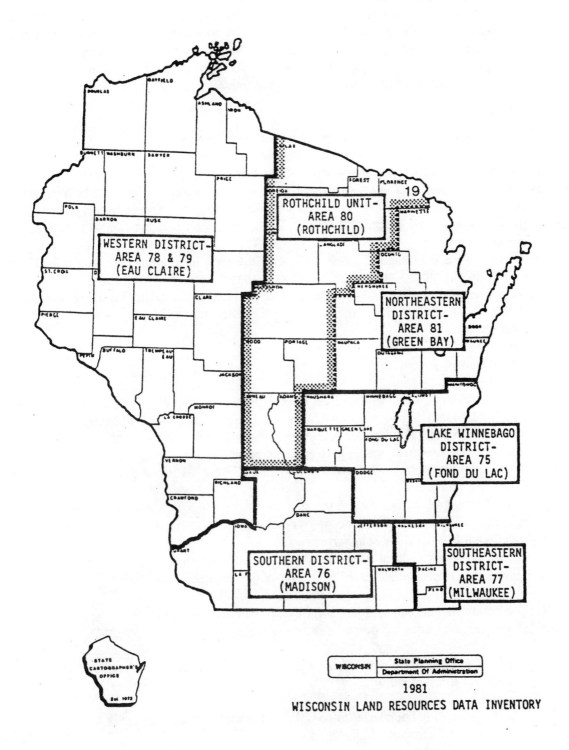

Figure 13-10. Revenue/Manufacturing Districts -- Wisconsin 1981. Source: Wisconsin
Department of Administration.

Ontario Regions.--The province has provided leadership in developing metropolitan regions to deliver services to urbanized areas as well as combining counties into stronger local units of government. Yet, the situation of the proliferation of non-uniform service boundaries still exists. Single purpose regions, it can be argued, have a beneficial role in a society. However, without basic regional boundary compatibility, the economic and social benefits which uniform boundaries provide for data collection, analysis and community interest spirit building, are lost.

The Quest for Better

The problem of overlapping boundaries of single-purpose regions is not new nor is the attempt by governments and their agencies to change boundaries in order to provide better service at a reasonable cost. The evolution of county boundaries during the pioneer period common to each state/province is a historic precedent today for further boundary modification as demographic and settlement conditions change (Figs 13-11, 13-12). The Michigan county boundaries changed about twenty-seven times between 1837 and 1897 when the state population rose from 30,000 to 2.5 million. Yet, in the 20th Century, as population soared to over nine million, no county boundary changes have taken place. Thus, like all other districts in the Basin, Michigan is moving into the Global Village/Information Age of the 3rd millennium with an outdated political geographic organization.

Attempts to Modernize

During the economic stress of the Great Depression and World War II it became clear that the pioneer era local boundaries were unsuitable for the future. Thus, the states enacted regional organization statutes which allowed for the combining of local government areas. It was envisioned that such actions would enable local political-economic areas to sufficiently enlarge and keep government "close to home" which would also curtail the need for larger state and federal bureaucracies in the capitals.

The proliferation of scores of service regions across the Basin attests to the fact that "regional organization" is an accepted concept. The complexity explosion is centered on the fact that the regions do not have *uniform boundaries*.

If regional or enlarged local government units are to strengthen the democratic form of government, some choices can be addressed especially in the US area of the Basin:

1. Election, rather than appointment, of representatives to "regional" government leadership posts;

2. Direct funding at the regional or enlarged local area level rather than indirect state and federal funding;

3. Fitting township boundaries to consolidated school district boundaries to reduce social-economic fragmentation;

4. Eliminate "another layer of government out of touch with local citizens" (a common criticism of regionalism) by designating the "regions" as enlarged counties with the time tested county government organization and designate the school district boundaries as new township boundaries;

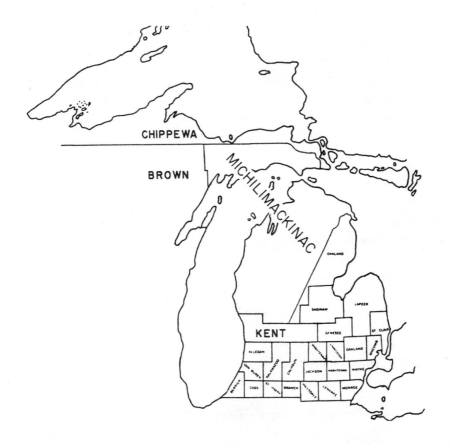

Figure 13-11. Michigan County Boundaries 1836. Source: R. Welsh, *County Evolution in Michigan 1790-1897*. Michigan Department of Education, 1972.

Figure 13-12. Michigan County Boundaries 1867. Source: R. Welsh, *County Evolution in Michigan 1790-1897*. Michigan Department of Education, 1972.

5. Reorganize the county based sheriff units into service districts.

Most of the planning and service regions so far created have dysfunctional boundaries because they are usually based on the political expedient of quick straight line geometric borders using *old* county lines for *new* political geographic units (Fig 13-13). A better fit would be to use school district or township lines. Never-the-less, the regions established in the 1970's roughly based on communities of interest could be used as a first step toward 21st century political geographic county reorganization.

The value of adopting uniform regions as enlarged counties, school districts as townships and both as local communities of interest are:

1. Improved communication between people, governments and levels of government based on a lower number;

2. Economy in providing services by elimination of duplication of activities;

3. Greater local citizen ability to design and finance programs to their local situation;

4. Creation of common information units for data analysis and local delivery of services.

In determining contemporary service areas and communities of interest, several factors can be used including:

1. Circulation of node city (metropolitan market center) newspapers;

2. Journey to work commuting patterns;

3. Minimum traffic flow break points;

4. Gravity Models -- a mathematical measure of attraction of shoppers based on population, commercial retail floor space, travel time and distance to major shopping malls;

5. Agricultural production and marketing patterns.

Summary and Conclusion

This chapter has briefly outlined several quality of life concerns that have developed as a result of the enduring generational quests to make life comfortable. Particularly stressful situations are related to acid rain, disposal of radioactive waste, sanitary landfills, crime, correctional facility costs and out moded local geographic boundaries for units of government. In the attempt to deliver governmental services, numerous regions have been established, but in an un-coordinated manner which leaves the need for the creation of functional/direct representation uniform regions

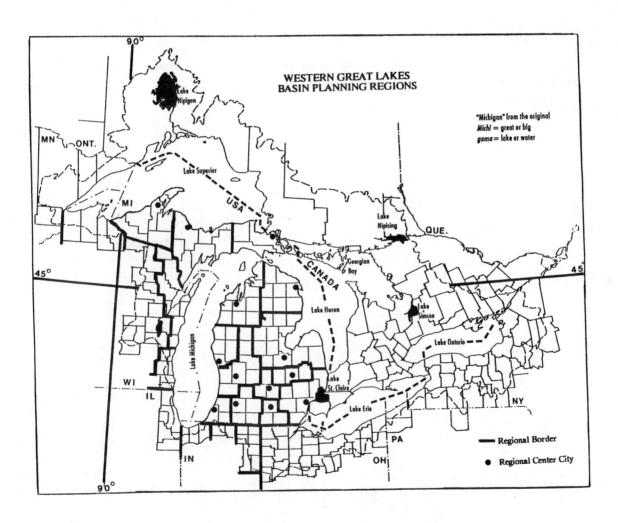

WESTERN GREAT LAKES
BASIN PLANNING REGIONS

"Michigan" from the original
Michi = great or big
gama = lake or water

——— Regional Border

● Regional Center City

Figure 13-13. Western Great Lakes Basin Planning Regions.

as enlarged counties to help preserve local democracy[11]. Throughout the Basin the increasing impact of the women's equality movement is apparent; however, place names provide evidence of the historic lack of honoring women's contributions.

Perhaps in evolving change Henry Wadsworth Longfellow's 1839 *Hyperion* words provide reassurance:

> "Look not mournfully into the Past.
> It comes not back again. Wisely improve
> the Present. It is thine. Go forth
> to meet the shadowy Future, without
> fear..."

[11]See also James Burke, *The Day the Universe Changed*, (London: British Broadcasting Corporation, 1985).

Reflections and Self-Learning: Chapter 13

1. Evaluate the core cultural goal of the region. Is it a reasonable ethic or continuously attainable goal? Why yes, why no?

2. What are the primary environmental stresses of the Basin?

3. What is pH? How is it related to the food chain?

4. Describe the nuclear waste concern and options for disposal. What is a reasonable solution: Why?

5. What are the historic concerns with town dumps?

6. What is re-cycling? What is a Mt. Trashmore?

7. How do you think the cultural landscape would be different if women had been the primary architects during the last century?

8. What are the places named for females in your area?

9. What is a third order stream?

10. How does crime change or help to shape the cultural landscape?

11. Compare Michigan and Ontario index crime statistics -- why the difference given the same cultural hearth and physical environment?

12. Evaluate the number of police reporting units in Michigan, Ontario and the United Kingdom.

13. Evaluate the pros and cons of locating a prison in your community -- where would you site one? If you have a prison in your community evaluate its economic impact.

14. Evaluate the boundaries and changes in political geographical units of your area. What would you recommend as the best community borders to provide local government service at a fair tax cost?

15. Why have social services buildings on the landscape become so numerous in the post World War II years?

16. Evaluate making rural township and the local school district boundaries the same -- list advantages and disadvantages.

17. Determine for your state/province area the legal right to use deadly force in varying spatial situations to protect life or property.

Geographic -- Spatial Relationships of Diffusion of Urban Weapons and Violence Great Lakes Basin

Evaluation of rights to use deadly force to defend and protect private property and life:

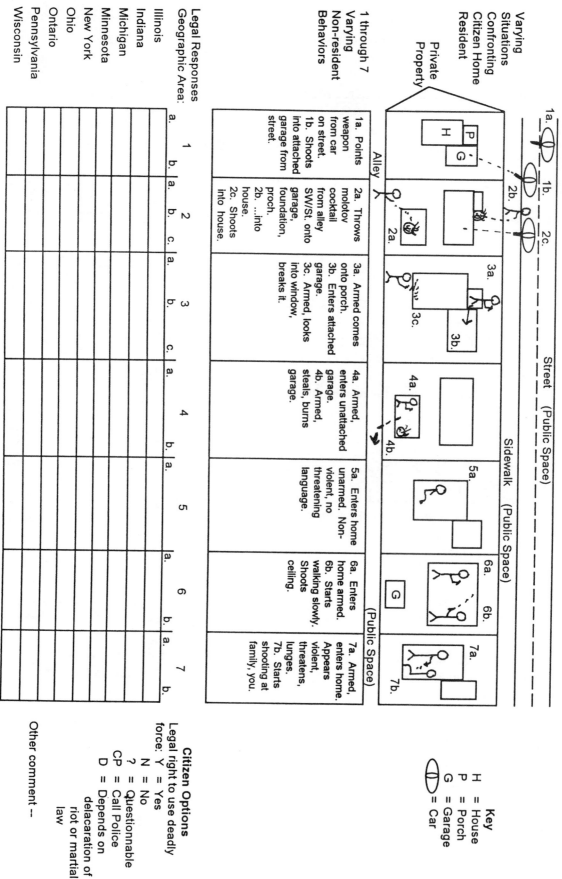

Key
H = House
P = Porch
G = Garage
C = Car

Citizen Options
Legal right to use deadly force: Y = Yes
N = No
? = Questionnable
CP = Call Police
D = Depends on delacaration of riot or martial law

Other comment --

360

Chapter Fourteen

BEYOND JOINT COMMISSIONS, PEACE AND AMBASSADOR BRIDGES

The preceding chapters have provided a comprehensive description of the Great Lakes Basin with a primary focus on past and present land uses, physical features and human activities found in the watershed. The organization of this material comes from the time tested holistic generalist interdisciplinary method of exploration and geography which inter-relates and borrows from the specialized bodies of knowledge of both the physical and social sciences. The technical fields of cartography and photography have also been used to illustrate points and places, and to complement the written descriptions. Perhaps as a result of this text, the work of earlier explorers has been expanded and modernized.

Because there are no comprehensive texts which focus on the *entire* Basin, this description of it can perhaps best be used, as most explorers' work, as a forerunner-preliminary guide for further holistic description of this critical freshwater area of the planet. Further, it provides an opportunity to initiate a spirit of place or Great Lakes *geocentrism* to help foster wise use of the Basin's resources now and forever. This concluding chapter directs thinking to the future.

On the Path Away from Warfare to Peace

In Western culture the unrelenting quest for equality in rights and privileges can be traced to the Magna Charta signed at Runnymede in 1215. The concepts of liberty, freedom, equality, independence and power of authority were tested in the agonies of the Revolutionary War which divided the people of the Basin. The subsequent U.S. Constitution (1787) and Northwest Ordinance (1787) laid more foundation stones for freedom and equality. The deaths and destruction of the War of 1812 fought in part on the land and waterways of the Basin assured the American independence. Significantly and not to be overlooked, and perhaps more important in moving away from warfare and towards equality and peace, is the Canadian experience where people gained political independence through conflict resolution, based on the process of negotiation-mediation-firm patience which resulted in the British North American Act of 1867 and Canadian Constitution of 1982. Notable also is the fact that former British colonies in Australia, New Zealand and Africa all gained national independence evolutionally, that is without death dealing revolutionary wars. The inter-Basin reformation of friendships, absence of cross border warring, relatively unfortified borders, military cooperation, plus the 20th Century International Joint Commission, Ambassador and Peace bridges, provide further examples that serious conflicts can be healed and resolved without wars while at the same time nurturing independence. While some may observe that all the national examples cited have British antecedents which may favor an evolutionary versus revolutionary war process, both Canada and the United States are plural societies with huge non-British immigrant stock. Thus, given the precedents of the past and the enriching philosophy of the present generation, the people of the Basin are on an excellent pathway to provide world leadership in moving toward peaceful means of resolving conflicts, as well as, peacefully resolving intra-Basin conflicts.

The War System and Changed Thinking

Realities of the past perhaps need to be recalled however, to temper sophomoric enthusiasm that peaceful means of conflict resolution are easy or automatic.

> I am not saying this to alarm you, but the world war was a pathetic disappointment...it revealed no progress for making the world safe for democracy. Other wars will follow.[1]

These words by a U.S. Senator, in a 1927 Memorial Day speech at Ionia, Michigan proved prophetic and the list of wars involving citizens of the Great Lake Basin lengthened to include World War II, Korea, Vietnam, Lebanon, Granada and Persian Gulf.

In the seemingly blinding prosperity of rising stocks and of peace, the January 18, 1926, *Congressional Record* carried this description of the planet power system.

> Even with huge armies and navies, nations do not feel secure. So they form military alliances. Alliances lead to counter alliances culminating in the balance-of-power system, with continents divided into great armed camps. Under this regime occasions for war, as in 1914, will continue to arise. It is clearly evident that the nationalist, competitive system is a menace to world peace. It is imperative, therefore, that some way should be found to break the vicious circle -- nationalism, imperialism, militarism, alliance, balance-of-power, crisis, war.[2]

A hint of the answer possibly for today as contemporary leaders toil with the complexities of defense budgets and Star Wars costs again, comes from an individual who migrated from the impoverished height of land at the edge of the Basin to its heart:

> I would make the hideous wars so costly that nations wouldn't want them.[3]

Albert Einstein's attention to physical scientific relationships led to his descriptive theory of relativity and advanced the earth into the atomic age with such common descriptive terms as over-kill and mutual assured destruction "MAD". Yet, before his death in 1955, he wrote his warning and tried to point humanity onto the path of changed thinking:

> The unleashed power of the atom has changed everything save our mode of thinking, and we thus drift toward unparalleled catastrophes.[4]

---

[1]Roy Newton, ed., *Life and Works of W. N. Ferris*, Bound, typewritten manuscript, Ferris State University Archives, 1960, p. 279.

[2]Irene E. Wade, *An Analysis of the Speeches of Woodbridge Ferris*, Michigan State University, Master's Thesis, 1946, p. 39.

[3]Newton, *op. cit.*, p. 243.

[4] *New York Times Magazine*, "The Einstein Letter That Started It All," August 2, 1964, p. 54.

In spite of these historical realities, given the precedents for political evolution, open-peaceful borders and an educated human resource base, the people of the Great Lakes Basin have an opportunity again for leadership by responding to the need for institutionalizing changed modes of thinking.

Education for the Future

Birds, fish and plants continue to provide evidence that the Basin's food chain and environment are not healthy. Riot and institutions for war, crime, mental health, marriage counseling and abuse indicate failure to solve problems without violence. Now respected education leaders and scientists have provided adequate warnings that survival of Homo sapiens depend on a break with past thinking patterns, methods of decision-making and problem solving. Reassuringly, shifts in ways of thinking are not unprecedented when one reviews the impact of the thoughts and teachings of Aristotle, Copernicus, Newton or Christ.

A New Concept in Education

The opening of the University of Michigan as a public institution in 1817, the establishment of the University of Notre Dame as a religious teaching center in 1842, opening of Heidelberg College to female students in 1852, the creation of Eastern Michigan University as a forerunner teacher education school in 1849, the innovation of Land Grant Institutions at Michigan State University in 1855 plus the organization of the public junior-community college system in the 20th century with private antecedents dating from the late 19th century, provide a respected evolutionary education foundation for further advancement.

Now, Michigan, the heart of the Great Lakes, with Ontario, heart of Canada, plus other districts of the Basin, have an opportunity to cooperatively assert innovative leadership by establishing the *world's first public international water-grant college*. Such a college's role and mission would be to complement the other 325 institutions of higher education in the Basin. None of the existing institutions address themselves by charter to focusing research and dissemination of knowledge on freshwater or focus in a holistic manner. Nor do any existing institutions have a charge to provide services on a watershed systems basis (Table 14-1).

An International Freshwater Grant College

Summarized below are the need and situations relating to a new institution of higher education devoted to the wise use of freshwater.

1. Freshwater is basic to human health and survival.

2. The Great Lakes Basin holds a disproportionate share of the planet's freshwater resources.

363

TABLE 14-1

**Contemporary and Future Institutions of
Higher Education Great Lakes Basin**

PUBLIC -- In Place (See Appendix One)
    Mega-universities
    Regional-Teacher Education Universities
    Agricultural Universities and Colleges
    Mining-Engineering Universities
    Technical-Professional Colleges/Universities
    Military College
        Law Schools
        Medical Schools
        Optometry Schools
        Engineering Schools
    Junior/Community Colleges
        Maritime Academy
    *Land Grant Institutions -- 19th Century Innovation

PRIVATE -- In Place (See Appendix One)
    Major Religious Affiliated Universities and Colleges
        (male-female and co-ed heritage)
    Liberal Arts Colleges
    Theological and Bible Institutions
    Specialized Colleges: Business, Podiatry, etc.

FUTURE -- Complementing NEED
    *Freshwater Grant International Institution -- 21st Century Innovation

---

3.   The past and current education-economic-religious-legal systems have not been able to protect the Basin's freshwater from toxic contamination which continues to reach into the food chain via fish, birds, surface and ground water.

4.   There is little evidence that the current fragmented system of monitoring, researching and political management of the lakes, if continued, will result in adequate Basin-wide protection of the freshwater resources.

5.   One of the significant weaknesses of current freshwater resource management is that it is lake and lakeshore oriented rather than total Basin ecosystem focused.

6.   The source of the Great Lakes is the watershed from the *land* by the Basin's hundreds of rivers and creeks.

7.   A positive transitional step is the current Sea Grant College Program, but it is limited in scope to focusing on lake and lakeshore areas.

8.   To manage the freshwater resources of the Basin holistically presents the need and opportunity to solve continuous conflicts. These conflicts are, and can be expected to be, not unlike the historic resource wars and violent family feuds because of the historic fragmentation of the Basin's local river watersheds into 230 counties, the division of the Basin into 2 nations and nine state/provinces, conflicting demand for water use by homeowners, food producers, municipalities, commercial-industrial-shipping interests, lakeshore structure owners, recreational and environmental groups.

9.   The problems of conflict can be expected to both continue and increase with population growth and non-compatible economic development, as well as demands from sun-drought belt citizens for more freshwater from the "national resource treasury" --the Great Lakes Basin.

10.   Currently little is known about the condition or potential of the individual watersheds of the Basin.

11.   Currently little is known about the combined long-term relationships of repeated spreading of a variety of chemicals in separate applications on the food lands of the Basin, especially in relationship to soils, run-off and ground-well water.

12.   There is a lack of comprehensive analysis, data and research focused on fitting the Great Lakes Basin freshwater resources effectively, environmentally wisely and economically profitably into the emerging global economic/social system.

13.   Currently there is no public higher education institution in the world with the specific mission to research and disseminate knowledge about freshwater watersheds.

14.   Michigan and Ontario, because they are situated in the heart of the world's freshwater resource and have a history of peaceful relationships, share a *de facto* leadership responsibility to assure the protection and non-violent wise use of the earth's life-supporting water resource with the seven other Basin state-districts.

In addition to the Sea Grant Program, the Great Lakes Commission and International Joint Commission efforts during the 20th Century, several other organizations have maintained interests in the Great Lakes which can, in part, be used as an initial base for developing holistic education materials on the Basin's ecosystem (Table 14-2). The University of Michigan's Global Rivers

Environmental Education Network (GREEN) is an anti-pollution effort which has grown to monitoring 180 rivers in the United States and several more in 50 other nations.

TABLE 14-2

Selected List of Great Lakes Interest Organizations

Canada Centre for Inland Waters - Burlington, Ontario
Council of Great Lakes Governors - Lansing and other capitals
Environment Canada - Ottawa
Great Lakes Biolimnology Laboratory - Burlington, Ontario
Great Lakes Carriers Association - Cleveland
Great Lakes Commission - Ann Arbor
Great Lakes Environmental Research Laboratory, NOAA - Ann Arbor
Great Lakes Fisheries Commission - Ann Arbor
Great Lakes Forest Research Station - Sault Ste. Marie, Ontario
Great Lakes Marine Water Center, U. of Mich. - Ann Arbor
Great Lakes Tomorrow - Hiram, Ohio
Great Lakes United - Buffalo
Great Lakes Waterways Development Association - Ottawa
International Joint Commission - Detroit, Washington, Ottawa
Large Lakes Research Station, EPA - Grosse Isle
Office of the Great Lakes, MDNR - Lansing
Sea Grant College Program, NOAA - Ann Arbor, St. Paul, Albany, Madison, Columbus
Sea Lamprey Control Center -- Sault Ste. Marie, Ontario
St. Lawrence Seaway Development Corporation, U.S. D of T. - Washington, DC

Recommendations and Purpose.--

1.   Establishment of a separate public international/ intra-Basin water grant college.

2.   The college's purpose or mission would be to provide a campus center for the holistic-comprehensive primary research and dissemination of knowledge on freshwater, its economic uses and the skill development of non-violent resolution of conflicts within watersheds.

3.   The college would adapt the concept of the land grant system with: (a) a strong focus on a specific range of topics -- freshwater and conflict resolution rather than agriculture and applied sciences, (b) research and degree programs in the applied tradition, (c) the organization of a well-supported system of *watershed based* extension agents and local offices, and (d) a firm commitment to basic general education through life-long learning.

4.   It is envisioned that the Water Grant College concept has a growth
      potential to expand into a system to serve all freshwatersheds of the world.

Location.-- The following are location options:

1.   The campus could be located on a new site with new buildings.

2.   The adaptation of a current community college may be a better choice.

3.   Forming the new college as a unit of an existing university would have the
      advantage of in place education resources with the advantages and
      disadvantages of traditional campus power structures.

4.   The adaption of a community college and linking it to an institution with
      an established reputation of excellence.

5.   The adaptation of a community college or newly built campus with a
      specific period of direct linkage to an institution with an established
      reputation of excellence.

Initial discussion locations for a site: Port Huron, Sarnia, Windsor, Monroe, or Toledo.

Funding.--

1.   Student tuition and fees.

2.   Per capita tax (with exchange rate adjustment) based on residency by
      state/province area within the Basin, adjusted annually to cost of living
      index, or

3.   State/province funding based on a percent of total higher education budget
      support.

4.   Private and federal grants and aids as available annually.

Target Student Body.--

1.   Great Lakes Basin high school graduates or college graduates and transfer
      students.

2.   A reasonable amount of non-Basin and foreign secondary school graduates
      especially from other "great lake" or major fresh watershed areas.

3.   Mix of traditional and non-traditional age students open to all races, sexes
      and religious beliefs.

4.   Target enrollment: variable.

Degree Levels.--Degrees awarded for successful programs completed, minimum baccalaureate and higher as institution becomes established.

Target Faculty and Administration.-- Best qualified and hirable with a goal of equality between sexes and races in proportion to Basin's total population.

Initial Programs to Support Mission.--

1.   Economic Development of Freshwater Resources (shipping, manufacturing, recreation, sub-surface, hydro-power, food and diversions).

2.   Freshwater Sciences (chemistry, biology).

3.   Freshwater Fisheries (large lake, inland lake, sport, commercial, rivers).

4.   Geography of the Great Lakes Watershed (cultural, physical, historical and contemporary relationships), Coastal Zone Management programs, International Trade.

5.   Political Science (water/land use inventory and management practices, international and interstate laws, planning and zoning, public and private Great Lakes organizations.

6.   Conflict Resolution (non-traditional, dynamic approach, integrated inter-disciplinary study and research), non-traditional resolution systems, para-legal, mediation and negotiation, counseling, holistic and all levels focus: interpersonal, private institutional, public institutions-intergovernmental, international, religious cross-cultural.

7.   Arts in the Great Lakes Basin.

8.   Watershed Extension and Continuing Programs (office based in each watershed).

9.   The Art and Techniques of Thinking[5].

Conclusion and Commencement

Whether observed from outer space, automobile, airplane, canoe, bicycle or tramping the rocky/muddy portages of the early explorers, the Great Lakes Basin clearly reveals to the visionary its unique beauty, richness and vast opportunities. Yet, as with all people in all times, enormous challenges and change face today's inhabitants of the Basin.

---

[5]Great Lakes United, *Unfulfilled Promises*, (Buffalo: Great Lakes United Water Quality Task Force, February 1987), p. 24.

Perhaps the biggest challenge is to understand the Basin's ecosystem, appreciate the lakes and wisely use their watersheds. In underscoring the importance of the Great Lakes Region and its resources maybe Anna Howard Shaw's words put things in final perspective. After campaigning for nine months in South Dakota she concluded:

> Many days, and in all kinds of weather, we rode forty and fifty miles in uncovered wagons. Many nights we shared a one-room cabin with all the members of the family. *But the greatest hardship we suffered was the lack of water.*[6]

Not the end, but a commencement.

[6]Shaw, *op. cit.*, p. 201.

Reflections and Self-Learning: Chapter 14

1. Summarize the main sections of the book.

2. Why are cartography and photography important to geographic writing?

3. Define geocentrism.

4. What is the Basin's heritage of peace? Why might it be valuable as a role model for other parts of the world?

5. Contrast the United States and Canada's route to independence from the British government.

6. Evaluate Ferris' and Einstein's quotes.

7. Describe the Basin's contribution to innovative or world class higher education. Why might these contributions be used as a basis for further innovation?

8. Evaluate the "Water Grant College" concept and proposal.

9. Where would you locate a water grant institution? Why?

10. What was not presented in the book which you need now to seek additional information on independently?

11. Review the list of sources -- select five entries of which to study further.

12. Why does the author conclude with -- "Not the end, but a commencement"?

APPENDIX ONE

Selected Colleges and Universities of the Great Lakes Basin
by Name and Community

Group I: Four Year to Post Terminal Degree Institutions:

Institution/City	Institution/City

ILLINOIS

Adler Sch. of Pro. Psychology - Chicago
American Cons. of Music - Chicago
Barat Col. - Lake Forest
Catholic Theological U. - Chicago
Chicago Col. of Osteopathic Med. - Chicago
Chicago State U. - Chicago
Chicago Theological Sem. - Chicago
Columbia Col. - Chicago
Concordia Col. - River Forest
DePaul U. - Chicago
East-West U. - Chicago
Garrett-Evangelical Sem. - Evanston
Illinois Col. of Optometry - Chicago
Ill. Inst. of Technology - Chicago
Kendall Col. - Evanston
Lake Forest Col. - Lake Forest
Loyola U. - Chicago
Lutheran Sch. of Technology - Chicago
McCormick Theological Sem. - Chicago

NAES College - Chicago
Nat'l. Col. of Education - Evanston
North Park Col. & Theo. Sem.
Northwestern U - Evanston
Roosevelt U - Chicago
Rosary Col. - River Forest
Rush U. - Chicago
St. Xavier Col. - Chicago
Dr. Wm. M. Scholl C. Podiatric Med. - Chicago
Shimer Col. - Waukegon
Spertus Col. of Judaica - Chicago
Telshe Yeshiva Chicago - Chicago
Trinity Christian Co. - Chicago
U. of Chicago - Chicago
U. of Health Science - The Chicago Med. School
   - North Chicago
U. of Ill. at Chicago - Chicago
Vandercook Col. of Music - Chicago

INDIANA

Bethel Col. - Mishawaka
Calumet Col. - Whiting
Concordia Theological Sem. - Ft. Wayne
Goshen Biblical Sem. - Elkhart
Goshen Col. - Elkhart
Ind. Inst. Tech. - Ft. Wayne
Ind. U. Northwest - Gary

Ind. U. - Purdue U. at Ft. Wayne - Ft. Wayne
Ind. U. at South Bend - South Bend
St. Francis Col. - Ft. Wayne
St. Mary's Col. - Notre Dame
Tri-State U. - Angola
U. of Notre Dame - Notre Dame

MICHIGAN

Public Institutions
Central Mich. U. - Mt. Pleasant
Eastern Mich. U. - Ypsilanti
Ferris State U. - Big Rapids
Grand Valley State U. - Allendale
L. Superior State U. - Sault Ste. Marie
Mich. State U. - East Lansing
Mich. Tech. U. - Houghton
Northern Mich. U. - Marquette

Oakland U. - Rochester
Saginaw Valley U. - Univ. Center
U. of Mich. - Ann Arbor
U. of Mich. - Dearborn
U. of Mich. - Flint
Wayne State U. - Detroit
Western Mich. U. - Kalamazoo

Institution/City	Institution/City

MICHIGAN

Independent Institutions

Adrian Col. - Adrian	Jordon Col. - Cedar Springs
Albion Col. - Albion	Kalamazoo Col. - Kalamazoo
Alma Col. - Alma	Kendall School of Design - Grand Rapids
Andrews U. - Berrien Springs	Lawrence Inst. of Tech. - Southfield
Aquinas Col. - Grand Rapids	Madonna U. - Livonia
Calvin Col. - Grand Rapids	Marygrove Col. - Detroit
Calvin Theological Sem. - Grand Rapids	Northwood Inst. - Midland
Center for Creative Studies - Detroit	Olivet Col. - Olivet
Cleary Col. - Ypsilanti	Reformed Bible Col. - Grand Rapids
Concordia Col. - Ann Arbor	Sacred Heart Sem - Detroit
Cranbrook Academy of Art - Bloomfield Hills	St. Mary's Col. - Orchard Lake
Detroit Col. of Business - Dearborn	Siena Heights Col. - Adrian
Detroit Col. of Law - Detroit	Spring Arbor Col. - Spring Arbor
General Motors Inst - Flint	Suomi Col. - Hancock
Grace Bible Col. - Grand Rapids	Thomas Cooley Law School - Lansing
Great Lakes Bible Col. - Lansing	U. of Detroit Mercy - Detroit
Grand Rapids Baptist - Grand Rapids	Walsh Col. of Accountancy
Hillsdale Col. - Hillsdale	and Business Admin. - Troy
Hope Col. - Holland	Western Theological Sem. - Holland

MINNESOTA

Col. of St. Scholastica - Duluth	U. of Minn. - Duluth - Duluth

NEW YORK

Alfred U. - Alfred	Roberts Wesleyan Col. - Rochester
Canisius Col. - Buffalo	Rochester Inst. of Tech. - Rochester
Christ the King Sem. - E. Aurora	St. John Fisher Col. - Rochester
Colgate Roch. Divinity &	SUNY - Buffalo - Buffalo
Sch. B. Hall-Crozer	SUNY - Buffalo Health Sci. - Buffalo
Theological Sem. - Rochester	SUNY - Upstate Med. Cen. - Syracuse
Cornell U. - Ithaca	SUNY - Brockport - Brockport
Daemen Col. - Amherst	SUNY Col. - Buffalo - Buffalo
D'Youville Col. - Buffalo	SUNY Col. - Cortland - Cortland
Hobart & Wm Smith Cols. - Geneva	SUNY Col. - Fredonia - Fredonia
Houghton Col. - Houghton	SUNY Col. - Genesee - Genesee
Ithaca Col. - Ithaca	SUNY Col. - Oswego - Oswego
Medaille Col. - Buffalo	Syracuse - Syracuse
Nazareth Col. of Rochester - Rochester	U. of Rochester - Rochester
Niagara U. - Niagara U.	

Group I: Four Year to Post Terminal Degree Institutions: (Cont'd.)

Institution/City	Institution/City

OHIO

Baldwin-Wallace Col. - Berea
Bluffton Col. - Bluffton
Bowling Green St. U. - Bowling Green
Case Western Reserve U. - Cleveland
Cleveland Col. of Jewish St. - Cleveland
Cleveland Inst. of Art - Cleveland
Cleveland St. U. - Cleveland
Defiance Col. - Defiance
Dyke Col. - Cleveland
Findlay Col. - Findlay
Heidelberg Col. - Tiffin
Hiram Col. - Hiram
John Carroll U. - Cleveland
Kent State U. - Kent
Lake Erie Col. - Painesville

Lourdes Col. - Sylvania
Medical Col. of Ohio - Toledo - Toledo
NE Ohio U. Col. of Med. - Rootstown
Notre Dame Col. - Cleveland
Oberlin Col. - Oberlin
Ohio Col. Podiatric Med. - Cleveland
Ohio Northern U. - Ada
OSU - Lima - Lima
St. Mary's Sem. - Cleveland
Tiffin U. - Tiffin
U. of Akron - Akron
U. of Findlay - Findlay
U. of Toledo - Toledo
Winebrenner Theo. Sem. - Findlay

ONTARIO

Universities
Brock U. - St. Catherines
Lakehead U. - Thunder Bay
Lauarentian U. of Sudbury - Sudbury
McMasters U. - Hamilton
Queen's U. - Kingston
Trent U. - Peterborough
U. of Waterloo - Waterloo
U. of Western Ontario - London
U. of Guelph - Guelph
U. of Toronto - Toronto
U. of Windsor - Windsor
Wilfred Laurier U. - Waterloo
York U. - North York

Agricultural Colleges
Alfred C. of A. & Food Tech. - Alfred
Centralia C. of A. & T. - Huron Park
Ontario Ag. Col. - Guelph
Ridgetown C. of A. - Ridgetown

Colleges of Applied Arts and Technologies
Cambrian Col. - Sudbury
Canadone C.A.A.&T. - North Bay
Centennial C.A.A.&T. - Scarborough
Conestoga C.A.A.&T. - Kitchener
Confederation C.A.A.&T. - Thunder Bay
Fanshawe C.A.A.&T. - London
Geo. Brown C.A.A.&T. - Toronto
Georgian C.A.A.&T. - Barrie/Orillia/Owen
    Sound/Parry Sound
Humber C.A.A.&T. - Rexdale/Toronto/Weston
Lambton C.A.A.&T. - Sarnia
Loyalist C.A.A.&T. - Belleville
Mohawk C.A.A.&T. - Hamilton
Niagara C.A.A.&T. - Welland
Ourham C.A.A.&T. - Oshawa
St. Clair C.A.A.&T. - Windsor
The Sault C.A.A.&T. - Sault Ste. Marie
Seneca C.A.A.&T. - North York
Sheridan C.A.A.&T. - Oakville
Sir Sandford Fleming C.A.A.&T. -
    Peterborough/Lindsey/Haliburton/Cobourg

PENNSYLVANIA

Gannon U. (RC) - Erie
Mercyhurst C. (RC) - Erie

Penn State U. - Behrend - Erie

Group I: Four Year to Post Terminal Degree Institutions: (Cont'd.)

Institution/City	Institution/City

WISCONSIN

Bellin Col. of Nursing - Green Bay	Mt. Mary Col. - Milwaukee
Cardinal Stritch Col. - Milwaukee	Northland Col. - Ashland
Carroll Col. - Waukesha	Ripon Col. - Ripon
Carthage Col. - Kenosha	St. Norbert Col. - DePere
Columbia Col. of Nursing - Milwaukee	Silver Lake Col. - Manitowoc
Inst. of Paper Chemistry - Appleton	U. of Wis. - Green Bay - Green Bay
Lakeland Col. - Sheboygan	U. of Wis. - Milwaukee - Milwaukee
Lawrence U. - Appleton	U. of Wis. - Oshkosh - Oshkosh
Marquette U. - Milwaukee	U. of Wis. - Parkside - Kenosha
Medical Col. Wis. - Milwaukee	U. of Wis. - Superior - Superior
Mil. Sch. of Engineering - Milwaukee	Wis. Lutheran Col. - Milwaukee

Group II: Two Year Undergraduate Degree Institutions:

Institution/City	Institution/City

ILLINOIS

City Colleges of Chicago(8) - Chicago	Prairie State Col. - Chicago Heights
Ill. Tech. Col. - Chicago	St. Augustine Col. - Chicago
MacCormac Jr. Col. - Chicago	

INDIANA

Holy Cross J.C. - Notre Dame	International Business Col. - Ft. Wayne
Ind. Vo. Tech. Col. North Central - South Bend	ITT Tech. Inst. - Ft. Wayne
Ind. Vo. Tech. Col. Northeast - Ft. Wayne	Purdue U. North Central - Westville
Ind. Vo. Tech. Col. Northwest - Gary	

MICHIGAN

<u>Public Community and Junior Colleges</u>

Alpena Com. Col. - Alpena	Macomb County Com. Col. - Warren
Bay de Noc Com. Col. - Escanaba	Mid-Mich. Com. Col. - Gladwin
C. S. Mott Com. Col. - Flint	Monroe Co. Com. Col. - Monroe
Delta Col. - Univ. Center	Montcalm Com. Col. - Sidney
Glen Oaks Com. Col. - Centerville	Muskegon Com. Col. - Muskegon
Gogebic Com. Col. - Ironwood	North Central Mich. Col. - Petoskey
Grand Rapids Jr. Col. - Grand Rapids	Northwestern Mich. Col. - Traverse City
Henry Ford Com. Col. - Dearborn	Oakland Com. Col. - Bloomfield Hills
Highland Park Com. Col. - Highland Park	St. Clair Co. Com. Col. - Port Huron
Jackson Com. Col. - Jackson	Schoolcraft Col. - Livonia
Kalamazoo Valley Com. Col. - Kalamazoo	Southwestern Mich. Col. - Dowagiac
Kellogg Com. Col. - Battle Creek	Washtenaw Com. Col. - Ann Arbor
Kirtland Com. Col. - Roscommon	Wayne Co. Com. Col. - Detroit
L. Mich. Col. - Benton Harbor	West Shore Dom. Col. - Scottville
Lansing Com. Col. - Lansing	

Group II: Two Year Undergraduate Degree Institutions: (Cont'd.)

Institution/City	Institution/City
MICHIGAN	
Independent Institutions	
Baker Col. of Business - Flint/Muskegon/Owosso	Davenport Col. of Business - Grand Rapids
	Lewis Col. of Bus. - Detroit
MINNESOTA	
Arrow Head Com. Col. - Hibbing	
NEW YORK	
Briggs & Stratton Bus. Ins. - Rochester	Genesee Com. Col. - Batavia
Briggs & Stratton Bus. Ins. - Buffalo	Hilbert Col. - Hamburg
Briggs & Stratton Bus. Ins. - Syracuse	Maria Regina Col. - Syracuse
Cayuga Co. Com. Col. - Auburn	Niagara Co. Com. Col. - Sanborn
Cazenovia Col. - Cazenovia	Onondaga Com. Col. - Syracuse
Com. Col. of Finger Lakes - Canandaigua	SUNY A-T - Alfred - Alfred
Erie Com. Col. - Buffalo	SUNY A-T - Morrisville - Morrisville
Erie Com. Col. - Williamsville	Tompkins-Cortland Com. Col. - Dryden
Erie Com. Col. - Orchard Park	Villa Maria Col. - Buffalo
OHIO	
BGSU - Firelands - Huron	Lorain Co. Com. Col. - Elyria
Cuyahoga Com. Col. - Cleveland	NW Tech. Col. - Archbold
Davis Jr. Col. - Toledo	Northwestern Col. - Lima
Kent State U. - Ashtabula - Ashtabula	Owens Tech. Col. - Toledo
Lakeland Com. Col. - Mentor	Terra Tech. Col. - Fremont
Lima Tech. Col. - Lima	
ONTARIO	
Pre-University and Junior Colleges	
Algoma Col. - Sault Ste. Marie	Kingsway Col. - Toronto
Assumption U. - Windsor	Mt. Carmel Col. - Niagara Falls
Brescia Col. - London	Ontario Col. of Arts - Toronto
Canadian Mem. Chiropractic Col. - Toronto	Osgoode Hall Law School - Toronto
Can. Baptist Sem. & Bible Col. - Toronto	Philathea Col. - London
Canterbury Col. - Windsor	Queen's Tehological Sem. - Kingston
Emmanuel Col. of Victoria - Toronto	Royal Military Col. - Kingston
Hearst Col. - Hearst	Regis Col. - Toronto
Huron Col. - London	Victoria U. - Toronto
Institute for Christian Studies - Toronto	Waterloo Lutheran - Waterloo
King's Col. - London	Wycliffe Col. - Toronto
WISCONSIN	
Fox Valley Tech. Col. - Appleton	NE Wis. Tech. Col. - Green Bay
Gateway Tech. Col. - Kenosha	Stratton Col. - Milwaukee
Lakeshore Tech. Col. - Cleveland	Waukesha Co. Tech. Inst. - Pewaukee
Nicolat Tech. Col. - Rhinelander	

SOURCES: *The hep Higher Education Directory*, (Washington, DC and Falls Church VA, Higher Education Publications, Inc., 1986 and 1993). Ontario Ministry of Education and Ministry of Colleges and Universities. *Michigan Statistical Abstract 1984*, Table IV-12, pp. 111-115, Official State Transportation Maps and Community Publications.

APPENDIX TWO

Air photo of the Great Lakes - St. Lawrence River Divide/Height of Land three and one-half miles north of LaVase Creek the Brulè and Champlain route into the Great Lakes watershed. Trout Lake drains east into the Ottawa River. Delaney Lake (lower left) drains west into Lake Nippissing. City of North Bay, Widdifield and West Ferris townships, Ontario. SOURCE: Ontario Ministry of Environment, AP77-4614, 10-137.

APPENDIX THREE

Maps of the Bottom Topography of the Great Lakes.

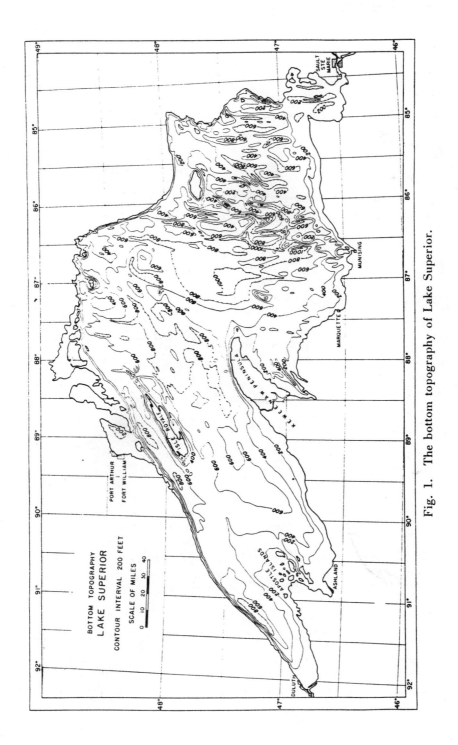

Fig. 1. The bottom topography of Lake Superior.

1. Lake Superior. SOURCE: *Great Lakes Basin*. H. J. Pincus, editor, Washington, DC: American Association for the Advancement of Science, Publication Number 71, copyrighted 1962 by AAAS. (Used with permission.)

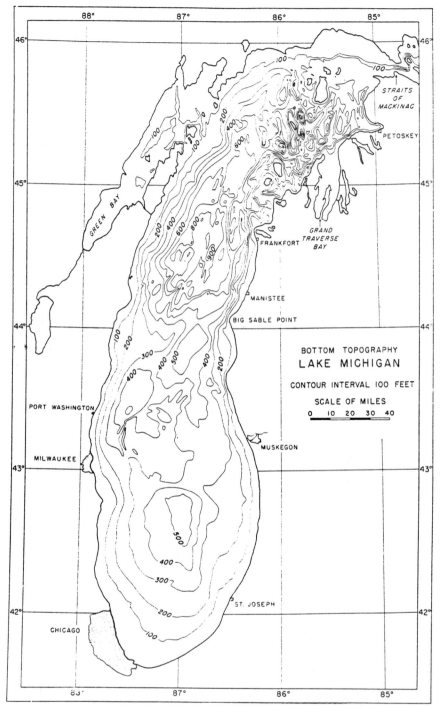

Fig. 2. The bottom topography of Lake Michigan.

2. Lake Michigan. SOURCE: *Great Lakes Basin*. H. J. Pincus, editor, Washington, DC: American Association for the Advancement of Science, Publication Number 71, copyrighted 1962 by AAAS. (Used with permission.)

380

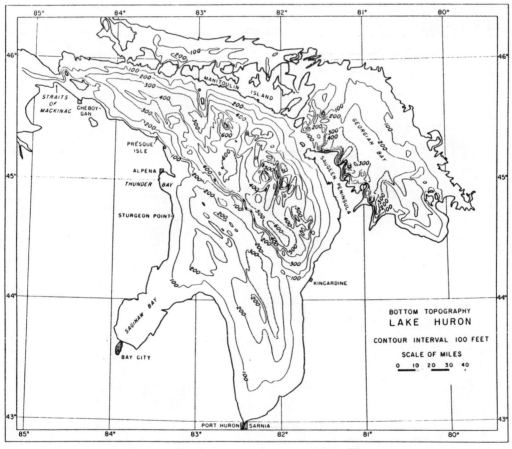

Fig. 3.   The bottom topography of Lake Huron.

3. Lake Huron. SOURCE: *Great Lakes Basin*. H. J. Pincus, editor, Washington, DC:
American Association for the Advancement of Science, Publication Number 71, copyrighted 1962
by AAAS. (Used with permission.)

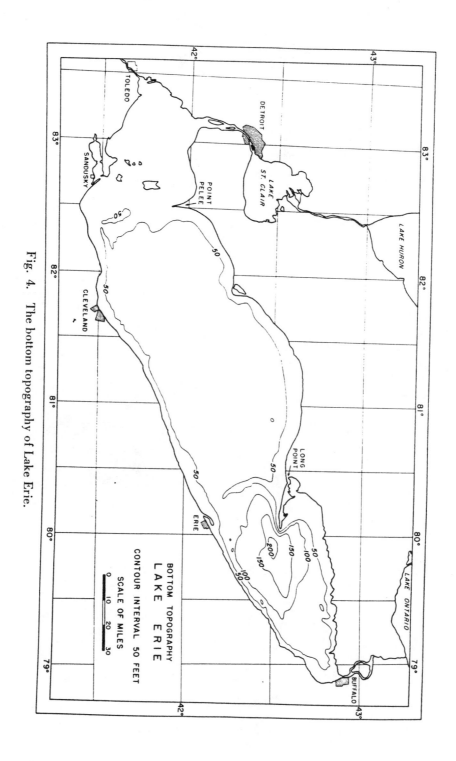

Fig. 4. The bottom topography of Lake Erie.

4. Lake Erie. SOURCE: *Great Lakes Basin*. H. J. Pincus, editor, Washington, DC: American Association for the Advancement of Science, Publication Number 71, copyrighted 1962 by AAAS. (Used with permission.)

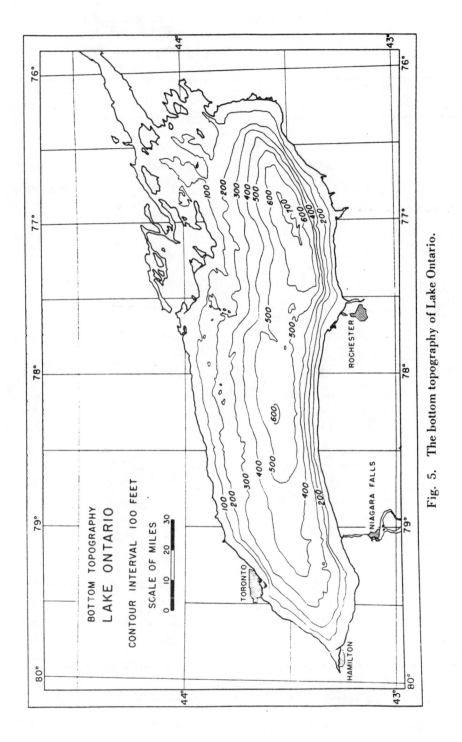

Fig. 5.   The bottom topography of Lake Ontario.

5. Lake Ontario. SOURCE: *Great Lakes Basin*. H. J. Pincus, editor, Washington, DC:
American Association for the Advancement of Science, Publication Number 71, copyrighted 1962
by AAAS. (Used with permission.)

APPENDIX FOUR

Historic Great Lake Water Levels
Highs-Lows 1879-1961
Plus June 1986 and 1987

High		Low	
Level*	Year	Level*	Year
Lake Superior			
603.7	1916	600.0	1926
603.6	1899-1900, 1950-1952	600.5	1911
603.5	1943	600.6	1925
603.4	1903, 1944	600.9	1800, 1924
601.7	1986	600.7	1987
Lake Michigan-Huron			
583.6	1886	577.3	1926
583.3	1883, 1885	577.4	1934
583.0	1884	577.7	1959
582.7	1952	579.0	1895-96
581.1	1986	580.3	1987
Lake Erie			
574.7	1952	569.4	1934-36
574.3	1929, 1947	569.9	1926
574.2	1883	570.4	1942
574.1	1882, 1884 1887,1943 1955	570.7	1895, 1902
573.7	1986	572.8	1987
Lake Ontario			
249.3	1952	242.7	1934
249.0	1947	242.9	1936
248.8	1943	243.4	1895, 1933
246.7	1986	245.6	1987

*Elevation above mean tide at New York City in feet.

SOURCE: *The Great Lakes Basin*, American Association Advancement of Science, 1962. *Water Impacts* - Vol. 8, No. 7. Institute of Water Research, East Lansing: Michigan State University, July 1987, p. 3, citing: Detroit District Corps of Engineers; see also: *Focus*, Vol. 12, No. 1, International Joint Commission, March/April 1987, p. 3. (Data varies between sources.)

Figure 5. Historic Water Level Fluctuations in metres and feet.

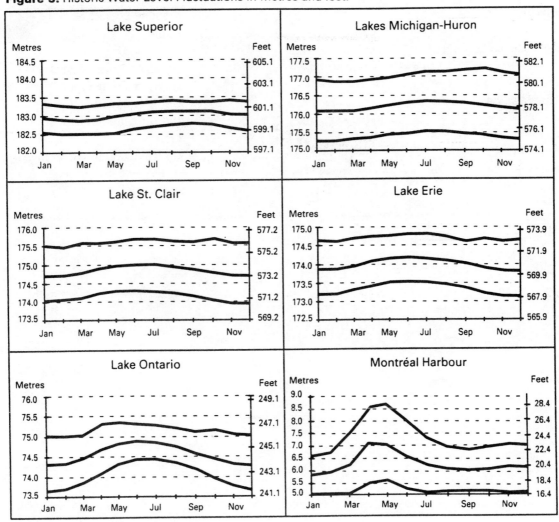

Historic monthly water level fluctuations of the Great Lakes and Montrèal Harbour. SOURCE: *Levels Reference Study: Great Lakes - St. Lawrence River Basin.* International Joint Commission, March 31, 1993, p. 10.

APPENDIX FIVE

Selected National Holidays of Great Lakes Basin

United States	Canada	Date
New Year's Day	New Year's Day	1 January
Martin L. King Day	---	3rd Monday in January
Presidents' Day	---	3rd Monday in February
Good Friday	Good Friday	Varies
Easter Sunday	Easter Sunday	Varies
---	Victorian Day	Monday nearest 25 May
Memorial Day	---	Monday nearest 30 May
---	Canada Day	1 July
Independence Day	---	4 July
---	Civic Holiday	1st Monday in August
Labor Day	---	1st Monday in September
Columbus Day	---	2nd Monday in October
---	Thanksgiving	2nd Monday in October
Veteran's Day	Remembrance Day	11 November
Thanksgiving	---	4th Thursday in November
Christmas Day	Christmas Day	25 December
---	Boxing Day	26 December

LIST OF SOURCES

In an attempt to make this List of Sources easier to use, it has been divided into eight sections: General References; Maps-Atlases-Guides; Canada-Ontario; individual states; Physical Environment, Culture-Education-Economic Activities; Polar Bears and Miscellaneous Sources.

General References

Academic American Encyclopedia. Princeton: Arete Publishing Co., 1980.

Adler, Mortimer J. *Six Great Ideas.* New York: Collier Books -- MacMillan Publishing Co., 1981.

American Library Directory. 38th ed. Vol. 1 & 2. Edited by Jacques Cattell Press. New York: R. R. Bonker Co., 1985.

Ballert, Albert C. *Great Lakes Research Checklist.* Ann Arbor, Michigan: The Great Lakes Commission. July 1985.

Barry, James P. *The Fate of the Lakes: A Portrait of the Great Lakes.* Grand Rapids, Michigan: Baker Book House, 1972.

Bartlett, John. *Familiar Quotations*, 15th ed. and 125th anniversary ed., Emily Morison Beck ed. Boston: Little, Brown and Co., 1980.

Belt, Don. "The World's Great Lake." Washington, DC: *National Geographic*, June, 1992, pp. 2-39.

Borman, Frank. Commander's Message Apollo 8 Lunar Mission, December, 1968

Brown, Ralph H. *Historical Geography of the United States.* New York: Harcourt, Brace and World, Inc., 1948.

Butzer, Karl W. *The Americas before and after 1492: Current Geographical Research.* Washington, DC: *Annals* of the Association of American Geographers, September, 1992.

Chermayeff, Serge and Tzonis, Alexander. *Shape of Community: Realization of Human Potential.* Harmondsworth, England, U.K.: Penguin Books Ltd., 1971.

Cobb, Charles E. Jr. "The Great Lakes' Troubled Waters." *National Geographic.* Vol. 172, No. 1. July, 1987, pp. 2-31.

Coleridge, Samuel D. *The Rime of the Ancient Mariner,* 1798 in Stevenson, Burton. *Home Book of Verse*, 9th Ed. New York: Holt, Rinehart and Winston, 1953.

"Communication on the Health of the Ecosystem is Stressed at the 1986 World Conference on Large Lakes." *Focus.* Vol. 11, No. 2. Windsor, Ontario: International Joint Commission, 1986.

Decisions for the Great Lakes. Edited by A. D. Misener and Glenda Daniel. Hiram, Ohio: Great Lakes Tomorrow, 1982.

Doolittle, William E. "Agriculture in North America on the Eve of Contact: A Reassessment." Washington, DC, *Annals* of the Association of American Geographers, September, 1992, pp. 386-401.

Entine, Lynn. *Our Great Lakes Connection: A Curriculum Guide for Grades Kindergarten Through Eight.* Madison, Wisconsin: University of Wisconsin - Extension Environmental Resources Center, 1985.

Ferguson, Caryl B. and Santer, Richard A. *The Sayings of W. N. Ferris.* Big Rapids, Michigan: Ferris State University Centennial Task Force, 1983.

Frost, Robert. *Robert Frost's Poems.* New York: Pocket Books, Inc. 1955. "Going for Water," "Sand Dunes," "A Drumlin Woodchuck."

Garland, John H. ed. *The North American Midwest: A Regional Geography.* New York: John Wiley and Sons, Inc., 1955.

Garreau, Joel. *The Nine Nations of North America.* Boston: Houghton-Mifflin Co., 1981.

"Garrett Hardin Reexamines the Human Predicament." *The Woodlands Forum.* Vol. 2, No. 2. Fall 1985, pp. 16-17.

Great Lakes Basin. Extension Bulletin E-1865. East Lansing, Michigan: Michigan Sea Grant College Program, Michigan State University, 1985.

Great Lakes Basin Compact (with State and Federal Legislative History) PL 90-419, July 24, 1968. Ann Arbor, Michigan: Reprinted by Great Lakes Commission.

The Great Lakes Commission: A Briefing Paper. Ann Arbor, Michigan: Great Lakes Commission, April 1984.

The Great Lakes Communicator. Vol. 8 - Vol. 11. Ann Arbor, Michigan: Great Lakes Basin Commission, 1977-1981.

Great Lakes Basin: A Symposium Presented at the Chicago Meeting of the American Association for the Advancement of Science 29-30 December, 1959. Pub. No. 71. Washington, DC.: American Association for the Advancement of Science, 1962.

Great Lakes Basin Framework Study: Appendix 13 Land Use and Management. Ann Arbor, Michigan: Great Lakes Basin Commission, 1974.

The Great Lakes Economy: A Resource and Industry Profile of the Great Lakes States. Prepared by: The Federal Reserve Bank of Chicago in cooperation with The Great Lakes Commission @ October 1985. Harbor House Pub. Inc.: Boyne City, Michigan.

Great Lakes Governors Task Force. *Water Diversion and Great Lakes Institutions.* Madison: Council of Great Lakes Governors, January 1985.

"Great Lakes Management Changes Needed." *Water Impacts.* E. Lansing: Institute of Water Research, Michigan State University, January, 1988, pp. 4-5.

Halsey, John R. *Beneath the Inland Sea.* Lansing: Michigan Department of State, Bureau of History, 1990.

Hatcher, Harlan and Walter, E. A. *A Pictorial History of the Great Lakes.* New York: Bonanza Books, 1968.

Helm, June. Vol. ed. *Handbook of North American Indians.* Vol. 6 Subarctic. Washington, DC.: Smithsonian Institution, 1981.

The Hep: Higher Education Directory. Edited by Constance H. Torregrosa. Washington, DC and Falls Church, VA: 1986 and 1993.

Herbert, Paula. *Great Lakes Nature Guide.* Lansing, Michigan: Michigan United Conservation Clubs, ca. 1980.

The Holy Bible. Red Letter Edition, Authorized King James Version. Cleveland: The World Publishing Co.

Institute for Future Studies. "The Emerging Context for Life in America." Warren, Michigan: Macomb Community College, c. 1992, a folder.

International Joint Commission. 1983-1984 Activities Report International Joint Commission: Canada - United States. Windsor, Ontario: International Joint Commission, 1985.

International Joint Commission. "Final Report: 42 Recommendations for Actions." *UPDATE.* March 31, 1993.

Jager, Ronald. *Eighty Acres: Elegy for a Family Farm.* Boston: Beacon Press, 1990.

Kenton, Edna. *Black Gown and Redskins: Early Jesuit Missionaries 1610-1791.* New York: Longmans, Green and Co., 1956 (Published in Great Britain under title Jesuit Relations and Allied Documents, 1926). 527 pp.

Lake Erie. Extension Bulletin E-1869. East Lansing, Michigan: Michigan Sea Grant College Program, Michigan State University, 1985.

Lake Huron. Extension Bulletin E-1868. East Lansing, Michigan: Michigan Sea Grant College Program, Michigan State University, 1985.

Lake Michigan: The Bulletin of the Lake Michigan Federation. Chicago: Lake Michigan Federation, Summer, 1985.

Lake Michigan. Extension Bulletin E-1867. East Lansing, Michigan: Michigan Sea Grant College Program, Michigan State University, 1985.

Lake Ontario. Extension Bulletin E-1870. East Lansing, Michigan: Michigan Sea Grant College Program, Michigan State University, 1985.

Lake Superior. Extension Bulletin E-1866. East Lansing, Michigan: Michigan Sea Grant College Program, Michigan State University, 1985.

Lane, Ferdinand C. *The World's Great Lakes.* Garden City, NY: Doubleday and Company Inc., 1948.

"Lester Brown: New Global Concerns Emerge Even as Old Problems Remain Unsolved," *The Woodland Forum.* Vol. 3, No. 2. Summer 1986. pp. 1-4.

The Marine Advisory Service. Extension Bulletin E-1871. East Lansing, Michigan: Michigan Sea Grant College Program, Michigan State University, 1985.

McCarthy, Ann. *The Great Lakes*. New York: Crescent Books, 1985.

McDonald, James R. *A Geography of Regions*. Dubuque, Iowa: William C. Brown, 1972.

McGuffey's Second Eclectic Reader. New York: Van Nostrand Reinhold Company, Inc., 1879, 160 pp.

Michigan Sea Grant College Program. *Institutional Arrangements for Great Lakes Management: Past Practices and Future Arrangements*. Ann Arbor: University of Michigan, c. 1992.

Moon, William L. H. *Blue Highways: A Journey into America*. New York: Fawcett Crest Book, Ballantine Books, 1982.

"National Hub for environmental research sought." Big Rapids: *Pioneer*, February 8, 1993, p. 1.

Parkman, Francis. *The Jesuits in North America in the Seventeenth Century*. Boston: Little, Brown and Co., 1925.

Pierce, Neal R. and Hagstrom, Jerry. *The Book of America*. New York: Warner Books Edition by W. W. Norton and Co., Inc., 1984.

People and Projects 1985-86. Ann Arbor, Michigan: Michigan Sea Grant College Program, 1986.

Proceedings of the Second Federal Conference on the Great Lakes. Ann Arbor, Michigan(?): Great Lakes Basin Commission with Argonne National Laboratory, March 1975.

Schoolcraft, Henry R. *The Indian Tribes of the United States*. Edited by F. S. Drake. Philadelphia: J. B. Lippincott and Co., 1884.

Sea Grant Association. *The National Sea Grant College Program: 1987-1992*. Washington, DC: Washington Sea Grant Program, undated c. 1993.

Shaw, Anna Howard. *The Story of a Pioneer*. New York: Harper and Brothers Publishers, 1915; Kraus Reprint Co., 1970.

Slater, C. M. and Hall, E. G. *1993 County and City Extra*. 2nd ed. Lanhan, MD Bernan Press, 1993.

TEF Data. No. 17. Washington, DC.: The Environmental Fund, February 1985.

Tenterden Explored: An Architectural and Townscope Analysis. Maidstone, Kent County, England, United Kingdom: Kent County Council, 1967.

Trigger, Bruce G., Vol. ed. *Handbook of North American Indians*. Vol. 15, Northeast. Washington, DC.: Smithsonian Institution, 1978.

United States Department of Commerce. Characteristics of the Population Number of Inhabitants: United States Summary. Washington, DC.: Bureau of Census, 1980.

United States Department of Commerce. *County and City Data Book 1983: A Statistical Abstract Supplement*. 10th ed. Washington, DC.: Bureau of Census, 1983.

United States Department of Commerce. *Statistical Abstract of the United States*. 105th ed. and 112th ed. Washington, DC.: Bureau of the Census, 1985 and 1992.

United States Government. EPA Superfund: What it is How it Works. Washington, DC.: United States Environmental Protection Agency Office of Solid Waste and Emergency Response, July 1982.

Upwellings. Vol. 7, No. 3. Ann Arbor, Michigan: Michigan Sea Grant College Program. Summer/Fall 1985.

Walker, Barbara G. *The Woman's Encyclopedia of Myths and Secrets*. San Francisco: Harper & Row, 1983.

Waller, Robert J. *Bridges of Madison County*. New York: Warner Books, 1992

Wharton, Clifton R. Jr. "Taking Teaching Seriously: Taking *Teachers* Seriously." Chicago: Closing Plenary Address, American Association for Higher Education, March 4, 1987. 11 pp. mimeographed.

White, C. L., Foscue, E. J., McKnight, T. L. *Regional Geography of Anglo-America*, 6th ed. Englewood Cliffs, New Jersey: Prentice-Hall, Inc., 1985.

Winklepleck, Julie. ed. *Gale Directory of Publications and Broadcast Media*. Detroit: Gale Research, Inc., 1993.

The World Book Encyclopedia. Chicago: Field Enterprises Educational Corporation, 1973.

Zim, H. S. and Gabrielson, I. N. *Birds: A Guide to the Most Familiar American Birds*. New York: Golden Press and Racine: Western Publishing Co., 1956.

Maps, Atlases, Guides

Agnew, Julianne and Lydecker, Ryck. *A Boater's Guide to Lake Superior Launch Ramps.* (with maps) Duluth, Minnesota: University of Minnesota Sea Grant Extension Program, ca. 1985.

Ashley, Laura R. ed. *Traveling Through Time: A Guide to Michigan's Historical Markers.* Lansing: Michigan Department of State Bureau of History, 1991.

Association of American Geographers. "Land Claims by Tribes." *Annals.* June 1972. Map Supplement 16, Vol. 16 No. 2.

Bergen, John V. "Sources of Ohio Maps for teaching geography and history." *Journal of Geography.* Vol. 81, No. 1. January-February 1982, pp. 20-29.

Brewer, L. G., Hodler, T. W. and Raup H. *Presettlement Vegetation of Southwestern Michigan.* Kalamazoo: Western Michigan University, 1984. Map 38x24 inches.

Borchert, J. R. and Gustafson, N. C. *Atlas of Minnesota Resources and Settlement.* 3rd ed. Minneapolis, Minnesota: University of Minnesota and Minnesota State Planning Agency, 1980.

Canada Government. *Adventure Tours off the Trans-Canada Highway.* Ottawa: Ministry of Industry, Trade and Commerce, undated.

Canada Government. *The National Atlas of Canada.* 4th ed. Toronto: The MacMillan Company Limited in association with Ottawa: Department of Energy, Mines and Resources, 1974.

"Canada Indian Bands with Linguistic Affiliations." Ottawa: Department of Indian Affairs and Northern Development, 1968.

Chicago. Map of Old Chicago Portage. Chicago: William E. Rose and Associates, Inc., ca. 1980.

"Closing the Tax Gap." *Grand Rapids Press*, May 1, 1993, p. C1. (Map: U.S. Census Bureau.)

Combination Atlas Map of Lenawee County, Michigan. Chicago: Everts & Stewart, 1874. From Atlas Reprints sponsored by Lenawee County Historical Society, Inc., ca. 1976.

Epenshade, Edward B., Jr. ed. *Goodes World Atlas.* 14th 15th and 16th ed. Chicago: Rand McNally.

"Food Baskets Under Siege." *Grand Rapids Press*, May 31, 1992, p. F6.

Indiana 1985: State Highway System. Indianapolis: Department of Highways, 1985.

"Indians of North America." *National Geographic Magazine*, December 1972. Map Supplement to Vol. 142 No. 6.

Joint Publication. *The Great Lakes: An Environmental Atlas and Resource Book.* Environment, Canada and U.S. Environmental Protection Agency, Chicago/Toronto, 1987.

Karpinski, Louis C. *Bibliography of the Printed Maps of Michigan 1804-1880: Constituting An Historical Atlas of the Great Lakes and Michigan.* Lansing: Michigan Historical Commission, 1931.

"Major Highways." Windsor: Windsor - Essex County Development Commission, ca. 1985.

Martin, Helen M. *Map of the Surface Formations of the Southern Peninsula of Michigan.* Publication 49. Lansing: Michigan Department of Conservation, 1955.

Michigan Government. *Mapbook of Michigan Counties.* Lansing: Michigan Department of Natural Resources, 1984.

Michigan Government. Mapping and Photography Directory. Lansing: Department of Natural Resources, Office of Land Use, 1976.

Michigan Government. *Warm Weather Travel Planner.* Lansing, Michigan: Michigan Travel Bureau, Department of Commerce, 1986.

Michigan Government. *Yes Michigan: Official Transportation Map.* Lansing, Michigan: Michigan Department of Transportation, 1985.

Michigan Travel Pages. Troy, Michigan: Ameritech Publishing Enterprises, Spring/Summer 1986.

Minnesota Government. *Minnesota: Official Highway Map.* St. Paul: Minnesota Department of Highways, 1976.

Muskegon River, Michigan. (6 sheets). Milwaukee, Wisconsin: United States Army Corps of Engineers, April 3, 1931.

"National Topographic System Maps of Canada." Index 1. Ottawa: Department of Energy, Mines and Resources, 1984.

Nelson Atlas of Canada. G. J. Matthews, cartographer. Canada: The Canadian National Institute for the Blind, 1978.

The New Canadian Oxford Atlas. Edited by Walter G. Kemball. Don Mills, Ontario: Oxford University Press (Canada), 1985.

I Love New York Rochester - Monroe County Travel Guide. Rochester, New York: Rochester Area Chamber of Commerce and Rochester, Monroe County Convention Visitors Bureau, 1985. (a pamphlet)

New York Government (?). I "Love" NY Seaway Trail 1985 Tour Guide. (The only Official Touring Guidebook to the Seaway Trail) Albany, New York ?: 1985.

New York Government. I "Love" NY. State Travel Guide. Albany, New York: New York State Tourism, 1985.

Ohio: the heart of it all. Official Transportation Map. Columbus, Ohio: Ohio Department of Transportation, 1985-1986.

Olsenius, R. and Zerby, J. A.; Andrews, S. K. Cartographer. *Wisconsin Travel Companion*. Wayzata, Minnesota: Bluestem Productions/Mijaz, Inc.,

Ontario Government. Map: District Health Council Areas (Southwestern, Central West, Central East, Eastern, Northeastern, Northwestern). Toronto: Ontario Ministry of Health, 1985.

Ontario Government. *KWIC Index to Your Government Services: 1984*. Toronto: Ministry of Government Services, 1984.

Ontario Government. *Ontario Official Road Map*. Toronto: Ontario Ministry of Transportation and Communication, 1984-85 and 1986-87.

Ontario Government. Map: Conservation Areas (Watershed Outdoor Recreation Facilities). Toronto: Ministry of Natural Resources, 1985.

Ontario Government. *Traveler's Encyclopedia*. Toronto: Ministry of Tourism and Recreation, 1985, with maps.

Ontario Government. *Map Sources -- Ontario Canada*. Toronto: Ontario Travel, Ministry of Tourism and Recreation, 1985.

Pennsylvania Government. *Official Transportation Map of Pennsylvania*. Harrisburg: Department of Transportation, ca. 1985.

Pennsylvania Government. Presque Isle State Park. Harrisburg: Office of Resources Management Bureau of State Parks, ca. 1985.

Portage County (Wisconsin) Road Map. Stevens Point, Wisconsin: Portage County Clerk's Office, 1985.

"Railways." Windsor: Windsor - Essex County Development Commission, ca. 1985.

Ride Guide - Toronto. Toronto: Toronto Transit Commission, May 1984.

Road Atlas: United States, Canada, Mexico. Chicago: Rand McNally and Company, 1980.

Robinson, A. H. and Culver, J. B., ed. *The Atlas of Wisconsin: General Maps and Gazetteer*. Madison: The University of Wisconsin Press, 1974.

Rooney, J. F., Jr., Zelinsky, W., Louder, D. R. *This Remarkable Continent: An Atlas of the United States and Canadian Society and Culture*. College Station, Texas: Texas A and M University Press, 1982.

Scharfenberg, Doris. *The Long Blue Edge of Summer*. Grand Rapids: William B. Eerdmans Publishing Co., 1982.

"Self-Guided Tour of Our City's Trees." Big Rapids Garden Club, 1982. (A folder with map.)

Senninger, Earl J., Jr. *Atlas of Michigan*. 3rd ed. Flint: Flint Geographical Press, 1970.

Small Boat Guide: Eastern Lake Ontario Thousand Islands -- Seaway Region, 3rd Printing. Watertown, New York: Black River - St. Lawrence Resource Conservation & Development Council, May 1985 (originally prepared by L. A. LaPointe and Media Services, Cornell University).

The Society for Human Exploration. *The Nuclear War Atlas*. Victoriaville, Quebec: P.O. Box 532, 1982.

Sommers, Lawrence M., ed. *Atlas of Michigan*. East Lansing: Michigan State University Press, 1977.

Thinking About Canada. Edited by G. J. A. deLeeuw, R. J. B. Carswell, H. W. Castner. Toronto: Hosford Publishing Ltd., 1981.

Tioga County, New York Highway Map. Owego, New York: The Tioga County Highway Department and The Tioga County Chamber of Commerce, 1985.

Tip of the Arrowhead. Grand Maris, Minnesota: Tip of the Arrowhead Association, ca. 1985.

University of Michigan. Thomas Jefferson 1743-1943: A Guide to the Rare Books Maps & Manuscripts exhibited at the University of Michigan. Ann Arbor, Michigan: The William L. Clemets Library, 1943.

United States Government. "Probable Locations of Indian Tribes North of Mexico About 1500 AD.", "Culture Areas and Approximate Locations of Tribes Today." "Indian Reservations of the United States, 1948." Washington, DC: Bureau of Indian Affairs, Department of Interior, 1948. 3 maps.

Wisconsin Coastal Atlas 1977. Madison: Wisconsin Coastal Management Program, 1977.

Wisconsin Government. *Wisconsin Official Highway Map*. Madison: Wisconsin Department of Transportation, ca. 1985.

Wisconsin Government. *Wisconsin Land Resources Data Inventory*. Madison: Department of Administration, State Planning Office, 1981.

Wisconsin Muskellunge Waters. Kau Kauna, Wisconsin: Clarkson Map Co., 1979.

1992 Commercial Atlas and Marketing Guide. Skokie, IL: Rand McNally, 1992.

Canada - Ontario

Anderson, Richard. "Garbage Disposal in the Greater Toronto Area: A Preliminary Historical Geography." *The Operational Geographer*. Toronto: Canadian Association of Geographers, March 1993, pp. 7-13.

Barnes, Michael. *Gateway City: The North Bay Story*. North Bay: North Bay and District Chamber of Commerce, 1982.

Blair, W. L. and Blake, F. G. "Niagara Planning Area Official Plan Partial Referral (urban area boundaries). Toronto: Ontario Municipal Board Report, 9, February 9, 1979. pp. 286-307.

Bunge, W. W. and Bordessa, R. *The Canadian Alternative: Survival, Expeditions and Urban Change*. Geographical Monograph 2. Toronto: Department of Geography, Atkinson, College York University, 1975.

Canada Government. *Canada's Mental Health*. Vol. 32, No. 4. Tunney's Pasture, Ottawa: Ministry of Health and Welfare, 1985.

Canada Government. "Energy from Forest Biomass." *Forestry Newsletter*. Canada Forestry Service, Toronto, Spring 1985.

Canada Government. *Immigration Statistics 1983*. Ottawa: Employment and Immigration Canada, 1985.

Canada Government. *The Land Planning Framework of Canada: an Overview*, Working Paper No. 28. Ottawa: Land Use Policy and Research Branch, 1984.

Canada Government. Report of Hearing and Decision, Re: Development of 1005 Acres Between Etobicoke Creek and Caledon-Brampton Municipal Boundary. Toronto: Ontario Municipal Board, Minister's File No. 21-08-0019-038, August 8, 1984.

Canada, Lands, Directorate. *Stress on Land*. Ottawa: Ministry of Supply and Services, 1983.

Canadian Almanac & Directory. Toronto: Copp Clark Pitman, Ltd. 1986 and 1993.

"Canadian Bulk Fleet - 20 year Profile." *Transport of Thunder Bay*, Fall 1992, p. 7 (a graph).

Canadian Government. *Canada Today*. Washington, DC. Canadian Embassy, 1993.

"Canadian repairs to Welland Canal total $126 million." *Grand Rapids Press*, November 30, 1986, p. A18.

Carruthers, Clark. "Light at the end of the tunnel?." *Transport of Thunder Bay*, Spring 1993, pp. 10-11.

Chapman, L. J. and Putnam, D. F. *The Physiography of Southern Ontario*, 2nd ed. Toronto: Ontario Research Foundation by the University of Toronto Press, 1973.

Chapman, L. J. and Putnam, D. F. *The Physiography of Southern Ontario*, 3rd ed. Ontario Geological Survey Special Volume 2. Toronto: Ministry of Natural Resources, 1984.

Choquette, Robert. *Ontario: An Informal History of the Land and its People*. Toronto: Ontario Ministry of Education, 1984.

Environment Canada. *Acid Precipitation and Forest Ecosystems*. Sault Ste. Marie, Ontario: Canadian Forestry Service and Great Lakes Forest Research Centre, March 1980.

Environment Canada. *Alternatives in Forest Insect Control*. Proceedings. Sault Ste. Marie, Ontario: Canadian Forestry Service and Great Lakes Forest Research Centre, June 1973.

Environment Canada. *Black Spruce Symposium*. Proceedings. Sault Ste. Marie, Ontario: Canadian Forestry Service and Great Lakes Forest Research Centre, December 1975.

Environment Canada. *Boreal Mixedwood Symposium*. Proceedings. Sault Ste. Marie, Ontario: Canadian Forestry Service and Great Lakes Forest Research Centre, April 1981.

Environment Canada. *Canadian Containerized Tree Seeding Symposium.* Proceedings. Sault Ste. Marie, Ontario: Canadian Forestry Service and Great Lakes Forest Research Centre, 1982.

Environment Canada. *Climatic Atlas Canada.* Map Series 1 -- Temperature and Degree Days. Ottawa: Ministry of Supply and Services, 1984.

Environment Canada. *Ecotour: Thunder Bay to White River; Ecotour: White River to Sault Ste. Marie; Ecotour: Sault Ste. Marie -- North Bay.* Sault Ste. Marie, Ontario: Great Lakes Forest Research Centre, 1976 and 1979.

Environment Canada. *Jack Pine Symposium.* Proceedings. Sault Ste. Marie, Ontario: Canadian Forestry Service and Great Lakes Forest Research Centre, 1984.

Environment Canada. *The Management of Southwestern Ontario Hardwoods.* Proceedings. Sault Ste. Marie, Ontario: Canadian Forestry Service and Great Lakes Forest Research Centre, March 1975.

Environment Canada. *Mechanization of Silviculture in Northern Ontario.* Proceedings. Sault Ste. Marie, Ontario: Canadian Forestry Service and Great Lakes Forest Research Centre, February 1975.

Environment Canada. *Plantation Establishment Symposium.* Proceedings. Sault Ste. Marie, Ontario: Canadian Forestry Service and Great Lakes Forest Research Centre, December, 1977.

Environment Canada. Prescribed Fire. Sault Ste. Marie, Ontario: Great Lakes Forest Research Centre, August 1982, 1 sheet.

Environment Canada. *Remote Sensing Symposium.* Proceedings. Sault Ste. Marie, Ontario: Canadian Forestry Service and Great Lakes Forest Research Centre, April 1980.

Environment Canada. *Rural Lands and Landowners of Ontario.* Toronto: Canadian Forestry Service and Ontario Ministry of Natural Resources, <u>ca.</u> 1981.

Environment Canada. *The Spruce Budworm Problem in Ontario -- Real or Imaginary?* Proceedings. Sault Ste. Marie, Ontario: Canadian Forestry Service and Great Lakes Forest Research Centre, 1983.

Environment Canada. *Tree Improvement Symposium.* Proceedings. Sault Ste. Marie, Ontario: Canadian Forestry Service and Great Lakes Forest Research Centre, April 1979.

Essex County Sketches. Windsor: Essex County (Ontario) Tourist Association, 1974.

Facts and Figures on Sarnia, Canada. Sarnia: Sarnia and District Chamber of Commerce, December 1984.

Fasolino, Karl and Bardecki, M. J. "Ontario Environmental Assessment Act and the Private Sector: Policy Considerations...Waste Management." *The Operational Geographer.* Canadian Association of Geographers, December 1992, pp. 2-5.

Freeman, E. B. and Sado, E. V. *Field Trip Guide F1 Physiography, Geology and Land Use Toronto to Madoc.* Toronto: National Council for Geographic Education and Ontario Association of Geographers and Environmental Educators, October 1984.

The Geography of the Peterborough Area, occasional paper. Peterborough, Ontario: Department of Geography Trent University, 1982.

Glazebrook, G. P. det. *Life in Ontario: A Social History.* Toronto: University of Toronto, 1975.

Key to Kingston. Vol. 5, No. 4. Kingston: Kingston Publications, August 1985.

Krueger, Ralph R. Urbanization of the Niagara Fruit Belt." *Canada Geographer,* XXII, March 1978.

Krueger, R. R. "The Destruction of a Unique Renewable Resource: The Case of the Niagara Fruit Belt," from *Managing Canada's Renewable Resources.* Krueger, R. R. and Mitchell, D. M., ed. Toronto: Methuen, 1977. pp. 132-148.

London, City of. *Industrial Data and General Information: London, Ontario.* A packet with maps. London: Economic Development Department, 1985.

Mauro, Joseph M. *A History of Thunder Bay.* Thunder Bay: Lento Printers Limited, April 1981.

Moving to and Around Southwestern Ontario. Vol. 12, No. 4. Don Mills, Ontario: Moving Publications, Ltd., 1985.

National Council for Geographic Education. "Special Issue on Canada." *Journal of Geography.* Vol. 83, No. 5, September-October 1984. pp. 193-260.

"1985 Navigation Season at Thunder Bay." Thunder Bay: Port of Thunder Bay News Release, January 17, 1986.

North Bay, City of. City of North Bay Gateway to Opportunity: Market Data and Fact File. A packet with map. North Bay: Economic Development Department, 1985.

Ontario Geography. No. 10. London: University of Western Ontario, 1976.

Ontario Geography. "Department of Geography." London: The University of Western Ontario, <u>ca.</u> 1985. 7 pp. mimeographed.

Ontario Government. *Agricultural Code of Practice.* Toronto: Ministry of Agriculture and Food, Ministry of Environment, Ministry of Housing, 1976.

Ontario Government. *Agricultural Statistics for Ontario 1983.* Pub. 20. Toronto: Ministry of Agriculture and Food. 1984.

Ontario Government. *Annual Report Ontario Ministry of Industry and Trade 1983-84.* Toronto: Ministry of Industry and Trade, 1984.

Ontario Government. *The Case Against the Rain.* Toronto: Ministry of the Environment, October 1980 and insert 1982.

Ontario Government. *Coal in Ontario.* Toronto: Ministry of Energy, 1980.

Ontario Government. *Community and Social Services.* 52nd Report, for 1982-83 and 1983-84. Toronto: Ministry of Community and Social Services, 1985.

Ontario Government. *Directory of Community Mental Health Services Programs 1984.* Toronto: Ontario Ministry of Health, 1984.

Ontario Government. *Ferris Provincial Park: Ontario.* Folder and maps. Toronto: Ministry of Natural Resources, 1985.

Ontario Government. *Food Land Guidelines: A Policy Statement of the Government of Ontario on Planning for Agriculture 1978.* Toronto: Ministry of Agriculture and Food, 1978, 27 pp.

Ontario Government. *Futures in Water: Proceedings, Ontario Water Resources Conference.* Toronto: Province of Ontario, June 12-14, 1984.

Ontario Government. *Hospital Statistics 1982/83: Public and Private Hospitals Mental Health Services.* Toronto: Ontario Ministry of Health, <u>ca.</u> 1984.

Ontario Government. *Lake Nipigon Provincial Park: Ontario.* Folder and maps. Toronto: Ministry of Natural Resources.

Ontario Government. *Lake Superior Provincial Park: Ontario.* Folder and maps. Toronto: Ministry of Natural Resources, 1985.

Ontario Government. "Ministry Tightens Food Land Guide-Lines," news release. Toronto: Ontario Ministry of Agriculture and Food, February 23, 1983, 2 pp.

Ontario Government. *Municipal Directory, 1993.* Toronto: Ministry of Municipal Affairs, 1993.

Ontario Government. *Ontario Hospitals Directory, 1984.* Toronto: Ontario Ministry of Health.

Ontario Government. *Ontario Provincial Police Annual Statistical Report, 1982.* Toronto: Ontario Provincial Police, Policy and Planning Branch, 1982.

Ontario Government. *Ontario Statistics 1984.* Toronto: Ministry of Treasury and Economics, 1984.

Ontario Government. *Private Land Forests: A Public Resource.* Toronto: Ministry of Natural Resources, 1985.

Ontario Government. *Report of the Minister of Education 1983-84.* Toronto: Minister of Education, 1984.

Ontario Government. "Revision to Food Land Guidelines Policy Regarding Mineral Aggregate Extraction." Toronto: Ontario Ministry of Agriculture and Food, Section 3.16 added with 3 maps, February 1983.

Ontario Government. *Solicitor General Annual Report 1981.* Toronto: Ministry of Solicitor General, 1981, with maps.

Ontario Government. *Update.* "Ontario's Farmland in Perspective -- Setting the Record Straight." Toronto: Ministry of Agriculture and Food, February 1984.

Ontario Government. *Water Quantity Resources of Ontario.* Toronto: Ministry of Natural Resources, June 1984.

Ontario Government. *White Lake Provisional Park: Ontario.* Folder and maps. Toronto: Ministry of Natural Resources, 1985.

Ontario Hydro: Information Kit. Fact sheets, pamphlets -- nuclear. Toronto: Ontario Hydro, 1985.

Ontario Northland Marine Services. *Come Sail A Legend: Chief Commanda II.* Timetable. Toronto: Ontario Northland Transportation Commission, 1985.

Owen Sound, City of. *Basic Information and Statistics Regarding Owen Sound.* Owen Sound: Department of Economic Development.

Parks Canada. *Historic Trent-Severn Waterway*. A folder. Toronto: Ministry of the Environment, 1985.

Parks Canada. Plant Checklist for Pukaskwa National Park. Canada: 1974-77 data, (typed copy).

Parks Canada. *Pukaskwa National Park: Ontario*. Folder and map. Ottawa: Ministry of Environment, 1984.

Parks Canada. *Rideau Canal between Kingston and Ottawa*. Folder and map. Ottawa: Ministry of Environment, 1985.

Parks Canada. *Trent-Severn Waterway: Ontario*. Folder and map. Toronto: Ministry of the Environment, 1985.

Payne, R. J. *et. al.* "Measuring the Leisure Action and Activity spaces of Older Adults in small Ontario Towns." Toronto: *The Operational Geographer*, April 1992, pp. 18-21.

Phillips, Brian A. M. "Characteristics of Raised Cobble Ridges in the Terrace Bay Area." *Canadian Geographer*. Vol. 26, No. 2, 1982, pp. 128-141.

Plant, A. L. *Pre-contact and Contact Period Archaeological Sites and Their People: Petagwana to Pele'*. 2nd ed. Windsor: Standard Printing, 1983.

Pryke, K. G. and Kulisek, L. L. *The Western District*. Papers from the Western District Conference. Windsor: Essex County Historical Society and the Western District Council, 1983.

Putnam, D. F. and Putnam, R. G. *Canada: A Regional Analysis*. Revised metric edition. Canada: J. M. Dent & Sons, Ltd., 1978.

Royal Military College. Kingston: Information and Public Relations Office Royal Military College, ca. 1985.

Sewell, John. "Life Vibrant in North Bay." *The Globe and Mail*. Toronto, July 10, 1985, p. 5.

Statistics Canada. *Canada's Changing Population Distribution*. Ottawa: Ministry of Supply and Services, 1984.

Sudbury, City of. *Sudbury Ontario*. Sudbury: Convention and Visitors Services of Sudbury.

Thunder Bay: Come Grow with Us. Thunder Bay: Thunder Bay Economic Development Corporation, ca. 1985.

Thunder Bay Fact Book. Thunder Bay: Economic Development Corporation, ca. 1985.

Thunder Bay, Port of. *Port of Thunder Bay*. A packet. Thunder Bay: Port of Thunder Bay - Lakehead Harbor Commission, 1985.

Trans Port of Thunder Bay: ... Annual Report 1985. Vol. 4, No. 1. Thunder Bay: Port Authority, Spring 1986.

"The University of Western Ontario: Campus Facts 1985." London: Department of University Relations and Information.

University of Western Ontario. *Report of the President 1983-1984*. London: The University of Western Ontario, 1984.

Veitch, Isobel G. *Geographical Papers: Completed Theses and Undergraduate Senior Reports*. No. 52. London: Department of Geography, The University of Western Ontario, 1985.

Volgenau, Gerald. "Cigarette crackdown dries up tobacco farms in Canada." *Detroit Free Press*. July 27, 1986, pp. E1 & E4.

Wall, Geoffrey. *Recreational Land Use in Southern Ontario*. Pub. Series 4. Waterloo: Department of Geography, University of Waterloo, 1979.

"Western." *Saturday Toronto Star*. Part 13. August 17, 1985. P.M4.

Windsor-Essex County Manufacturers Directory, 1984. Windsor: Windsor-Essex County Development Commission, 1984.

Wrightman, N. M. and W. R. "Road and Highway Development in Northwestern Ontario, 1850 to 1990." *The Canadian Geographer*. Canadian Association of Geographers, Winter, 1992. pp. 366-380 (with maps).

Indiana

"Average City, USA." (an Editorial) *South Bend Tribune*. October 3, 1983.

Bloom, Phil. "More range, more days boost Hoosier turkey hunting." *Fort Wayne Journal-Gazette*, May 23, 1993, p. B10.

Claflin, B. and Bauer E. "State Park Eyed for Downtown." *The Journal-Gazette*. Fort Wayne. September 29, 1985, p. C1.

Elkhart, Indiana. Woodland Hills, California: Windsor Publications for the Greater Elkhart Chamber of Commerce, ca. 1982.

The City of Ft. Wayne: A Summary of Data. Ft. Wayne, Indiana: Chamber of Commerce, 1985.

Fun in the Steuben County Area. Angola, Indiana: Steuben Printing Company, ca. 1976.

Haynes, Lisa. "Northeast Indiana 'Hot' for Economic Development." *Indiana Business*, October 1984, pp. 16-26.

Heritage Country: Guide to Indiana Amish County. Spring/Summer 1983. Middlebury, Indiana:

Higdon, Hal. "Splashing Through South Bend." *Ford Times*, April 1986, pp. 33-37.

Major Economic Activities: Fort Wayne, Indiana. Fort Wayne, Indiana: Chamber of Commerce, February 23, 1984.

"Management Guide to Workers' Compensation and Occupational Diseases." Indianapolis: Indiana Chamber of Commerce, 1986.

McCord, Shirley (compiler). Travel Accounts of Indiana 1679-1961. Indianapolis: Indiana Historical Society, 1970.

Michiana Monthly. Mishawaka, Indiana: Michiana Monthly Publications, August 1985.

Northern Indiana: Community Analysis of South Bend, Indiana. Hammond, Indiana: Northern Indiana Public Service Co., 1985.

The Murals of Luigi Gregori. Notre Dame, Indiana: Department of Information Services, 1985. (2 pp. typed)

Schlereth, Thomas J. *The University of Notre Dame: A Portrait of its History and Campus*. Notre Dame, Indiana: University of Notre Dame Press, 1977.

Shipshewana Flea Market and Area Visitor's Guide. New 1985 edition. LaGrange, Indiana: LaGrange Publishing Co., 1985.

The Call of the Whitewater; South Bend's East Race Waterway. South Bend, Indiana: Office of Community Affairs, 1985. (a pamphlet)

Unemployment Compensation in Indiana. Indianapolis, Indiana: Indiana Chamber of Commerce, 1985. (a folder)

Veltema, Eugene. "An Odor Alert." *Grand Rapids Press*, February 19, 1985, P. A10.

Workmen's Compensation and Unemployment Compensation Programs: Indiana and Surrounding States. Indianapolis: Indiana State Chamber of Commerce, for years 1983, 1984, 1985.

Illinois

Conzen, Michael P. "The Changing Character of Metropolitan Chicago." *Journal of Geography*. Washington, DC. National Council for Geographic Education, Sept.-Oct. 1986, pp. 224-236.

Cutler, Irving, *Chicago: Metropolis of the Mid-Continent*. 2nd ed. Dubuque, Iowa: Kendall/Hunt Publishing Co. for The Geographic Society of Chicago, 1973. 210 pp.

United States Department of the Interior. "Chicago Portage National Historic Site." National Register of Historic Places Inventory -- Nomination Form. Cook County Forest Preserve, Illinois, 1958.

Michigan

Allen, Robert S. "His Majesty's Indian Allies: Native Peoples. The British Crown and the War of 1812." Mt. Pleasant: *The Michigan Historical Review*, Fall 1988, pp. 1-24.

Bald, F. Clever. *Michigan in Four Centuries*. New York: Harper and Brothers, 1954.

Blain, Judy. "Anguish in Agland." *West Michigan Magazine*, August 1987, pp. 28-31.

Books, Kathryn J. with Santer, R. A. Consultant. *Michigan Studies Program*. Tallahassee, Florida: Graphic Learning Corporation, 1983.

Brant, G. W. and Schafer, C. E., Illustrator. *Michigan Wildlife Sketches*. Lansing: Michigan Department of Natural Resources, 1972.

Bredin, Jim. "Rouge Rescue '86." *Natural Resources Record*. Vol. 6, No. 7. Lansing: Michigan Department Natural Resources, July 1986, pp. 14-15.

Brazaier, H. E. and Larsen, D. S. eds. *Michigan Fiscal and Economic Structure*. Ann Arbor: The University of Michigan Press, 1982.

Bunge, William. *Fitzgerald: Geography of a Riot Area.* Cambridge, Massachusetts: Schenkman Publishing Co., Inc., 1971.

"Community Awareness runs high in river clean up." *The Adrian Daily Telegram*, October 4, 1985, p. 1.

"Community Development Efforts for Underwater Preserves Increasing." *Water Impacts*, Institute of Water Research, Michigan State University, January, 1991, pp. 1-2.

Cornell, George L. "Indian Treaties and the Origins of Michigan." *The Michigan Connection*. Lansing: Michigan Council for the Humanities, 1986, p. 17-19.

Detroit Field Trip Guide. Detroit: Association of American Geographers, April 1985.

Dorr, J. A. and Eschman, D. F. *Geology of Michigan*. Ann Arbor: The University of Michigan Press, 1971.

Dunbar, Willis F. *Michigan: A History of the Wolverine State*. Grand Rapids, Michigan: William B. Eerdmans Publishing Co., 1966.

Economic Base Analysis City of Port Huron, Michigan. Detroit, Michigan: Parkin, Rogers Assoc., Inc. for Port Huron Planning Commission, February 1974.

Egginton, Joyce. *The Poisoning of Michigan*. New York: W. W. Norton and Company, 1982. 351 pp.

Ewew, Lynda Ann. *Corporate Power and Urban Crisis in Detroit*. Princeton: Princeton University Press, 1978.

Ferris, Woodbridge N. "The Spirit of the Times." An address delivered at the Annual Meeting of the Michigan Pioneer and Historical Society, Lansing, May 25, 1916. (stenographically reprinted) pp. 29-40.

Fitting, James E. *The Archaeology of Michigan*. Bloomfield Hills, Michigan: Cranbrook Institute of Science, 1975.

Flott, Leslie W. "Augustus Herring ... Aviation Pioneer." *Chronicle* of Historical Society of Michigan. Vol. 10, No. 3, 1974, pp. 2-8.

A Guide to the Michigan Environmental Protection Act. Troy, Michigan: East Michigan Environmental Action Council, 1980.

Holdane, Neal. "End of the Mine." *Michigan Natural Resources*, November-December 1985, pp. 40-45.

Harris, Fran. *Focus: Michigan Women 1701-1977*. Lansing: Michigan Coordinating Committee of the National Commission on the Observance of Women's Year, 1977.

Hubbard, Bela. *Memorials of a Half-Century*. New York: G. P. Putnam's Sons, 1888; Republished: Gale Research Company, Detroit, 1978.

Hudgins, Bert. *Michigan: Geographic Backgrounds in the Development of the Commonwealth*. 4th ed. Detroit: Edward Brothers of Ann Arbor, 1961.

Irwin, Jim. "The Vanishing Land." *The Grand Rapids Press*. February 9, 1986, p. A17.

Irwin, Jim. "20 Years After Great Riot." *The Grand Rapids Press*. July 12, 1987, p. A18.

Kaplan, Deborah. "What Have We Done to the Rouge?" *Detroit* Supplement of the *Detroit Sunday Free Press*, July 27, 1986, pp. 10-13.

Kyser, Dewayne. "The American Indian in Isabella County." *The Peninsula*. Vol. 1 (1974), pp. 14-19.

Martin, Thomas, Ridenour, Julie. "New Office Coordinates Michigan's Stand on Great Lakes." *Grand Rapids Press*, January 13, 1986, p. C3.

The Michigan Economy. Vol. 1 - Vol. 5. Detroit: Wayne State University, Bureau of Business Research, 1980-1986.

Michigan Government. *Agriculture Across Michigan*. Lansing: Michigan Department of Agriculture, United States Department of Agriculture, November 15, 1989; January 15, 1991; May, 1993.

Michigan Government. *Michigan Agricultural Land Requirements: A Projection to the Year 2000 A.D.* Lansing: Michigan Department of Agriculture, February 1973. Mimeographed, 11 pp.

Michigan Government. *Michigan Agricultural Statistics 1985*, also for 1982, 1983, 1984). Lansing: Michigan Department of Agriculture, 1985 (1982, 1983, 1984).

Michigan Government. *Michigan Airport Directory: 1986*. Lansing, Michigan: Michigan Department of Transportation, 1986.

Michigan Government. *Michigan Equine Survey: 1984*. Lansing: Michigan Department of Agriculture, 1984.

Michigan Government. *Michigan Natural Resources Magazine*. A Tribute to the Great Lakes Special Edition. Lansing, Michigan: Michigan Department of Natural Resources, May-June 1986.

Michigan Government. *Michigan Natural Resources Magazine* (Sand Dunes special feature). Lansing: Michigan Department of Natural Resources, July-August 1985.

Michigan Government. Michigan State Parks. Lansing: Department of Natural Resources, 1985. (a pamphlet)

Michigan Government. *Natural Resources Register*. Vol. 6, No. 7 (Kirtlands Warbler, Sichuan Pheasant, Michigan Earthquakes, Rouge River). Lansing: Michigan Department of Natural Resources, July 1986.

Michigan Government. *Natural Resources Register*: Vol. 7. No. 6 (Islands). Lansing: Michigan Department of Natural Resources, July, 1987. p. 7.

Michigan Government. *State of the Great Lakes*. Annual Report for 1985. Lansing: The Office of the Great Lakes, 1985.

Michigan Government. Wildflowers of Michigan. Lansing, Michigan: Michigan Department of Transportation and Department of Natural Resources, 1985.

Moore, Michael D. "Timber Treasure." *Michigan Natural Resources Magazine*. Lansing, Michigan: Department of Natural Resources, January-February 1986, pp. 48-53.

Muskegon Shoreline Magazine. Vol. 1, No. 11. Muskegon, Michigan: Muskegon Magazine Inc., August 1985.

"New Office Coordinates Michigan's Stand on Great Lakes." *The Grand Rapids Press*. January 13, 1986, p. C3.

Newnom, Clyde L. *Michigan's Thirty-Seven Million Acres of Diamonds*. Detroit: The Book of Michigan Co., 1927.

Peters, Bernard C. "Hypocrisy on the Great Lakes Frontier: The use of Whiskey by the Michigan Department of Indian Affairs." Mt. Pleasant: *The Michigan Historical Review*, Fall 1992, pp. 2-13.

"Pine Martens Welcomed Back to Michigan North." *Natural Resources Register*. Vol. 6, No. 1. Michigan Department of Natural Resources, January 1986, pp. 12-13.

Port Huron (Michigan) Economic Base. Detroit: Parkins, Rogers and Associates, Inc. for The Port Huron Planning Commission, 1974.

Port Huron Land Use Plan. Port Huron, Michigan: Port Huron Planning Commission, 1974.

Port Huron, Michigan: Market Analysis. Columbia, Maryland: American City Corporation, 1982.

Quaternary Geomorphology: Michigan Field Trip Guide. East Lansing, Michigan: East Lakes Division of the Association of American Geographers, October 10, 1986.

Records of Decision: Final Environmental Impact Statement Huron-Manistee National Forests. Cadillac, Michigan: U.S. Department of Agriculture, Forest Service - Eastern Region, 1986 (U.S. Government Printing Office 641-110/20052).

Rieck, R. L. and Winter, H. A. "Characteristics of a Glacially Buried Cuesta in Southeast Michigan." *Annals of the Association of American Geographers*. Vol. 72, No. 4, December 1982. pp. 482-494.

Rosen, James. "Michigan Waste Disposal 'Host'". *The Pioneer*. Big Rapids, Michigan, July 1, 1987, p. 1.

Santer, R. A. *Michigan: Heart of the Great Lakes*. Dubuque: Kendall/Hunt Publishing Co., 1977.

Schallau, Con H. *Small Forest Ownership in the Urban Fringe Area of Michigan*, Station Paper No. 103. Lake State Forest Experiment Station: U.S. Department of Agriculture, August 1962.

Schoolcraft, Henry R. *Travels through the Northwestern Regions of the United States 1820*. (Reprint) Ann Arbor: University Microfilms, Inc., 1966. from original, Albany, New York: E. and E. Hosford, 1821.

Sinclair, Robert. *The Face of Detroit -- A Spatial Synthesis*. Detroit: Wayne State University - National Council for Geographic Education. U.S. Office of Education, 1970.

Soil's Our Thing: Periodic Newsletter of the Mecosta Soil Conservation District. Big Rapids, Michigan: Mecosta Soil Conservation District, August 1986.

Sommers, Lawrence M. *Michigan: A Geography*. Boulder, Colorado: Westview Press, 1984.

Spencer, J. W. "Origins of the Basins of the Great Lakes." *American Geologist*, Vol. 7, 1891, pp. 86-97.

Struthers, F. and Lewando, R. *The Michigan Food System: Increasing Dependence or Self-Reliance*. Emmaus, Pennsylvania: The Cornucopia Project of Rodale Press, 1982.

Waldron, Clara. *One Hundred Years a Country Town: The Village of Tecumseh, Michigan 1824-1924*. Tecumseh, Michigan Thomas A. Riordan, 1968.

"Waste Disposal Methods Reviewed" *Water Impacts*, Vol. 8 No. 5. E. Lansing: Institute of Water Research, Michigan State University, May, 1987. p. 2.

Water Impacts. Vol. 6 - Vol. 7. East Lansing, Michigan: Institute of Water Research, Michigan State University, 1985-1986.

Welch, Richard W. *County Evolution in Michigan 1790-1897*. Lansing: Michigan Department of Education, 1982.

United States Department of Agriculture. *Soil Survey of Mecosta County Michigan*. Washington, DC.: Soil Conservation Service, 1984.

United States Department of Commerce. *Climate of Michigan by Stations*. East Lansing: Michigan Weather Service, 1963.

Zeman, Henry. "Moose Introduction Doomed to Failure." *The Grand Rapids Press*. January 16, 1986. p. C8.

Minnesota

Catfish Festival. Floodwood, Minnesota: Floodwood Area Development Corporation, 1985. (a pamphlet)

Dilley, Robert S. *et. al.* "Duluth and Thunder Bay: A Study of Mutual Tourist Attraction." Toronto: *The Operational Geographer*, December, 1991, pp. 9-13.

Duluth Business Indicators. Vol. 6, No. 1. Duluth: University of Minnesota-Duluth, School of Business and Economics, 1985.

Duluth Facts: Current Facts Concerning Minnesota's Third Largest City. Duluth: Duluth Area Chamber of Commerce, 1985.

Duluth Government. This is Duluth. Duluth: Office of Business Development, 1985.

Ebbott, Elizabeth. *Indians of Minnesota*. Minneapolis: University of Minnesota Press, 1985.

Johnson, Elden. *The Prehistoric Peoples of Minnesota*. Minnesota Prehistoric Archaeology Series No. 3. Rev. 2nd ed. St. Paul, Minnesota: Minnesota Historical Society, 1978.

Lake Superior Port Cities Magazine. (Special edition A Lake Superior Experience). Vol. 7, No. 1. Duluth, Minnesota, Summer 1985.

Miller, A. L. "Butler Taconite grinds to a halt; 450 jobs lost." Duluth *News-Tribune and Herald*. July 29, 1985. p. 1A.

Northeastern Minnesota Labor Market Review. Duluth: Duluth Area Chamber of Commerce, June 1985.

Phillips, Brian A. M. "Shoreline Inheritance in Coastal Histories: Cook County, Minnesota." *Science*. Vol. 195, January 7, 1977, pp. 11-16.

Tip of the Arrowhead: Minnesota's Northland. Grand Marais, Minnesota: Tip of the Arrowhead Association, 1985.

Tip of the Arrowhead: A Part of the Nation's Last Wilderness. Grand Marais, Minnesota: Tip of the Arrowhead Association, 1985.

United States National Park Service. *Grand Portage*. Washington, DC.: United States Department of the Interior, 1984, reprint of 1976. (a pamphlet)

New York

Dunkirk, New York Report 3. Dunkirk, New York: Department of Development, 1985.

Dunkirk Government. *Profile of Dunkirk, New York*. Dunkirk, New York: Dunkirk City Planning Office, 1985.

Fort Drum, New York. Watertown, New York: Greater Watertown Chamber of Commerce, ca. 1985. (2 pp. typed)

Kodak in Rochester. Rochester, New York: Eastman Kodak Company, 1986.

Metro Buffalo: Facts and Figures. Buffalo, New York: Buffalo Area Chamber of Commerce, 19085. (a pamphlet)

Lamb, Richard F. "The Morphology and Vitality of Business Districts in Upstate New York Villages." *The Professional Geographer,* May 1985, pp. 162-172.

Oswego. Franklin Square Oswego, New York: A Walking Tour. Oswego, New York: Heritage Foundation of Oswego County, 1985. (a pamphlet)

1985 Oswego Chamber of Commerce Directory Government Directory. Oswego, New York: Oswego Chamber of Commerce, 1985.

Prospectus for Opportunity: Buffalo, New York. Buffalo, New York: Buffalo Area Chamber of Commerce, 1985.

Roberts, Susan M. and Schein, R. H. "The Entrepreneurial City: Fabricating Urban Development in Syracuse, New York." *The Professional Geographer.* Washington, DC: Association of American Geographers, February, 1993, pp. 21-33.

Sackets Harbor Central School Graduates 1982. Historic Sackets Harbor. Sackets Harbor, New York: Sackets Harbor Area Cultural Preservation Foundation, Inc., ca. 1985.

Tioga County, NY. Worth Looking Into .... Owego, New York: Broome/Tioga Industry Council, 1985. (a packet)

Tioga County. 1984 Community Directory (Tioga County, New York). Owego, New York: Owego Pennysaver Press, 1984.

Thompson, John H., editor. *Geography of New York State.* Syracuse, New York: Syracuse University Press, 1966.

VanDiver, Bradford B. *Upstate New York.* Dubuque, Iowa: Kendall/Hunt Publishing Co., 1980.

Watertown. One Million dollars a Day (Fort Drum, NY.). Watertown, New York: WWNYTV7, ca. 1985. (4 pp. typed)

"Watertown, NY. Community Economic Profile." Syracuse: Economic Development Department, Niagara Mohawk Power Company, ca. 1985.

Watertown Government. Resource Conservation and Development. Watertown, New York: Black River - St. Lawrence Resource Conservation and Development, 1985. (a pamphlet)

Welcome to Historic Mormon Country. Rochester, New York: The Church of Jesus Christ of Latter Day Saints, 1985. (a pamphlet)

Welcome to Kodak Park this is our story. Rochester, New York: Eastman Kodak Company, 1986.

Ohio

(Armstrong) *Neil Armstrong Air and Space Museum.* Columbus, Ohio: Ohio Historical Society, 1985.

Ashtabula County Tourism -- Visitor's Guide: 1985. Ashtabula, Ohio: Ashtabula County Tourism Association, 1985.

Cleveland, Ohio. Research Publications and Reports (data, life, maps). Cleveland: Greater Cleveland Growth Association, varying dates.

Easterly, Nathan W. *The Oaks of the Oak Openings.* Toledo: The Metropolitan Park District of the Toledo Area, undated.

Ferguson, William A. "Stan Hywet Hall and Gardens." *Toledo Blade,* May 23, 1993, p. G1.

Findlay (Ohio) 2000: A Comprehensive Land Use Plan. Findlay, Ohio: Hancock Regional Planning Commission, ca. 1980.

Findlay Hancock County Ohio. Findlay, Ohio: Findlay Area Chamber of Commerce, 1982.

Lake Erie. Cleveland: The Greater Cleveland Growth Association, 1983.

Ohio Almanac. Lorain, Ohio: The Lorain Journal Company, 1977.

Ohio Government. *Ohio is the Greatest.* Columbus, Ohio (?): Regional Graphics, ca. 1980.

Raup, H. F. and Smith, C. *Ohio Geography: Selected Readings.* Dubuque: Kendall/Hunt Publishing Co., 1973.

Rosenboom, E. H. and Weisenburger, F. P. *A History of Ohio*. Columbus: The Ohio Historical Society, 1973.

Tiffin Ohio. Tiffin, Ohio: Tiffin Area Chamber of Commerce, 1985.

"Toledo heads Lake Erie office." Big Rapids: *Pioneer*, September 23, 1991, p.2.

(Toledo Packet) Capabilities that Link the World. Toledo: Port of Toledo, 1985.

Toledo. *Guide to Your Nine Metroparks* (Toledo). Toledo: Metropark Naturalist Headquarters, 1985.

Toledo. Toledo: Toledo Area Chamber of Commerce, - Windsor Publications, Inc., 1981.

Pennsylvania

The Cornucopia Project. *The Pennsylvania Food System: Crash or Self-Reliance?* Emmaus, Pennsylvania: Rodale Press, 1981.

"Erie Area Development Report." Section 2. *Pittsburgh Business Times Journal*, July 22-28, 1985, pp. 1-24.

"Erie History." Erie Pennsylvania: Chamber of Commerce,
(4 page typed) undated.

"Erie Growth Report." *Pittsburgh Business Times-Journal*, July 22, 1985, p. 125, p. 225.

The Erie Labor Market Profile. Erie, Pennsylvania: Greater Erie Industrial Development Corporation, @ 1985.

(Erie) *You'll Love Erie*. Economic and History Packet. Erie, Pennsylvania: Erie Area Chamber of Commerce, <u>ca.</u> 1985.

Wisconsin

Abrams, Lawrence and Kathleen. *Exploring Wisconsin*. Chicago: Rand McNally and Co., 1981.

Bayfield County: Wisconsin's Best Kept Secret. Washburn, Wisconsin: Bayfield County Tourism and Recreation Department, 1985.

Wisconsin Government. *Economic Profiles*. (for the Counties of Kenosha, Milwaukee, Ozaukee, Walworth, Washington, Waukesha) Madison: Wisconsin Department of Development, <u>ca.</u> 1984.

Wisconsin Government. *Economic Profile: The Region as a Whole* (Southeast Wisconsin Regional Planning Commission). Madison: Wisconsin Department of Development, <u>ca.</u> 1984.

Fox Cities Profile. Appleton and Neenah, Wisconsin: Fox Cities Chamber of Commerce and Industry, <u>ca.</u> 1985.

Green Bay Area Market Guide. Green Bay, Wisconsin: Green Bay Area Chamber of Commerce, <u>ca.</u> 1985.

Hale, Frederick. *Danes in Wisconsin*. Madison: The State Historical Society of Wisconsin, 1981.

Hunt, Jane N. ed. *Brevets Wisconsin Historical Markers and Sites*. Sioux Falls, South Dakota: Brevet Press, 1974.

Hurley Reaches 100 Years: 1884-1984. Hurley, Wisconsin: Hurley, Wisconsin Centennial Committee, 1984.

Martin, Lawrence. *The Physical Geography of Wisconsin*. Madison: The University of Wisconsin Press, 1965. (1st edition 1916).

Menominee Planning Department. *Population Characteristics of the Menominee Reservation and Labor Force Survey 1984*. Menominee Reservation, Wisconsin: Menominee Tribal Office, 1984.

Ourada, Patricia K. *The Menominee Indians. A History*. Norman: University of Oklahoma Press, 1979.

Port of Milwaukee 1985 Directory Great Lakes Overseas Shipping Services. Milwaukee: Port of Milwaukee, 1985.

Port of Milwaukee Economic Impact Study. Milwaukee: Port of Milwaukee, 1982.

1984 Annual Report: Bay-Lake Regional Planning Commission. Green Bay, Wisconsin: Bay-Lake Regional Planning Commission, 1984.

1984 Annual Report: Northwest Regional Planning Commission. Spooner, Wisconsin: Northwest Regional Planning Commission, 1984.

1984 Population Characteristics of the Menominee Reservation and Labor Force Survey. Menominee Reservation, Wisconsin: Department of Planning, 1984.

1978 Upgraded Overall Annual Economic Development Report: Northwest Wisconsin. Spooner, Wisconsin: Northwest Regional Planning Commission, 1978.

Overall Economic Development Program: East Central Wisconsin. Menasha, Wisconsin: East Central Wisconsin Regional Planning Commission, 1981.

"Rural County is Thriving in Wisconsin." *Chicago Tribune*, February 8, 1993, Section 1 p. 3.

Sturgeon Bay, Door County Wisconsin, 1985. (a 12 page traveler information booklet), 1985.

Three Year Annual Report of the Human Services Board of Forest, Oneida and Vilas Counties: 1981-1983. (Mental Health, Developmental Disability Chemical Dependency, and Systems Management Services). Rhinelander, Wisconsin: Human Services Board of Forest, Oneida and Vilas Counties, 1984.

Urban Waterfronts: an Assessment. (Staff Report). Madison: Office of Coastal Management, Wisconsin Department of Administration, March 1981. (mimeographed)

Wisconsin Government. *Reading Wisconsin's Landscape.* 2nd ed. Madison: Wisconsin State Department of Public Instruction, 1962.

Wisconsin Department of Administration. *Urban Waterfronts an Assessment.* Madison: Office of Coastal Management, 1981.

Wisconsin Historical Markers and Sites. Edited by N. Jane Hunt. Garretson, South Dakota: Sanders Printing Co., 1974.

Physical Environment

"American bald eagles making comeback in Lower Peninsula." *Grand Rapids Press*, February 15, 1990, p. B7.

Ankey, Robert. "Clean-up plan for Rouge River." *Detroit News.* February 12, 1993, p. B1.

Ashbaugh, Rosalie. "The gypsy moth invasion." Big Rapids: *Pioneer*, August 21, 1990, p. D1.

BeVier, Thomas. "Cormorants." *Detroit News*, May 9, 1993, p. C3.

BeVier, Thomas. "Sinkholes aren't just holes to him." *Detroit Free Press*, April 27, 1983.

BeVier, Thomas. "Fish Stories - Uneasy Peace." *Detroit.* Detroit Free Press, July 26, 1987, pp. 10-15.

Bogue, M. B. and Palmer, V. A. *Around the Shores of Lake Superior: A Guide to Historic Sites.* Madison, Wisconsin (?): The University of Wisconsin Sea Grant College Program, 1979.

Bradshaw, Michael and Weaver, Ruth. *Physical Geography.* St. Louis: Mosby - Year Book, Inc. 1993.

Buol, S. W. *et. al. Soil Genesis and Classification.* Ames: Iowa State University Press, 1973.

Campbell, B. and Stanton, B. "The Blobs: A Crisis bubbling Up?" *The Grand Rapids Press*, March 2, 1986, p. B1.

Clark, T. H. and Stearn, C. W. *Geological Evolution of North America.* 2nd ed. New York: The Ronald Press, Co., 1968.

"Cleaner Rivers Triggers Comeback of Fish Killing Lamprey." *Grand Rapids Press*, June 8, 1987, p. 3.

Cohen, Stewart J. "Climatic Change, Population Growth, and Their Effects on Great Lakes Water Supplies." *The Professional Geographer.* Washington, DC: Association of American Geographers, November 1986, pp. 317-323.

Coping with Drought. E. Lansing: Michigan Cooperative Expension Service and Michigan Farm Bureau, Summer, 1988.

Doerr, Arthur. *Fundamentals of Physical Geography*, 2nd ed. Dubuque, IA: Wm C. Brown Publishers, 1993.

Drake, R. H. and Reinking, R. L. "Sources of Sediment Pollution in the Lake Macatawa Drainage Basin, Michigan." *Michigan Academician.* Vol. X, No. 3, Winter 1978, pp. 265-272.

Dufresne, Jim. "DNR is hunting fish heads." (tagged chinook salmon) *Detroit News*, April 19, 1992, p. C3.

Eichenlaub, Val L. *Weather and Climate of the Great Lakes Region.* Notre Dame: University of Notre Dame Press, 1979. Cartography by: Thomas W. Hodler.

Ferrett, R. L. and Ojala, C. F. "Seasonal Variation in Michigan's Precipitation in the Last Century." *Michigan Academician*, Spring 1993, p. 244.

"Foreign fish puts crimp in fishery." *Grand Rapids Press*, October 3, 1992, p. D4.

Francis, Mary. "Fungus Fancy: The big mushroom." *Grand Rapids Press*, May 3, 1992, pp. A1 and 10.

"Global Warning: State temps show opposite effect." Big Rapids: *Pioneer*, November 19, 1990, p. A1.

"Great Lakes Water Level Update." *Water Impacts*, Vol. 8. No. 7. Institute of Water Research (East Lansing: Michigan State University), July 1987.

Guthrie, D. and Hoogterp, E. "New Roles for Weather Service draw mixed reviews." *Grand Rapids Press*, March 29, 1992, p. A1.

Gwizdz, Bob. "DNR changes direction, will allow pheasant hunting in stocked area." *Grand Rapids Press*, April 17, 1993, p. D2.

Gwizdz, Bob. "Restoration project gives a closer look at moose." *Grand Rapids Press*, January 9, 1993, p. D1.

Gwizdz, Bob. "State's elk herd growing fast." *Grand Rapids Press*, February 13, 1993, p. D1.

Hill, Richard L. "Scientists doubt benefit of replacing old-growth forests." *Grand Rapids Press*, February 18, 1990, p. C5.

"Hungrier, bigger mussel invades the Great Lakes." *Grand Rapids Press*, August 18, 1992, p. A9.

"Information Office Established to Answer Zebra Mussel Questions." *Water Impacts*. E. Lansing: Institute of Water Research, Michigan State University, February, 1992.

Kaplan, Deborah. "What have we done to the Rouge? Can Jim Murray Save the Dirtiest River in Michigan?" *Detroit: Sunday Supplement of the Detroit Free Press*, July 27, 1986, pp. 10-13.

Kearns, Kim. "Biological Control of Purple Loosestrife Studied." *Water Impacts*. E. Lansing: Institute of Water Research, Michigan State University, November/December, 1992, pp. 3-4.

Kromn, D. E. and White, S. E. *Conserving the Ogallala: What Next?*. Manhattan, Kansas (?): Kansas State University, 1985.

Lacy, Mary L. "Michigan Seeks Recovery of Gray Wolf." *Jack Pine Wabler*, Michigan Audubon Society, May/June 1993, p. 13.

"Lake Sturgeon May Be Making Comeback." *Grand Rapids Press*, July 12, 1987, p. D1.

Lamm, Tom. "A Real Crisis in Real Country". *American Land Forum*. Vol. V, No. 2, Spring 1985, pp. 10-12.

"Lighting Underrated As a Killer." *Grand Rapids Press*, August 7, 1986, p. D6.

McCarthy, Tom. "Mexico polluting Great Lakes, EPA official says." *Grand Rapids Press*, September 22, 1992, p. B8.

McKenzie, A. "Explaining and Exploiting a winter worry." (frost heave), *Science*, December 23 and 30, 1989, p. 407

McKnight, Tom L. *Physical Geography: A Landscape Appreciation*. 2nd Ed. Englewood Cliffs, NJ.: Prentice-Hall, Inc. 1984.

Magner, Mike. "Air-monitoring system checks for pollution." *Grand Rapids Press*, April 26, 1992, p. A21 (with map).

Magner, Mike. "Great Lakes Coastal Barrier Act." *Grand Rapids Press*, April 2, 1989, p. F1.

Magner, Mike. "State braces for change in watershed rules." *Grand Rapids Press*, March 21, 1993, p. C5.

Magner, Mike. "Zebra mussels suspected in decline of walleye." *Grand Rapids Press*, April 23, 1993, p. C2.

Mainville, Frank W. "Return of the Grayling." *Michigan Natural Resources*. Vol. 56, No. 4, July-August, 1987, pp. 4-9.

Meyerson, Howard. "Bear problems in wild largely man-made, professor contends." *Grand Rapids Press*, February 6, 1993, p. D1.

Meyerson, Howard. "Zebra mussel populations gaining strength." *Grand Rapids Press*, May 1, 1993, p. D3.

Michigan Department of Natural Resources. *Protecting Inland Lakes: A Watershed Management Guidebook*. Lansing: State of Michigan, 1990.

Milstein, Randall. "Past Tales Describe Michigan Earthquakes." *Natural Resources Record*. Vol. 6, No. 7. Lansing: Michigan Department Natural Resources, July 1986, pp. 19-21.

Moore, Raymond C. *Introduction to Historical Geology.* 2nd ed. New York: McGraw Hill Book Co., Inc., 1958.

"New Studies Contribute to Understanding of Zebra Mussels." *Water Impacts.* E. Lansing: Institute of Water Research, Michigan State University, April 1991.

"Northern Michigan woodlands disappearing." Big Rapids: *Pioneer*, January 4, 1992, p. 2.

"Oft-feared mussels aid in cleanup of harbor." *Grand Rapids Press*, November 7, 1992, p. A4.

Ojakangas, R. W. and Matsch, C. L. *Minnesota's Geology.* Minneapolis: University of Minnesota Press, 1982.

Paulson, Gerald A. *Wetlands and Water Quality.* Chicago: Lake Michigan Federation, 1985. Paull, R. K. and Paull, R. A. *Geology of Wisconsin and Upper Michigan.* Dubuque, Iowa: Kendall/Hunt Publishing Co., 1977.

Peters, Bernard C. "The Remaking of an Image," Geographical Survey, Blue Earth Geographical Society, Mankato, Minnesota, Vol. 3. No. 1, January, 1974, pp. 38-44.

Peters, Bernard C. "No Trees on the Prairie: Persistence of Error in Landscape Terminology," *Michigan History*, Vol. 54, Spring 1970, p. 26. Citing E. Larkin Brown, "A Poem for the Dedication of the Ladies Library Building at Schoolcraft, Michigan," Regional History Collection Western Michigan University Library.

Peterson, Susan. "The Great Toxic Lakes." *Environmental Action Magazine.* June 1985.

"Plan Calls for State to Buy Out Commercial Fishers." *Grand Rapids Press*, July 12, 1987, p. A19.

"Plant Identification Appropriate Prior to Treatment." *Water Impacts.* E. Lansing: Institute of Water Research, Michigan State University, June, 1990, pp. 6-7.

"Plight of the Wolf on Isle Royale." *Water Impacts.* Michigan State University: Institute of Water Research, January, 1989, pp. 4-5.

"Population Growth and the Toxic Contamination of the Great Lakes." *TEF data*, No. 17. The Environmental Fund: Washington, DC., February 1985.

Poulson, David. "Natural enemies are killing Michigan Trees." *Grand Rapids Press*, January 11, 1993, p. A1.

"Questions on Nuclear Wastes." *The Wilson Quarterly.* Winter 1983, pp. 34-35.

Raffel, John. "Area residents spot bald eagles." Big Rapids: *Pioneer*, May 2, 1991, p. A6.

Raphael, C. Nicholas. "Prehistoric and Historic Wetland Heritage of the Upper Great Lakes." *Michigan Academician.* Vol. XIX No. 3, Summer 1987, pp. 331-365.

Rieck, R. L. and Winters, H. A. "Lake, Stream and Bedrock in South Central Michigan." *Annals of the Association of American Geographers.* Vol. 69, 1979, pp. 276-288.

Santer, Richard A. *Final Report of Findings Concerning an August, 1991 Remembrance of an Alleged Wolf Attack During the 1930's in Big Rapids, Michigan.* Yellowstone National Park, Wyoming, October 15, 1992, 5 pp. typed (unpublished for N. A. Bishop, Research Interpreter).

"Save the Dunes, Leave the Oil." *Grand Rapids Press*, April 28, 1986, p. A10.

Schaaf, Miv. "Dreaming About Lost Orange Groves." *Los Angeles Times*, March 27, 1986, p. V.2.

"*Science* Magazine Reports on Acid Rain." *The Woodlands Forum.* Vol. 2, No. 2. Fall 1985, p. 18.

"Search for a Chunk from Space." *Detroit Free Press*, December 21, 1990, p. C3.

Shaver, Robert H. *Adventures with Fossils.* Circular No. 6. Bloomington, Indiana: Geological Survey, 1959.

Sheskin, Ira M. A geographic approach to the Study of natural gas." *Journal of Geography.* Vol. 79, No. 3. March 1980, pp. 86-99.

Sloane, Eric. A Reverence for Wood, Our Vanishing Landscape, An Age of Barns

Sommers, Lawrence, *et. al.* Fish in Lake Michigan. East Lansing, Michigan: Michigan Sea Grant Program, 1981.

Spiers, S. and Thornburn, G. "Interim Report Presented to Governments on Methods to Alleviate High Great Lakes Water Levels." *Focus*, Windsor: International Joint Commission, Vol. 12. No. 1. March/April 1987, pp. 2-3.

"State Closes Some North Beaches." *Grand Rapids Press*, June 28, 1986, p. D6.

Swart, Jennifer and Meehan, Chris. "They don't relish job or killing pets." *Grand Rapids Press*, March 15, 1993, p. A5.

"Tern Population Under Watchful Eye." *Grand Rapids Press* July 26, 1987, pp. D1-2.

"Trout From Yellowstone." *Grand Rapids Press*, June 1, 1987, B3.

"U-M water clean-up program used world wide." *Detroit News*, June 17, 1991, p. E3.

United States Government. *Great Lakes Water Level Facts*. Washington, DC.: Detroit District, U.S. Army Corps of Engineers, 1985.

United States Government. *Record of Decision*. Huron- Manistee National Forests. Cadillac, Michigan: United States Department of Agriculture, Forest Service --Eastern Region, 1986.

United States Government. *Stockholder Report FY1986*. Huron- Manistee National Forests. Cadillac, Michigan: United States Department of Agriculture, Forest Service --Eastern Region, May, 1987.

Weeks, George. *Sleeping Bear*. Glen Arbor, MI: Cottage Book Shop of Glen Arbor and Historical Society of Michigan, 1988.

Wells, J. R. and Thompson, P. W. *Ecological and Floristic Survey of P. J. Hoffmaster State Part*. Bloomfield Hills, Michigan (?): Cranbrook Institute of Science, October 1983.

"Zebra Mussels in the Great Lakes." (a fact sheet). E. Lansing: The Michigan Sea Grant College Program, Rev. January 4, 1991.

Zeman, Henry. :"Moose Introduction Doomed to Failure." *Grand Rapids Press*, January 18, 1986, p. C8.

Culture, Education and Economic Activities

"Aging munitions threaten sites." *Grand Rapids Press*, April 20, 1993, p. A3.

"Another boost in state support for education." *Voice: MEA*. Michigan Education Association, August 5, 1985, p. 3.

Auto '93. Lincolnwood, IL: Consumer Guide, 1993.

Brown L. and Jacobson, J. L. "The Future of Urbanization: Facing the Ecological and Economic Constraints." *World Watch Paper 77*. Washington, DC.: Worldwatch Institute, May 1987.

Choosing a Future: Steps to Revitalize the Mid-American Economy. Menlo Park, California: Public Policy Center SRI International for AmeriTrust Corporation, 1984.

Cornell, George C. "Unconquered Nations: the Native People of Michigan." *Michigan: Visions of Our Past*. E. Lansing: Michigan State University Press, 1989, pp. 24-40.

Cornell, Stephen. "The New Indian Politics." *The Wilson Quarterly*. Vol. X, No. 1. New Year's 1986, pp. 113-131.

"Cruise Ship Starts Runs to Fayette." *Grand Rapids Press*, June 14, 1987, P.E.G.

Cuttler, S. L., Holcomb, H. B., Shatin, D. "Spatial Patterns of Support for a Nuclear Weapons Freeze." *Professional Geographer*. Vol. 38, No. 1. February 1986, pp. 42-52.

Deupree, Joseph E. *A Century of Opportunity: A Centennial History of Ferris State College*. Big Rapids, Michigan: Joseph E. Deupree, 1982.

Eckert, Kathryn B. *Buildings of Michigan*. New York: Oxford University Press (Society of Architectural Historians), 1993.

Eckman, Bev. "Bring racing to the people." *Detroit News*, July 11, 1993, p. E9.

Ewing, Gordon O. "The Bases of Differences Between American and Canadian Cities." *The Canadian Geographer*, Canadian Association of Geographers, Fall 1992.

Flory, Bradley. "Integrity...horse racing Probe." *Grand Rapids Press*, April 12, 1993, p. B2.

Green, Milford B. "A Geography of Institutional Stock Ownership in the United States." *Annals*. Association of American Geographers, March 1993, pp. 66-89.

Hacker, David. "Up town cheers as national park gets OK." *Detroit Free Press*, October 7, 1992, p. B1.

Hart, John F. "Population Change in the Upper Lake States." *Annals of the Association of American Geographers*. Vol. 74, No. 2. June 1984, pp. 221-243.

Hart, John F. "Small Towns and Manufacturing." *Geographical Review*. New York: American Geographical Society, July 1988, pp. 272-287.

Hayden, Dolores. "What Would a Non-Sexist City Be Like? Speculations on Housing, Urban Design, and Human Work." *Signs*. Vol. 5. Spring 1980, pp. S170-S187.

Heidelberg: and International Community for an International World. Tiffin, Ohio: Heidelberg College, 1985.

Heidelberg College Catalog: 1985-1986. Tiffin, Ohio: Heidelberg College, 1985.

Heidelberg Resource Book 1985-85. Tiffin, Ohio: Heidelberg College, 1985. (map)

"Holdings of Research Libraries in U.S. and Canada 1990-91." *The Chronicle of Higher Education Almanac*, August 26, 1992, p. 36. and *CHE* May 6, 1992, p. A14.

Hornbeck, Mark. "The going rate." (Taxes), *Detroit News*, April 15, 1993, p. 3BNE. (Map).

Hudson, John C. "North American Origins of Middlewestern Frontier Populations." *Annals.* Washington, DC: Association of American Geographers, September, 1988, pp. 395-413. (w/maps).

Investing in the Future: A Prospectus for MidAmerica. Cleveland: AmeriTrust Corporation, 1986.

Kaniewski, David. "Fur trappers upset, frustrated." *Detroit News*, February 4, 1990, p. C5.

Koschik, Pat "Hopes Rise for High-Speed Rail Service." *Grand Rapids Press*, May 31, 1987, p. F9.

Lake Carriers Association. *Great Lakes Shipping.* Cleveland: 1982.

Lake Michigan Carferry Service: Ludington-Kewaunee. Ludington, Michigan: Michigan-Wisconsin Ferry Service, 1985, 1986.

Lemley, Brad. "What Does Your Garbage Say About You?" *Parade Magazine.* June 14, 1987, p. 20.

LesStrang, Jacques. *The Great Lakes/St. Lawrence System.* Maple City, Michigan: Harbor House Publishers Seaway Review, Inc., 1984.

"Logging in national forests." *Grand Rapids Press*, March 13, 1990, p. B4.

Longcore, Kathleen. "Desperate cherry group." *Grand Rapids Press*, February 4, 1990, p. A1-4.

Longcore, K. and Schmidt, W. "Land act aids farmers." *Grand Rapids Press*, December 14, 1987, p. C1.

Lund, Robert. *ABRACADABRA: Michigan and Magic.* Ann Arbor: Historical Society of Michigan, C. M. Burton Memorial Lecture, 1991.

MacNeill, Brendon. "Shipwrecks of the Great Lakes." Unpublished report, Ferris State University, November 1992.

McCarthy, Colman. "Teaching peace not such a silly goal." *Grand Rapids Press*, citing Washington Post Writers Group, February 1, 1990, p. A11.

McLuhan, T. C. *Touch the Earth: A Self-Portrait of Indian Existence.* New York: Promontory Press, 1971.

McWhirter, Nickie. "Some Community Needs Can't Wait for the Future." *Detroit Free Press*, June 6, 1986, p. B1.

Mazey, M. E. and Lee, D. R. *Her Space Her Place: A Geography of Women.* Washington, DC: Association of American Geographers, 1983.

Magner, Mike. "West Michigan farms are among nation's endangered." *Grand Rapids Press*, July 14, 1993, p. A1. (Map).

Michigan History Division. *Historic Sites in Michigan.* Lansing: Michigan Department of State, undated, 104 pp.

"Midwest farmers can taste big gains in Mexico trade." *Chicago Tribune*, May 2, 1993. Sec. 7 p. 2.

Nevala, Amy E. "Appreciation of Great Lakes Shipwrecks." *Water Impacts*, Institute of Water Resources, Michigan State University, May, 1993, p. 6.

Nye, Russel B. *Ferris Comes of Age: The Years of Transition 1946-1963.* Big Rapids, Michigan: Ferris State College Centennial Task Force, 1983.

O'Hare, William P. "America's Minorities -- The Demographics of Diversity." *Population Bulletin.* Washington, DC: Population Reference Bureau, December 1992.

O'hUallacháin, Breandan. "Regional and Technological Implications of the Recent Buildup in American Defense Spending." *Annals of the Association of American Geographers*, June, 1987, pp. 208-223.

"Once-mighty Great Lakes Shipping." *Grand Rapids Press*, October 10, 1992, p. B8.

Perlman, Lisa. "Benton Harbor showing life signs." *Grand Rapids Press*, October 1, 1989, p. E1.

"Prisons, military bring wealth." *Grand Rapids Press*, November 24, 1988, p. D2.

"Remove the Seaway toll disadvantage." Duluth *News-Tribune and Herald.* June 26, 1985, p. 8D.

Rensberger, Boyce. "Huge genetic experiment." *Grand Rapids Press*, March 21, 1993, p. A4.

Ross, Sonya. "Five medium-sized cities have worst poverty." Big Rapids *Pioneer*, March 19, 1993, p. A3.

Rubenstein, James M. "The Changing Distribution of U.S. Motor Vehicle Parts Suppliers." *Focus.* New York: American Geographical Society, Winter 1988, pp. 10-14.

St. Lawrence Seaway. Washington, DC: U.S. Department of Transportation, St. Lawrence Seaway Corporation, 1983.

St. Lawrence Seaway Traffic Report for the 1984 Navigation Season. Ottawa and Washington, DC.: St. Lawrence Seaway Development Corporation and The St. Lawrence Seaway Authority, 1985.

Swartz, Robert D. "Hispanic and Polish Commercial Strips in Detroit." *The Michigan Academician.* Ann Arbor: Michigan Academy of Science Arts and Letters, Fall, 1992, pp. 31-45.

"Tourism's Effect on Community." *Mecosta County Area Chamber of Commerce,* Special 50th Anniversary Issue, Big Rapids, Michigan, Feb/March 1987.

"Tribes legal attempt." *Grand Rapids Press,* November 2, 1988, p. A4.

Schenker, E., Mayer, H. M. and Brocket, H. C. The Great Lakes Transportation System. Technical Report 230. Madison: University of Wisconsin Sea Grant College Program, January 1976.

"Saviors of the People Mover." (Special Report), *Detroit Free Press.* July 26, 1987, pp. G1, 4-7.

United States Government. *U.S. Senate Concurrent Resolution 76.* Washington, DC: 100th Congress 1st Session, 1987.

United States Government. *Zip + 4 Codes ....* Notice 186. Washington, DC.: United States Postal Service, September 1984.

Vinge, C. L. and A. G. *Economic Geography.* Totowa, NJ: Littlefield, Adams and Co., 1966.

Polar Bears

Anderson, Godfrey. "The Polar Bears, a Memoir." *The Grand River Valley Review.* Vol. 4, No. 1. F/W 1982, pp. 2-15.

"Bears' Meet for Last Time." Big Rapids: *The Pioneer.* May 23, 1983, p. 2A.

Doolen, Richard M. *Michigan's Polar Bears.* Ann Arbor: The University of Michigan, 1965.

Halliday, E. M. *The Ignorant Armies.* New York: Harper and Bros., 1958.

Hunt, B. D. Capt. *Canada and Armed Intervention in Russia 1918-1919.* A Thesis for MA Degree. Kingston: Department of History, Royal Military College, February 1967.

MacLaren, Roy. *Canadians In Russia, 1918-1919.* Toronto: The MacMillan Co. of Canada Ltd., 1976.

1919-1941. *American Military History 1607-1953.* ROTCM 145-20. Department of the Army, July 1956, pp. 362-363.

Strakhovsky, Leonid I. "The Canadian Artillery Brigade in North Russia 1918-1919." *The Canadian Historical Review.* Vol. XXXIX, No. 2, June 1958, pp. 125-146.

Miscellaneous Sources

Baumgartner, John. Chairman Whitefish Point Bird Observatory, Kalamazoo, Michigan, January, 1987.

Cooper, Wililam. Phone Conversation. Department of Zoology, Michigan State University. Project Director Underlake Research. September 3, 1987.

Ceremsik, Karen. Phone Conversation. Public Relations Section, Eastern Airlines, Miami, Florida, February 1987.

Goodrich, Marie A. (Boyce). Letter to author, January 24, 1986, from Fort Wayne, Indiana. Letter to author, November 7, 1985, from Fort Wayne, Indiana.

Harlow, Richard. Phone conversation. Administrator of PA116-74, Michigan Department of Natural Resources, July 27, 1993.

Hesberg, Father Theodore, WJR Radio: "Focus With J. P. McCarthy," Detroit, April 22, 1986.

Kerkhof, Janet. Letter to Editor, *Grand Rapids Press,* March 27, 1987, p. A14. (Canada Information)

Sauer, Serge. Map Curator-Geographer, University of Western Ontario, July 17, 1985.

Taylor, Mildred, Big Rapids. Phone conversation, October 1985.

Thackham, Dorothy, Plymouth, Michigan, December 17, 1981.

Author's Background Music While Thinking and Writing

(Selection/Album. Artist/Group/Composer, Producing Firm, Date.)

American Hammered Dulcimer. The Original Dulcimer Players Club, Traditional Records, Cosby, Tennessee, Ca 1975.

American Hammered Dulcimer Volume Two: 25 years with the O.D.P.C., Evart, MI; L.D.P.C., Inc., 1988.

Around the World with Sanderjord Jentekor. Sanderjord Girls Choir, EMI/Odeon, Oslo, Norway Ca. 1975.

A Sampler of Michigan Women. Candace Anderson, Hermonikher Records, 1985.

Bach Greatest Organ Music. Michael Schneider, Organist, Sine Qua Non, Fall River, Mass., 1973.

Brahm's Fourth and Academic Festival Overture. Cleveland Orchestra, Great Performances--CBS, New York, 1982.

Eric Robertson Present Piana Hits. Silver Eagle Records, Willowdale, Ont., 1982.

Greatest Hits. Volume II, The Mormon Tabernacle Choir and The Philadelphia Orchestra, Columbia Masterworks, New York, Ca. 1965.

The Hammered Dulcimer Album. Jay Round and Friends, Grandville, Michigan, 1974.

Hymns on the Crystal Cathedral Organ. Fredrick Swann Organist, Gothic Records, Tustin, Ca., 1985.

I Have a Dream/Voulez-Vous. Abba, Polar Music Studio, Stockholm, 1979.

Mid-Western Conference on Vocal and Instrumental Music. Big Rapids Symphonic Band, Mark Custom Records, Livonia, Michigan, 1979.

Morning Has Broken/Cat Steven's Greatest Hits. A&M Records, Beverly Hills, California, 1975.

Now is the Hour-Songs of the South Pacific. The New Zealand Maori Chorale, Monitor Record, New York, 1978.

Old Favorites on the Hammered Dulcimer. Wes Linenkugel with Jack Lewis, L-Three Music, Inc. Toledo, Ohio, 1982.

Organ Masterworks. Lenough Anderson, Oryx-Exploring the World of Music, Peerless, Middlesex, UK, 1961 Recital.

Peaceful Evening. (Tape) David and Steve Gordon, Sequoia Records, Canoga PK., Ca. 1984.

Pianoscapes. (Tape) Michael Jones, Narada Productions, Haarlen, Holland, 1983.

Quiet Hour, 101 Strings. Somerset Records, Media, Pov., 1958.

The Singing Zither Request Album. Willie Dittrich, Homestead, Iowa, Ca. 1968.

Songs of Praise. First Mennonite Church, Berne, Indiana-Columbia Special Products, 1977.

The Voices of the LaSalle: Expedition II, LaSalle Expedition II. Chicago, Ill., 1977.

Voice of the Pioneer (Canada). Bill McNeil, Tapestry Records and Tapes, Toronto, Ont., 1982.

Wes Linenkugel Interprets Hammered Dulcimer. Lou Linenkugal and Jack Lewis, L-Three Music, Inc. Toldeo, Ohio, 1978.

INDEX

NOTE: The following grouped categories have not been individually indexed -- counties, rivers, parks, education institutions and forests. For **county names** see Table 4-1, pages 68-75; **rivers** Table 6-3, pages 141-151; **parks** and **forests** Tables 6-3 and 6-4, pages 141-151 and 156; **and education institutions** Appendix One..

ABOUT THE AUTHOR

Professor Richard Santer, Ph.D. has taught Geography at Ferris State University in Big Rapids, Michigan since 1969. He grew up in northwest Detroit and graduated from Burt Elementary and Detroit Redford High (1955) of that city's public school system. His ancestors migrated to Michigan Territory Bucklin Township (now Redford) in 1828 from Ontario County, New York. He earned his Bachelor of Science (1959) degree in geography from Eastern Michigan University. He completed his Master's degree course work at the University of Iowa under a National Defense Education Grant. That degree, however was awarded at Eastern Michigan (1965) after completing major research focused on the Status of Tree Farms in Michigan.

He served as a Lieutenant in the Regular United States Army 1959-1962. He gained experience in teaching at Wyandotte Roosevelt High School (1963-1966) where he was a World Region and Cultural Geography instructor. In 1970 he earned the doctorate in geography from Michigan State University with assistance from the Cold War-Vietnam Era G.I. Bill. His dissertation was a *Historical Geography of the City of Jackson, Michigan 1825-1969*.

The faculty of Ferris recognized him in 1981 as its Distinguished Professor. The following year the Michigan Association of Governing Boards awarded him similar status. Prior to this work he authored *Michigan: Heart of the Great Lakes* (1977) and later "Michigan" *Academic American Encyclopedia* and "The Land and People of Freshwater" Chapter One in *Michigan: Visions of Our Past* (1989) -- a sesquicentennial history of Michigan.

He has served on the local Township and County Planning and Zoning Commissions plus the Bicentennial of the United States Committee. At Ferris he chaired the university's Centennial Task Force (1980-84), the Celebrate III Committee to observe the bicentennials of the US Constitution and Northwest Ordnance and Michigan's Sesquicentennial (1987). In 1980 he coordinated the Governors Upper Great Lakes Small Cities and Rural Areas Growth Conference. He is listed in *Who's Who in America; Mid-West*.